Research & Education Association

The Best Teachers' Test Preparation for the

AEPA®
Elementary Education
(Field 01)

Anita Price Davis, Ed.D.

And the Staff of
Research & Education Association

Visit our Educator Support Center at:
www.REA.com/teacher

The competencies presented in this book were created and implemented by the Arizona Department of Education. For further information visit the Arizona Department of Education website at *www.ade.state.az.us/certification*.

For all references in this book, AEPA® and Arizona Educator Proficiency Assessments® are trademarks of the Arizona Department of Education and Pearson Education, Inc. or its affiliates.

Research & Education Association
61 Ethel Road West
Piscataway, New Jersey 08854
E-mail: info@rea.com

The Best Teachers' Test Preparation for the Arizona Educator Proficiency Assessments® (AEPA®) Elementary Education Test (Field 01)

Library of Congress Control Number 2006938944

ISBN-13: 978-0-7386-0168-7
ISBN-10: 0-7386-0168-3

REA® is a registered trademark of Research & Education Association, Inc.

About Research & Education Association

Founded in 1959, Research & Education Association is dedicated to publishing the finest and most effective educational materials—including software, study guides, and test preps—for students in middle school, high school, college, graduate school, and beyond.

REA's Test Preparation series includes books and software for all academic levels in almost all disciplines. Research & Education Association publishes test preps for students who have not yet entered high school, as well as for high school students preparing to enter college. Students from countries around the world seeking to attend college in the United States will find the assistance they need in REA's publications. For college students seeking advanced degrees, REA publishes test preps for many major graduate school admission examinations in a wide variety of disciplines, including engineering, law, and medicine. Students at every level, in every field, with every ambition can find what they are looking for among REA's publications.

REA presents tests that accurately depict the official exams in both degree of difficulty and types of questions. REA's practice tests are always based upon the most recently administered exams, and include every type of question that can be expected on the actual exams.

REA's publications and educational materials are highly regarded and continually receive an unprecedented amount of praise from professionals, instructors, librarians, parents, and students. Our authors are as diverse as the fields represented in the books we publish. They are well-known in their respective disciplines and serve on the faculties of prestigious high schools, colleges, and universities throughout the United States and Canada.

Today REA's wide-ranging catalog is a leading resource for teachers, students, and professionals.

We invite you to visit us at *www.rea.com* to find out how "REA is making the world smarter."

About the Author

Dr. Anita Price Davis is the Charles A. Dana Professor Emerita of Education and was the Director of Elementary Education at Converse College, Spartanburg, South Carolina, before retiring in 2005. Dr. Davis earned her B.S. and M.A. from Appalachian State University and her doctorate from Duke University. She also received a postdoctoral fellowship to Ohio State University for two additional years of study.

Dr. Davis worked more than 36 years at Converse College, where she served as the faculty adviser for Kappa Delta Epsilon, a national education honor organization. She also worked 5 years as a public school teacher.

Dr. Davis has received wide recognition for her work, including a letter of appreciation from the U.S. Department of the Interior, inclusion in *Contemporary Authors*, and a citation of appreciation from the Michigan Council of the Social Studies. She has authored/coauthored 23 funded grants for Converse College. She has served as a mentor and was a two-time President of the Spartanburg County Council of the International Reading Association. The state of South Carolina twice named her an outstanding educator, and she was twice a nominee for the CASE U.S. Professor of the Year.

Dr. Davis has authored, coauthored, and edited more than 80 books. She has written two college textbooks, titled *Reading Instruction Essentials* and *Children's Literature Essentials*. Dr. Davis has published several history books and is also the author of more than 80 papers, book reviews, journal articles, and encyclopedia entries.

Acknowledgments

In addition to our author, we would like to thank Larry B. Kling, Vice President, Editorial, for supervising development; Pam Weston, Vice President, Publishing, for setting the quality standards for production integrity and managing the publication to completion; Anne Winthrop Esposito, Senior Editor, for project management and preflight editorial review; Caroline Duffy for copyediting the manuscript; Ellen Gong for proofreading; Terry Casey for indexing; Christine Saul, Senior Grapic Designer, for cover design; Caragraphics for typesetting; and Jeff LoBalbo, Senior Graphic Designer, for postproduction file mapping.

CONTENTS

CHAPTER 3: MATHEMATICS   71

CHAPTER 4: SCIENCE   101

Elementary Education

Introduction

Passing the AEPA Elementary Education Test

▶ About This Book

REA's *The Best Teachers' Test Preparation for the Arizona Educator Proficiency Assessments (AEPA): Elementary Education (Field 01)* is a comprehensive guide designed to assist you in preparing to take the AEPA Elementary Education Test. This examination is not the only one that Arizona requires of elementary candidates applying for teacher certification; elementary candidates must pass the following:

- A subject knowledge test that matches the desired type of certification or endorsement (in this case elementary education)
- A professional knowledge test
- The Constitutions of Arizona and the United States test—unless they have completed successfully course work that the Arizona Department of Education has approved for exemption of this requirement

The AEPA is a **criterion-referenced test (CRT)**. In CRTs, each student is measured against uniform objectives or criteria; candidates are not scored in relation to the scores of the other examinees, as they are in **norm-referenced tests (NRTs)**. CRTs allow for the possibility that all students can score 100 percent, because the students can determine ahead of time the concepts on the examination. If students properly study for the test, their scores should be high. This type of test is noncompetitive, because students are not in competition with one another for a high score; there is no limit to the number of candidates who can score well.

The purpose of the AEPA is to identify the certification candidates who demonstrate the skills and the professional knowledge that the Arizona Department of Education considers to be important for a state educator who will (1) enhance student achievement and (2) meet the needs of the changing and diverse student population in the Arizona schools.

The candidates for teacher certification in the state of Arizona should check with their preparatory institution, National Evaluation Systems, Inc. (NES), and the Arizona Department of Education for the latest information about certification requirements, test dates, and so forth.

AEPA Program
National Evaluation Systems, Inc.
PO Box 660
Amherst, MA 01004-9011
800-239-8105 or 413-256-2883
7 a.m.–6 p.m. (Mountain Standard Time)
413-256-8032 (TTY)
www.aepa.nesinc.com

Arizona Department of Education
Certification United States
PO Box 6490
Phoenix, AZ 85005-6490
www.ade.az.gov/certification

This book helps in your preparation for the AEPA Elementary Education Test. This test guide does the following:

- Identifies the 38 objectives in five subject areas (language arts, mathematics, science, social studies, and the arts) that form the foundation of the content of the AEPA. Objectives are broad statements whose language is a reflection of the professional knowledge, skills, and understandings that a beginning educator needs for effective performance in the elementary classroom in Arizona.

- Provides an explanation of the skills and the knowledge that the objective covers in a statement that follows each objective; these objectives and statements reflect Arizona's curriculum standards and materials, certification standards, and teacher preparation programs.

- Identifies some of the important information about the AEPA Elementary Education Test.

- Presents an accurate and complete overview of the AEPA.

- Summarizes the content of the AEPA for a quick review of content.

- Provides sample questions in the AEPA format.

- Suggests tips and strategies for successfully completing standardized tests.

- Provides two practice tests that (1) replicate the format of the AEPA Elementary Education test, (2) provide an opportunity for the candidate to rehearse before the test date, and (3) represent the types and the levels of difficulty of the questions that appear on the AEPA.

- Supplies the correct answer and detailed explanation for each question on the two practice tests included in this book. This explanation feature enables you not only to identify correct answers but also to understand why they are correct and, just as important, why the other answers are incorrect.

- Provides sample performance assignment responses and the score that the response would typically receive on the test.

In producing this guide, the editors considered the most recent test administrations, other test guides, and professional standards; they also researched information from the Arizona Department of Education, professional journals, textbooks, other educators, and the most recent information from National Evaluation Systems (NES).

In addition to guiding your preparation for certification, recertification, out-of-field certification, or multiple certifications, this book is a valuable source for college and university personnel and in-service trainers. They will find the guide helpful as they construct help sessions and recommend resources for a test candidate. The guide may even suggest topics or content to include in a college course syllabus.

Although this book is intended to help you succeed on the AEPA, you should not consider it a replacement for any college course, a duplicate of the test, or a complete source of subject matter to master. Like knowledge itself, the AEPA test can change.

This book includes the best test preparation materials based on the latest information available from test administrators. The number and distribution of questions can vary from test to test. Accordingly, prospective examinees should pay strict attention to their strengths and weaknesses and not depend on specific proportions of any subject areas appearing on the actual exam.

▶ About the Test

Who Must Take the AEPA Elementary Education Test?

In November 1997 the State of Arizona adopted certain rules and regulations governing the evaluation

of educators applying for state teacher certifications, endorsements, and credentials. One of these rules requires candidates for teacher certification to pass certain tests: the subject matter test that matches the certification or endorsement area, a professional knowledge test, and the Constitutions of the United States and Arizona test. To obtain an elementary education teaching certificate, then, a prospective elementary teacher must demonstrate mastery of subject matter knowledge, as indicated by a passing score on the AEPA Elementary Education test (01) and on the AEPA Professional Knowledge Test: Elementary (91).

People taking the test typically include (1) individuals seeking initial teacher certification in Arizona and (2) educators who are making changes in their teaching career.

How Is the Test Scored?

On the AEPA, the selected-response (multiple-choice) section counts for 90 percent of your total score, while the performance assignment (essay) counts for 10 percent. Once you take the test, your raw score—based on the number of questions you answer correctly—is converted to a scaled score based on a weighting value unique to the administration of your particular test. The scaled scores possible on the AEPA range from 100 to 300; 240 or higher is a passing score. (Your actual scaled score is provided only if you do not pass the test.) For all practical purposes, on the sample tests in this book, if you write a good essay and correctly answer roughly 70 percent of the questions, you will approximate a passing score on the AEPA.

What If I Do Not Pass the Test?

If you do not achieve a passing score on the AEPA test, you should not panic! Instead, as a serious test taker, plan to retake the test. The test schedule usually makes the assessments available six times during a calendar year (September–July). The waiting period enables you to do additional work to improve your score on the next test.

Retaking the AEPA Test

Remember, a low score on the AEPA is not an indication that you should change your plans about a teaching career. The low score does indicate, however, that you need to review and study before entering the examination setting again. Remember, the AEPA is a reliable test; this means that the instrument will give consistent results with repeated measurements. Just as a reliable bathroom scale will give almost identical weights for the same person measured three times in a morning, the AEPA test will give you similar scores each time you take it—unless you change some things (like the preparation you make before you retake the test). Adequate preparation is what this book should help you accomplish.

There is a limited amount of time between the date of the mailing of the score report and the registration date for the new administration. A special dispensation occurs when the two dates occur in the same week. In that case, if you must retake the test, no late registration fee applies if you register to take the test by the late registration deadline; this waiver is applicable only for the late registration period of the next test date and for the same test that you failed. No refunds are applicable, however, if you register to retake the test before the receipt of your initial test score and then find that you earned a passing score on that initial test.

Who Designs the Test?

A content validation was an essential part of the development of the set of AEPA test objectives. Randomly selected Arizona school personnel and Arizona college and university faculty members participated in the content validation. Participants in the elementary survey were proficient in their area of review; they considered only the objectives for their field of certification. Their goals were (1) to determine whether the objectives were important to the profession of an Arizona educator and (2) to ensure that the objectives were indicative of the skills, standards, and knowledge necessary to Arizona educators. The test questions and answers thus reflect the objectives that the Arizona educators validated.

National Evaluation Systems (NES) developed the AEPA. NES is a company that develops and administers tests customized for teacher certification programs and higher-education assessment programs. NES has developed assessments in more than 100 content fields, in professional teaching, and in the basic skills: reading, writing, and mathematics. In addition to tests for the state of Arizona, NES has developed tests for the states

of California, Colorado, Illinois, and New York, among others.

When Should I Take the AEPA Test?

Most teacher certification candidates take the test in time for their test results to accompany their certification applications. Some colleges and institutions have rules about the dates by which students must have taken and passed the examination. Consult the rules of the college or university where you are enrolled to determine whether any stipulations exist.

The Arizona Department of Education establishes the tests you must take for certification; it also sets the deadlines by which you must complete the tests for certification purposes. Rules and regulations change with time. You must generally adhere to the rules and regulations in effect at the time you are applying for certification, so it is important to stay up to date.

Typically, there are six administrations of the AEPA Elementary Education test during a calendar year: September, November, January, April, June, and July. Students may take the test at several locations throughout the state of Arizona. The state of Arizona and NES often plan alternative test dates to accommodate test takers whose schedules might conflict with the typical testing schedule because of religious obligations, for instance. In addition, a test candidate who has a disability and cannot take the test under standard testing conditions may request special accommodations. Such candidates need to check with NES in Amherst, Massachusetts, about rules for requesting special arrangements.

You can access up-to-date information about the AEPA from the websites, phone numbers, and addresses listed earlier in this book.

Is There a Registration Fee?

To take the AEPA, you must pay a $35 registration fee that is nonrefundable; the fee for the subject knowledge test is $70. Additional fees apply for late registration and for emergency registration, as well as for change of registration, additional score reports, rescoring the multiple-choice section, disputed payments, and performance assignment sections.

Payment method depends on the registration method. If you register or make changes to the registration by telephone or the Internet, you can use only a MasterCard or Visa credit card. If you pay via the U.S. mail, checks or money orders are appropriate. Should any payment fail to clear, you may not register for future tests until you have paid an additional penalty charge and have cleared the account by cashier's check or money order.

▶ How to Use This Book

The following sections outline ways you can use this study guide and take the practice tests to help you prepare for the AEPA.

How Do I Begin Studying?

1. Review the organization of this test preparation guide.
2. Follow the "AEPA Elementary Education Test Study Schedule" presented at the end of this chapter. The schedule is for a seven-week independent study program, but you can condense or expand the schedule according to the time you have available.
3. Take Practice Test 1 under timed, simulated testing conditions.
4. Score Practice Test 1. Be sure to study the explanations for why the answers are correct, as well as why the other answer choices are wrong.
5. Review the section of this chapter titled "Format of the AEPA Test," which provides the format of items on the sample test and a replica of the types of questions.
6. Review the suggestions for test taking presented later in this chapter.
7. Pay attention to the information about the objectives, competencies, skills, content, and topics on the test.
8. Spend time reviewing those topics that seem to warrant more study.
9. Take Practice Test 2 under timed, simulated testing conditions.

10. Score Practice Test 2 and study those competencies that your test scores indicate need more review.

11. Follow the suggestions presented later in this chapter for the day before and the day of the test.

Studying thoroughly the subject area reviews in chapters 2 through 6 of this guide will reinforce the basic skills you need to do well on the exam. Taking the practice tests under timed, simulated testing conditions will help you become familiar with the format of the AEPA and the procedures involved in taking the actual test.

When Should I Start Studying?

It is never too early to start studying for the AEPA. (Actually, you started preparing when you began your first college course and internship.) The earlier you begin using this guide, however, the more time you will have to sharpen your skills. Do not procrastinate! Cramming is not the most effective way to study; it does not give you the time you need to study the objectives, think about the content, review the competencies, and take the practice tests. Although you do not want to cram, it is important to review the material one last time the night before the test administration.

▶ Format of the AEPA Test

The AEPA Elementary Education test is a four-hour exam. On each test day, the test is available in the afternoon. There will be two types of questions on the exam: selected response (multiple choice) and written performance. There are 100 selected-response questions on the test, but only 80 of the questions are for scoring purposes; the other 20 are for field testing and do not contribute to or detract from the test taker's score. The written performance item also contributes to the test score. A passing score, again, is 240 points or higher.

You should have plenty of time to complete the AEPA during the four-hour examination period, but you will need to be aware of the amount of time you spend on each question. You do not want to find you

have run out of time before you finish all the questions. Although speed is not very important, a steady pace is necessary when answering the questions. You can allocate your time during the exam period as you need; you can, therefore, spend as much time as you wish on the test sections as long as you do not go over the four-hour limit. Pacing yourself is very important. Using the practice tests will help you set your pace.

▶ Format of the Performance Assignment

The AEPA Elementary Education test includes at least one assignment that requires an extended, written response. The test will present you with an issue and a task. The assignment may, for example, ask you to compare and contrast proposals or even present you with a problem to which you must present a solution and justify your response. Therefore, you must be prepared to think about an issue, organize your thoughts, give a response, and justify the presented response.

▶ Format of Multiple-Choice Questions

Each of the multiple-choice questions has four answer options: A, B, C, and D. You will receive an answer sheet on which you will mark your responses by filling in the "bubbles." Individual test items require levels of thinking, ranging from simple recall to evaluation, analysis, and problem solving.

Two types of multiple-choice questions may appear on the exam. Your test might have both types of questions or just one of the types. It is important, however, for you as a test taker to study both types of questions. The question types are (1) the single-question format and (2) questions with stimulus material.

Single-Question Format

The **single-question format** comprises two question types: the direct question and the sentence comple-

tion. With the direct question, the question stem ends in a question mark, and you must select the answer choice that best answers the question. Consider the following examples:

1. Which of the following is a trait of effective professional development?

    A. a continuous plan of lifelong learning
    B. activities developed solely by the principal
    C. a one-hour, stand-alone workshop
    D. a totally theory-based program

2. What is one way of incorporating nonperformers into a discussion?

    A. Ask a student to respond to a previous student's statement.
    B. Name a student to answer a question.
    C. Only call on students with their hands raised.
    D. Allow off-topic conversations.

With the sentence completion, a portion of the sentence is omitted; you must choose the answer that *best* completes the statement. Here is an example:

3. Teachers convey emotion through

    A. body language, eye contact, and verbal cues.
    B. verbal contact and cues.
    C. voice levels.
    D. the way they listen.

Questions with Stimulus Material

For **questions with stimulus material**, a direct question follows a stimulus. The stimulus could be a classroom scenario, a reading passage, and/or a visual representation, such as graph, chart, table, or map. One or more questions follow the stimulus; a direction line states how many questions refer back to the given stimulus.

Scenario. For a scenario stimulus, you must examine a case study, scenario, or problem and answer the question, diagnose the problem, or suggest the best

course of action from the provided options. Try these examples:

4. A student describes an analysis of a recent presidential address for the class. The teacher replies, "You have provided us with a most interesting way of looking at this issue!" The teacher is using

    A. simple positive response.
    B. negative response.
    C. redirect.
    D. academic praise.

5. While waiting for students to formulate their responses to a question, a student blurts out an answer. The teacher should

    A. ignore the answer entirely.
    B. respond immediately to the student's answer.
    C. silently acknowledge the student's response and address the response after someone else has answered the question.
    D. move on to another question without comment.

Graph or map. Other stimulus questions will ask you to identify or interpret a graph or map by choosing the response that best answers the question:

The following graph shows sales totals for each region of the state in thousands of dollars; the graph shows the totals by yearly quarters.

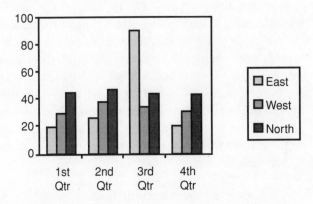

6. The region with the largest total sales for the year is

    A. the east.

B.   the north.
C.   the west.
D.   the south.

Graphics. Again, you must choose the response that best answers a question about a number line, a geometric figure, a chart, a graph of lines or curves, or a table—but not the typical maps and graphs of the previous question type.

Troubled by what seems to be an increase in gang-type activity among increasingly younger children, Bill wants to find out what his students think and know about gangs. He wants to learn the most he can about the students' thinking on this topic in the smallest amount of time. He wants all students to have the chance to share what they think and know, yet he also wants to maximize interaction among students. The students will spend the entire morning reading, talking, and writing a group report about this subject.

7.   Which of the following seating arrangements would best help Bill meet his objectives?

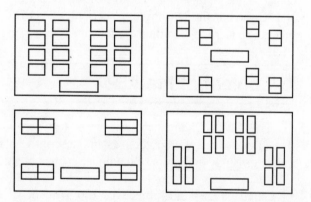

A.   the upper-left diagram
B.   the lower-left diagram
C.   the upper-right diagram
D.   the lower-right diagram

Word problem. Some stimulus problems ask you to apply mathematical principles to solve a real-world problem. Here is an example:

Examine the following addition problems worked by an elementary school student. Analyze what error pattern the student's work is exhibiting.

$$74 + 56 = 1,210 \qquad 35 + 92 = 127$$
$$67 + 18 = 715 \qquad 56 + 97 = 1,413$$

8.   If the student worked the problem $88 + 39$ using the error pattern exhibited in the above equations, what answer would the student give?

A.   127
B.   131
C.   51
D.   1,117

Answers

1.   **A**

Effective professional development is not a one-time workshop, nor can it be satisfied within a specified amount of time (C). To effect growth in children, teachers must grow and develop as well (A). This learning must extend throughout the teacher's career and beyond. In addition, effective professional development relies on meeting the needs of those involved and therefore cannot be dictated solely by one individual (B). Finally, in addition to being theory and research based, the learning gained from professional development activities must be practical and applicable (D). Otherwise, the learning cannot be used at the school site, and the training is rendered useless.

2.   **A**

Nonperformers are students who are not involved in the class discussion at that particular moment. Asking students to respond to student statements (A) is the only option that describes a way of incorporating nonperformers into a class discussion.

3. A

Even without saying a word, teachers can communicate a variety of emotions with their body language, eye contact, and verbal cues (A). Smiles, verbal cues (such as the intonation of voice), movement, posture, and eye contact with students can convey the enthusiasm of an effective teacher. Body language—maintaining eye contact and leaning in to the conversation—can convey that teachers are actively listening to their students.

4. D

Academic praise (D) is composed of specific statements that give information about the value of the object or about its implications. A simple positive response (A) does not provide any information other than the praise, such as the example "That's a good answer!" There is nothing negative (B) about the teacher's response. A redirect (C) occurs when a teacher asks a student to react to the response of another student.

5. C

If the teacher ignores the answer entirely (A) or moves on to another question (D), it devalues the student's response. If the teacher responds immediately to the digression (B), the disruptive behavior has been rewarded. The correct answer is (C).

6. B

To figure out the answer to any question involving a bar graph, you need to look at the graph carefully. The numbers on the left of the graph in this question are in increments of 20, which would be $20,000; these large increments make it difficult to get a precise answer. The first reaction is that the east (A) might be the correct answer. The largest bar is in the color for the east. If you look more closely, however, you see that during the first quarter, the sales in the east were $20,000; sales were about $28,000 during the second quarter. The third-quarter sales in the east amounted to about $90,000; add this sum to the $20,000 for the fourth quarter, and you get a total of about $158,000. The totals for the north (B) were $42,000, $42,000, $42,000, and $42,000; this gives a total of $168,000. The sales for the west (C) were $30,000, $38,000, $37,000, and $25,000; that gives a total of $130,000. The reader has no idea of sales figures for the south (D).

7. B

Placing the students in small groups in which they meet face-to-face (B) will allow Bill to maximize the students' interaction while giving each student the maximum opportunity to speak. Placing students in the traditional rows facing the front (A) discourages student interaction and minimizes each student's opportunity to speak. Although placing students in pairs (C) maximizes each student's opportunity to speak, it limits the sources of interaction; each student can share thoughts with only one other student. In contrast, a group of four allows the student to interact as part of three dyads, two triads, and a tetrad. When placing the students in cooperative groups, teachers are wise to arrange the desks within the physical space of the classroom in such a way that each group's talking does not distract the members of other groups (D).

8. D

You should note that the student is failing to carry (regroup) in both the ones and tens places. The equation $(56 + 97)$, for example, is being treated as $(5 + 9 = 14)$ and $(6 + 7 = 13)$. The two answers are then combined, for a total of 1,413. Choice A presents the correct answer to the addition problem and therefore does not exhibit the error pattern. Choice C exhibits switching from addition to subtraction $(9 - 8 = 1)$ and $(8 - 3 = 5)$. Also, the child subtracts the top number from the bottom one in the first step. In choice B, the child subtracts 8 from 9, subtracts 3 from 8, and then adds to the 8 in the tens place. Only choice D illustrates the pattern of recording the sum and not carrying.

► Content of the AEPA

The AEPA Elementary Education test comprises five subject areas, with objectives and descriptive statements for study and preparation under each subject:

- Language arts: 11 objectives (30 percent of the questions)
- Mathematics: 9 objectives (24 percent of the questions)
- Science: 6 objectives (16 percent of the questions)
- Social studies: 7 objectives (19 percent of the questions)
- Arts: 4 objectives (11 percent of the questions)

These identified objectives and statements are the basis for the AEPA Elementary Education test. You can use these objectives and statements as an inventory of information to consider when preparing to take the test. The subject area reviews—in addition to the objectives and statements—in chapters 2 through 6 of this book can help in preparation for the AEPA.

About the Subject Area Reviews in This Book

The subject area reviews in chapters 2 through 6 will help you sharpen the basic skills you will need when you take the AEPA. In addition, the reviews provide you with strategies for attacking the test questions. Each teaching area has its own chapter; subtopics in each chapter include the objectives within the subject area and statements on the skills within the objectives.

Your education has already provided much of the information you need to score well on the AEPA. Education classes and internships have given you the know-how to make important decisions about situations that teachers face. The reviews in this book will help you fit the information you have already acquired into the specific objective and statement components. Reviewing class notes and textbooks and using the reviews, objectives, tests, scoring guides, and statement reviews in this book will provide excellent preparation for passing the AEPA.

Other important parts of the book are the two practice tests, which will help develop your test-taking skills. Although the review chapters and the practice tests will help prepare you for the AEPA, this guide is not an all-inclusive source of information or a substitute for course work. The practice test items cannot be exact representations of questions that actually appear on the test.

Using the Practice Tests

There are 100 multiple-choice questions and one essay question on both of the AEPA practice tests. Only 80 of the 100 multiple-choice questions on the actual AEPA

apply to your test score; the other 20 are field-test questions. On the practice tests, you should answer all the questions, just as you will on the actual test; this will help you pace yourself and judge your time on the test day.

Your main objective on these practice tests is to answer the questions in the allotted time and to check your answers. You should study carefully the detailed explanations for the right and wrong answers. Pay particular attention to the questions you answered incorrectly, note the types of questions you missed, consider the related objectives, and reexamine the corresponding review section. After further study, you might want to retake the practice tests.

Studying for the AEPA Test

Choose a study time and study place that suit the way you live and learn. Some people set aside some time early in the morning to study; others choose to study at night before going to sleep. Busy test candidates study at random times during the day: while standing in line for coffee, while eating lunch, or while waiting for their next class to begin. Only you can determine the study plan that is best for you.

It is important to study consistently and to use your time wisely. After you work out a study routine, stick to it. It is crucial not to wait until the last minute and not to cram.

When you take the practice tests in this book, observe the time constraints and try to simulate the conditions of the actual test as closely as possible. Turn off the television, the phone, and the radio. Sit down at a table in a quiet room free from distraction.

After you complete a test, score your performance. Keeping track of your scores will enable you to gauge progress and discover general weaknesses in particular sections.

Reviewing thoroughly the explanations to the questions you answered incorrectly and also noting the reasons for the correct answers will help you master the material. Concentrating on just one problem area at a time, give extra attention to the review sections that

cover the areas of difficulty you have noted; you will want to build skills in those areas. Paying special attention to competencies and skills related to your areas of weakness is an effective learning tool and will help increase your knowledge and confidence in subject areas that initially gave you difficulty.

Using small note cards to record facts and information for future review is a good way to study and keep the information at your fingertips in the days to come. You can easily pull out the cards and review them at random moments: during a coffee break or meal, on the bus or train as you head home, or just before falling asleep. Using the cards gives you essential information at a glance, keeps you organized, and helps you master the materials. Ultimately, you gain the confidence you need to succeed.

▶ Before the Test

If the test center is not located in an area familiar to you, you might want to make a trial run to ensure that you do not get lost on that important test day and to make certain that there are no detours. It is always a good idea to check your registration slip to verify the time and place. Before leaving for the test center, be sure you have your admission ticket and two forms of identification, one of which must contain a recent photograph, your name, and signature (for example, your driver's license). You will not be permitted to enter the test center without proper identification.

It is helpful to arrive at the test center early. This allows you some time to choose a suitable seat, relax, and avoid the anxiety that might come with a late arrival. If you are late, you will not be admitted to the testing room. If you are absent, you will not receive a credit or refund. You will need to reregister and take the test at a later date.

You should plan what to wear ahead of the test day. It is important to dress comfortably and in layers; that way you can remove a sweater or add a jacket if the room is too hot or too cool. Dressing in layers ensures that the room temperature will not divert your concentration while taking the test.

▶ What to Take—and What Not to Take—to the Test Center

You must supply your own pencils. It is a good idea to bring several sharpened No. 2 pencils with erasers, because the test monitors will not provide any at the test center. You do not want to have to get up during the test to sharpen a pencil; another test taker may forget a pencil and may ask you to share, so it is best to have a supply on hand.

You should wear a watch to the test center. However, you cannot wear a watch that makes noise, because it can disturb the other test takers. The proctor will remind test takers of the total time for the session; because you know how many questions are in the booklet and how many minutes are in the afternoon session, you can gauge time accurately for each question.

As an added precaution, do a very quick check of the page numbers. If your booklet is incorrectly stapled, it is better to find this out at the beginning—not the end—of the test.

You cannot bring dictionaries, textbooks, notebooks, calculators, briefcases, or packages. Food, drinks, and cigarettes or other smoking implements must also remain at home. Some test sites *may* allow you to have water bottles in the testing room, provided that the containers are clear, do not have a label, have a secure lid, and are kept under the seat—not on your desk.

▶ During the Test

The AEPA Elementary Education test is a four-hour exam. To maintain test security, test takers and the proctor must follow certain procedures. Once you enter the test center, you must follow all the rules and the instructions that the proctor gives. Test takers who do not adhere to the rules risk dismissal from the test and cancellation of their test scores.

After distributing the testing materials, the proctor will give the directions for filling out the answer sheet.

It is important to fill out the sheet carefully, because the information you provide will appear on the score report.

Once the test begins, you should be sure to fill in answers darkly and neatly, mark only one answer per question, and completely erase unwanted answers and marks.

▶ Test-Taking Tips

This book will acquaint you with the test and help alleviate test-taking anxieties. Listed here are ways you can get ready to take the AEPA, and perhaps other tests as well:

Tip 1. **Become comfortable with the format** of the AEPA. Use the sample tests, simulate the conditions under which you will be taking the actual test, try to stay calm, and pace yourself. In fact, after simulating the test only once, you will boost your chances of doing well and will be able to sit down for the actual AEPA with much more confidence.

Tip 2. **Read all the possible answers.** Even if the first response appears to be the correct answer, the savvy test taker will read all the choices and not automatically assume that the first is the best answer. Read through each choice to be sure that you are not making a mistake by jumping to conclusions.

Tip 3. **Use the process of elimination** by going through each answer to a question and discarding as many of the answer choices as possible. For instance, if you eliminate two of the four answer choices, the chances of getting the item correct have increased; you have only two choices left from which to make a guess—a 50-50 chance of choosing the correct answer.

Tip 4. **Cross out *in the test booklet* (not on the answer sheet) any answer you know is not the appropriate one.** Crossing out the incorrect answer will prevent your having to reread it if you need to look over the question again. This will save you time.

Tip 5. **Never leave a question unanswered.** There is no penalty for guessing, so even if you are unsure of an answer, do not leave it blank.

Tip 6. **Work quickly and steadily when taking the AEPA.** The actual test consists of roughly 100 multiple-choice questions and one essay question, and you will have four hours to complete the test. You will need to work at a constant pace over a long period of time. Wearing a watch and referring to the time occasionally will help you gauge the time left.

Tip 7. **Do not focus on any one question too long.** You need to use your time wisely.

Tip 8. **Take the diagnostic and practice tests in this guide** to help you practice budgeting the precious time allotted for the test session.

Tip 9. **Study the directions and the format of the AEPA.** Familiarity breeds confidence. By becoming acquainted with the instructions and with the structure of the test, you can save time when you actually begin taking the test. In addition, you can cut your chances of having any unwanted surprises. When you sit for the test, it should be just as you thought it would be. By studying the directions and format ahead of time, you can avoid both anxiety and the mistakes a case of the jitters causes.

Tip 10. **During the test, you should constantly check the answer sheet** to be sure that the number beside the answer bubble matches the number beside the question in the test booklet.

Tip 11. **Enter your answers carefully.** The AEPA is a multiple-choice test graded by machine. If you skip a bubble or enter an answer twice, the rest of the answers on the answer sheet may be incorrect and may seriously affect your score.

Tip 12. **Place a question mark in your answer booklet—not on the answer sheet—beside any question for which you had to guess.** If you have extra time, you can always recheck those questions you marked. Do not, however, make stray marks on the answer sheet.

▶ After the Test

When time is up, hand in the materials. The proctor will dismiss all the people taking the test. You are then free to go home and relax—a well-deserved treat!

▶ AEPA Elementary Education Test Study Schedule

The study schedule below allows for thorough preparation to pass the AEPA test. The course of study suggested here is seven weeks, but you can condense or expand your preparation program to match the time you have available for study. In any case, it is vital that you adhere to a structured plan and set aside ample time each day to study. Depending on your time frame, you might find it easier to study throughout the weekend or during the week. No matter what timetable you plan, the more time you devote to studying for the AEPA, the more prepared and confident you will be on the day of the actual test.

Week	Activity
1	**Take Practice Test 1.** The score will indicate your strengths and weaknesses. Make sure that you take the test under simulated exam conditions and observe the time guidelines. After taking the test, score it and review the explanations, particularly for the questions you answered incorrectly.
2	**Review the explanations for the questions you missed, and choose the review sections in the chapters that will provide information in your areas of weakness.** Useful study techniques are to highlight key terms and information, to take notes on the material in the review sections as you work, and to put new terms and information on note cards to help you retain the information.
3 and 4	**Reread the note cards you created in preparation for the test, look through your college textbooks, and read over your class notes from past courses.** In addition, you may find it helpful to reread the competencies and skills that the test emphasizes; a summary of this information is in the review sections of this guide. This is the time to consider any materials and information that your counselor or the Arizona Department of Education offers. (Be sure to review the website for the Arizona Department of Education at *www.ade.az.gov/certification*.)
5	**Begin to condense your notes and findings.** A structured list of important facts and concepts—based on the AEPA Elementary Education competencies and skills and written on index cards—will help you as you review for the test. Have a relative, friend, or colleague quiz you by using the index cards you wrote in the previous week.
6	**Take Practice Test 2, adhere to the time limits, and replicate actual testing conditions as closely as possible.** Review the explanations for both the incorrectly and correctly answered questions.
7	**Review your areas of weakness by using study materials in this book, references, and notes.** This is a good time to retake the sample tests by using the extra answer sheets provided in the back of the book.

AEPA®

Arizona Educator Proficiency Assessments®

Elementary Education

Review

Language Arts

It is important for the potential test taker to review the content of the language arts and reading curriculum. Approximately 30 percent of the AEPA Elementary Education test comes from the content areas of reading and the language arts. Some salient points are worthy of special review.

▶ Objective 0001:
Understand the Reading Process

Interaction Among the Reader, the Text, and the Context to Construct Meaning

Reading is about bringing meaning to the page and taking meaning from the page. Reading and comprehension are actually interactions among the reader, the text, and the **context**; context can be the pictures or the parts of a sentence, paragraph, story, or passage that occur just before and after a specified word or passage and that help to determine the exact meaning.

As children progress in their skills and confidence, teachers might encourage them to use picture clues and previously read materials to predict what word would make sense. To help children make their predictions, the teacher can give them a clue, like the first sound of the word. Another way a teacher can provide context clues

is to mask words or portions of words with a "magic window"—a sturdy piece of cardboard with a small rectangle cut out of the center. This allows the teacher to single out a letter or syllable for the children to consider. The teacher can also cover up words or parts of words on a transparency sheet on the overhead (Combs 2006).

Cultural, Social, Linguistic, Developmental, and Environmental Factors Affecting Reading

Reading does not occur in a vacuum. The students bring to the classroom their culture, their social background, their linguistic achievements, their developmental levels, and environmental factors. Upon their arrival, the students encounter the culture, social climate, linguistic and developmental expectations, and the environment of the school, the educators, and the curriculum materials. Differences between the child's culture, social background, linguistic and developmental factors, and environment and that which he or she encounters in the educational environment may affect learning and achievement.

The culture and the family are important to the work of the school. The U.S. Department of Education recognizes that "parents are their children's first and most

influential teachers" (Bennett 1987, 5). The department further notes that "what parents do to help their children learn is more important to academic success than how well-off the family is" (Bennett, 7). After reviewing many studies, the department reports the following:

> The best way for parents [and adults] to help their children become better readers is to read to them—even when they [the children] are very young. Children benefit most from reading aloud when they discuss the stories, learn to identify letters and words, and talk about the meaning of words. (Bennett, 7)

The department also found that

> . . . children whose parents simply read to them perform as well as those whose parents use workbooks or have had training in reading. . . . Kindergarten children who know a lot about written language usually have parents who believe that reading is important and who seize every opportunity to act on that conviction by reading to their children. (Bennett, 7)

Jim Trelease (1985) reinforces that parents and teachers should read aloud regularly to children. The reasons Trelease cites for reading aloud include "to reassure, to entertain, to inform or explain, to arouse curiosity, and to inspire" (68). Trelease also explains that reading aloud to a child can strengthen writing, reading, and speaking skills and the child's entire civilizing process. Another important reason for reading to children while they are young is that at that age, children want to imitate what they hear and see adults do. In his book *The Read-Aloud Handbook*, Trelease suggests stories and books ideal for reading aloud.

The Southern Regional Education Board (1994) recommends that schools help parents to become actively involved in their children's education and that schools adopt formal policies to improve communication between parents (or caregivers) and schools.

It is important for the school environment to be accepting of all cultures and social backgrounds, learning styles, linguistic elements, and developmental stages. Ideally, the school will promote multiculturalism and cultural pluralism.

According to Denise Ann Finazzo (1997), **cultural pluralism** "recognizes that in diversity lies strength and in acceptance of different races, ethnicities, languages, and cultures [lie] understanding and growth" (203). **Multiculturalism**, by contrast, "speaks to the issue of many cultures combining to form a better society" (203).

Multiculturalism reflects both assimilationism and pluralism. **Assimilationism** is a view that promotes a "national culture" and considers microcultures as deficient until they become part of the national culture. **Pluralism** suggests that a functional society should recognize and accept microcultures as they are (Finazzo 1997, 204). The teacher who subscribes to multiculturalism combines some elements of both pluralism and assimilationism in the curriculum and does not take extreme or radical stands on either issue.

Finazzo (1997, 205) suggests that an educator promotes multiculturalism in the classroom by emphasizing the following:

* The diversity in American culture
* The influence of cultures on society
* The many various cultures in the world
* The origins of rhymes, stories, games, and riddles

Oral Language Foundation of Reading

The school curriculum, especially the Language Experience Approach, should help the students to see:

* That what I say, I can write
* That what I can write, I can read
* That what others write, I can read (Davis 2004)

With the Language Experience Approach (LEA), the teacher attempts to facilitate the students' language development through the use of experiences, rather than printed material alone. After the class participates in an experience or event, the students as a group record what happened (often with the help of the teacher). The teacher writes exactly what the students say—even if they do not use Standard American English. The teacher may talk at this time about alternative ways to say what the students do not say in Standard American English.

In summary, many forms of language exist, but the school should not try to eradicate the culture or the language of its students.

The Language Arts: Reading, Writing, Listening, and Speaking

The language arts include all the subjects related to communication. The school curriculum often gives most attention to reading, writing, literature, and spelling; listening and speaking are other essential parts of the language arts curriculum. A balanced language arts curriculum addresses each topic. Ideally, reading, writing, spelling, listening, speaking, and even the literature are integrated into other content areas.

▶ Objective 0002:
Understand Skills and Strategies Related to Decoding, Word Identification, and Vocabulary Development

Decoding

In their beginning work with reading and reading materials, students should find in their texts many **decodable words**, which are words that follow a regular pattern and have a predictable sound, such as the long final vowel sounds in *so*, *he*, and *be*. The beginning readers can practice their decoding skills as they read and become more confident; they should also be progressing with their handwriting skills and becoming more independent in spelling the words they need in writing (Combs 2006).

Phonics

The most commonly used method of teaching reading in the United States from colonial times through the 1920s was the phonics method. Other reading methods—the sight word method, modified alphabet approach, and the whole language approach, for example—came into prominence after the 1920s. However, phonics is still an important part of reading instruction in the United States and has many **advantages**.

The phonics method of teaching reading emphasizes the association between the **grapheme** (the written symbol) and the **phoneme** (the speech sound). The phonics method attempts to relate spelling rules to the process. Because English is not entirely a phonetic language, students must simply memorize the spelling of some words.

William Holmes McGuffey and Rudolf Flesch were proponents of the phonics method. McGuffey produced his series of reading books in 1836. The readers used phonics while teaching morals to students; the series was a cultural force, not just a reading textbook. By 1920, sales of McGuffey readers had reached 122 million. In 1955, Flesch wrote *Why Johnny Can't Read— And What You Can Do About It* to warn parents that the reason many children cannot read is that the schools are not using the phonics approach.

Phonics is, of course, useful in attacking and decoding many unknown words; this is a definite advantage of the method. Because the phonics approach involves phoneme–grapheme associations, auditory learners— those who learn best through the sense of sound—often prefer to read using phonics; this is a second advantage to phonics instruction. A third advantage of this method, with its emphasis on sound–symbol relationships, is that phonics readers can often transfer their skills to spelling, another one of the language arts subjects. Spelling involves associating sounds with letters; it is the opposite of phonics, which associates symbols with sounds. Phonics readers are often good spellers (Davis 2004).

At its January 1997 meeting, the board of directors of the International Reading Association (IRA) passed a position statement titled "The Rule of Phonics in Teaching Instruction." The key assertions were that phonics is an important aspect in beginning reading instruction, primary teachers value and teach phonics, and effective phonics is integrated into the total language arts program ("IRA takes a stand on phonics" 1997). Phonics awareness includes experiences with rhyming, blending, and segmenting sounds.

There are, however, **disadvantages to the phonics method**. A major disadvantage of phonics is that visual learners may not read well by this method. A second disadvantage of the method is that the rules do not hold

true all the time. In his now classic study, Theodore Clymer (1963) reported that he found few phonic generalizations that held true in more than 50 percent of the cases in the primary grades. Four years later, however, Mildred Hart Bailey (1967) found in her study of phonic rules that 27 of the 45 generalizations identified by Clymer held true in 75 percent of the words appearing most often in reading materials for grades 1 through 6.

A third disadvantage of the phonics method is that some students are confused when they learn a phonics rule and then encounter frequent exceptions; inconsistencies pose a problem for them. Some educators, though not all, note a fourth disadvantage to the phonics method: they believe that there is no basis for the view that there are subskills, such as phonics, that students need in order to read; they see the skills as mythical (Davis 2004).

To help children learn phonics, many teachers find certain **techniques for teaching** the method especially helpful. Students should have opportunities to practice the phonics rules and generalizations in context; instructors should make every effort to illustrate the transfer of the phonics rules and generalizations to everyday materials and to other subjects. **Analytic phonics** (using phonics in context with actual materials), as opposed to **synthetic phonics** (phonics taught in isolation from meaningful books and materials, often using worksheets), seems to be the more helpful technique.

Teachers can introduce a phonics rule or generalization as it appears, but such an **incidental approach** does not ensure that all students meet and practice the most frequently encountered phonics rules. A **structured, systematic, sequential phonics program** helps ensure that readers have at their disposal an arsenal of skills to decode new words and spell the words correctly. Such a plan of presenting the rules and regulations of phonics can help eliminate gaps in students' word attack skills (Davis 2004).

Marie Carbo (1993), nationally known for her work with reading styles, recognizes the importance of making available phonics instruction in any reading program. She particularly warns, "A good whole language program does include phonics" (*Schools of Thought II: Reading Styles and Whole Language*. VHS.).

In *Becoming a Nation of Readers*, the Commission on Reading (1986) stresses that phonics is an essential strategy for beginning reading. Teachers should use a systematic approach and present the skills in meaningful sentences, passages, and materials, not just as words in isolation.

A word of caution for teachers of phonics is that in the beginning, students may read slowly. When students begin to commit high-frequency words to memory, however, reading speed and, in turn, comprehension will increase (Davis 2004). The young child begins recognizing letters and their sounds. These skills will help the child with reading and spelling. Another technique that will help the child in attacking unknown words is analyzing the structure of the words, or structural analysis (Davis 2004).

Word Identification

A technique that will help the child in word identification is analyzing the structure of the words, or structural analysis (Davis 2004).

Breaking a word into its parts, or syllables, is called **structural analysis**. By dividing a word into its syllables and sounding out these smaller parts, students are often able to pronounce longer, unknown words that they previously did not recognize. There are many rules for dividing words into syllables; some of these rules often hold true, but some of the rules do not. As mentioned earlier, Bailey (1967) found in her study of phonics rules that 27 of 45 syllabication rules hold true in 75 percent of the words a child frequently encounters in grades 1 through 6.

Children do not work with all the rules for structural analysis in the early years. Usually, children begin work mainly with adding word endings to words that are already a part of their sight vocabulary or word families. Some of the endings that children encounter first are the suffixes -*ed*, -*s*, -*es*, and -*ing* (Davis 2004). Fry (1980) says that six suffixes cause a large percentage of the variants: -*ed*, -*s*, -*er*, -*ly*, -*est*, and -*ing*.

Young children are constantly encountering new words. Even though some texts try to limit the new words a child meets at a given time (**controlled vocabulary**), most children do not experience such a protected environment. All the words a child sees may not be

those in the list of sight words the child already knows. It is important for the child to have some word attack skills to decipher new, unknown words.

Separating the prefix and/or the suffix from the root word is an example of structural analysis. After separating these word parts, the child may be able to sound out the word. Examples include *un•tie*, *re•peat*, and *sing•ing* (Davis 2004).

Another important rule for separating words into parts is the compound word rule. With this rule, the child divides a compound word into its parts. The child and the teacher can work together to sound out each part. Examples include *cow•boy* and *foot•ball* (Davis 2004).

Two essential rules for structural analysis are the v/cv and the vc/cv rules. Teachers introduce these rules and encourage the students in the later stages of reading development to employ these attack skills. To use the rules successfully, the child must first determine whether each letter in a word is a vowel (v) or a consonant (c). The child can write the label over each letter in the word. Looking for the v/cv or vc/cv pattern, the child separates the word at the appropriate place. Examples of the v/cv rule are *o•ven* and *bo•dy*. Examples of the vc/cv rule are *sum•mer* and *ig•loo* (Davis 2004).

Some rules of structural analysis, such as the following, are complex but useful for advanced readers (Davis 2004):

1. When *-le* comes at the end of the word and a consonant comes before it, the consonant goes with the *-le*, as in the words *pur•ple* and *bub•ble*. (An exception to this rule is when the word contains a *ck*; one would not separate the *c* and the *k*, as in the word *pick•le*.)
2. The ending *-ed* forms a separate syllable if *d* or *t* comes before the *-ed*, as in *skidd•ed* and *mist•ed*.

A **running record** is a way to assess students' word identification skills and fluency in oral reading. As the teacher listens to a student read a page, the teacher uses a copy of the page to mark each word the child mispronounces. The teacher will write the incorrect word over the printed word, draw a line through each word the child does not know, and draw an arrow under repeated words.

After determining the words that the child did not read successfully, the teacher can analyze the missed words to determine the reason that the child missed them. This assessment of missed words is **miscue analysis**. The teacher is looking for a pattern in the student's mistakes so that the teacher can provide help to the student.

Vocabulary Development

Vocabulary instruction is important to the teaching of the language arts—and other subjects. Teachers identify important vocabulary words in their units and often single these words out for study.

Vocabulary study is more than memorizing definitions, however. Effective teachers employ many strategies to increase the vocabulary of their students. They post new words on the word wall as reminders of the new vocabulary words. The teachers develop lessons about idioms, the use of dictionaries and glossaries, multiple meanings of words, antonyms, synonyms, homonyms, figurative meanings, word parts, and other word-study techniques.

Effective instruction includes making connections to the background of the students. Repetition, meaningful use, and encouraging independent reading work also help to enhance vocabulary development (Tompkins 2006, 196–213).

Combs (2006) reminds the educator that children seem to acquire vocabulary when the adult provides explanations of the new words encountered in context. To enhance the learning, the children should have ample opportunities to review and use that knowledge, especially in other contexts. Shared reading, especially, aids in vocabulary development (Combs, 190).

Our environment is rich with words. People see signs advertising everything from fast foods to fast cars. Television shows display many words, and newspapers and magazines depend on words to sell their products and to communicate their messages. Around swimming pools, playgrounds, recreation centers, and movie theaters are printed signs and cautions to help ensure the safety of customers and users. Becoming aware of these environmental words is important to children. They

should begin to notice and try to recognize these important words at an early age. Noting the signs and words around them will help children feel comfortable with words and make them aware of the importance of reading in our society.

Anita P. Davis and Thomas R. McDaniel (1998) identify current words that they consider essential for physical safety, social acceptability, and the avoidance of embarrassment. Some of these "essential words" are *exit*, *danger*, *high voltage*, *stop*, *beware*, *keep out*, and *no trespassing*. Being able to read these words is vital. Davis and McDaniel advocate that teachers and adults help children notice and master these words in their environment.

Edward Dolch (1960) identifies the most frequently used vocabulary words from preprimer level to grade 3. Listing the words by grade in the Dolch Word List, the author recommends teaching them to primary children to develop their reading vocabulary. Because Dolch advocates teaching the beginning reader to read the words quickly and to "pop" them off immediately, many teachers call the words the "Popper Words."

Students who are not proficient in speaking English (limited English proficient, or LEP) require special consideration. The English language consists of many slang and multidefinitional words that can confuse students. To build the vocabulary of LEP students, teachers need to employ such tactics as matching concrete pictures to vocabulary, rewording complex statements, simplifying instructions, and modeling correct vocabulary. It is important to remember that students learn to speak a language long before they are proficient at writing in that language.

▶ Objective 0003:
Understand Skills and Strategies Involved in Reading Comprehension

Reading is more than calling words. Reading must result in **comprehension**, or understanding.

Comprehension skills include the ability to identify supporting details and facts, the main idea or essential message, the author's purpose, fact and opinion, point of view, inference, and conclusion. To help students de-velop these skills, teachers can consistently emphasize meaning in the classroom and should focus on the four levels of comprehension: literal, interpretive, critical, and creative.

The **literal level of comprehension**, the lowest level of understanding, involves **reading the lines**, or reading and understanding exactly what is on the page. Students may give back **facts** or **details** directly from the passages as they read. For example, a teacher works with students as they make their own play dough and use the recipe to practice **authentic reading** (Davis 2004). The teacher might question the students on the literal level as they mix their ingredients. Here are some sample questions:

Factual question. How much salt do you add to the mixture?

Sequence question. What is the first step in making the play dough?

Contrast question. Do you add more or less salt than you did flour?

The **interpretive level of comprehension**, the second-highest level of understanding, requires students to **read between the lines**. At this level, students must explain figurative language, define terms, and answer interpretive or inferential questions. **Inferential questions** require the students to **infer**, or figure out, the answers. Asking students to determine the **author's purpose**, **the main idea** or **essential message**, **the point of view**, and **the conclusion** are examples of inferential questions. Inferential questions may require students to draw conclusions, generalize, derive meaning from the language, speculate, anticipate, predict, and summarize. All such questions are from the interpretive level.

Here are some examples of interpretive questions the teacher could ask at the cooking center while students are making play dough:

Contrast. How is the dry measuring cup different from the liquid measuring cup? Why are they different?

Deriving meaning. What does the term *blend* mean?

Purpose. What is the purpose of making play dough at home? Why would you want to make play dough instead of buying it?

Cause and effect. Why do the directions say to store the play dough in a covered, airtight container?

The **critical level of comprehension** requires a high level of understanding. The students must judge the passage they have read. The critical level is one of the two highest of the levels of understanding; it requires students to **read beyond the lines**. Having students determine whether a passage is true or false, decide whether a statement is a fact or an opinion, detect propaganda, or judge the qualifications of the author for writing the passage are examples of activities that use the critical level of comprehension. Here are some examples of questions the teacher could ask students as they make play dough to encourage their thinking and understanding at the critical and creative levels:

Checking author's reputation. The recipe for the play dough comes from a book of chemistry experiments. A chemist wrote the book. Do you think that a chemist would be a good person to write about play dough? Why, or why not?

Responding emotionally. Do you prefer to use the play dough we made in class or the play dough that the local stores carry?

Judging. Do you think that the recipe for play dough that is on the recipe card will work? Why, or why not?

The **creative level of comprehension** is at the highest level of understanding. As with the critical level of comprehension, the student must **read beyond the lines**. The student must often make judgments about other actions to take. Answers may vary among the students. The teacher may not want to stifle creativity by saying one action is better than another. For instance, a teacher may suggest that after making a batch of cookies a student finds that the baked cookies do not fit in the cookie jar; the teacher may ask, "What can the student do?" Answers may include "Donate the extras to the first-graders," "Give some to the teacher," "Share with my little sister," or "Put them in a plastic storage bag." All these answers are creative; the teacher should not judge one as better than another.

Teachers need to be explicit about teaching students to be aware, to check for understanding, and to use reading comprehension strategies to determine meaning. To monitor and repair students' understanding, teachers should explicitly teach students to do the following (Goudvis and Harvey 2000):

- Track their thinking through coding with sticky notes, writing, or discussion.
- Notice when they lose focus.
- Stop and go back to clarify thinking.
- Reread to enhance understanding.
- Read ahead to clarify meaning.
- Identify and articulate what is confusing or puzzling about the text.
- Recognize that all of their questions have value. (There is no such thing as a stupid question.)
- Develop the disposition to question the text or author.
- Think critically about the text and be willing to disagree with its information or logic.
- Match the problem with the strategy that will best solve it.

There are various levels of understanding.

Bloom's Taxonomy

Bloom describes six levels of comprehension in his Taxonomy. The teacher may wish to develop questions at each level to increase comprehension, prepare a series of questions for thought and discussion, or prepare a test (Krathwohl, Bloom, and Masia 1964):

Level 1. **Knowledge**. Students give back the information that is on the page.

Level 2. **Comprehension**. Students show that they can give the meaning of terms, idioms, figurative language, and other elements of written material.

Level 3. **Application**. After reading a story about how a class raised money for playground equipment, the students discuss some ways that they might improve their own playground.

Level 4. **Analysis**. Students examine the parts or components of a passage. For example, students might examine a menu and locate food groups, or they might identify terms in a word problem to determine the operations they should use.

Level 5. **Synthesis**. Students move from specifics to generalities. For instance, the class might develop a solution to the overcrowding problem suggested in a story, or students might construct a platform for

the main character to use if she should run for class officer in the school described in another story.

Level 6. **Evaluation**. Students judge if a passage is fact or opinion, true or false, biased or unbiased.

In the 1990s, a group of psychologists revised Bloom's Taxonomy. They reversed the order of the two highest levels; they made *synthesis* (creating) higher than *evaluating*; in fact, they designated synthesis as the highest level of intellectual behavior. (See *http://web. odu.edu/educ/llschult/blooms_taxonomy.htm*.)

Assessing Comprehension

A frequent device for assessing comprehension is the use of oral or written questions. A question may be **convergent**, which indicates that only one answer is correct, or **divergent**, which indicates that more than one answer is correct. Most tests, however, include a combination of question types.

Another device for checking comprehension is a **cloze test**, a passage with omitted words the test taker must supply. The test maker must decide whether to require the test taker to supply the exact word or to accept synonyms. Passing scores reflect which type of answer is acceptable. If meaning is the intent of the exercise, the teacher might accept synonyms and not demand the surface-level constructs, or the exact word.

The speed at which a student reads helps determine comprehension, *up to a point*. The faster that a student reads, the better that student comprehends, *up to a point*. The slow reader who must analyze each word does not comprehend as well as the fast reader. It is possible, however, to read too fast. Most students have had the experience of having to reread materials. For example, a student reading a physics chapter in preparation for a test might read more slowly than when reading a novel but not slowly enough to note every important detail.

A teacher might ask students to read a passage and record their reading times. Then the teacher might give the students a quiz on the passage. After scoring the quizzes, the teacher could meet with each student to discuss the student's reading speed and its relation to the quiz grade. For students who received low quiz scores, the teacher could assign another passage and at-tempt to have the student slow down, or perhaps even accelerate, the speed of reading.

▶ Objective 0004:

Understand Reading Instruction and Study and Research Skills in the Content Areas

---

Reading in the Content Areas and Activating and Developing Prior Knowledge

An important part of helping the students read and comprehend effectively in a content area book is helping them to be aware of the **patterns of organization** of various books, the **text structure**, and the use of **book parts**. Since book parts and organization may vary, particularly from one content area to another, the effective teacher will develop methods and/or materials to introduce the students to the texts and/or other materials that they will be using. The teacher will make sure that students know the purpose of bold font, the index, the contents page, and so forth.

Clay (1985) developed a formal procedure for sampling a child's reading vocabulary and determining the extent of a child's print-related concepts. For instance, her assessment checks whether a child can find the title of a book, show where to start reading it, and locate the last page or end of the book. These components may differ from those typically considered essential before children can begin to read, like discriminating between sounds and finding likenesses and differences in print (Davis 2004; Finn 1990). A teacher or parent might hand a book to a child with the back of the book facing the child and in a horizontal position. The adult would then ask questions such as "Where is the name of the book?" "Where does the story start?" "If the book has the words *the end*, where might I find those words?" (Davis 2004).

When reading in the content area for information, activating and developing prior knowledge is important. The teacher may guide the student in prereading instruction. The teacher and class together may set up a K-W-L chart. The chart may list what they already

know (K) about the topic or the story; what they *want* (W) to know and find out as they read; and—after the reading—what they have *learned* (L).

Looking at strategies used by proficient readers helps teachers make skillful choices of activities to maximize student learning in subject area instruction. Anne Goudvis and Stephanie Harvey (2000) offer the following list:

Activating prior knowledge. Readers pay more attention when they relate to the text. Readers naturally bring their prior knowledge and experience to reading, but they comprehend better when they think about the connections they make between the text, their lives, and the larger world.

Predicting or asking questions. Questioning is the strategy that keeps readers engaged. When readers ask questions, even before they read, they clarify understanding and forge ahead to make meaning. Asking questions is at the heart of thoughtful reading.

Visualizing. Active readers create visual images based on the words they read in the text. These created pictures enhance their understanding.

Drawing inferences. Inferring is when the readers take what they know, garner clues from the text, and think ahead to make a judgment, discern a theme, or speculate about what is to come.

Determining important ideas. Thoughtful readers grasp essential ideas and important information when reading. Readers must differentiate between less important ideas and key ideas that are central to the meaning of the text.

Synthesizing information. Synthesizing involves combining new information with existing knowledge to form an original idea or interpretation. Reviewing, sorting, and sifting important information can lead to new insights that change the way readers think.

Repairing understanding. If confusion disrupts meaning, readers need to stop and clarify their understanding. Readers may use a variety of strategies to "fix up" comprehension when meaning goes awry.

Confirming. As students read and after they read, they can confirm the predictions they originally made. There is no wrong answer. One can confirm nega-

tively or positively. Determining whether a prediction is correct is a goal.

Using parts of the book. Students should use book parts—like charts, diagrams, indexes, and the table of contents—to improve their understanding of the reading content.

Reflecting. An important strategy is for students to think about, or reflect on, what they have just read. Reflection can be just thinking, or it can be more formal, such as a discussion or writing in a journal.

While providing instruction in a subject area, the teacher needs to determine if the reading material is at the students' level of reading mastery. If not, the teacher needs to make accommodations either in the material itself or in the manner of presentation.

Studying in the Content Areas

To ensure that the students master the material, the teacher may develop **process guides** to help the students as they read. In a process guide, the teacher develops specific aids for a section of the text that the students are going to read and that the teacher believes might cause some problems for specific students. The teacher might seek to anticipate the problem areas for the students and might include in a process guide for a particular chapter the following information:

- A list of key terms for the students to identify as they read
- A list of key people for the students to identify as they read
- A list of new vocabulary for the students to identify as they read
- A guide to relational words in the passages
- Questions to call the readers' attention to graphic aids in the passage

It is true that process guides are time consuming to develop, but because schools use most texts and other materials for more than one year, the teacher may be able to reuse them from year to year if there are sections of the text that continue to be applicable to the subject and to the students of later years. After the teacher calls the students' attention to certain features of the text and how to read it, the students may be able to develop process guides for themselves or for the person whom they

tutor; preparing the guides may serve as a learning/organizing experience (Davis 2000; Karlin 1971).

Before, during, and after instructional input, the students preview, rehearse, or apply what they have learned. In **guided reading**, the teacher watches carefully to make sure students realize what they are to observe during their reading and that they have grasped the material correctly. Because the teacher is on hand to assess student responses, he or she is able to provide correction or additional input if necessary. During independent practice, students work independently. At the end of each lesson (or at the end of the class), the teacher or students summarize or review what has been learned (Davis 2004).

The teacher might acquaint students with several plans to help them read content materials. Many of these plans already exist, and the teacher and the students can simply select the plan(s) that works best for them with various subjects. Students may use **mnemonic devices**, or memory-related devices, to help them remember the steps in reading a chapter effectively. Students often use plans like the following SQ3R plan when reading text in content areas:

Survey. Before reading a passage or an entire section of the text, the student should look over the assigned page or chapter and consider some questions: Are there illustrations, charts, or diagrams? What are some of the chapter headings? Are some words in bold type?

Question. The student may wish to devise some questions that the chapter will probably answer. If an assigned chapter has questions at the end, the student can look over the questions before reading the chapter; the questions serve as a guide to the text.

Read. The student now reads the passage to answer the questions at the end of the chapter or to answer the questions that the student developed before reading the chapter.

Recite. The student attempts to answer orally or in writing the student-developed questions or the questions at the end of the chapter.

Review. The student reviews the material to "double-check" the answers given in writing or orally at the previous step.

Vacca and Vacca (1989) express doubt that most students actually use a study plan. Even though an instructor may try to teach the "formula" for reading and studying a passage by having a class memorize the steps, practice the procedure several times, and view the formulas as a lifelong activity, Vacca and Vacca contend that a study system "evolves gradually within each learner" and that the SQ3R plan is difficult even for junior high school students (227). They suggest that students need to become "text smart" and learn to preview, skim for the main idea, and organize information through mapping or outlining.

Other reading authorities disagree. Richardson and Morgan (1990) suggest that students can use the SQ3R plan by fifth or sixth grade. Gunning (1996, 316) reminds teachers that SQ3R has been around since the 1930s; he describes the method as "a widely used and effective study strategy incorporating five steps" (319). Michaelis and Garcia (1996) suggest that students can create their own self-directed reading strategies. They cite PROVE as an example:

Purpose. Establish a purpose or set up questions to guide your reading.

Read. Read the passage to try to achieve the purpose or answer the questions.

Organize. Outline; place details under main ideas.

Vocabulary. Note any new vocabulary or concepts that you master.

Evaluate. Evaluate to determine if you achieved your purpose.

Depending on the situation, instructors may use these strategies across the curriculum, in any subject area.

The use of graphic organizers such as story maps, Venn diagrams, fishbone organizers, and double-entry journals can also be helpful to enhancing understanding.

Story mapping or webbing helps students think about a reading passage and its structure. Webs or maps, in which the student charts out a concept or section of text in a graphic outline, are useful organizers. The web begins with the title or concept written in the middle of the page and branches moving out in web fashion; students will note specific bits of information on the branches or strings of the web. Arrows or lines in other formats can make connections from one bit of information to another. Some typical devices in good narrative fiction and that might be useful on a story map or web

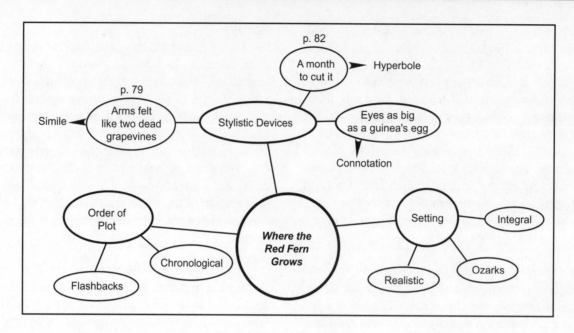

Figure 1-1. Story Map

include setting, stylistic devices, characters, and plot. A class reading Wilson Rawls's *Where the Red Fern Grows* (1961/1976) created the story map shown here in Figure 1-1.

Venn diagrams (two overlapping concentric circles; see Figure 1-2) enable the reader to compare two characters, concepts, places, or things by placing specific criteria or critical attributes for one in the left circle, for the other in the right circle, and attributes or characteristics that are shared by the two in the overlapping section in the center.

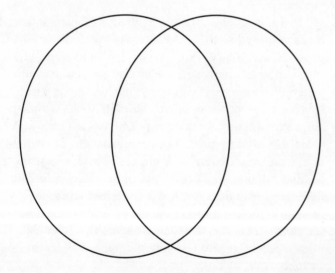

Figure 1-2. Venn Diagram

Another useful graphic organizer is the **fishbone organizer** (Figure 1-3). This type of graphic can help the reader to illustrate cause and effect. A reader viewing the fishbone chart can immediately see the cause and the direct result of the cause.

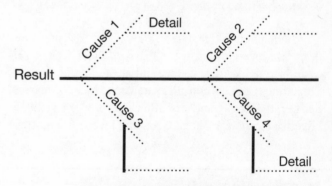

Figure 1-3. Fishbone Organizer

These and many other graphic organizers can help students gain understanding of a text by making it visual and more concrete. As students manipulate information in writing, they have a better opportunity to deal with it effectively and more concretely (Barry et al. 2005).

Double-entry journals are another graphic method for enhancing understanding. The student enters direct quotes from the text (with page number) in the left column and enters "thinking options"—such as "This is

important because," "I am confused because," "I think this means"—in the right column (Barry et al. 2005).

The effective teacher maintains a climate that promotes the lifelong pursuit of learning. One way to do this is to encourage students to practice research skills that will be helpful throughout life. All subject areas can promote the skills of searching for information to answer a question, filtering it to determine what is appropriate, recording the findings (whether in the form of bar graphs, charts, written findings, notes, outlines, pie graphs, and so forth), and using what is helpful and important to solve a problem.

The effective teacher also facilitates a positive social and emotional atmosphere and promotes a risk-taking environment for students. He or she sets up classroom rules and guidelines for how he or she will treat students, how students will treat him or her, and how students will treat each other. In part this means that he or she does not allow ridicule or put-downs, either from the teacher or among the students. It also means that the teacher has an accepting attitude toward student ideas, especially when the idea is not what he or she was expecting to hear. Sometimes students can invent excellent ideas that are not always clear until they explain how they arrived at them.

Students should feel free to answer and ask any questions that are relevant to the class, without fear of sarcasm or ridicule. Teachers should always avoid sarcasm. Sometimes teachers consider sarcasm to be mere teasing, but because some students often interpret it negatively, effective teachers avoid all types and levels of sarcasm.

► Objective 0005:
Understand Characteristic Features of Children's Literature and Strategies to Promote Students' Literary Response and Analysis

Genres of Children's Literature and Their Attributes

Literary genres include poetry, prose, novels, short stories, plays or drama, and personal narratives or essays.

Poetry

Poetry is a genre that is difficult to define for children, except as "not prose." **Poetry** is the use of words to capture something: a sight, a feeling, or perhaps a sound. Poetry needs to be chosen carefully for a child, as poetry ought to elicit a response from the child—one that connects with the experience of the poem. All children need poetry in their lives. Poetry needs to be celebrated and enjoyed as part of the classroom experience, and a literacy-rich classroom will always include a collection of poetry to read, reread, savor, and enjoy. Some children enjoy the discipline of writing in a poetic format.

Poetry is perhaps the oldest art and has been a part of people's lives through the centuries. Like the ancient listeners who thrilled to Homer's poetry and the tribes who chanted invocations to their gods, today's generation listens to song lyrics and finds itself, sometimes despite itself, repeating certain rhythmic lines. An advertisement that listeners chuckle over—or say they hate—has a way of repeating itself as listeners use the catchy phrase or snappy repetition. Both lyricists and advertisers cleverly use language and play on people's ability to pick up on a repeated sound or engaging rhythm or inner rhyme—a part of poetry.

Children love poetry: nursery rhymes, ball-game rhythms, jump-rope patterns. Even with no idea of the meaning of the words (like "Little Miss Muffet sat on a tuffet"), a child can respond to the sounds and the pattern they form.

Prose

Prose is another literary type. Students are sometimes confused as to what exactly prose is. Basically, **prose** is not poetry. Prose is what people write and speak most of the time in everyday intercourse: unmetered, unrhymed language. This does not mean, however, that prose does not have its own rhythms; language, whether written or spoken, has cadence and balance. Certainly prose can have instances of rhyme or assonance, alliteration, or onomatopoeia. Language is, after all, phonic. Furthermore, prose may be either fiction or nonfiction. A novel (like a short story) is fiction; an autobiography is nonfiction. Although a novel (or short story) may have autobiographical elements, most readers regard an autobiography as entirely factual.

Textbooks are generally nonfiction prose. Reading textbooks (**basals**) may contain both fiction and nonfiction, poetry and prose.

The **narrative** is a common style of prose that can be fiction or nonfiction. A narrative tells a story or gives an account of an incident or a series of incidents. The account may be autobiographical to make a point, as in George Orwell's essay "Shooting an Elephant."

Narrative fictional children's literature is either traditional or modern in form. **Traditional literature** is composed of ancient stories, and it has a set form. People passed these stories down through the centuries by word of mouth. Later others, like Joel Chandler Harris, the Grimm Brothers, and Charles Perrault, recorded the stories for future generations. **Modern literature**, on the other hand, is, as the name suggests, much more recent; its categories can overlap some of the categories of traditional literature and can include additional forms of literature.

Seven Types of Traditional Literature. There are seven types of traditional fiction: parables, fables, fairy tales, folktales, Noodle-head tales, myths, and legends. Each has certain characteristics that set it apart from the others.

A **parable** is a story that is realistic and has a moral. The story is **didactic**, meaning it teaches a lesson. Unlike the fable, the parable could be—but is not necessarily—true. The biblical figure Jesus often taught with parables. One of his best known parables is "The Prodigal Son" (Lk 16:11–32); others include "The Good Samaritan" (Lk 10:30–36), "The Lost Coin" (Lk 15:8–11), and "The Parable of the Seeds on Rich and Fallow Ground" (Mk 4:3–8; Lk 10:30–36).

A **fable** is a nonrealistic story with a moral. The fable often has animals as main characters. **Aesop**, a Greek slave supposedly born around 600 B.C.E., often receives credit for developing the fable; however, whether he actually did so—or ever even existed—is debatable. Charlotte Huck, the noted children's literature authority and one of the authors of *Children's Literature in the Elementary School*, states that fables were actually in Greek literature as early as 800 B.C.E. (Huck, Hepler, and Hickman 1993, 362–364). "The Fox and the Crane," "The Fox and the Crow," and "The Fox and

the Grapes" are among the best-known fables. Some scholars use the classification **beast tale** for fables in which animals behave as humans do.

Translators changed Aesop's Fables from Greek to Latin and to English. William Caxton published these fables in England in 1484. It was sometime after the publication of these fables that the Grimm Brothers (1800s) and Charles Perrault (1697) secured the publication of fairy tales.

Fairy tales have the element of magic; they do not necessarily have fairies in them. They often have a certain pattern and may present an "ideal" to the listener or the reader. For instance, fairy tales such as "Cinderella," "Snow White," and "Rapunzel" convey a message about the "proper" woman. According to these tales, the ideal woman is beautiful, kind, and long-suffering; she waits for her prince to come and to save her from any disappointment or disaster that may occur.

Charles Perrault recorded the French fairy tales in the 1600s (Haviland 1959). It was not until the 1800s that the Grimm Brothers recorded German fairy tales, Joseph Jacobs recorded British fairy tales, Peter Asbjornsen and Jorgen Moe recorded Scandinavian fairy tales, and Aleksandr Nikolaevich Afanas'ev recorded Russian fairy tales.

Sometimes, writers, such as Nathaniel Hawthorne, use the term **wonder tales** to refer to these fairy tales with their magical elements. Such elements are often embodied in the characters of witches, wizards, and talking beasts and other magical animals. The use of the **"magic three"** is another frequent feature of the fairy tale; for instance, the stories often involve three wishes, three attempts at achieving a goal, or three siblings.

Another characteristic of a fairy tale is that the listener or reader knows that good will always win out over evil. A youngster may find frightening witches, wicked ogres, and evil forces, but in the end the protagonist (the hero or heroine) ". . . will live happily ever after."

Stereotyping is another characteristic of the fairy tale. As soon as the storyteller or the reader says the word *stepmother*, for instance, the listener knows that the woman is wicked. Likewise, mere mention of the setting as being in the *woods* conveys a message of fear,

impending doom, and evil. The word *prince* causes one to envision a young, handsome man on a white horse! The *princess* is usually the youngest in the family, beautiful, soft-spoken, kind, inactive, and waiting for her prince to come. The demure female characters of the fairy tale stand in direct contrast to the assertive female characters of the folktale.

Folktales are in the language of the people. The stories do not necessarily have a moral. In fact, entertainment is often the main purpose of folktales. In the 1600s and 1700s, early residents of the Appalachian Mountains, for instance, brought many of the fairy tales of England, Scotland, and Ireland with them to the "new" country. The fairy tale "Cinderella" became "Ashpet" in the Appalachians (Chase 1948, 119). The quiet, passive Cinderella became the hard-working, smart, active Ashpet, a character more like the mountain women who had to work and assist their men. "The Bremen Town Musicians" (Grimm and Grimm 1968, 301–304) became "Jack and the Robbers" in another mountain tale (Chase 1943, 40–46).

Another example of the humorous folktales is the Noodle-head stories. **The Noodle-head stories** are those tales that have a character or characters whom the listener can outsmart. The listener often finds these stories particularly humorous because they make the listener feel superior. "Epaminondas" (Bryant 1938) is an example of a Noodle-head story.

The humor in folktales may be coarse, and the diction is often that of the particular group of people who originated the tales. Richard Chase collected many of the Appalachian folktales. He transcribed the tales on paper and told them in personal appearances, on records, and on tapes for the public. He was always careful to use the mountain dialect. His *Jack Tales* (1943) and *Grandfather Tales* (1948) are among his best-known works.

Likewise, other cultures around the world have their own unique folktales and fairy tales. For instance, Charles Perrault's French tale of "Cinderella" is "Tattercoats" in Joseph Jacobs's (1959) collection; in this British version the prince falls in love with a dirty, ragged girl—not a beautiful, well-dressed figure at the ball. The Norwegian tale *East o' the Sun and West o' the Moon* (Asbjornsen and Moe 1946) tells the story of Cinderlad,

not Cinderella. The Jewish folktale of "Zlateh the Goat" (Singer 1966; illustrated by Maurice Sendak) tells of the survival of a young boy and his goat in a snowstorm.

Myths are stories to explain things that the teller does not understand. Greeks and Romans used the story and its associated heroes and heroines to explain thunder, fire, and the "movements" of the sun. Norse myths, too, explain phenomena—especially those associated with the frost, snow, and the cold climate of the north. Likewise, Native American myths explain such phenomena as why the rabbit does not have a tail and why the constellations exist. (Some of these Native American myths are referred to as *legends* instead of the correct name, *myths*.) Another name for these explanations is **pourquoi tales**. Most cultures have their own myths.

Legends are stories—usually exaggerated—about real people, places, and things. George Washington, for instance, was a real person. However, not all the stories about him are true. For example, because there were no silver dollars minted during the American Revolution, it would have been impossible for him to have tossed a American silver dollar across the Potomac. Paul Bunyan (Kellogg 1938/1986) may actually have been a logger or lumberjack, but it is doubtful that he owned a blue ox or had a pancake griddle large enough that his cook could tie hams on his feet and skate on it. The careful reader of literature realizes that though legends are generally a part of traditional literature, they continue to spring up, with modern figures, animals, and places as their central elements.

Four Classifications of Modern Literature. An easy way of classifying modern literature is simply to decide if a book is **realistic** or **fanciful**. There are times, however, when a more discrete classification method is in order. In this case, modern fiction may fall into four categories: novels, romance, confession, or Menippean satire.

Novels are realistic stories depicting events that could really happen or could really have happened. A novel has a realistic setting and realistic characters. The setting could be any planet, any city, or any country—as long as the author can convince the reader that the setting is real. Anyone can serve as a main character as long as the author can convince the reader that the character is believable.

A **romance**, on the other hand, presents an idealized view of life and even of the setting. The story may—or may not—involve love, but the story does involve fantasy. The characters and the setting are better than real life. An ocean cruise in a romance book might, therefore, involve characters who are young, handsome or beautiful, and rich; the romantic characters might also possess all the qualities of the elite. The weather would, of course, be clear and pleasant for the entire cruise.

In a **confession**, one character reveals thoughts and ideas. This particular character is a **round character**, one whom the reader knows in detail. In Laura Ingalls Wilder's *Little House in the Big Woods* (1953), for example, the reader knows exactly what the main character (Laura) is thinking; the reader, however, does not know what Mary (Laura's sister) is thinking. In this case, the confession allows the reader to view the inner thoughts and feelings of only one character.

A **Menippean satire** allows the reader to see the world through the eyes of another. In Roald Dahl's *Charlie and the Chocolate Factory* (1972), the reader sees the world through Charlie's eyes. The desire for candy becomes almost overpowering for the reader—just as it does for Charlie. The reader has a different outlook on life, candy, and others as a result of experiencing *Charlie and the Chocolate Factory*.

Strategies to Promote Understanding of Children's Literature

Most sources agree that it is imperative that teachers **scaffold**, or support, children of all ages in order to promote instruction and reading. Scaffolding involves demonstrating, guiding, and teaching; the amount of support the teacher provides should depend on the instructional support needed and the individual child. Five stages that mark scaffolding are—moving from greatest to the least as students assume more and more responsibility—the modeled, shared, interactive, guided, and independent levels of support (Tompkins 2006).

An instructor can teach reading strategies explicitly to students in a carefully orchestrated manner. First, the teacher should model the strategy, explain it, and describe how to apply the strategy successfully.

It helps if the teacher "thinks aloud" while modeling the strategy for students. Second, the teacher should practice the strategy with the students. It is important to scaffold the students' attempts and support their thinking by giving feedback during conferencing and classroom discussion. In this case, it helps if the students "think aloud" while practicing the strategy. Third, the teacher should encourage the students to apply the strategy and should give them regular feedback. Fourth, once the students clearly understand the strategy, they should apply it on their own in new reading situations. While monitoring students' understanding of the subject matter, the teacher should become aware of students' thinking as they read and as they detect obstacles and confusions that derail their understanding. The teacher can suggest, teach, or implement strategies to help students repair meaning when it breaks down.

Promoting Respect for and Appreciation of Cultural Diversity and Pluralism Through Children's Literature in the Classroom

Dolores B. Malcolm, president of the International Reading Association (IRA) in the late 1990s, states

> Only through the acceptance of the presence of "all" will the true concept of pluralism be realized. . . . Every culture has a heritage, and all children need to know and respect their own heritage and that of other people. (Micklos 1995–1996, 8)

Teachers can heighten students' appreciation for the importance of cultural pluralism—as opposed to separatism or elitism—using activities like the following:

1. Give students the opportunity to look at a situation through several viewpoints. *Faithful Elephants* (Tsuchiya 1988) requires the reader to consider war through its impact on animals, particularly the animals in Japan. *Sadako and the Thousand Paper Cranes* (Coerr 1977) enables the reader to consider war through the eyes of an innocent child. *Maniac Magee* (Spinelli 1990) asks the reader to consider prejudice in America through a child's eyes.

2. Invite members of the community to share their diverse backgrounds.

3. Establish a cooperative work environment in the classroom and the schools.

4. Explore the history of rhymes, riddles, superstitions ("unlucky 13"), customs, symbols (Yule logs, menorahs), chants, songs ("Star-Spangled Banner"), foods, dances, and games.

5. Identify authors who present diverse cultures, like the Cuban writer Carmen Deedy in her narrative *Growing Up Cuban in Decatur, Georgia* (Deedy 1995).

6. Read books about various cultures, such as the southern African American community in *Roll of Thunder, Hear My Cry* (Taylor 1976).

7. Explore various family organizations, such as the matriarchal family and the extended family.

8. Compare and contrast the "melting pot" view with the "salad bowl" view of American society.

9. Show successful individuals from various cultural groups.

10. Experiment with writing haiku (an ancient Japanese verse form), make origami cranes after reading *Sadako and the Thousand Paper Cranes* (Coerr 1977), and experiment with rope rhymes after reading Eloise Greenfield's poem "Rope Rhyme" (Greenfield 1972, 15).

Exceptionalities

Schools have progressed from ignoring children with special needs, to isolating children with special needs in special schools, to providing separate classrooms for exceptional students within the public schools, to mainstreaming the students into the classrooms, and finally to including those with exceptionalities into the "regular" class. Because biases and prejudices sometimes exist as a result of or even before this inclusion, teachers must help construct a working environment that meets each student's basic needs, including a feeling of belonging, a feeling of safety, and a place where each student feels loved and accepted.

Children's literature can show others how it feels to be different in some way and can emphasize that everyone has the same basic needs. For instance, *Crow Boy* (Yashima 1955) helps the students to see what it is like to be excluded because of being "different." *The Flunking of Joshua T. Bates* (Shreve 1984) explores the impact that failing a class has on a student. *Discover-*

ies, by Anita Price Davis and Katharine S. Slemenda, provides numerous biographical sketches of successful people who are deaf. The book establishes effective role models, discourages labeling, and presents individuals who have overcome obstacles in their lives.

Many activities are useful for encouraging the acceptance of others. For instance, teachers can have students role-play situations in which they feel different or in which they encounter another who feels different or left out of the activities. The students can model their responses and discuss their feelings when they respond. Teachers should encourage all students to express worries, fears, and concerns. The teacher could work toward a constructivist classroom.

Bibliotherapy—giving the right book to the right child at the right time, or treating problems with books—is particularly helpful in constructing a cooperative classroom. Students might read and discuss such books as *I Have a Sister—My Sister Is Deaf* (Peterson 1977) about deafness and *The Summer of the Swans* (Byars 1970) about academic problems. These books and others can serve as springboards for discussions of exceptionalities. *The Bookfinder* (Dreyer 1977) is a particularly good source for locating books for bibliotherapy on individual topics.

Multicultural Poems and Poets

Although the poetry of Eloise Greenfield, Nikki Giovanni, Gwendolyn Brooks, and Lee Bennet Hopkins has not yet lasted a century, the quality of their works ensures that their poems will become classics. Their poems (and prose) honor and make others aware of their rich African American heritage.

In Daddy's Arms I Am Tall: African Americans Celebrating Fathers edited by Javaka Steptoe (1997) is a recent Coretta Scott King Award winner. The book of poetry emphasizes the African American experience. Javaka Steptoe's father was author/illustrator John Steptoe. The multicultural literature of father and son are important contributions to children's literature.

Teachers must make certain to include poetry of all cultures in their classrooms. Cynthia Rylant has written many poems on growing up in the Appalachian Mountains. Charlotte Pomerantz writes about her winters in Puerto Rico. Louise Bennett writes of Jamaica. Hai-

ku—a type of poetry in which the poem has three lines with six, seven, and five syllables, respectively—is specific to the Japanese culture. The teacher and students should research other poems about various cultures and experiences.

Elements of Literary Analysis

Plot

The **plot** of a book is the story line and is usually the element that holds the reader's attention. The plot has a definite order, involves conflict, and has a structure. There are several orders.

Order: Chronological, Flashback, or Foreshadowing. The events of the plot can occur either randomly or in **chronological**, or sequential, order. In some books or stories, the plot carries the reader from the present to events in the past; this is called a **flashback**. The plot may carry the reader to and from the past once or several times. There may even be **foreshadowing**, a hint of what is to come. In *The Chocolate War*, the narrator uses foreshadowing and gives the reader a hint of what is to come: "They shouldn't have picked Frankie Rollo for an assignment, of course" (Cormier 1974/1977, 130).

Conflict. There must be **conflict**, or unsettled issues, in the plot to keep the reader interested. The conflict can be with self, others, society, or nature. Of course, *Robinson Crusoe* (Defoe 1719/1972) is an excellent example of conflict with nature. In *Gulliver's Travels* (Swift 1726/1945), the protagonist encounters conflict with the Lilliputians, small people though they are. Vera and Bill Cleaver present a family of children who are fighting society and its rules to remain together in *Where the Lilies Bloom* (1969). Jerry Renault, the main character in *The Chocolate War* (Cormier 1974/1977), faces conflicts with himself (Am I strong enough to refuse to sell the chocolates that the rest of the school is selling?), with others who try to force him to sell, and with society because the entire school community is at odds with him for not selling candy to support the school.

Pattern: Suspense, Cliffhanger, Foreshadowing, Sensationalism, Climax, or Denouement. A book or story that has **suspense** keeps the reader in doubt or uncertain as to the outcome until the end. For instance, in *The Island of the Blue Dolphins* (O'Dell 1960), the reader does not know until the end of the book whether the main character, Karana, will stay on the island.

A **cliffhanger** is an exciting, unsolved event designed to keep the reader turning the page. Cliffhangers are often used in television programs and movies. The television series *Batman*, for example, originally aired on Tuesday and Thursday nights; the viewer had to wait until the Thursday night episode to find out the outcome of the Tuesday night episode. Of course, the story lines featured on soap operas are excellent examples of cliffhangers, as are the Saturday radio serials that were especially popular in the 1940s. The open endings of *The Borrowers* by Mary Norton (1953) and *The Indian in the Cupboard* by Lynne Reid Banks (1980) kept many readers eager for the sequels to those books.

Sensationalism is a literary style in which the author graphically depicts shocking events in order to excite the reader. "Hansel and Gretel," with its tragically vivid scenes of a father abandoning his children in the woods, the children's ill-fated attempts to make their way home, and their capture by and dramatic escape from an evil witch, is an example of sensationalism in traditional literature. Many action movies, such as *Raiders of the Lost Ark*, also contain elements of sensationalism.

The **climax** is the point of highest dramatic tension or the major turning point in a book or story. At the climax, the reader says, "Ah-ha! Now I am sure of the outcome of the conflict!" Sometimes a story has a **false climax** that leads readers to believe they have their questions answered, only to find that the story has new twists and turns. In "Hansel and Gretel," some readers think the conflict is resolved when the children find their way home after their father leaves them in the forest the first time. However, the questions raised in the story are not answered until later.

The **denouement** is the final outcome of the major conflict in a book. There are two types of denouement: open and closed. An **open denouement** is one in which readers do not have all their questions answered. A **closed denouement** is one in which all the questions are resolved. Each story in Howard Garis's volume *Uncle Wiggly's Adventures* (1912/1915) contains an open

ending, which keeps the reader turning the pages. For instance, this is how the first story ends:

> But then, all of a sudden, a harsh voice cried out: "Ha! Now I have you! I was just wishing someone would come along with my dinner, and you did! Get in there, and see if you can find your fortune, Uncle Wiggly!"
>
> And with that a big, black bear, who had been hiding in the stump, pushed Uncle Wiggly into a dark closet, and locked the door! And there the poor rabbit was, and the bear was getting ready to have him for dinner.
>
> But don't worry, I'll find a way to get Uncle Wiggly out. And in case we have ice cream pancakes for supper, with strawberry jam pudding sauce, I'll tell you, in the next story, how Uncle Wiggly got out of the bear's den, and went fishing. (14)

The open endings of some horror movies are what keep viewers attending numerous sequels. *Friday the 13th, Nightmare on Elm Street, Halloween*, and *I Know What You Did Last Summer* are some examples. Of course, the *Rocky* series is also a good example of movies with open denouements, and television soap operas are notorious for their open endings. The American public waited a whole summer to find out "Who shot J. R.?" when the last episode of the 1979–1980 season of the television show *Dallas* had an unsettled ending.

Structure: Progressive or Episodic. Plots are either progressive or episodic. A **progressive** plot is one in which the reader must finish the book or story to find the answers to the questions the plot poses. For instance, to find out who created the statue in *From the Mixed-up Files of Mrs. Basil E. Frankweiler* (Konigsburg 1967), readers must read every page (unless, of course, they cheat and skip to the end). In contrast, Robert Newton Peck's *Soup* series (beginning with *Soup*, published in 1974) contains chapters, each of which is a complete story, or episode, in itself. The chapters in *Soup*, therefore, are **episodic**.

Setting

The **setting**—the time and place where a story or book occurs—is important in juvenile literature. An essential element of the setting is its believability. The plot and the setting together make up the structure of the story.

A setting may be either backdrop or integral. A **backdrop** setting is not essential to the text. The setting in many of the Nancy Drew books is a backdrop setting because the plot could have happened in almost any American city. Most backdrop settings are **figurative**, meaning they serve as illustrations.

An **integral** setting is essential to the plot. Wilson Rawls's novel *Summer of the Monkeys* (1977) has an integral setting: the Ozark Mountains. This novel's setting is also **literal**, meaning the story could actually have occurred where the author set it. Rawls's description of the novel's mountain setting gives readers the feeling they are reading a biography:

> It was in the late 1800s, the best I can remember. Anyhow—at the time, we were living in a brand-new country that had just been opened up for settlement. The farm we lived on was called Cherokee land because it was smack dab in the middle of the Cherokee Nation. It lay in a strip from the foothills of the Ozark Mountains to the banks of the Illinois River in northeastern Oklahoma. (9–10)

Characterization

As important as the plot and action may be to a story, the **characters** are what make many books live on for generations. It is Tom Sawyer, Long John Silver, and Meg, Beth, Jo, and Amy who have made *The Adventures of Tom Sawyer* (Twain 1876/1989), *Treasure Island* (Stevenson 1883/1981), and *Little Women* (Alcott 1868/1968) classics; the characters have withstood the test of time.

Characters can be **round** (fully developed, described, or revealed) or **flat** (undeveloped). In addition, characters are either dynamic or static. A **dynamic** character undergoes some kind of change in the course of the story and becomes more fully revealed as the plot develops. **Static** characters do not change in significant ways—that is, in ways that relate to the plot that is structuring the novel. Even if a character dies—that is, changes from alive to dead—that character is static unless the death is central to the narrative.

Major characters are protagonists or antagonists. The terms come from the Greek word *agon*, meaning "struggle." The **protagonist** struggles for someone or something; the **antagonist** is the enemy or the rival struggling against the protagonist. In "The Three Little Pigs," for instance, the wolf is the antagonist fighting against the pigs, who are the protagonists trying hard to keep their homes and each other safe from the wicked wolf.

Stock characters are characters that exist because the plot demands them. For instance, the ball scene in "Cinderella" must include many men and women who do nothing more than attend the dance; these partygoers are stock characters. A Western novel featuring a gunman who robs a bank may have several stock characters: the banker's lovely daughter, the tough but kindhearted barmaid, the cowardly white-shirted citizen who sells out the hero to save his own skin, and the young freckle-faced lad who shoots the bad guy from a second-story hotel window.

A character can be a **stereotype**, a generalized representation of a certain type of person. For instance, in many fairy tales, the oldest daughter is ugly and mean, whereas the youngest daughter is beautiful—on both the outside and the inside. The small-town Southern sheriff, the brawny football player, the bespectacled librarian, or the cruel commandant of a prisoner-of-war camp are some examples of stereotypes.

A character can also act as a **foil**, someone who serves as a contrast to another character and, in so doing, helps the reader see that other character more clearly. A classic example is in Mark Twain's *The Adventures of Tom Sawyer* (1876/1989). Tom is the romantic foil for Huck Finn's realism. In Harper Lee's *To Kill a Mocking-bird* (1960/1982), Scout serves as the naive observer of events that her older brother, Jem, comes to understand from the perspective of the adult world.

Some characters are **allegorical**, standing for qualities or concepts rather than for actual personages. In C. S. Lewis's *The Lion, the Witch, and the Wardrobe* (1950/1988), the Lion stands for good.

Revealing Characters. Writers use a variety of means to reveal characters to the readers. The writer may **tell about the character**. For instance, here is a description of the dog Lassie, the main character in Eric Knight's *Lassie Come Home* (1938/1966):

> Greenall Bridge was like other Yorkshire villages. Its men knew and understood and loved dogs, and there were many perfect ones that walked at men's heels; but they all agreed that if a finer dog than Sam Carralough's tricolor collie had ever been bred in Greenall Bridge, then it must have been long before they were born. (11)

Another effective device is to **describe the character in the character's surroundings**. In the following passage from *Never Cry Wolf*, Farley Mowat (1963/1984) gives readers a feeling of what it might be like to be an Eskimo:

> This country belonged to the deer, the wolves, the birds and the smaller beasts. We two were no more than casual and insignificant intruders. Man had never dominated the Barrens. Even the Eskimos, whose territory it had once been, had lived in harmony with it. The little group . . . was the last of the inland people, and they were all but swallowed up in this immensity of wilderness. (126)

The writer might also **show the character in action**. The following excerpt from *To Kill a Mockingbird* (Lee 1960/1982) describes Atticus, the lawyer and father, in action when a rabid dog enters their neighborhood:

> Atticus pushed his glasses to his forehead; they slipped down, and he dropped them in the street. In the silence, I heard them crack. Atticus rubbed his eyes and chin; we saw him blink hard. . . . With movements so swift they seemed simultaneous, Atticus's hand yanked a ball-tipped lever as he brought the gun to his shoulder. (96)

The **speech**, or dialect or diction, of a character can aid the author in revealing the character. The language of the gang members in *Durango Street* (Bonham 1965/1975) helps to disclose Tojo's and Rufus's attitudes:

> Tojo smiled. "Esscuse me, brothers. I meant bloods."

Rufus rocked his head. "That's all right, greaseballs—Esscuse *me:* I mean Spanish-Americans."

"Mexicans," Tojo snapped.

"Sure, man," Rufus said. "Well, if you beans change your minds, you know where to find us. But don't come into Durango unless you're ready to talk business. *Adiòs,* huh?" (105)

The author often **reveals the thoughts of a character** to further inform the reader about the character. Billie Jo in Karen Hesse's 1998 Newbery Award winner *Out of the Dust* (1997/1999) expresses her thoughts in her diary: "From the earliest I can remember I've been restless in this little Panhandle shack we call home, always getting in Ma's way with my pointy elbows, my fidgety legs" (4).

A **character's appearance** can help the reader to understand the character. Dori Sanders uses this device in her book *Clover* (1991):

> They dressed me in white for my daddy's funeral. White from my head to my toes. I had the black skirt I bought at the six-dollar store all laid out to wear. I'd even pulled the black cross-grain bows off my black patent leather shoes to wear in my hair. But they won't let me wear black. (1)

What others say about the character gives the reader additional insight into the character. S. E. Hinton uses this device in *The Outsiders* (1967/1983) to tell the reader about Dallas:

> He had quite a reputation. They have a file on him down at the police station. He had been arrested, he got drunk, he rode in rodeos, lied, cheated, stole, rolled drunks, jumped small kids—he did everything. I didn't like him, but he was smart and you had to respect him. (13)

What others say to the character is another way of revealing the character to the reader. In *Brighty of Grand Canyon* (Henry 1953/1967), Uncle Jim—a prospector—speaks to the burro as if it were a human. The reader comes to believe that the burro can understand. When a mountain lion cuts Brighty, Uncle Jim explains how he is helping the burro:

"I've an idee!" he crowed, eyes twinkling in triumph. He took out his pocketknife and pierced the denim just above one knee. Then he cut his way around the pants leg and stepped out of it. "Y'see, boy," he said, "if we hide yer cuts, you can't pick at 'em so easy, and they'll heal nice and clean." (57–58)

Sometimes the author gives the reader **information about the character**. Mary Mapes Dodge in *Hans Brinker* (1963) gives the reader an idea of the time, the place, and the character Hans by her description:

> These queer-looking affairs [homemade skates] had been made by the boy Hans. His mother was a poor peasant woman, too poor even to think of such a thing as buying skates for her little ones. Rough as these were, they had afforded the children many a happy hour upon the ice; and now as with cold, red fingers our young Hollanders tugged at the strings— their solemn faces bending closely over their knees—no vision of impossible iron runners came to dull the satisfaction glowing within. (1–2)

The **reactions of different characters to one another** can help the reader gain insight into each of the characters. Anne's reactions to Marilla and Marilla's reactions to Anne help the reader to know both characters in the classic *Anne of Green Gables* (Montgomery 1908/1935):

> "Will you please call me Cordelia?" she [Anne] asked eagerly.
>
> "*Call* you Cordelia! Is that your name?" [Marilla]
>
> "No-o-o, it's not exactly my name, but I would love to be called Cordelia. It's such a perfectly elegant name."
>
> "I don't know what on earth you mean. If Cordelia isn't your name, what is?"
>
> "Anne Shirley," reluctantly faltered forth the owner of that name. "But oh, please do call me Cordelia. It can't matter much to you what you call me if I'm only going to be here a little while, can it? And Anne is such an unromantic name."

"Unromantic fiddlesticks!" said the unsympathetic Marilla. "Anne is a real good plain sensible name. You've no need to be ashamed of it." (34)

Whatever method the writer chooses to reveal a character, a careful writer will avoid stereotyping. As discussed earlier, **stereotyping** is creating a character based on generalizations regarding factors such as nationality, religion, size, or age. Gender, too, has been a way of stereotyping characters in children's books. Traditionally, fewer female than male characters have appeared in books for children. The female characters who have been portrayed usually exhibit poorer reasoning skills and lead a more placid existence than the males, according to the findings of Suzanne M. Czaplinski (1972). Many female characters depend on males to rescue them and are more passive than their male counterparts. Anita P. Davis and Thomas R. McDaniel (1999) report some gains for girls in the way that Caldecott Award–winning picture books depict female characters, but the researchers were perplexed that books awarded the Caldecott in the 1950s included more female characters than did books from the supposedly more "liberated" decades that followed.

Some teachers who discover stereotyping in a juvenile book may wish to exclude it from the required reading lists for their classrooms. Other teachers may make a point of including such books as a way of helping students become aware of stereotyping and indicating to students the weaknesses of such pigeonholing.

Theme

The **theme** is the main point of the book. The three most common themes in traditional children's literature are the survival of the unfittest theme, the picaresque theme, and the reversal of fortune theme. These themes are also found frequently in modern juvenile literature as well. Whether the theme is **implicit** (suggested) or **explicit** (stated), the reader should immediately recognize these common themes.

The **survival of the unfittest** theme appears in *Gulliver's Travels* (Swift 1726/1945) and *Robinson Crusoe* (Defoe 1719/1972), two books that were published in the 1700s for adults but have become classics for children. In the satire *Gulliver's Travels* and the religious writing *Robinson Crusoe*, Gulliver and Crusoe face many life-threatening situations; in reality, a person would probably not survive the dangers and hardships these two characters encounter. Yet, with the survival of the unfittest theme prevailing, Gulliver and Crusoe manage to endure.

The **picaresque** theme features a traveling or roguish character; *picaro* is Spanish for "rogue." Typically lowborn but clever, the rogue wanders in and out of adventures at all social levels. Though punctuated by broad humor and satire, stories with the picaresque theme have the serious intent of ridiculing social elitism. Examples of picaresque novels are *Uncle Wiggly* by Howard Garis (1912/1915), *Don Quixote* by Miguel de Cervantes (1605, 1615/1950), *Tom Jones* by Henry Fielding (1749/1960), and *Moll Flanders* by Daniel Defoe (1722/1964).

The **reversal of fortune** theme, which focuses on the changing circumstance of a character or characters, is a frequent feature of modern juvenile literature. *Heidi* (Spyri 1884/1982) is an example of a book in which the main character experiences a reversal of fortune. The young girl Heidi goes to live in the mountains with her grandfather, finds herself in the city with a foster family, and then goes back to the mountains with her friend to live with Grandfather. Not only is Heidi's fortune reversed, but so is the fortune of her crippled friend, whom the mountain air, fresh food, and proper exercise healed.

Style

Another criterion for evaluating juvenile fiction is the writing style of the author. A writer can employ many devices to enhance the flow of the words, make the writing more appealing, and clarify the meaning. These stylistic devices include denotation, connotation, irony, humor, figurative language (similes, metaphors, personification), alliteration, consonance, assonance, onomatopoeia, rhythm, imagery, hyperbole, understatement, allusion, word play (pun), parody, and diction. All these stylistic devices appear in Homer Hickam Jr.'s autobiography *October Sky* (1999), the story of some West Virginia high school students who manage to launch their own rockets in the late 1950s and pursue their life dreams.

Denotation. The **denotation** of a word is its precise meaning. Denotation is evident throughout

October Sky, which seems logical because as a scientist, Hickam would use accurate, clear descriptions and would say precisely what he means. Homer uses denotation when he describes Emily Sue's family and where they live:

> Emily Sue lived in a house built on the side of a nearly vertical mountain across the creek and not more than a hundred yards from Big Creek High School. Her father owned a big scrap yard in War [the name of a town], and her mother was the third-grade schoolteacher at War Elementary. (232)

Connotation.   The **connotation** of a word is the impression or feeling a word gives beyond its exact meaning. Sometimes the reader must have some prior knowledge to understand the term. For example, Homer's statement that "Mr. Turner was a banty-rooster type of man" (94) gives a unique impression of Mr. Turner. However, a reader with no previous experience with a banty rooster may not get much insight into the character of the man.

Irony.   **Irony** is the incongruity between what one expects and what actually happens. When Homer uses a telescope to try to look at his own town of Coalwood, he is unable to do so—an unexpected happening:

> I went back to the telescope and tried to use it to look at Coalwood, but discovered I couldn't focus it close enough. I thought how ironic it was that Jake's telescope could see stars a million light-years away, but not the town it was in. Maybe I was that way myself. I had a clear vision of my future in space, but the life I led in Coalwood sometimes seemed to blur. (162)

Humor.   **Humor** is precise and exacting; it is *funny*! When Homer wears his Sunday shoes to the creek, his mother punishes him:

> For punishment, she dictated that the next week I had to go to church in my stocking feet. It didn't take long before everybody in town got wind of what I was going to have to do. I didn't disappoint, walking down the church aisle in my socks while everybody nudged their neighbor and snickered. The thing was, though, I had

picked out the socks, and my big toe poked through a hole in one of them. Mom was mortified. Even the preacher couldn't keep a straight face. (49)

Figurative Language.   **Figurative language** includes the use of similes, metaphors, and personification. It is a way of adding information and description to the writing and of encouraging the reader to think about the text. All the details are not "spoon-fed" to the reader.

A **simile** is a comparison between two things and uses *like*, *than*, or *as*. In describing Jake Mosby, the new junior engineer, Homer remarks, "'He's got more money than Carter's got little liver pills'" (145). Homer overhears a secretary tell some other women that "'he looks just like Henry Fonda'" (146). Homer's mother notes that on one occasion Jake is "'drunk as Cooter Brown'" (146). This figurative language brings imagery to the mind of the reader, requires the reader to think, and adds information to the description.

A **metaphor** is a comparison in which one thing is likened to some other thing. For example, Jake calls the *McDowell County Banner* "'a grocery-store rag'" (154). Homer calls the rocket fuel "rocket candy" because of its sweet odor (181). He also refers to a cord as "a thick electrical umbilical" (199).

Personification is the attribution of human characteristics or behavior to animals, ideas, inanimate objects, and so on. For instance, Homer states that the "big golden moon hovered overhead" (53). Later he says that "a shuttle car darted in, its crablike arms sweeping up the coal thrown out" (199).

Alliteration.   **Alliteration** is the repetition of the same initial sound or letter of words that appear near each other in text. In Homer's description of riding the bus to school on a snowy morning, he uses the repetition of the *s* sound.

> Cresting the top of Coalwood Mountain, we were faced with a steep, straight stretch followed by a series of curves that dipped and turned. Jack slipped into a low gear and we trundled slowly through them, coming out at a short straight stretch that bottomed out into a

wide inside curve, a rocky cliff looming over it. (228)

Consonance. **Consonance**, like alliteration, is the repetition of sounds—in this case, consonant sounds. The short, staccato sound of the hard *c* builds tension when Homer reports that the mining town is about to experience change that may result in the loss of jobs and company housing for Coalwood residents: "In May, the company announced that its big new coal-preparation plant in Caretta was complete, and all the coal from both the Coalwood and Caretta mines would henceforth be loaded into coal cars over there" (148).

Assonance. **Assonance** is the repetition of vowel sounds. In *October Sky*, the school fight song uses assonance: "On, on, green and white. . . . We are right for the fight tonight! Hold that ball and hit that line, every Big Creek star will shine. We'll fight, fight, fight for the green and white" (133–134).

Onomatopoeia. **Onomatopoeia** is a stylistic device in which the word that the writer uses imitates the sound. Cartoons often use onomatopoeic words like *pow*, *bop*, *splat*, and *pop* in their sound effects; sometimes the words even appear on the screen.

October Sky contains many instances of onomatopoeia. For instance, Homer wonders if *Sputnik* will "zip along or dawdle" and notes that his father "plopped on his hat" (37). Later, Homer remarks that Roy Lee growled an "'Ughhhh'" (133) and that his father's "door banged open and I heard him thumping down the stairs. . . . At the bottom of the stairs he started to cough, a racking, deep, wet hack" (54).

Rhythm. The **rhythm**, or flow or cadence, of the words can help create a **mood**, or feeling, in the reader. When Homer and the Rocket Boys attempt to launch their first rocket, the sentences and thoughts that follow the "blast off" are short and choppy—almost staccato—evoking the tension and excitement the boys felt. These brief sentences and concise thoughts are in marked contrast to Hickam's typical style of longer, more descriptive sentences:

Wooden splinters whistled past my ears. Big clunks of the fence arced into the sky. Burning debris fell with a clatter. A thunderous

echo rumbled back from the surrounding hollows. Dogs up and down the valley barked and house lights came on, one by one. People came out and huddled on their front porches. (45)

The reader senses the tension subsiding when Hickam returns to his more usual style of longer, less stressful sentences:

Later, I would hear that a lot of them were wondering if the mine had blown up or maybe the Russians had attacked. At that moment, I wasn't thinking about anything except a big orange circle that seemed to be hovering in front of my eyes. When I regained some sensibility and my vision started to come back, the circle diminished and I started to look around. (45)

Imagery. **Imagery** is a description of the smells, feelings, sounds, or sights of a person, place, thing, or event. Hickam employs imagery to describe many of the places and events surrounding the activities of the Rocket Boys. Particularly important are his descriptions of the town of Coalwood and how the town appeals to the many senses of its inhabitants:

Every weekday, and even on Saturday when times were good, I could watch the black coal cars rolling beneath the tipple to receive their massive loads and then smoke-spouting locomotives straining to pull them away. All through the day, the heavy thump of the locomotives' steam pistons thundered down our narrow valleys, the town shaking to the crescendo of grinding steel as the great trains accelerated. Clouds of coal dust rose from the open cars, invading everything, seeping through windows and creeping under doors. Throughout my childhood, when I raised my blanket in the morning, I saw a black, sparkling powder float off it. My socks were always black with coal dirt when I took my shoes off at night. (2)

Hickam's description of Buck, a football player, employs the senses of seeing, smelling, hearing, and feeling:

"You really are a little sister, ain't you?" He pulled his face in close to us, his chin prickly

with whiskers. There was a brown chewing-tobacco stain in the lower left corner of his mouth. I could smell its sweetness on his breath. (93)

Hyperbole. A **hyperbole** is an exaggeration. Hickam makes use of many of these in *October Sky*. Here is one example: "There was . . . a huge flash in the Hickams' yard and a sound like God Himself had clapped his hands" (44). Another exaggeration occurs when Homer finds out that the Russians have sent the dog Laika into space. Homer begins to consider the size of his dog, Poteet:

> Mom saw me and came outside. "What are you doing to that dog?"
>
> "I just wondered how big a rocket it would take to put her into orbit."
>
> "If she don't stop peeing on my rosebushes, she's going into orbit, won't need any rocket," Mom said. (40)

Understatement. Whereas a hyperbole exaggerates or embellishes to the maximum, an **understatement** is a comment that minimizes. For example, Homer remarks that "I did as I was told with the enthusiasm of a prisoner going to his own beheading" (48). Dreaming about the girl he secretly loves, Homer says, "'I wonder if I crawled over there and kissed her feet if she'd pet me on the head?'" (29).

Allusion. An **allusion** is a reference to a historical, literary, or otherwise generally familiar character event that helps make an idea understandable. Hickam employs this device when he refers to the family pets with the names Daisy Mae (a character in a comic strip popular in the 1950s) and Lucifer (another name for the devil). The pets' names give the readers a hint of the "characters" of the animals. Homer mentions that he "got barely a glimpse of J. Fred Muggs" on the *Today Show* before a snowball hit the window. The allusion to the chimpanzee cohost of the morning television show that began in the late 1950s helps set the time frame of the upcoming events of the story.

Word Play. Hickam makes use of a **word play**, or a pun, when he describes Homer losing a wheel off his wheelbarrow and telling his mother "that I'd spotted some great flower dirt up in the mountains and would've

brought Mom some home with me 'if this blame ol' 'wheelbare' hadn't fallen apart!'" (47).

Parody. A **parody** is a humorous imitation of a musical or literary work. While the Rocket Boys work, they mimic the song "When I Was a Lad" from Gilbert and Sullivan's *H.M.S. Pinafore*.

> "I'm not the carpenter or the carpenter's son," he chanted as we sawed and drove nails, "but I'll do the carpentryin' until the carpenter comes." (139)

At another point in *October Sky*, the principal announces that the football team will not be able to compete for the year and that there will be a concentrated curriculum and more homework than ever. The principal calls the cheerleaders to the front and tries to make the occasion into a happy pep rally—a parody.

Diction. **Diction** is the writer's or speaker's choice of words. Hickam's diction in *October Sky* informs the reader of the words used by the people of Coalwood:

> "We ought to just shoot that damn Sputnikker down." There was a pause while the men all thoughtfully spat tobacco juice into their paper cups, and then one of them said, "Well, I'll tell you who we oughta shoot. Makes me madder'n fire"—he pronounced the word as if it rhymed with *tar*—"them damn people up in Charleston who's tryin' to cheat Big Creek out of the state champs. I'd like to warp them upside the head." (32)

Homer's mother states that his dad "'would have a hissy'" (51), and Roy Lee tells Homer to "'have at it'" (37) when Homer says he plans to build a rocket. Quentin, unlike most of the residents of the West Virginia town, speaks in his own dialect: "'O'Dell,' Quentin replied, in all sincerity, 'I'm worried that your insatiable cupidity will ultimately prove to be something less than a virtue for our club'" (105).

Symbolism

Symbolism is the use of one person, place, or thing to represent another. A common symbol in juvenile literature is the loss or death of an animal to represent the death of childhood; this symbol appears in *Old Yeller*

(Gipson 1956), *The Yearling* (Rawlings 1938), *Where the Red Fern Grows* (Rawls 1961/1976), and *The Biggest Bear* (Ward 1952).

Authenticity

An essential element in juvenile books is **authenticity**. Although the juvenile book might be fiction, it is essential that the elements of the book be believable and convincing. This means that the components (setting, characters, diction, details) must be accurate for the time and place—or at least believable to the reader. A story may, for example, take place on the planet Mars, but as long as the facts, setting, and characters are valid, the story meets one criterion of good literature.

Summary

Juvenile fiction can be categorized as modern or traditional fiction. Under each of these broad categories are several types of literature. For instance, traditional literature includes parables, fables, fairy tales, folktales, noodlehead tales, myths, and legends; modern fiction includes novels, romance, confession, and Menippean satire.

One important element of fiction is the plot and its order (chronological, flashback, foreshadowing), conflict, pattern (suspense, cliffhanger, foreshadowing, sensationalism, climax, denouement), and structure. Another important element is the **setting** (the time and place), which may be one of two types: backdrop (figurative, could occur almost anywhere, not vital to the story) or integral (basic to the plot and occurring in only one place and time).

Character revelation is one of the necessary elements of a good juvenile novel. An author may reveal a character in a variety of ways, such as following them in action or allowing them to speak; most authors use more than one method. The characters may be round or flat, dynamic or static. The characters, however, should not be stereotypical.

The theme may be implicit or explicit. The three main types of theme in children's literature are survival of the unfittest, picaresque, and reversal of fortune.

One of the essential elements in good writing is the use of stylistic devices. Some of the common stylistic devices used in good juvenile books are denotation, connotation, irony, humor, figurative language (similes and metaphors), personification, alliteration, consonance, assonance, onomatopoeia, rhythm, imagery, hyperbole, understatement, allusion, word play, parody, diction, symbolism, and authenticity.

▶ Objective 0006:
Understand Skills and Strategies Involved in the Writing Process

---

The Writing Process

Teachers in the early 1970s were very concerned with spelling and punctuation in students' papers. The teacher did all the "correcting" and watched carefully for grammatical, spelling, and punctuation errors. In the late 1970s, writing "experts" denounced students' compositions as being too dull. The schools began to foster creative writing and encouraged teachers to provide opportunities for creative writing each week. However, many teachers began to view the creative writing as lacking in structure. **Process writing** has since become the "buzz" word in writing. With process writing, students engage in several activities (Noyce and Christie 1989):

Prewriting stage. During the first stage in the writing process, the students begin to collect information for the writing that they will do.

Composing or writing stage. The classroom resembles a laboratory. Students may consult with one another and use various books and materials to construct their papers. At this stage, the student-writers do not worry about spelling and mechanics. This is the drafting stage.

Some students will use invented spelling as they try to apply their understanding of spelling rules. The students may later edit and revise the words, but on a first writing draft, they can simply record the word quickly and go on to the next word in the sentence.

Revising stage. Writers polish and improve their compositions.

Editing/evaluation/postwriting stage. Students read and correct their own writing and the works of others. The teacher does not have to do all the evaluating. Students use a dictionary, a thesaurus, their peers, and even the spell-check program on the classroom computers.

Rewrite stage. After their self-evaluations and after their classmates and teachers share praise and constructive criticisms, including spelling and punctuation, the students rewrite their compositions.

In some classes, the students **publish** their own works and even have an **author's chair** from which the writers can tell some things about themselves, discuss their writing process, and read their compositions aloud (Noyce and Christie 1989). According to research, the most effective writing process includes at least the pre-writing, composing, revising, and editing/evaluation/postwriting stages (Bennett 1987).

Several software tools can be extremely useful to teachers and students when they are writing. Word processing programs allow teachers and students to write, edit, and polish assignments and reports. Most programs have a spelling checker or even a grammar checker to enhance written products. Students in all subjects can use word processors to write term papers or reports of their research. Many word processors allow writers to put the text into columns so that students can produce newsletters with headlines of varying sizes. For example, a reading class could write a series of reviews of *Charlotte's Web* (1952), add information about E. B. White and his times, then collect everything into a newsletter as a class project. There are also desktop publishing programs that allow users to integrate text and graphics to produce publications, such as a class newsletter and school newspapers and yearbooks.

▶ Objective 0007:
Analyze and Revise Written Work in Relation to Style, Clarity, Organization, and Intended Audience and Purpose

Writing serves many different functions. The main functions, however, are to narrate, to describe, to explain, and to persuade. Students need to be aware of each of these types of literature. In any event, the four categories are neither exhaustive nor mutually exclusive.

As discussed earlier, a **narrative** tells a story or gives an account of an incident or a series of incidents. It may be fiction or nonfiction.

The purpose of **descriptive** writing is to provide information about a person, place, or thing. Descriptive writing can be fiction or nonfiction. E. B. White uses descriptive writing to relate what the barn is like in *Charlotte's Web* (1952); the story itself, however, is fiction. Realtors use descriptive writing when they advertise a house in a local newspaper; the general public expects the descriptions of events in the local paper to be factual.

The purpose of **expository** writing is to explain and clarify ideas. Students are probably most familiar with this type of writing. Although the expository essay may have narrative elements, the storytelling or recounting aspect is minor and subservient to that of the explanation element. Expository writing is typically found in many textbooks; for instance, a textbook on how to operate a computer would likely be expository.

The purpose of **persuasive** writing is to convince the reader of something. Persuasive writing fills current magazines and newspapers and permeates the Internet. The writer may be trying to push a political candidate, to convince someone to vote for a zoning ordinance, or even to promote a diet plan. Persuasive writing usually presents a point; provides evidence, which may be factual or anecdotal; and supports the point. The structure may be very formal, with counterpositions and counterarguments. Whatever the organizational pattern, the writer's intent is to persuade readers of the validity of some claim. Nearly all essays have some element of persuasion.

Authors choose their form of writing not necessarily just to tell a story but to present an idea. Whether writers choose the narrative, descriptive, expository, or persuasive format, they have something on their minds that they want to convey to their readers. When readers analyze writing, they often seek first to determine its form.

There are other types of writing, of course. For instance, **speculative** writing is so named because, as its Latin root *speculari* ("to examine") suggests, it looks at ideas and explores them rather than merely

explaining them, as expository writing does. The speculative essay might be meditative; it often makes one or more points, and the thesis may not be as obvious or clear-cut as that in an expository essay. The writer deals with ideas in an associative manner and plays with ideas in a looser structure than the writer might do in an expository format. This "flow" may even produce intercalary paragraphs, which present alternately a narrative of sorts and thoughtful responses to the recounted events.

The genres of novels, short stories, poetry, and drama require from the reader a different kind of involvement than does the essay. Rather than presenting a story from which the reader may discern meaning through the skillful analysis of character, plot, symbol, and language, the essay presents a relatively straightforward account of the writer's opinion on a specific topic. Depending on the type of essay, the reader may become informed (expository essay), provoked (argumentative essay), convinced (persuasive essay), enlightened (critical essay), or acquainted with the writer through a personal story (autobiographical or fictitious).

Satire

Satire, properly speaking, is not a genre at all but rather a mode of writing. Writers of various genres—poetry, drama, fiction, and nonfiction—use satire. It is less a product than a perspective that the reader must try to understand through critical thinking. Satire is a manifestation of the writer's attitude (tone) and purpose.

Satire mainly exposes, ridicules, derides, and denounces vice, folly, evil, and stupidity; those qualities manifest themselves in people, groups, ideas, institutions, customs, and beliefs. Although satirists have many techniques at their disposal, only two types of satire are available—gentle or harsh; the type the author uses depends on the author's intent, audience, and methods.

Selection of the Appropriate Mode of Writing for a Variety of Occasions, Purposes, and Audiences

The writer must consider the audience, the occasion, and the purpose when choosing the writing mode.

The writer's responsibility is to write clearly, honestly, and cleanly for the reader's sake; the **audience** is very important. After all, writing would be pointless without readers.

Why write? Why add evidence, organize your ideas, or correct bad grammar? The reason to do any of these things is that someone out there—an audience—needs to understand what you mean to say.

The teacher can designate an audience for students' writing. Knowing those who will read their work, students can modify their writing to suit the intended readers. For instance, a fourth-grade teacher might suggest that the class take their compositions about a favorite animal to second-graders and allow the younger children to read or listen to the works. The writers will realize that they need to use manuscript—not cursive—writing, to employ simple vocabulary, and to omit complex sentences when they write for their young audience.

The **occasion** helps to determine the elements of the writing. The language should fit the occasion; particular words may have certain effects, such as evoking sympathy or raising questions about an opposing point of view. The students and teacher might try to determine the likely effect on an audience of a writer's choice of a particular word or words.

The **purpose** helps to determine the format (narrative, expository, descriptive, persuasive) and the language of the writer. The students, for instance, might consider the appropriateness of written material for a specific purpose: a business letter, a communication with residents of a retirement center, or a thank-you note to parents. The teacher and students might try to identify persuasive techniques used by a writer in a passage.

In selecting the mode of writing and the content, the writer might ask the following:

- What would the audience need to know to believe you or to accept your position? Imagine someone you know (visualize her or him) listening to you declare your position or opinion and then saying, "Oh yeah? Prove it!"

- What evidence do you need to prove your idea to this skeptic?

- With what might the audience disagree?
- What common knowledge does the audience share with you?
- What information do you need to share with the audience?

The teacher might wish to have the students practice selecting the mode and the language by adapting forms, organizational strategies, and styles for different audiences and purposes.

Identifying Strategies to Teach a Variety of Informational and Literary Text Structures

Informational writing and literary text commonly use several patterns of organization or structure: descriptive writing, ordered list, sequence, cause and effect, comparison, contrast, chronological order, and problem and solution.

To set the scene for a novel or to describe a place in a geography text, for example, a writer often uses **descriptive writing**. Typically, the writer of fiction describes a time and the characteristics of the setting. The time can be thousands of years in the future, for example, as long as the writer makes the setting believable for the reader. Descriptions should encourage readers to feel some kind of connection to the information. Descriptive writing is usually in paragraph form and differs from the ordered list or sequence (Combs 2006).

The **ordered list** is typical in content area textbooks. Using an ordered list, the author can present facts and information more quickly and concisely than is possible using the paragraph format. Text clues of an ordered-list structure are numbers, bullets, letters, or word clues like *first* and *second* (Combs 2006).

Sequence organization can occur in both fiction and nonfiction writing. A writer can organize a sequence to suit the purpose: for instance, alphabetical order, order of occurrence, or geographical placement, among others. A reader who quickly determines the sequence can gain understanding (comprehension) of the material more easily. A perceptive reader watches for word clues like *first, next, before, after,* and *last* (Combs 2006).

Cause-and-effect writing does not necessarily have to progress from cause to effect; a writer might decide that presenting the effect and then discussing the cause is the most effective way to present the material. In a social studies text, for instance, the writer might mention the American Revolution first and discuss the causes afterward; an alternative structure, however, would be to give the causes first and then indicate the effect: the American Revolution. Teachers can guide students to watch for key words that indicate the cause-and-effect structure, including *because, resulting in, why, as a result, therefore, if . . . then, cause,* and *effect*.

Comparison writing occurs when the writer explains the similarities between two or more things. The reader can often identify this type of writing by looking for cue words such as *alike, same as,* and *similar to*.

Sometimes it is helpful for the writer to use a structure that **contrasts** things or indicates how they are different. The cue words that a reader can watch for include *different from, on the other hand,* and *opposite of*.

History books, biographies, and many narratives relate their information in the order in which they happened, or **chronological order**. Watching for words like *first, next, then,* and *last* may cue students that the arrangement is chronological, beginning at the start of the action.

Some writers structure their material according to a **problem-and-solution** organization. The writer can state the problem and then either offer several solutions or present the best answer for the reader (Combs 2006; Tompkins 2006).

▶ Objective 0008:
Use Knowledge of English Grammar and Mechanics to Revise Writing

Writing Skills Review

The AEPA Elementary does not require you to memorize grammatical terms. However, it is important to understand grammatical concepts in order to write and revise text. It is not necessary to memorize all of the following rules, but if you have problems with certain

areas of your writing, be sure to study the appropriate review sections.

Grammar and Usage

The requirements for informal spoken English are much more relaxed than the rigid rules for "standard written English." Although slang, colloquialisms, and other informal expressions are acceptable and sometimes very appropriate in casual speech, they are inappropriate in academic and business writing.

You should watch for errors in grammar, spelling, punctuation, capitalization, sentence structure, and word choice. Remember that this is a test of written language skills; therefore, you should base your responses on what you know to be correct for written work, not what you know to be appropriate for a casual conversation.

Sentence Structure Skills

Parallelism. Parallel structure helps express matching ideas. It refers to the grammatical balance of a series of any of the following:

- Phrases:

    The squirrel ran *along the fenc*e, *up the tree*, and *into his burrow* with a mouthful of acorns.

- Adjectives:

    The job market is flooded with *very talented*, *highly motivated*, and *well-educated* young people.

- Nouns:

    You will need a *notebook*, *pencil*, and *dictionary* for the test.

- Clauses:

    The children were to decide *which toy they would* keep and *which toy they would* give awa*y*.

- Verbs:

    The farmer *plowed*, *planted*, and *harvested* his corn in record time.

- Verbals:

    Reading, *writing*, and *calculating* are fundamental skills that all of us should possess.

- Correlative conjunctions:

    Either you will do your homework *or* you will fail.

- Repetition of structural signals (such as articles, auxiliaries, prepositions, and conjunctions):

    INCORRECT: I have quit my job, enrolled in school, and am looking for a reliable babysitter.

    CORRECT: I *have quit* my job, *have enrolled* in school, and *am looking* for a reliable babysitter.

(*Note*: Repetition often is formal and is often not necessary.)

Misplaced and Dangling Modifiers. A misplaced modifier is one that is in the wrong place in the sentence. Misplaced modifiers come in all forms—words, phrases, and clauses. Sentences containing misplaced modifiers are often very comical: *Mom made me eat the spinach instead of my brother*. Misplaced modifiers, like the one in the preceding sentence, are usually too far away from the word or words they modify. This sentence should read: *Mom made me, instead of my brother, eat the spinach*. Modifiers such as *only*, *nearly*, and *almost* should be next to the word they modify and not in front of some other word, especially a verb, that they do not modify.

A modifier is misplaced if it appears to modify the wrong part of the sentence or if the reader cannot be certain what part of the sentence the writer intended it to modify. To correct a misplaced modifier, move the modifier next to the word it describes:

INCORRECT: She served hamburgers to the men on paper plates.

CORRECT: She served hamburgers *on paper plates* to the men.

A squinting modifier is one that may refer to either a preceding or a following word, leaving the reader uncertain about what it is intended to modify. Correct a squinting modifier by moving it next to the word it is intended to modify:

INCORRECT: Snipers who fired on the soldiers often escaped capture.

CORRECT: Snipers who *often* fired on the soldiers escaped capture.

OR:

Snipers who fired on the soldiers escaped capture *often*.

A dangling modifier is a modifier or verb in search of a subject. The modifying phrase appears to modify the wrong word or has nothing to modify. It is literally dangling at the beginning or the end of a sentence. The sentences often look and sound correct: *To be a student government officer, your grades must be above average.* In this example, the verbal modifier has nothing to describe. Who is *to be a student government officer*? Your grades?

To correct a dangling modifier, reword the sentence by either (1) changing the modifying phrase to a clause with a subject, or (2) changing the subject of the sentence to the word that should be modified:

INCORRECT: Shortly after leaving home, the accident occurred. (Who is leaving home? The accident?)

CORRECT: Shortly after *we* left home, the accident occurred.

Fragments. A fragment is an incomplete construction, which may or may not have a subject and a verb. Specifically, a fragment is a group of words pretending to be a sentence:

INCORRECT: Traffic was stalled for ten miles on the freeway. Because repairs were being made on potholes.

CORRECT: Traffic was stalled for ten miles on the freeway *because* repairs were being made on potholes.

Run-On or Fused Sentences. A run-on or fused sentence is not necessarily a long sentence or a sentence that the reader considers too long; in fact, a run-on may be two short sentences: *Dry ice does not melt it evaporates.* A run-on results when the writer fuses or runs together two separate sentences without using any correct mark of punctuation to separate them:

INCORRECT: Knowing how to use a dictionary is no problem each dictionary has a section

in the front of the book telling how to use it.

CORRECT: Knowing how to use a dictionary is no problem. *Each* dictionary has a section in the front of the book telling how to use it.

Even if one or both of the fused sentences contains internal punctuation, the sentence is still a run-on.

Comma Splices. A comma splice is the use of only a comma to combine what really is two separate sentences:

INCORRECT: One common error in writing is incorrect spelling, the other is the occasional use of faulty diction.

CORRECT: One common error in writing is incorrect spelling; the other is the occasional use of faulty diction.

Sentence Order Skills
Subordination, Coordination, and Predication. Suppose you want to combine the information in these two sentences to create one statement: *I studied a foreign language. I found English quite easy.* How you decide to combine this information should be determined by the relationship you'd like to show between the two facts. *I studied a foreign language, and I found English quite easy* seems rather illogical. The *coordination* of the two ideas (connecting them with the coordinating conjunction *and*) is ineffective. Using *subordination* (connecting the sentences with a subordinating conjunction) clearly shows the degree of relative importance between the expressed ideas: *After I studied a foreign language, I found English quite easy.*

When using a conjunction, keep in mind the following rules:

- *While* is precise when it refers to time; one should exercise care in writing it in its other senses: *although, and,* or *but*. It can be used

    1. to denote simultaneity:

        He wrote the script *while* I assembled the slides.

    2. to denote undertaking:

        He wrote the script *while* I assembled the slides.

(There is ambiguity if one is reading the sentence, so it is preferable to write: *He wrote the script* and *I assembled the slides.*)

- *Where* refers to place and should not be used as a substitute for *that*:

  INCORRECT: We read in the paper *where* they are making great strides in DNA research.

  CORRECT: We read in the paper *that* they are making great strides in DNA research.

- After words such as *reason* and *explanation*, use *that*, not *because*:

  INCORRECT: His explanation for his tardiness was *because* his alarm did not go off.

  CORRECT: His explanation for his tardiness was *that* his alarm did not go off.

Use of Verbs: Verb Tenses

In effective writing, the sense sequence indicates a logical time sequence. Verb tense indicates the time frame of the action:

- **Present tense** is proper

  — in statements about the present:
  I *am* tired.

  — in statements about habitual conditions:
  I *go* to bed at 10:30 every night.

  — in statements of universal truth:
  I learned that the sun *is* 93 million miles from the earth.

  — in statements about the contents of literature and other published works:
  In this book, Sandy *becomes* a nun and *writes* a book on psychology.

- **Past tense** is used in statements of the finished past:
  He *wrote* his first book in 1949, and it *was published* in 1952.

- **Future tense** is used to indicate an action or condition expected in the future:
  I *will* graduate next year.

- **Present perfect tense** describes an action that began in the past but continues into the future:
  I *have lived* here all my life.

- **Past perfect tense** is used for an earlier action that is mentioned in a later action:
  Cindy ate the apple that she *had picked*. (First she picked it, then she ate it.)

- **Future perfect tense** indicates an action that will have been completed at a specific future time:
  By May I *shall have* graduated.

- **Present participle** is used for action that occurs at the same time as the sentence's main verb:
  Speeding down the interstate, I saw a cop's flashing lights.

- **Perfect participle** is used for action that occurred before the main verb:
  Having read the directions, I started the test.

- **Subjunctive mood** is used

  — to express a wish or state a condition contrary to fact:
  If it were not raining, we could have a picnic.

  — in *that* clauses after verbs like *request, recommend, suggest, ask, require,* and *insist* and after such expressions as *it is important* and *it is necessary*:
  It is necessary that all papers *be* submitted on time.

Use of Pronouns

Pronoun Case.   Appropriate pronoun case is essential to effective, understandable essay writing. Pronoun case can either be nominative or objective.

Nominative Case	Objective Case
I, we	*me, us*
you	*you*
he, she, it, they	*him, her, it, them*
who	*whom*

Use the **nominative case** for

- the subject of a sentence:

We students studied until early morning for the final.

- pronouns in apposition to the subject:

  Only two students, Alex and *I*, reported on the meeting.

- the subject of an elliptical clause:

  Molly is more experienced than *he*.

- the subject of a subordinate clause:

  Robert is the driver *who* reported the accident.

- the complement of an infinitive with no expressed subject:

  I would not want to be *he*.

Choose the **objective case** for

- the direct object of a sentence:

  Mary invited *us* to her party.

- the object of a preposition:

  Just between you and *me*, I'm bored.

- the indirect object of a sentence:

  Walter gave a dozen red roses to *her*.

- the appositive of a direct object:

  The committee elected two delegates, Barbara and *me*.

- the object of an infinitive:

  The young boy wanted to help *us* paint the fence.

- the object of a gerund:

  Enlisting *him* was surprisingly easy.

- the object of a past participle:

  Having called the other students and *us*, the secretary went home for the day.

- a pronoun that precedes an infinitive (the subject of an infinitive):

  The supervisor told *him* to work late.

When a conjunction connects two pronouns or a pronoun and a noun, removing the *and* and the other pronoun or noun can help you determine the correct pronoun form. For example, consider this sentence: *Mom gave Tom and myself a piece of cake.* Remov-ing the words *Tom and* reveals that *myself* is not acceptable.

When deciding between *who* and *whom*, try substituting *he* for *who* and *him* for *whom*; follow these easy transformation steps:

1. Isolate the *who* clause or the *whom* clause: Whom we can trust?

2. Invert the word order, if necessary: We can trust whom.

3. Read the final form with the *he* or *him* inserted: We can trust him.

When a pronoun follows a comparative conjunction like *than* or *as*, complete the elliptical construction to help you determine which pronoun is correct:

> She has more credit hours than me [do].
> She has more credit hours than I [do].

Pronoun-Antecedent Agreement. Using the appropriate pronoun antecedent is very important to the effective essay. An **antecedent** is a noun or pronoun to which a pronoun refers. Here are the two basic rules for pronoun-antecedent agreement:

1. Every pronoun must have a conspicuous antecedent.

2. Every pronoun must agree with its antecedent in number, gender, and person.

When an antecedent is one of dual gender—for example, words such as *student, singer, artist, person, citizen,* and so forth—use the expression *his or her.* Some careful writers change the antecedent to a plural noun to avoid using the sexist, singular masculine pronoun *his:*

INCORRECT: *Everyone* hopes that *he* will win the lottery.

CORRECT: Most *people* hope that *they* will win the lottery.

Ordinarily, the relative pronoun *who* is used to refer to people, *which* and *that* to refer to things and places, and *where* to refer to places. There is a grammatical distinction between *that* and *which.*

When differentiating something from a larger class of which it is a member, use *that*. When the subject is not being distinguished from a larger class, use *which*:

> I bought the sweater *that* was on sale.
>
> There were many sweaters, all of *which* were on sale.

Many writers prefer to use *that* to refer to collective nouns:

> A family *that* traces its lineage is usually proud of its roots.

Correct Use of Adjectives and Adverbs

Adjectives are words that modify nouns or pronouns by defining, describing, limiting, or qualifying those nouns or pronouns. **Adverbs** are words that modify verbs, adjectives, or other adverbs and that express such ideas as time, place, manner, cause, and degree. Use adjectives as subject complements with linking verbs; use adverbs with action verbs. Here are some examples:

ADJECTIVE: The old man's speech was *eloquent*.
ADVERB: Mr. Brown speaks *eloquently*.
ADJECTIVE: Please be *careful*.
ADVERB: Please drive *carefully*.

Correct Use of *Good* and *Well*. *Good* is an adjective; its use as an adverb is colloquial and nonstandard:

INCORRECT: He plays *good*.
CORRECT: He looks *good* for an octogenarian.

Well may be either an adverb or an adjective. As an adjective, *well* means "in good health":

ADVERB: He plays *well*.
ADJECTIVE: My mother is not *well*.

Correct Use of *Bad* and *Badly*. *Bad* is an adjective used after sense verbs (*look, smell, taste, feel,* or *sound*) or after linking verbs (*is, am, are, was,* or *were*):

INCORRECT: I feel *badly* about the delay.
CORRECT: I feel *bad* about the delay.

Badly is an adverb that can be used after all other verbs:

INCORRECT: It doesn't hurt very *bad*.
CORRECT: It doesn't hurt very *badly*.

Correct Use of *Real* and *Really*. *Real* is an adjective that means "genuine"; its use as an adverb is colloquial and nonstandard:

INCORRECT: He writes *real* well.
CORRECT: This is *real* leather.

Really is an adverb meaning "very":

INCORRECT: This is *really* gold.
CORRECT: Have a *really* nice day.

Correct Use of *Sort Of* or *Kind Of*. Rather than using *rather* or *somewhat,* some writers incorrectly use the expressions *sort of* and *kind of*:

INCORRECT: Jan was *kind of* saddened by the results of the test.
CORRECT: Jan was *somewhat* saddened by the results of the test.

Use of Faulty Comparisons. Sentences containing faulty comparisons often sound correct because their problem is not one of grammar but of logic. Make sure that like things are being compared, that the comparisons are complete, and that the comparisons are logical.

When comparing two persons or things, use the **comparative** form of an adjective or an adverb; when comparing more than two persons or things, use the **superlative** form. Most one- and two-syllable words form their comparative and superlative degrees with *-er* and *-est* suffixes, respectively. Adjectives and adverbs of more than two syllables form their comparative and superlative degrees with the addition of *more* and *most*, respectively.

When comparing one thing or person with a group of which he, she, or it is a part, use *any, other,* or *else*.

Positive	Comparative	Superlative
good	*better*	*best*
old	*older*	*oldest*
friendly	*friendlier*	*friendliest*
lonely	*lonelier*	*loneliest*
talented	*more talented*	*most talented*
beautiful	*more beautiful*	*most beautiful*

Punctuation

The standard rules of punctuation help the writer to write with clarity and achieve the desired purpose and effect.

Correct Use of Commas

Series.   When more than one adjective describes a noun, use a comma to separate and emphasize each adjective; the comma takes the place of the word *and* in the series:

> the long, dark passageway
>
> an elaborate, complex, brilliant plan

Some adjective-noun combinations are thought of as one word. In these cases, the adjective in front of the adjective-noun combination needs no comma. If you were to insert *and* between the adjective-noun combination, it would not make sense:

> a stately oak tree
>
> a china dinner plate

The comma is also used to separate words, phrases, and whole ideas (clauses); it still takes the place of *and* when used this way: *She lowered the shade, closed the curtain, turned off the light, and went to bed.*

The only question that exists about the use of commas in a series is whether to use one before the final item. It is standard usage to do so, although many newspapers and magazines have stopped using the final comma. Occasionally, the omission of the comma can be confusing:

INCORRECT: We planned the trip with Mary and Harold, Susan, Dick, and Joan, Gregory and Jean and Charles.

CORRECT: We planned the trip with Mary and Harold, Susan, Dick and Joan, Gregory and Jean, and Charles.

Long Introductory Phrases.   Usually if a phrase of more than five or six words or a dependent clause precedes the subject at the beginning of a sentence, a comma is used to set it off:

> After last night's fiasco at the disco, she couldn't bear the thought of looking at him again.
>
> Whenever I try to talk about politics, my wife leaves the room.

If an introductory phrase includes a verb form functioning as another part of speech (a *verbal*), it must be followed by a comma:

INCORRECT: When eating Mary never looked up from her plate.

CORRECT: When eating, Mary never looked up from her plate.

Sentences with Two Main Ideas.   When a sentence contains more than two subjects and verbs (clauses) and the two clauses are joined by a conjunction (*and, but, or, nor, for, yet*), use a comma before the conjunction to separate the two clauses:

> I thought I knew the poem by heart, but he showed me three lines I had forgotten.

If the two parts of the sentence are short and closely related, it is not necessary to use a comma.

> Jane played the piano and Michael danced.

Be careful not to confuse a sentence that has a compound verb and a single subject with a compound sentence. If the subject is the same for both verbs, there is no need for a comma:

> Charles *sent* some flowers and *wrote* a long letter explaining why he had not been able to attend.

In general, words and phrases that stop the flow of the sentence or are unnecessary for the main idea are set off by commas.

Use of Nonrestrictive and Restrictive Elements.

Parts of a sentence that modify other parts are sometimes essential to the meaning of the sentence and sometimes not. When a modifying word or group of words is not vital to the meaning of the sentence, it is set off by commas and is called "nonrestrictive." Modifiers that are essential to the meaning of the sentence are called "restrictive" and are not set off by commas:

ESSENTIAL: The girl *who wrote the story* is my sister.

NONESSENTIAL: My sister, *the girl who wrote the story*, has always loved to write.

Commas are necessary in the following circumstances:

- Interjections:

  Oh, I'm so glad to see you.

- Direct address:

  Roy, won't you open the door for the dog?

- Tag questions:

  I'm really hungry, *aren't you*?

- Geographical names and addresses:

  The letter was addressed to Mrs. Marion Heartwell, *1881 Pine Lane, Palo Alto, California 95824*.

  (*Note:* No comma is needed before the zip code because it is already clearly set off from the state name.)

- Transitional words and phrases:

  You'll find, *therefore,* that no one is more loyal than I am.

- Parenthetical words and phrases:

  The Mannes affair was, *to put it mildly,* a surprise.

- Unusual word order:

  The dress, *new and crisp,* hung in the closet.

- Direct quotations:

  "I won't know what to do," *said Michael,* "if you leave me."

(*Note:* Commas always go inside the closing quotation mark, even if the comma is not part of the material being quoted.)

- Contrasting elements:

  It was a reasonable, *though not appealing,* idea.

- Dates:

  On *October 22, 1992,* Frank and Julie were married.

  (*Note*: One can express dates without commas: He left on 5 December 1980.)

Correct Use of Semicolons

Semicolons are often followed by conjunctive adverbs. Usually, a comma follows the conjunctive adverb. Note that a period can be used to separate two sentences joined by a conjunctive adverb. Some common conjunctive adverbs are *however* and *therefore*. One separates two independent clauses connected by a conjunctive adverb with a semicolon.

He took great care with his work; therefore, he was very successful.

He wanted to be successful; however, he did not take care in doing his work.

The semicolon can do the following:

- Separate independent clauses that are not joined by a coordinating conjunction

  I understand how to use commas; the semicolon I have not yet mastered.

- Combine two independent clauses connected by a coordinating conjunction if either or both of the clauses contain other internal punctuation

  Success in college, some maintain, requires intelligence, industry, and perseverance*; but* others, fewer in number, assert that only personality is important.

- Separate items in a series when each item has internal punctuation

  Call our customer service line for assistance: University of Graduate, 800-555-8020; College of Success, 800-555-8050; School of

Hope, 800-855-3140; or School of Academics, 800-555-8214.

Correct Use of the Colon

Although it is true that a colon precedes a list, one must also make sure that a complete sentence precedes the colon. The colon signals the reader that a list, explanation, or restatement of the preceding will follow. The difference between the colon and the period is that the colon is an introductory mark, not a terminal mark. Look at the following: *The Constitution provides for a separation of powers among the three branches of government . . .* The mark of punctuation after *government* is significant.

- **government.** The period signals a new sentence.

- **government;** The semicolon signals an interrelated sentence.

- **government,** The comma signals a coordinating conjunction followed by another independent clause.

- **government:** The colon signals a list. *The Constitution provides for a separation of powers among the three branches of government: executive, legislative, and judicial.*

The writer can correctly use the colon in the following instances:

- To introduce a list (one item may constitute a list)

    I hate this one course: English.

- To introduce a list preceded by *as follows* or *the following*.

    The reasons he cited for his success are as follows: integrity, honesty, industry, and a pleasant disposition.

- To separate two independent clauses, when the second clause is a restatement or explanation of the first

    All of my high school teachers said one thing in particular: college is going to be difficult.

- To introduce a word or word group that is a restatement, explanation, or summary of the first sentence

    These two things he loved: an honest man and a beautiful woman.

- To introduce a formal appositive

    I am positive there is one appeal which you can't overlook: money.

- To separate the introductory words from a quotation that follows if the quotation is formal, long, or paragraphed separately

    The actor then stated: "I would rather be able to adequately play the part of Hamlet than to perform a miraculous operation, deliver a great lecture, or build a magnificent skyscraper."

Correct Use of the Apostrophe

Apostrophes make a noun possessive, not plural. The following rules are necessary to show possession:

- Add *'s* to singular nouns and indefinite pronouns:

    Tiffany's flowers, the dog's bark

- Add *'s* to singular nouns ending in *s,* unless this distorts the pronunciation, as in the following:

    the boss's pen, Dr. Evans's office OR Dr. Evans' office

- Add *only an apostrophe* to plural nouns ending in *s* or *es*:

    two cents' worth, ladies' night

- Add *'s* to plural nouns not ending in *s*:

    men's room, children's toys

- Add *'s* to the last word in compound words or groups:

    brother-in-law's car, someone else's paper

- Add *'s* to the last name when indicating joint ownership:

    Joe and Edna's home, women and children's clinic

- Add *'s* to both names if you intend to show ownership by each person:

    Joe's and Edna's trucks

- Do *not* add an apostrophe to possessive pronouns: *her, hers; their, theirs; it, its.*

- Use the possessive form of a pronoun or a noun preceding a gerund:

    My bowling a strike irritated him.

    Do you mind *Jane's* stopping by?

- Add *'s* to certain letters, words referred to as words, and abbreviations with periods to show that they are plural:

    three A's on her report card, no's, Ph.D.'s

- Add *s* to decades, symbols, and abbreviations without periods to show that they are plural:

    VCRs, the 1800s

Correct Use of Quotation Marks

The most common use of double quotation marks (" ") is to set off quoted words, phrases, and sentences:

"All I've done is give you a book," she said. "You have to have the courage to learn what's inside it. Come on. You can walk me out to my car."

Single quotation marks are used to set off titles or quoted material within a quote:

"Shall I bring 'Rime of the Ancient Mariner' along with us?" she asked her brother.

Mrs. Green said, "The doctor told me, 'Go immediately to bed when you get home!'"

Double quotation marks can also be used in the following cases:

- To enclose words used as words (although sometimes italics serve this purpose)

    "Horse and buggy" and "bread and butter" can be used either as adjectives or as nouns.

- To enclose slang words or phrases used within more formal writing

    Harrison's decision to leave the conference and to "stick his neck out" by flying to Jamaica was applauded by the rest of the conference attendees.

- To signal to the reader that a word or phrase has an unusual or specific significance, for instance, irony or humor

    The "conversation" resulted in one black eye and a broken nose.

- To set off titles of TV shows, poems, stories, and book chapters

You will find Keats's "Ode on a Grecian Urn" in Chapter 3, "The Romantic Era," in Lastly's *Selections from Great English Poets*.

(*Note:* Titles of books, motion pictures, newspapers, and magazines are underlined when handwritten and italicized when typed.)

Correct Use of Capitalization

When a writer uses capitalization, the capital letter calls attention to itself. This attention should be for a good reason. There are standard uses for capital letters. In general, capitalize (1) all proper nouns, (2) the first word of a sentence, and (3) the first word of a direct quotation. Also capitalize the following:

- Names of ships, aircraft, spacecraft, and trains

    Apollo 13, DC-10, S.S. *United States*, Boeing 707

- Names of deities

    Allah, the Holy Spirit, Venus, Jehovah

- Geological periods

    Neolithic age, Cenozoic era, late Pleistocene times

- Names of astronomical bodies

    Mercury, Halley's comet, Ursa Major, North Star

- Personifications

    Reliable Nature brought her promised Spring.

    Bring on Melancholy in his sad might.

- Historical periods

    Middle Ages, Reign of Terror, Great Depression, Renaissance

- Names of organizations, associations, and institutions

    Girl Scouts, Kiwanis Club, League of Women Voters, Smithsonian Institution

- Government and judicial groups

    United States Court of Appeals, Senate, Committee on Foreign Affairs, Peace Corps

- A general term (such as *state* or *park*) that accompanies a specific name only if it follows the specific name. If it stands alone or comes before the specific name, it is put in lowercase. This rule does

not apply, however, when the general term directly precedes a person's name, thus acting as part of his or her title.

> Washington State, the state of Washington
>
> Central Park, the park
>
> Mississippi River, the river
>
> Pope John XXIII, the pope

- The first word in a sentence within a sentence

> We had only one concern: When would we eat?
>
> He answered, "We can only stay a few minutes."

- The first and last words of a title and all other major words. Do not capitalize conjunctions *(and, or, but)*, articles *(a, an, the)*, or short prepositions *(of, on, by, for)*, unless they are the first or the last word.

> *Of Mice and Men*
>
> *Rise of the West*
>
> "Rubaiyat of Omar Khayyam"
>
> "All in the Family"

- Newspaper and magazine titles

> *U.S. News & World Report, National Geographic, The New York Times, The Washington Post*

- Radio and TV station call letters

> KNX-AM, KQED-FM, WNEW, WBOP

- Names of specific regions, but not general areas, compass directions, or seasons

> the South, the Northeast, the West, Eastern Europe
>
> the south of France, the eastern part of town
>
> east, south
>
> summer, autumn

- Names of specific military units

> U.S. Army, 1st Infantry Division

- Names of political groups and philosophies, but not systems of government or individual adherents to a philosophy

> Democratic party, democracy
>
> Communist party, communist
>
> Libertarian party
>
> Transcendentalism
>
> fascist, agnostic

Correct Spelling

Many people learn to read English phonetically, by sounding out the letters of the words. However, many English words are not pronounced the way they are spelled; the oft-repeated mnemonic "*i* before *e* except after *c*, or when sounded as 'a' as in *neighbor* and *weigh*" presents a case in point. Further confounding phonetic spellers is the fact that the English language uses different spellings to create the same sounds. For example, consider the following spelling facts:

- Only three words in the English language end in -*ceed*: *proceed, succeed,* and *exceed.*

- There are several words that end in -*cede*: *secede, recede, concede, precede.*

- Only one word in the English language ends in -*sede*: *supersede.*

Thus, people who try to spell certain English words phonetically often make spelling errors. It is better to memorize the correct spelling of some English words than to rely on phonetics to spell correctly.

The following words are frequently misspelled. Study the spelling of each word and then have a friend or teacher drill you. Mark down the words that you misspelled and study those select ones again. (The words appear in their most popular spellings.)

Words That Are Commonly Misspelled

a lot	advisable	anxious	attendance	borrow
ability	advise	apologize	attention	bottle
absence	adviser	apparatus	audience	bottom
absent	aerial	apparent	August	boundary
abundance	affect	appear	author	brake
accept	affectionate	appearance	automobile	breadth
acceptable	again	appetite	autumn	breath
accident	against	application	auxiliary	breathe
accommodate	aggravate	apply	available	brilliant
accompanied	aggressive	appreciate	avenue	building
accomplish	agree	appreciation	awful	bulletin
accumulation	aisle	approach	awkward	bureau
accuse	all right	appropriate	bachelor	burial
accustomed	almost	approval	balance	buried
ache	already	approve	balloon	bury
achieve	although	approximate	bargain	bushes
achievement	altogether	argue	basic	business
acknowledge	always	arguing	beautiful	cafeteria
acquaintance	amateur	argument	because	calculator
acquainted	American	arouse	become	calendar
acquire	among	arrange	before	campaign
across	amount	arrangement	beginning	capital
address	analysis	article	being	capitol
addressed	analyze	artificial	believe	captain
adequate	angel	ascend	benefit	career
advantage	angle	assistance	benefited	careful
advantageous	annual	assistant	between	careless
advertise	another	associate	bicycle	carriage
advertisement	answer	association	board	carrying
advice	antiseptic	attempt	bored	category

ceiling	competition	council	descent	dissatisfied
cemetery	compliment	counsel	describe	dissection
cereal	conceal	counselor	description	dissipate
certain	conceit	courage	desert	distance
changeable	conceivable	courageous	desirable	distinction
characteristic	conceive	course	despair	division
charity	concentration	courteous	desperate	doctor
chief	conception	courtesy	dessert	dollar
choose	condition	criticism	destruction	doubt
chose	conference	criticize	determine	dozen
cigarette	confident	crystal	develop	earnest
circumstance	congratulate	curiosity	development	easy
citizen	conquer	cylinder	device	ecstasy
clothes	conscience	daily	dictator	ecstatic
clothing	conscientious	daughter	died	education
coarse	conscious	daybreak	difference	effect
coffee	consequence	death	different	efficiency
collect	consequently	deceive	dilemma	efficient
college	considerable	December	dinner	eight
column	consistency	deception	direction	either
comedy	consistent	decide	disappear	eligibility
comfortable	continual	decision	disappoint	eligible
commitment	continuous	decisive	disappointment	eliminate
committed	controlled	deed	disapproval	embarrass
committee	controversy	definite	disapprove	embarrassment
communicate	convenience	delicious	disastrous	emergency
company	convenient	dependent	discipline	emphasis
comparative	conversation	deposit	discover	emphasize
compel	corporal	derelict	discriminate	enclosure
competent	corroborate	descend	disease	encouraging

endeavor	explanation	government	ignorance	invitation
engineer	extreme	governor	imaginary	irrelevant
English	facility	grammar	imbecile	irresistible
enormous	factory	grateful	imitation	irritable
enough	familiar	great	immediately	island
entrance	fascinate	grievance	immigrant	its
envelope	fascinating	grievous	incidental	it's
environment	fatigue	grocery	increase	itself
equipment	February	guarantee	independence	January
equipped	financial	guess	independent	jealous
especially	financier	guidance	indispensable	journal
essential	flourish	half	inevitable	judgment
evening	forcibly	hammer	influence	kindergarten
evident	forehead	handkerchief	influential	kitchen
exaggerate	foreign	happiness	initiate	knew
exaggeration	formal	healthy	innocence	knock
examine	former	heard	inoculate	know
exceed	fortunate	heavy	inquiry	knowledge
excellent	fourteen	height	insistent	labor
except	fourth	heroes	instead	laboratory
exceptional	frequent	heroine	instinct	laid
exercise	friend	hideous	integrity	language
exhausted	frightening	himself	intellectual	later
exhaustion	fundamental	hoarse	intelligence	latter
exhilaration	further	holiday	intercede	laugh
existence	gallon	hopeless	interest	leisure
exorbitant	garden	hospital	interfere	length
expense	gardener	humorous	interference	lesson
experience	general	hurried	interpreted	library
experiment	genius	hurrying	interrupt	license

light	mischief	occasional	patience	pleasant
lightning	mischievous	occur	peace	please
likelihood	misspelled	occurred	peaceable	pleasure
likely	mistake	occurrence	pear	pocket
literal	momentous	ocean	peculiar	poison
literature	monkey	offer	pencil	policeman
livelihood	monotonous	often	people	political
loaf	moral	omission	perceive	population
loneliness	morale	omit	perception	portrayal
loose	mortgage	once	perfect	positive
lose	mountain	operate	perform	possess
losing	mournful	opinion	performance	possession
loyal	muscle	opportune	perhaps	possessive
loyalty	mysterious	opportunity	period	possible
magazine	mystery	optimist	permanence	post office
maintenance	narrative	optimistic	permanent	potatoes
maneuver	natural	origin	perpendicular	practical
marriage	necessary	original	perseverance	prairie
married	needle	oscillate	persevere	precede
marry	negligence	ought	persistent	preceding
match	neighbor	ounce	personal	precise
material	neither	overcoat	personality	predictable
mathematics	newspaper	paid	personnel	prefer
measure	newsstand	pamphlet	persuade	preference
medicine	niece	panicky	persuasion	preferential
million	noticeable	parallel	pertain	preferred
miniature	o'clock	parallelism	picture	prejudice
minimum	obedient	particular	piece	preparation
miracle	obstacle	partner	plain	prepare
miscellaneous	occasion	pastime	playwright	prescription

presence	quite	rhythm	sight	succeed
president	raise	rhythmical	signal	successful
prevalent	realistic	ridiculous	significance	sudden
primitive	realize	right	significant	superintendent
principal	reason	role	similar	suppress
principle	rebellion	roll	similarity	surely
privilege	recede	roommate	sincerely	surprise
probably	receipt	sandwich	site	suspense
procedure	receive	Saturday	soldier	sweat
proceed	recipe	scarcely	solemn	sweet
produce	recognize	scene	sophomore	syllable
professional	recommend	schedule	soul	symmetrical
professor	recuperate	science	source	sympathy
profitable	referred	scientific	souvenir	synonym
prominent	rehearsal	scissors	special	technical
promise	reign	season	specified	telegram
pronounce	relevant	secretary	specimen	telephone
pronunciation	relieve	seize	speech	temperament
propeller	remedy	seminar	stationary	temperature
prophet	renovate	sense	stationery	tenant
prospect	repeat	separate	statue	tendency
psychology	repetition	service	stockings	tenement
pursue	representative	several	stomach	therefore
pursuit	requirements	severely	straight	thorough
quality	resemblance	shepherd	strength	through
quantity	resistance	sheriff	strenuous	title
quarreling	resource	shining	stretch	together
quart	respectability	shoulder	striking	tomorrow
quarter	responsibility	shriek	studying	tongue
quiet	restaurant	siege	substantial	toward

tragedy	United States	vegetable	voice	weird
transferred	university	vein	volume	whether
treasury	unnecessary	vengeance	waist	which
tremendous	unusual	versatile	weak	while
tries	useful	vicinity	wear	whole
truly	usual	vicious	weather	wholly
twelfth	vacuum	view	Wednesday	whose
twelve	valley	village	week	wretched
tyranny	valuable	villain	weigh	
undoubtedly	variety	visitor		

▶ Objective 0009:
Understand Listening Skills and Strategies

Language is an intensely complex system for creating meaning through socially shared conventions. Very young children begin to learn language by listening and responding to the people in their life. This early listening provides a foundation for acquisition of language. Babies are active listeners. Long before they can respond in speech per se, they wave their arms, smile, or wriggle to encourage the person talking to them to continue. On the other hand, they are also capable of clearly communicating—by dropping eye contact or turning away, for example—when they have had enough.

Although listening is important in communication, it does not receive much attention at school. Most people seem to assume that listening develops naturally. Listening skills can and should be taught. In American society, citizens must often ignore environmental sounds (lawn mowers, traffic sounds, trains, plane engines). It seems that Americans often spend more energy "tuning out" than "tuning in." It is no wonder that many people in our society enter kindergarten, high school, and even college as poor listeners (Davis 2004, 65).

Most theorists link listening and attending skills to reading skills. They indicate that reading and listening make use of similar language comprehension processes. Listening and reading both require the use of skills in phonology, syntax, semantics, and knowledge of text structure; the same set of cognitive processes controls both. However, an additional factor occurs in listening: the recipient of the oral message can elect to listen passively or to listen actively; active listening is the desired goal. The skill of listening can be efficiently taught by engaging students in the kinds of activities that have been successful in developing reading, writing, and speaking proficiencies and skills: setting a purpose for listening, giving directions, asking questions about the selection heard, and encouraging children to forge links between the new information that they just heard and the knowledge already in place.

Perceptual strengths (learning modalities) refer to students' learning modalities, such as whether they are visual, auditory, tactile, or kinesthetic learners. Basically, these perceptual modalities refer to whether students learn best by seeing, hearing, or doing. Although less than 15 percent of the school-age population is auditory, much of the classroom instruction takes the form of teachers telling students information.

Girls are more likely to learn auditorially than are boys. Teachers should also keep in mind that whether students benefit from lectures is likely to depend on several other elements, such as whether the students like the teacher, whether they think the information being presented is important, and whether they think that listening to the teacher will help them to achieve their goals.

Most students (about 85 percent) do not learn auditorially. Teachers must help these students perfect their listening skills and profit from oral instructions and lecture.

On the other hand, there are students who do not seem to benefit much from lectures, textbook assignments, or visual aids. These students' perceptual strengths are tactile and kinesthetic. They learn from movement and motion—being able to touch, handle, and manipulate objects. Often these students may have been identified as having learning disabilities. Sometimes they have been relegated to shop or cooking classes or have found their success in athletics, music, or art. Interestingly, many of the hands-on skills that often identify a student for a career as an auto mechanic are also important skills for mechanical engineers and surgeons.

Teachers should be careful to instruct students on how to take notes while listening to a speaker; note taking is a skill students will use not only in school but also in their future careers, whether listening to instructions from a supervisor or to lectures at meetings and conferences. One way a teacher can teach note taking is to show students notes or an outline from the mini lecture he or she is about to present, or to write notes or an outline on the board or overhead while presenting the information. This activity requires careful planning by the teacher and will result in a more organized lecture. This type of structure is especially helpful for sequential learners: those who like organization. Such structure will also help random learners develop organizational skills. A web, map, or cluster is a more right-brained method of connecting important points in a lecture or a chapter. The effective teacher will use both systems and teach both to students so they have a choice of strategies.

A teacher who wants to emphasize careful listening from the students should model the skill for the class. The teacher should listen carefully to the students, ask for clarification if necessary, and respond appropriately to the student. Teachers should also monitor the effects of a message and make sure that the audience actually received and understood the message. An effective way to encourage students to be active and reflective listeners is by having each student summarize what another has said before making his or her own contribution.

Teachers must be cognizant of their treatment of high and low achievers in the classroom. When dealing with high achievers, as opposed to low achievers, teachers tend to listen more carefully, give them more time to answer, prompt or assist them more, call on them more often, give more feedback, and look more interested. The effective communicator will be careful not to differentiate communication based on a student's achievement level.

In calling on and responding to individual students in class, teachers must be especially mindful of personal biases to which everyone is susceptible. Do you tend to call on boys more than girls, or vice versa? Do you tend to call only on those who raise their hands? Should you ignore "call-outs"? The last question has no easy answer. If a student who is usually nonparticipatory calls out an answer on one occasion, it may be better to reward that student's willingness to participate by acknowledging the response. On the other hand, if a student frequently calls out without raising his or her hand, it is probably better to ignore the response until the student raises his or her hand and waits for the teacher's recognition.

▶ Objective 0010:
Understand Speaking Skills and Strategies

Children need coaching in the use of appropriate volume and speed when they speak. They need practice in how to participate in discussions and how to follow the rules of polite conversation, such as staying on a topic and taking turns. The teacher should provide opportunities for speaking.

Group work and response ensures that everyone is involved. Of course, the teacher should watch for the student who is not responding and encourage him or her to participate. Individual student responses give the

spotlight to particular students, increase their involvement in the class, and develop their ability and comfort in speaking in a group.

The teacher can employ eye contact to control interactions within the classroom. Teachers will often look directly at students to encourage them to speak or will look away to discourage them from speaking. "The stare" can be part of "the look" that a teacher uses for discipline reasons. Making eye contact with students is important when the teacher is giving instructions, sharing information, or answering questions. Many people make a habit of scanning the room with their eyes and pausing briefly to meet the gaze of many members of an audience. However, eye contact should last about four seconds to assure the person in the audience (or classroom) that the speaker has actually made contact.

Because people learn in different ways, the effective speaker uses a variety of presentation techniques and should encourage active listening from the audience. Being certain to include an introduction and conclusion can help bring a "set" to the topic under discussion and can summarize what the speaker has said. Many speakers employ the use of various methods of presentations (programs, overhead projectors, charts, and multimedia projectors) to enhance their speech and increase their audience's understanding and interest. The speaker may ask for analysis from the listener(s) to decide if further discussion or research is necessary.

It is essential also that the speaker be aware of body language and how one's movements convey messages to the listeners. For example, crossing the arms indicates a reluctance to accept information from others; standing or sitting with open arms indicates a willingness to listen and accept. A finger on the chin may indicate that the listener is considering what a speaker is suggesting.

▶ Objective 0011:
Understand the Use of Visual Media and Technological Resources in Communication

The most available tools in classrooms are the chalkboard and the overhead projector. Several prin-

ciples apply to both. The teacher must write clearly and in large letters. Overhead transparencies should never be typed on a regular typewriter because the print is too small. Computers allow type sizes of at least 18 points, which is the minimum readable size. Also, both boards and transparencies should be free of clutter. The teacher should remove old information before adding new information to a board or transparency. These tools work more effectively if the teacher plans ahead of time what he or she will write or draw on them. Using different colors will emphasize relationships or differences.

When schools began using computers, the early programs tended to be drill-and-practice exercises that allowed students to practice simple skills such as mathematics operations. Some of the more elaborate systems in use today include both instructional, practice, and testing exercises with management systems that allow teachers to keep track of how well the students are achieving. This type of software encourages practice; an advantage is immediate feedback so students know if they chose the correct answer. Many of these programs have a game format to make the practice more interesting. A disadvantage of these programs is the generally low-level nature of many of the activities.

Tutorials are a step above drill-and-practice programs because they include explanations and information. The student makes a response; the program branches to the most appropriate section, based on the student's answer. Tutorials not only provide remedial work but also are useful for instruction in English as a second language. Improved graphics and sound allow nonnative speakers of English to listen to correct pronunciation while viewing pictures of words. Tutorials supplement, not supplant, teacher instruction. Simulations or problem-solving programs provide opportunities for students and are useful instructional tools.

If the available screen is too small for large-group viewing, then the teacher might break the class into groups and have several different projects for them to do on a rotating basis. Some of the best graphic aids will be those that individual students or groups of students develop. Along with learning about subject area concepts, students will learn about design and presentation of information. Students can take pictures of their products to put in a portfolio or scrapbook.

Videodiscs provide a sturdy, compact system of storage for pictures and sound. They can store more than 50,000 separate frames of still images, up to 50 hours of digitized stereo music, or about 325 minutes of motion pictures with sound. An advantage of videodisc over videotape is that the presenter can access each frame separately and quickly. The simplest level of use involves commands to play, pause, skip forward, or skip back. The user can access individual frames by inputting their numbers.

A teacher can make programs interactive by linking them to a computer. The teacher can then individually access, sequence, and pace the information from the interactive system to design custom-made lessons that he or she can use repeatedly or easily revise. For example, an art teacher with a collection of pictures of the world's art treasures can choose which pictures to use and the order in which to show them. He or she might decide to develop a program on landscapes as portrayed in art during a certain period of time. By using the videodisc's reference guide, the teacher determines which pictures to use and the length of time he or she wants each displayed. Thus, the teacher can develop numerous lessons from one videodisc.

More comprehensive interactive programs can use the computer to present information, access a videodisc to illustrate main points, then ask for responses from the student. A computer multimedia production can include images, text, and sound from a videodisc, CD-ROM, graphics software, word-processing software, and a sound effects program. Teachers can develop classroom presentations, but students can develop presentations as part of their reports.

The cost of a multimedia system remains relatively high, but students can use it to develop high-level thought processes, collaborative work, and research skills, as well as content knowledge and understanding.

Computer Software Tools

Databases are like electronic file cards; they allow students to input data, then retrieve it in various ways and arrangements. History students can input data about various countries, for example, population, population growth rate, infant mortality rate, average income, and

average education level. They can then manipulate the database to call out information in a variety of ways. The more important step in learning about databases is dealing with huge quantities of information. Students need to learn how to analyze and interpret the data that they see so they can discover connections between isolated facts and figures and how to eliminate inappropriate information.

Online databases are essential tools for research. Students can access databases related to English, history, science—any number of subject areas. Most programs allow electronic mail so that students can communicate over the computer with people from around the world. There are also massive bibliographic databases that can help students and teachers find resources they need. Students can borrow many of the print materials through interlibrary loan. The use of electronic systems can exponentially increase the materials that are available to students.

Spreadsheets are similar to teacher grade books. Rows and columns of numbers can produce totals and averages. Formulas can connect information in one cell (the intersection of a row and column) to another cell. Teachers often keep grade books on a spreadsheet because of the ease in updating information. Once formulas are in place, teachers can enter grades and have completely up-to-date averages for all students. Students can use spreadsheets to collect and analyze numerical data, which can be sorted in various orders. Some spreadsheet programs also include a chart function so that teachers could display class averages on a bar chart to provide a visual comparison of the classes' performance. Students can enter population figures from various countries, then draw various types of graphs—bars, columns, scatters, histograms, pies—to convey information. This type of graphic information is useful in multimedia presentations. Various stand-alone graph and chart software packages are also available.

Graphics or paint programs allow users to draw freehand to produce any type of picture or to use tools to produce boxes, circles, or other shapes. These programs can illustrate classroom presentations or individual research projects. Many word-processing programs have some graphic elements. With the use of these relatively simple tools, teachers can create handouts and instructional materials with a very professional and polished appearance.

Today's teachers need to acquire and demonstrate skill in using presentation software (such as Microsoft PowerPoint) to prepare instructional lessons. In many classrooms, the use of presentation software makes the traditional use of transparencies on an overhead projector obsolete. Presentation software also makes it possible to provide students with instructional handouts and outlines to complement classroom instruction. In some situations and in some schools, web authoring experience and skills will prove useful.

Although it is very likely that prospective teachers have had some background in instructional design, some basic guidelines are helpful (Truehaft 1995). To begin, it is important that teachers consider the purpose of the presentation: What is the message? Teachers should avoid the temptation to include "bells and whistles" (or super-duper technologies) that are too dazzling and that detract from the message.

Second, it is important for the presentation to be consistent; that is, the transitions from slide to slide should, in general, be the same. The backgrounds (or templates) should remain the same. Type font and sizes should be consistent. The use of color to highlight or separate text should also be consistent.

Third, the audience (the students) must be able to see clearly. The presenter (the teacher) must make sure the type size is large enough: an image projected on a monitor will be smaller than one projected via an LCD projector. Each slide should have a limited amount of text: more than six or eight lines of type on a single slide will be hard to read. Lots of "white space" gives a presentation a clean and easily read appearance.

A presentation should feature only one or two fonts. If the presentation has only a small amount of text (a title or label), sans serif type may be best (such as Arial or Helvetica); however, for a passage of text, serif type (such as Times New Roman or Bookman) is easier to read.

When preparing the presentation slide, the presenter should include only one message or main point per slide. The presenter should also limit the number of graphic elements to only one or two per slide to enhance visibility. Whether or not the text is readable will depend on the contrast between the text color and the background: dark text on a light background or vice versa (such as black on white, or white on black) is best. An accent color (such as red) can add emphasis.

Before any presentation, teachers should ensure that they know how to use the computer and projection device controls. They should also check that all settings are as they need to be; for example, if the presentation includes sound, the teacher should set the volume ahead of time.

The Internet and the World Wide Web are having a profound effect on students and teachers alike. This very powerful learning tool is best viewed as a source of information. By linking computers around the world, the Internet serves as a network of networks. From 500 hosts in 1983, the Internet had grown to about 30 million hosts in 1998, and the number continued to mount at a dramatic rate. At the start of the twenty-first century, some 360 million people were believed to have access to the Internet. Oscar Wilde once argued that there is no such thing as a good or bad book, that a work of literature exists apart from issues of morality. One can apply the same logic to the Internet.

As any source of information, the Internet can be used well or badly. Because the amount of information available is so enormous, it is often difficult to find the exact information one is seeking. Also, with such large amounts of information and no quality control, a good deal of inaccurate and false information is available. With regard to the Internet, therefore, teachers must address critical thinking skills with their students and instruct the students on how to judge the accuracy of information, to look for evidence and substantiation of claims, and to separate facts from opinions. Educators, just as parents, must be concerned about the appropriateness of the information accessed by students; a wide range of material is available and some of it is unsuitable for children. To safeguard children and provide some kind of quality control, many public schools use Internet filters. These tools limit access to unsuitable material; however, because some of the filters do not discriminate adequately, students may sometimes access questionable material and may not be able to access some acceptable material. For this reason, teachers must carefully supervise the use of this powerful resource.

Teachers today should have acquired experience and expertise in using the Internet while completing their educational training. Basically, teachers should

be familiar with common Internet browsers (such as Microsoft Explorer and Netscape) and popular search engines (such as Yahoo, Excite, Lycos, and Google) that make it possible to research any topic. Many Web sites offer teaching tips and tools; teachers will want to investigate these and bookmark the ones that are most pertinent and reliable. Communicating with colleagues, parents, and even students is made convenient through electronic mail.

The Internet, then, is a common tool of the twenty-first century, used by both teachers and students. Internet sites are constantly being developed and renovated; sites that are popular today may be gone tomorrow. However, here are a few popular links for teachers:

www.ed.gov

www.education-world.com

www.nea.org

http://school.discovery.com/teachingtools

www.teachersfirst.com

As they find ways to use the Internet as a teaching tool, teachers must also be mindful of the Children's Internet Protection Act (CIPA) and the Neighborhood Children's Internet Protection Act (N-CIPA), which passed Congress in December of 2000. Both were part of a large federal appropriations measure (PL 106-554). There are three basic requirements in the legislation that applicants must meet, or be "undertaking actions" to meet:

1. The school or library must use blocking or filtering technology on all computers with Internet access. The blocking or filtering must protect against access to certain visual depictions, including obscenity, child pornography, and materials harmful to minors. The law does not require the filtering of text.

2. The school or library must adopt and implement an Internet safety policy that addresses the key criteria, including

   a. access by minors to inappropriate matter on the Internet and the Web;

   b. the safety and security of minors when using electronic mail, chat rooms, and other forms of direct electronic communications;

   c. unauthorized access, including so-called hacking, and other unlawful activities by minors online;

   d. unauthorized disclosure, use, and dissemination of personal identification information regarding minors;

   e. measures designed to restrict minors' access to materials harmful to minors.

3. The school or library must hold a public meeting to discuss the Internet safety policy; specifically, the law requires that the school or library "provide reasonable public notice and hold at least one public hearing or meeting to address the proposed Internet safety policy."

Copyright is a form of protection provided by the laws of the United States (Title 17, U.S. Code) to the authors of "original works of authorship," including literary, dramatic, musical, artistic, and certain other intellectual works. This protection is available to both published and unpublished works.

It is illegal for anyone to violate any of the rights provided by copyright law to the owner of the copyright. These rights, however, are not unlimited. Sections 107 through 121 of the 1976 Copyright Act establish limitations on these rights. In some cases, these limitations are specified exemptions from copyright liability. One major limitation is the doctrine of "fair use," which is given a statutory basis in section 107 of the 1976 Copyright Act.

The **fair use doctrine** allows limited reproduction of copyrighted works for educational and research purposes. In general, a teacher can copy a chapter from a book; an article from a periodical or newspaper; a short story, short essay, or short poem, whether or not from a collective work; and/or a chart, graph, diagram, drawing, cartoon, or picture from a book, periodical, or newspaper. For a classroom, a teacher can make multiple copies (not to exceed the number of students in the class) as long as the copying meets the following tests of brevity and spontaneity and meets the cumulative effect test and as long as each copy includes a notice of copyright.

Brevity generally refers to a poem of 250 words or less or a prose passage less than 2,500 words. *Spontane-*

ity refers to the need for a teacher to use a work without undertaking the normal time to obtain copyright permission. Finally, the *cumulative effect test* refers to copying material for only one class, from a single author and no more than nine times during a term. Suggested guidelines for fair use can be found at the University of Texas System Web site: *www.utsystem.edu/ogc/ intellectualproperty/clasguid.html.*

In regard to fair use of multimedia materials, in general, it is acceptable for faculty and students to incorporate others' work into a multimedia presentation and display or perform the multimedia work as long as it is for a class assignment. It is suggested that educators be prudent in the use of such materials by being conservative (using only small amounts of others' work) and not making unnecessary copies of such works. Complete information about copyright can be found at the official Web site of the U.S. Library of Congress Copyright Office: *www.loc.gov/copyright.*

Tools such as the Internet make available such a wide range of and substantial amount of content that today's teachers have a greater role than ever teaching students process skills (such as critical and creative thinking) rather than teaching mere content skills. Content will change and expand; however, thinking processes remain salient and necessary, regardless of the content.

Parents and other members of the community can be excellent local experts from which students can learn about any subject—mathematics from bankers, art and music from artists, English from public relations representatives, history from club or church historians or librarians, business from owners of companies. The list is endless. Effective teachers make sure that any guest who is invited to speak or perform understands the purpose of the visit and the goals or objectives the teacher is trying to accomplish. Preparation can make the class period more focused and meaningful. Field trips are excellent sources of information, especially about careers and current issues such as pollution control. One field trip can yield assignments in mathematics, history, science, and English, and often art, architecture, music, or health. Teachers can collaborate with each other to produce thematic assignments for the field trip or simply to coordinate the students' assignments. Often, a history report can serve as an English paper as well. Data can be analyzed in math classes and presented with the aid of computers.

The effective teacher uses criteria to evaluate audiovisual, multimedia, computer resources, and human resources. The first thing to look for is congruence with lesson goals. If the software doesn't reinforce student outcomes, then it should not be used, no matter how flashy or well done. A checklist for instructional computer software could include appropriate sequence of instruction, meaningful student interaction with the software, learner control of screens and pacing, and motivation. Other important factors include ability to control sound and save progress, effective use of color, clarity of text and graphics on the screen, and potential as an individual or group assignment.

In addition to congruence with curriculum goals, the teacher considers students' strengths and needs, their learning styles or preferred modalities, and their interests. Teachers can determine students' needs through formal or informal assessment. Most standardized tests include an indication of which objectives the student did not master. Computer or multimedia aids can assist students in mastering these objectives. Teachers can assess students' learning styles with a variety of instruments and models, including those that Rita and Kenneth Dunn advocate (Dunn and Dunn). Students with highly visual learning modes will benefit from audiovisuals. A questionnaire, either purchased or developed by the district, may reveal student interests. A knowledge of student interests will help the teacher provide resources to suit individual needs. The effective teacher can design activity choices that relate to class goals but also to student interests.

The effective teacher evaluates resources well in advance of the lesson and before purchase whenever possible. The teacher also evaluates the materials as students use them. When students have finished using the materials, the teacher can assess material usefulness by considering students' achievement levels and/or by asking students for their opinions.

▶ References

Aesop. 1950. *The fables of Aesop: Selected, told anew, and their social history traced by Joseph Jacobs.* New York: Macmillan.

Afanas'ev, Aleksandr Nikolaevich. 1975. *Russian fairy tales.* Trans. Norbert Guterman. New York: Pantheon.

Ainsworth, Larry, and Jan Christinson. 1998. *Student-generated rubrics: An assessment model to help all students succeed.* Upper Saddle River, NJ: Pearson.

Alcott, Louisa Mae. 1868/1968. *Little women.* Boston: Little, Brown.

Arbuthnot, May Hill. 1964. *Children and books.* Glenview, IL: Scott, Foresman.

Asbjornsen, Peter, and Jorgen Moe. 1946. *East o' the sun and west o' the moon.* Evanston, IL: Row, Peterson.

Bailey, Mildred Hart. 1967. The utility of phonic generalizations in grades one through six. *Reading Teacher* 20 (February): 413–418.

Banks, Lynne Reid. 1980. *The Indian in the cupboard.* Garden City, NY: Doubleday.

Barry, Leasha M., et al. 2005. *The best teachers' test preparation for the FTCE.* Piscataway, NJ: Research and Education Association.

Bennett, William. 1987. *What works: Research about teaching and learning.* Washington, DC: U.S. Department of Education.

Bonham, Frank. 1965/1975. *Durango Street.* New York: Dell.

Breinburg, Petronella. 1974. *Shawn goes to school.* New York: Crowell.

Bryant, Sara Cone. 1938. *Epaminondas and his auntie.* Boston: Houghton.

Byars, Betsy. 1970. *The summer of the swans.* New York: Viking Press.

Carbo, Marie. 1993. *Reading styles and whole language. Schools of thought II.* VHS. Bloomington, IN: Phi Delta Kappa.

Cervantes, Miguel de (John M. Cohen). 1976. *Don Quixote.* New York: Penguin.

Chase, Richard. 1943. *Jack tales.* New York: Houghton Mifflin.

———. 1948. *Grandfather tales.* New York: Houghton Mifflin.

Chudowsky, Naomi, and James W. Pellegrino. 2001. *Knowing what students know: The science and design of educational assessment.* Washington, DC: National Academy Press.

Clay, Marie M. 1966. Emergent reading behavior. PhD diss., University of Auckland, New Zealand.

———. 1979. *Reading: The patterning of complex behavior.* Auckland, New Zealand: Heinemann.

———. 1985. *The early detection of reading difficulties.* Portsmouth, NH: Heinemann.

Cleaver, Vera, and Bill Cleaver. 1969. *Where the lilies bloom.* New York: Lippincott.

Clymer, Theodore. 1963. The utility of phonic generalizations in the primary grades. *Reading Teacher 16* (January): 252–258.

Coerr, Eleanor. 1977. *Sadako and the thousand paper cranes.* New York: Putnam.

Combs, Martha. 2006. *Readers and writers in primary grades: A balanced and integrated approach.* Upper Saddle River, NJ: Pearson.

Commission on Reading. 1986 (September). *Becoming a nation of readers.* Washington, DC: U.S. Department of Education.

Cook, Jimmie E., et al. 1980. Treating auditory perception problems: The NIM helps. *Academic Therapy 15* (March): 473–481.

Cormier, Robert. 1974/1977. *The chocolate war.* New York: Dell.

Czaplinski, S. M. 1972. *Sexism in award winning picture books.* Pittsburgh: Know, Inc.

Dahl, Roald. 1972. *Charlie and the chocolate factory.* New York: Knopf.

Davis, Anita P. 2000. *Children's literature essentials.* Boston: American Press.

———. 2004. *Reading instruction essentials.* 3rd ed. Boston: American Press.

Davis, Anita P., and Ed Y. Hall. 1993. *Harriet Quimby: First lady of the air (an activity book for children).* Spartanburg, SC: Honoribus Press.

———. 1998. Harriet Quimby: *First lady of the air (an intermediate biography).* Spartanburg, SC: Honoribus Press.

Davis, Anita P., and Thomas R. McDaniel. 1998. Essential vocabulary words. *Reading Teacher 52* (November): 308–309.

———. 1999. You've come a long way, baby—or have you? *Reading Teacher* 52 (February): 532–535.

Davis, Anita P., and Marla Selvidge. 1995. *Focus on women*. Westminster, CA: Teacher Created Materials, Inc.

Davis, Anita P., and Katharine S. Slemenda. 1996/2005. *Discoveries*. Hillsborough, ID: Butte Publications.

De Angeli, Marguerite. 1946. *Bright April*. Garden City, NY: Doubleday.

Deedy, Carmen. 1995. *Growing up Cuban in Decatur, Georgia*. Atlanta, GA: Peachtree Publishers.

Defoe, Daniel. 1722/1964. *Moll Flanders*. New York: Signet.

———. 1719/1972. *Robinson Crusoe*. Boston: Houghton Mifflin.

Dodge, Mary Mapes. 1963. *Hans Brinker*. New York: Grosset and Dunlap.

Dolch, Edward William. 1960. *Dolch sight word list*. Champaign, IL: Garrard Press.

Dreyer, Sharon Spredemann. 1977. *The bookfinder: A guide to children's literature about the needs and problems of youth aged 2–15*. Circle Pines, MN: American Guidance Service.

Dunn, Rita, and Kenneth Dunn. 1978. *Teaching students through their individual learning styles: a practical approach*. Reston, VA: Reston Publishing Company.

Fielding, Henry. 1749/1950. *Tom Jones*. New York: The Modern Library.

Finazzo, Denise Ann. 1997. *All for the children*. Albany, NY: Delmar Press.

Finn, Patrick J. 1990. *Helping children learn to read*. New York: Longman.

Flesch, Rudolf Franz. 1955. *Why Johnny can't read—And what you can do about it*. New York: Harper.

Fry, Edward. 1980. *The new instant word lists*. Reading Teacher 34 (December): 264–289.

Garis, Howard. 1912/1915. *Uncle Wiggly's adventures*. New York: Platt and Munk.

Gilligan, C. 1982. *In a different voice: Psychological theory and women's development*. Cambridge, MA: Harvard University Press.

Gipson, Fred. 1956. *Old Yeller*. New York: Harper.

Goudvis, Anne, and Stephanie Harvey. 2000. *Strategies that work*. Portland, ME: Stenhouse.

Greenfield, Eloise. 1972. *Honey, I love*. New York: Thomas Y. Crowell Co., 15.

Grimm, Jacob, and Wilhelm Grimm. 1968. *Grimm's fairy tales*. Chicago: Follett.

Gunning, Thomas G. 1996. *Creating reading instruction for all children*. Boston: Allyn and Bacon.

Harmon, William, and C. Hugh Holman. 2002. *Handbook of literature*. Upper Saddle River, NJ: Prentice Hall.

Haviland, Virginia, ed. 1959. *Favorite fairy tales told in France: Retold from Charles Perrault and other French storytellers*. Boston: Little, Brown.

Hebert, Elizabeth A. 2001. *The power of portfolios: What children can teach us about learning and assessment*. Hoboken, NJ: Jossey-Bass.

Heckleman, R. G. 1969. *A neurological-impress method of remedial-reading instruction*. Academic Therapy IV (Summer): 277–282.

Henry, Marguerite. 1953/1967. *Brighty of the Grand Canyon*. New York: Scholastic.

Hesse, Karen. 1997/1999. *Out of the dust*. New York: Scholastic.

Hickam, Homer H., Jr. 1999. *October sky*. New York: Dell. (Orig. pub. 1998 as Rocket boys.)

Hildebrand, V., L. A. Phenice, M. M. Gray, and R. P. Hines. 2000. *Knowing and serving diverse families*. 2nd ed. Englewood Cliffs, NJ: Merrill.

Hinton, S. E. 1967/1983. *The outsiders*. New York: Dell.

Hollingsworth, Paul. 1978. An experimental approach to the impress method of teaching reading. *Reading Teacher* 31 (March): 624–626.

Huck, Charlotte S., Susan Hepler, and Janet Hickman. 1993. *Children's literature in the elementary school*. Fort Worth, TX: Harcourt Brace.

"IRA takes a stand on phonics." 1997. *Reading Today* (April/May): 1–4.

Jacobs, Joseph. 1959. *Favorite fairy tales told in England*. Boston: Little, Brown.

Karlin, Robert. *Teaching elementary reading*. New York: Harcourt Brace Jovanovich, 1971.

Kellogg, Steven. 1938/1986. *Paul Bunyan*. New York: Morrow.

Klein, Marvin L. 1985. *The development of writing in children pre-K through grade 8.* Englewood Cliffs, NJ: Prentice Hall.

Knight, Eric. 1938/1966. *Lassie come home.* New York: Scholastic.

Konigsburg, E. L. 1967. *From the mixed-up files of Mrs. Basil E. Frankweiler.* New York: Atheneum.

Krathwohl, David R., Benjamin S. Bloom, and Bertram B. Masia. 1964. *Taxonomy of educational objectives: The classification of educational goals.* Handbook II, Affective domain. New York: David McKay.

Larrick, Nancy. 1965. The all-white world of children's books. *Saturday Review* (September 11): 63–65.

Lee, Harper. 1960/1982. *To kill a mockingbird.* New York: Warner Books.

Lewis, C. S. 1950/1988. *The lion, the witch, and the wardrobe.* New York: Macmillan.

Marzano, Robert J., and Daisy E. Arredondo. 1986. *Tactics for thinking.* Aurora, CO: Mid-Continent Regional Education Laboratories.

Merleau-Ponty, Maurice. 1973. *Consciousness and the acquisition of language.* Trans. Hugh J. Silverman. Evanston, IL: Northwestern University Press.

Michaelis, John U., and Jesus Garcia. 1996. *Social studies for children: A guide to basic instruction.* Boston: Allyn and Bacon.

Micklos, B., Jr. 1995–1996. Multiculturalism and children's literature. *Reading Today* (December/January): 1, 8.

Montgomery, L. M. 1908/1935. *Anne of Green Gables.* New York: Farrar, Straus and Giroux.

Mowat, Farley. 1963/1984. *Never cry wolf.* Toronto: Bantam Books.

Norton, Mary. 1953. *The borrowers.* New York: Harcourt Young Classics.

Noyce, Ruth M., and James F. Christie. 1989. *Integrating reading and writing instruction in grades K–8.* Boston: Allyn and Bacon.

O'Dell, Scott. 1960. *Island of the blue dolphins.* New York: Houghton Mifflin.

Peck, Robert Newton. 1974. *Soup.* New York: Knopf.

Peterson, Jeanne Whitehouse. 1977. *I have a sister—My sister is deaf.* New York: Harper and Row.

Popham, W. James. 2001. *Classroom assessment: What teachers need to know.* 3rd ed. Upper Saddle River, NJ: Pearson, Allyn and Bacon.

Pyles, Thomas, and John Algeo. 1982. *The origins and development of the English language.* New York: Harcourt Brace.

Rawlings, Marjorie Kinnan. 1938. *The yearling.* New York: Scribner.

Rawls, Wilson. 1961/1976. *Where the red fern grows.* New York: Bantam.

———. 1977. *Summer of the monkeys.* New York: Dell.

Richardson, Judy S., and Raymond F. Morgan. 1990. *Reading to learn in the content areas.* Belmont, CA: Wadsworth.

Sanders, Dori. 1991. *Clover.* New York: Fawcett Columbine.

Shreve, Susan. 1984. *The flunking of Joshua T. Bates.* New York: Knopf.

Singer, Isaac Bashevis. 1966. *Zlateh the goat and other stories.* New York: Harper.

Southern Regional Education Board. Health and Human Services Commission. 1994. *Getting schools ready for children: The other side of the readiness goal.* Atlanta, GA.

Spinelli, Jerry. 1990. *Maniac Magee.* Boston: Little, Brown.

Spyri, Johanna. 1884/1982. *Heidi.* New York: Messner.

Steptoe, Javaka (ed.). 1997. *In daddy's arms I am tall: African Americans celebrating fathers.* New York: Lee and Low Books.

Steptoe, John. 1969. *Stevie.* New York: Harper and Row.

Stevenson, Robert Louis. 1883/1981. *Treasure island.* New York: Scribner.

Stiggins, Richard J. 2005. *Student involved assessment for learning.* 4th ed. Upper Saddle River, NJ: Prentice Hall.

Swift, Jonathan. 1726/1945. *Gulliver's travels.* Garden City, NY: Doubleday.

Tannen, D. 1991. *You just don't understand: Women and men in conversation.* New York: Ballantine Books.

Taylor, Mildred D. 1976. *Roll of thunder, hear my cry.* New York: Dial Press.

Tompkins, Gail E. 2006. *Literacy for the twenty-first century: A balanced approach.* 4th ed. Upper Saddle River, NJ: Pearson.

Trelease, Jim. 1985. *The read-aloud handbook.* New York: Penguin Books.

Truehaft, J. 1995. *Learning to Use Technology in Education.* Algonquin College, *www.algonquincollege.com/edtech/usngtech.html.*

Tsuchiya, Yukio. 1988. *Faithful elephants: A true story of animals, people, and war.* Boston: Houghton Mifflin.

Twain, Mark. 1876/1989. *The adventures of Tom Sawyer.* New York: Morrow.

Vacca, Richard T., and Jo Anne L. Vacca. 1989. *Content area reading.* 3rd ed. Glenview, IL: Scott, Foresman.

Ward, Lynd. 1952. *The biggest bear.* New York: Houghton Mifflin.

White, E. B. 1952. *Charlotte's web.* New York: Harper and Row.

Wilder, Laura Ingalls. 1953. *Little house in the big woods.* New York: Harper.

Wittgenstein, Ludwig. 1921/1974. *Tractatus logico-philosophicus.* Trans. D. F. Pears and B. F. McGuinness. London: Routledge.

———. 1958. *Philosophical investigations.* 3rd ed. Eds. G. E. M. Anscombe and Rush Rhees. Trans. G. E. M. Anscombe. New York: Macmillan.

Yashima, Taro. 1955. *Crow boy.* New York: Viking Press.

Mathematics

▶ Objective 0012:
Apply a Variety of Approaches to Interpret and Solve Mathematical Problems in Real-World Contexts

The ability to render some real-life quandaries into mathematical or logical problems—workable via established procedures—is a key to finding solutions. Because each quandary will be unique, so too will be your problem-solving plan of attack. Still, many real-world problems that lend themselves to mathematical solutions are likely to require one of the following strategies:

Guess and check. This is not the same as "wild guessing." With this problem-solving strategy, students make their best guess and then check the answer to see whether it is right. Even if the guess does not immediately provide the solution, it may help to get students closer to it so that they can continue to work on it. Here is an example:

Three persons' ages add up to 72, and each person is one year older than the last person. What are their ages?

Because the three ages must add up to 72, it is reasonable to take one-third of 72 (24) as the starting point. Of course, even though 24 + 24 + 24 gives a sum of

72, those numbers do not match the information ("each person is one year older"). So, students might guess that the ages are 24, 25, and 26. Checking that guess by addition, students would see that the sum of 75 is too high. Students might then try lowering their guesses by one each, trying 23, 24, and 25, which indeed add up to 72, giving students the solution. There are many variations of the guess-and-check method.

Make a sketch or a picture. Being able to visualize a problem can help to clarify it. Consider this problem:

Mr. Rosenberg plans to put a 4-foot-wide concrete sidewalk around his backyard pool. The pool is rectangular, with dimensions 12 feet by 24 feet. The cost of the concrete is $1.28 per square foot. How much concrete is required for the job?

Students with exceptional visualization abilities will not need a sketch. For most, however, a drawing like the one shown below may be helpful in solving this and many other real-life problems.

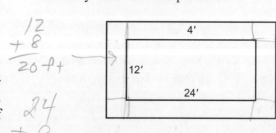

Make a table or a chart. Sometimes organizing the information from a problem into a table or a chart makes it easier to find the solution, as in the following example:

Pencils are two for 25 cents. How many pencils can Teresa buy for 75 cents?

One way to solve the problem is to set up a chart.

Pencils	Cost
2	25 cents
4	50 cents
x	75 cents

Make a list. Like a table or chart, a list can help organize information and perhaps provide or at least hint at a solution. The list-making strategy would work well for solving the following problem:

How many different outcomes are possible if you flip two regular two-sided coins?

Heads	Heads
Heads	Tails
Tails	Heads
Tails	Tails

Act it out. Sometimes literally "doing" a problem—with physical objects or even their bodies—can help students produce a solution. The following problem could be solved in this manner:

If five strangers meet and everyone shakes everyone else's hand once, how many total handshakes will there be?

Look for patterns. This technique encourages students to ask "What's happening here?" Spotting a pattern would be helpful in solving a problem such as this:

Nevin's weekly savings account balances for 15 weeks are as follows: $125, $135, $148, $72, $85, $96, $105, $50, $64, $74, $87, $42, $51, $60, and $70. If the pattern holds, what might Nevin's balance be the next week?

Work a simpler problem. By finding the solution to a different but simpler problem, students might spot a way to solve the harder one. **Estimating** can be thought of as working a simpler problem. To find the product of 23×184 when no calculator or pencil and paper are handy, students could estimate the product by getting the exact answer to the simpler problem 20×200.

Writing an open math sentence (an equation with one or more variables, or "unknowns") and then solving it. This is sometimes called "translating" a problem into mathematics. Here is a sample problem:

Tiana earned grades of 77%, 86%, 90%, and 83% on her first four weekly science quizzes. Assuming all grades are equally weighted, what score will she need on the fifth week's quiz to have an average (or mean) score of 88%?

Using the given information, students could set up and solve the following equation to answer the question:

$$\frac{(77+86+90+83+x)}{5} = 88$$

Work backward. Consider this problem:

If you add 12 to some number and then multiply the sum by 4, you will get 60. What is the number?

Students could find a solution by *starting at the end*, with 60. The problem states that the 60 came from multiplying a sum by 4. When 15 is multiplied by 4, the result is 60. The sum must be 15; if 15 is the sum of 12 and something else, the "something else" can only be 3.

As mentioned earlier, sometimes **finding the solution to a simpler problem** helps reveal a way to solve a hard one. Estimating is one technique for working a simpler problem. **Estimation** is thus a useful tool in predicting and in checking the answer to a problem. Estimation is at the second level in Bloom's Taxonomy—the *comprehension* level (see Table 3-1). Thinking at the comprehension level requires students not only to recall or remember information but also to understand the meaning of information and to restate it in their own words.

Table 3-1. Bloom's Taxonomy

Level of Question	Student Capability	Questioning Verbs
Level 1: Knowledge	Remembers, recalls learned (or memorized) information	define, describe, enumerate, identify, label, list, match, name, read, record, reproduce, select, state, view
Level 2: Comprehension	Understands the meaning of information and is able to restate in own words	classify, cite, convert, describe, discuss, estimate, explain, generalize, give examples, make sense out of, paraphrase, restate (in own words), summarize, trace, understand
Level 3: Application	Uses the information in new situations	act, administer, articulate, assess, chart, collect, compute, construct, contribute, control, determine, develop, discover, establish, extend, implement, include, inform, instruct, operationalize, participate, predict, prepare, preserve, produce, project, provide, relate, report, show, solve, teach, transfer, use, utilize
Level 4: Analysis	Breaks down information into component parts; examines parts for divergent thinking and inferences	break down, correlate, diagram, differentiate, discriminate, distinguish, focus, illustrate, infer, limit, outline, point out, prioritize, recognize, separate, subdivide
Level 5: Synthesis	Creates something new by divergently or creatively using information	adapt, anticipate, categorize, collaborate, combine, communicate, compare, compile, compose, contrast, create, design, devise, express, facilitate, formulate, generate, incorporate, individualize, initiate, integrate, intervene, model, modify, negotiate, plan, progress, rearrange, reconstruct, reinforce, reorganize, revise, structure, substitute, validate
Level 6: Evaluation	Judges on the basis of informed criteria	appraise, compare and contrast, conclude, criticize, critique, decide, defend, interpret, judge, justify, reframe, support

As mentioned earlier, in the 1990s a group of psychologists revised Bloom's Taxonomy. They reversed the two highest levels so that synthesis was the highest level of intellectual behavior (*http://web.odu.edu/educ/lschult/blooms_taxonomy.htm*).

▶ Objective 0013:

Understand Mathematical Communication and Use Mathematical Terminology, Symbols, and Representations to Communicate Information

The students must be able to convert among words, symbols, terms, and other representations.

The representations for numbers include the following:

Word names. For example, *four, one hundred, thirty-five*

Standard numerals. For example, 4, 100, 35

Pictorial models. For students in the lower grades, the number 4 may be represented by four drawings of a bird:

For students in the higher grades, pie graphs (like the one below), bar graphs, charts, and other pictorial representations can represent numbers.

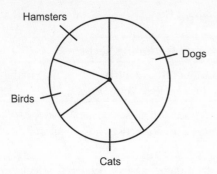

Operation	Key Words
Subtraction	Decreased by Minus Less Difference of Difference between Less than Fewer than
Multiplication	Of Times Multiplied by Product of Increased by a factor of Decreased by a factor of
Division	How many to each How many groups Share Separate Equal groups Divide Quotient

Counting numbers begin with the number 1 and continue 1, 2, 3, and so on. **Whole numbers** are the counting numbers plus zero (0, 1, 2, 3, and so on).

A **common fraction** is a number in the form *a/b*, where *a* and *b* are whole numbers. In the expression *a/b*, the dividend *a* is the **numerator**, and the divisor *b* is the **denominator**. A common fraction cannot have zero as a denominator, because **division by zero is undefined**.

Decimal numbers are fractions written in special notation. All decimal numbers are actually fractions whose denominators are powers of 10 (10; 100; 1,000; and so on). For instance, 0.25 can be thought of as the fraction 25/100, which reduces to 1/4.

Integers are numbers preceded by either a positive (+) or negative (–) sign. An integer without a sign is positive. (For example, 3 means +3.) On a number line, integers to the left of zero are negative, and integers to the right of zero are positive.

Operations indicate what one is to do with numbers. The four main operations are addition, subtraction, multiplication, and division. Words may provide a clue as to which operation to use. The following table highlights some examples of key words:

Operation	Key Words
Addition	Increased by More than Combined Together Total of Sum Added to

The following problem and the explanation that follows provide an example of how to change a word problem into a mathematical representation:

> The Acme Taxicab Company charges riders $3 just for getting into the cab, plus $2 for every mile or fraction of a mile driven. What would be the fare for a 10-mile ride?

One helpful approach when attempting to change a word problem into a mathematical representation is first to translate the problem into an equation (or, sometimes, an inequality). Translating the word problem into math results in the following algebraic expression:

$$x = 3 + (2 \times 10).$$

The equation can be read as "the unknown fare (*x*) is equal to $3 plus $2 for each of the 10 miles driven." Solving the equation gives 23 for *x*; $23 is the solution to the word problem.

Applying the Order of Operations

Some mathematical expressions indicate several operations. Simplifying that type of expression requires

following a universally agreed-upon order for performing each operation:

- First, compute any multiplication or division, left to right.
- Second, compute any addition or subtraction, also left to right.
- If an expression contains any parentheses, complete all computations within the parentheses first.
- Treat exponential expressions ("powers") as multiplication.

Thus, solving the expression $3 + 7 \times 4 - 2$ requires multiplying 7 by 4 *before* doing the addition and subtraction to obtain the result of 29.

The rules for performing operations on integers (whole numbers and their negative counterparts) and on fractions and decimal numbers in which at least one is negative are generally the same as the rules for performing operations on nonnegative numbers. The trick is to pay attention to the sign (the positive or negative value) of each answer.

The rules for both multiplication and division when at least one negative number is involved are as follows:

- Two positives or two negatives give a positive.
- "Mixing" a positive and a negative gives a negative. For example, $-5 \times 3 = -15$, and $-24 \div 3 = -8$.

For adding or subtracting when at least one negative number is involved, it may be useful to think of the values as money, considering adding as "gaining," subtracting as "losing," positive numbers as "credits," and negative numbers as "debts." Be careful, though: Adding or "gaining" –8 is actually losing 8.

▶ Objective 0014:

Understand and Apply Concepts and Skills Related to Whole Numbers, Number Theory, and Numeration

The Whole Number System, Whole Numbers, and Comparing and Ordering Numbers

A **number** is a concept or idea that indicates how many; a **numeral** is a symbol used to represent a num-

ber. The student must be able to read and to write the numerals. This skill is an important part of their early mathematical development. Children may memorize the counting numbers from 1 to 10 and be able to count by rote before they start going to school. After the students have some idea of the value of the numbers, they may arrange the numbers from largest to smallest, or smallest to largest.

Children may try counting by pairing the objects with a number on the number line; this will give a visual comparison. **Counting numbers** can be shown by the set $\{1, 2, 3, 4, \ldots\}$. Study the following number line below. Notice that the counting numbers start with 1 and that 0 is not in the set of counting numbers:

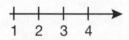

Whole numbers are the counting numbers, plus 0 $\{0, 1, 2, 3, \ldots\}$. Study the following number line below. Notice that 0 is a part of the set of whole numbers:

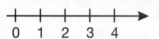

Children may try pairing objects with the numbers that they have memorized through rote; this is oral **counting**. After classifying objects, the child may try counting the objects in the groups. For example, if the teacher asks, "How many objects were soft?," the answer is a number that tells how many; the child will have to count to find the answer.

Students may also try another way of counting: skip counting. They may start with 1 and count only the odd numbers: 3, 5, 7, 9, and so on. **Odd numbers** are those that cannot be evenly divided by 2.

Students may also try skip counting with another beginning point; for instance, they may start with 2 and count only the even numbers: 4, 6, 8, 10, and so on. **Even numbers** are those that can be evenly divided by 2.

Another important part of mathematical learning and of language arts learning is being able to read and to represent the numbers not only in numerals but also in words: *one, two, three,* and so on.

Our numeration system uses the Hindu-Arabic numerals (0, 1, 2, 3, 4, 5, 6, 7, 8, 9) to represent numbers. Our numeration system follows a **base 10 place-value** scheme. As we move to the left in any number, each place value is ten times the place value to the right. Similarly, as we move to the right, each place value is one-tenth the place value to the left. For example, in the number 543, the place value of the 5 (100's) is ten times the place value of the 4 (10's). The place value of the 3 is one-tenth the place value of the 4.

Expanded notation can show the value of each number in its place. Using the same number 543, the values are

$$(5 \times [10 \times 10]) + (4 \times [10 \times 1]) + (3 \times 1).$$

Exponential notation can show the value of each number. Using the same number 543, the exponential values are

$$(5 \times 10^2) + (4 \times 10^1) + (3 \times 1^0).$$

Scientific notation is a method for showing any numbers using exponents (although it is most useful for very large and very small numbers). A number represented as between 1 and 10 times a power of 10 is in scientific notation. Thus, the number 75,000 in scientific notation is 7.5×10^4.

Rational numbers are all the numbers that can be expressed as the quotient of two integers. Rational numbers can be expressed as fractions, percents, or decimals.

As noted earlier, **common fractions** are in the form *a/b*, where *a* and *b* are whole numbers. **Integers** (whole numbers) can be expressed as fractions, but not all fractions can be expressed as integers. For example, the number 4 can be expressed as $^4/_1$. However, the fraction $^1/_4$ cannot be expressed as an integer, or a whole number. There are more fractions than whole numbers; between every integer is a fraction. Between the fraction and the whole number is another fraction, between the fraction and the other fraction is another fraction, and so on. Negative and positive fractions are not integers unless they are equivalent to whole numbers or their negative counterparts.

Decimal numbers are fractions written in special notation. For instance, 0.25 can be thought of as the fraction $^1/_4$. All decimal numbers are actually fractions. When expressed as decimals, some fractions terminate and some do not. For instance, 0.315 is a terminating decimal; 0.0575757 . . . is a repeating (nonterminating) decimal. All fractions, however, can be written as decimals. There are more decimals than integers.

Fractions, decimal numbers, and percents are different ways of representing values. It is useful to be able to convert from one to the other. The following paragraphs provide some conversion tips.

The practical method for changing a fraction into a decimal is by **dividing the numerator by the denominator**. For example, $^1/_4$ becomes 0.25 when 1 is divided by 4, as follows:

$$4\overline{)1.00}^{.25}$$

Naturally, this can be done longhand or with a calculator. (If the fraction includes a whole number, as in $2^3/_5$, the whole number is not included in the division.) The decimal number may terminate or repeat. Converting a simple fraction to a decimal number never results in an irrational number.

To convert a nonrepeating (terminating) decimal number to a fraction in lowest terms, write the decimal as a fraction with the denominator a power of 10, and then reduce to lowest terms. For example, 0.125 can be written as $^{125}/_{1,000}$, which reduces to $^1/_8$.

Any decimal number can be converted to a **percent** by shifting the decimal point two places to the right and adding the percent symbol (%). For instance, 0.135 becomes 13.5%. (If the number before the percent symbol is a whole number, there is no need to show the decimal point.)

To convert a percent to a decimal number, shift the decimal point two places to the left and drop the percent symbol. For example, 98% becomes 0.98 as a decimal.

To convert a percent to a fraction, put the percent (without the percent symbol) over 100 and then reduce. In this way, 20% is represented as $^{20}/_{100}$, which reduces to $^1/_5$.

The **natural numbers** include the set of counting numbers {1, 2, 3, 4, 5, . . .} and the set of whole numbers {0, 1, 2, 3, 4, 5, . . .}. The natural number of zero has special mathematical significance with respect to the operation of addition. Zero added to any natural number yields a sum that is the same as the other natural number; zero is, therefore, the **additive identity**, or the **identity element of addition**.

Applying Operations

Operations indicate what one is to do with numbers. As noted earlier, the four main operations are addition, subtraction, multiplication, and division.

Addition is an operation that, when performed on numbers of disjoint sets (sets with different members), results in a **sum**. One can show addition on a number line by counting forward. Addition is a **binary operation**, meaning it combines only two numbers at a time to produce a third, unique number. Adding two whole numbers always results in a whole number.

The **algorithm** of addition is the form in which we write and solve an addition example. Familiar short forms are

2 (addend) + 3 (addend) = 5 (sum)

and

$$\begin{array}{r} 2 \text{ (addend)} \\ +\ 3 \text{ (addend)} \\ \hline 5 \text{ (sum)} \end{array}$$

Like addition, **subtraction** is a binary operation; that is, we work on only two numbers at a time. The result is a third, unique number called the **difference**. Given two whole numbers, subtracting the smaller number from the larger one results in a whole number. However, subtraction of whole numbers does not result in a whole number if the larger whole number is subtracted from the smaller one.

The **algorithm** of subtraction is the form in which we write and solve a subtraction example. Familiar short forms are

$$5 - 3 = 2$$

and

$$\begin{array}{r} 5 \\ -\ 3 \\ \hline 2 \end{array}$$

Addition problems with a missing addend are solved with the operation of subtraction. For example

$\square$ (addend) + 3 (addend) = 5 (sum).

Relationships Among Operations

Multiplication is repeated addition. Division is repeated subtraction. The operation of subtraction is the **inverse** of addition because the operations "undo" one another.

Multiplication, like addition, is a binary operation: we work on only two numbers at a time. The result of the operation of multiplication is the **product**. The result of multiplying two whole numbers is always a whole number.

The operation of **division** has the same inverse relation to multiplication that subtraction has to addition. What multiplication does, division undoes. For example, multiplying 4 by 9 gives 36; dividing 36 by 9 "gives back" a **quotient** of 4. Teaching division should parallel teaching multiplication.

Properties of the Number System and Operations

Properties of Whole Numbers and the Whole Number System

Key properties of whole numbers (and some related terms) include the following:

Multiplicative identity property of 1. Any number multiplied by 1 remains the same. For instance, $34 \times 1 = 34$. The number 1 is called the **multiplicative identity**.

Property of reciprocals. Any number (except zero) multiplied by its reciprocal gives 1. The **reciprocal**

of a number is 1 divided by that number. Remember that dividing by zero is considered to have no meaning; avoid doing it when computing or solving equations and inequalities.

Additive identity property of zero. Adding zero to any number will not change the number. For instance, $87 + 0 = 87$. Zero is called the **additive identity**.

Commutative property for addition and multiplication. The order in which addends are added or factors are multiplied does not determine the sum or product. For example, 6×9 gives the same product as 9×6. Division and subtraction, however, are not commutative.

Associative property for addition and multiplication. Associating, or grouping, three or more addends or factors in a different way does not change the sum or product. For example, $(3 + 7) + 5$ gives the same sum as $3 + (7 + 5)$. Division and subtraction are not associative.

Distributive property of multiplication over addition. A number multiplied by the sum of two other numbers can be handed out, or distributed, to both numbers, multiplied by each of them separately, and the products added together. For example, 6 by 47 gives the same result as multiplying 6 by 40, multiplying 6 by 7, and then adding the products. That is, $6 \times (47) = (6 \times 40) + (6 \times 7)$. The simple notation form of the distributive property is

$$a(b + c) = (a \times b) + (a \times c).$$

Different Classes of Whole Number Operations

There are two ways to represent division: measurement and partition. With **measurement division**, students know how many in each group (set) but do not know how many sets. Consider this example: A homeowner has a group of 400 pennies; she plans to give each trick-or-treater 5 pennies. How many trick-or-treaters can receive a treat before the homeowner has to turn out the light? Again, the students know the number of pennies (measurement) each child will receive; they need to find the number of children.

Partitive division occurs when the students know the number of groups (sets), but they do not know the number of objects in each set. Here is an example: There is a plate of eight cookies on the table. There are four children at the table. How many cookies does each child get if they divide the cookies evenly? The question asks the students to determine how many in each group.

Division is the most difficult of the algorithms for students to use. Division begins at the left, rather than at the right. Also, to solve a division problem, students must not only divide but also subtract and multiply. Students must use estimation with the trial quotients; sometimes it takes several trials before the trial is successful. No properties of division—commutative, associative, and so on—hold true at all times.

Using a Variety of Methods, Models, and Materials in Mathematics Instruction

There are four ways to model the operations:

Concrete method. With the concrete method, the teacher allows the students to use real objects. The students can represent a set and take away objects from it (subtraction), or they can combine two sets with no common objects (addition).

Semiconcrete method. With the semiconcrete method, the students work with visual representations (pictures) instead of actual objects.

Semiabstract method. With the semiabstract method, the students work with one symbol (tally marks, x's, y's, and so forth) to represent objects; instead of actual objects, pictures, or abstract (numerical) representations, the students use one symbol. The semiabstract method can represent, for instance, a multiplication problem. Here is an example: If there are three rabbits and if each rabbit eats four carrots each day, how many carrots will the rabbits eat in one day? (Notice that the vertical representation shows the first number in the problem 3×4; notice also that one symbol—the x—represents carrots.)

Carrots Eaten in One Day			
Rabbit 1	x	x	x	x
Rabbit 2	x	x	x	x
Rabbit 3	x	x	x	x

Abstract method. With the abstract level, the student matches the elements of a given group with abstract numbers. To represent three rabbits eating four carrots daily, a student using the abstract method would set up the problem as 3×4.

Calculators, computers, and technology are important instructional and problem-solving tools. Their effectiveness, however, depends on the accuracy of the input and the ability of the user to operate the devices correctly.

The effective teacher includes resources of all types in the curriculum-planning process. The educator should be very familiar with the school library, the local library, education service center resources, and the library of any colleges or universities in the area. Another important set of resources is the audiovisual aids that the teacher can borrow: kits, films, filmstrips, videos, laser disks, and computer software, among others. Audiovisual aids can relate to curricular objectives. Many librarians have keyed their resources to objectives in related subject areas, and these keys enable the teacher to incorporate library holdings with ease into the lessons. However, teachers should never use resources with a class unless they have previewed and approved them. The teacher should include the list of resources for a lesson or unit in the curriculum guide or the lesson plan to make use more efficient.

The effective teacher determines the appropriate place in the lesson for audiovisual aids. If the material is especially interesting and thought provoking, the teacher can use it to introduce a unit. For example, a travel video on coral reefs or snorkeling might be an excellent introduction to the study of ocean depths and how to graph them.

Because textbooks do not stay up-to-date on batting averages and stock reports, local, state, and national newspapers and magazines, as well as the Internet, are important resources for teaching mathematics. Figuring batting averages and watching the stock reports are practical lessons in mathematics. Some newspapers and magazines provide special programs to help teachers use their products in the classroom. Local newspapers may even be willing to send specialists to work with students or act as special resource people.

Technology experts argue that tools such as the Internet make available such a substantial amount of wide-ranging content that today's teachers have a greater role than ever helping students acquire process skills (such as critical and creative thinking) rather than merely teaching content skills. Content changes and expands, but thinking processes remain salient and necessary, regardless of the content.

Spreadsheets are especially useful to the math classroom. The reader can see rows and columns of numbers linked to produce totals and averages. Formulas can connect information in one cell (the intersection of a row and column) to another cell. Teachers often keep grade books on spreadsheets because of the ease in updating information. Once formulas are in place, teachers can enter grades and have completely up-to-date averages for all students. Some spreadsheet programs also include charting functions that enable teachers to display class averages on a bar chart to provide visual comparisons of performance among various classes.

Students can use spreadsheets to collect and analyze numerical data and then sort the data in various orders. For example, students could enter population figures from various countries and then draw various types of graphs—lines, bars, pies, scatter plots, and so on—to convey information. This type of graphic information can also be used in multimedia presentations. Various stand-alone graphing and charting software packages are also available.

Graphics or paint programs allow users to draw freehand to produce any type of chart, graph, or picture. In addition, many word-processing programs have some graphic functions. Students can use these programs to produce boxes, circles, or other shapes to illustrate classroom presentations or individual research projects. For teachers, these relatively simple tools make it easy to create handouts and instructional materials with a very professional and polished appearance.

Today's teachers also need to acquire and demonstrate skill in using presentation software (such as Microsoft PowerPoint) to prepare instructional lessons. In many classrooms, the use of presentation software makes the traditional use of transparencies on an overhead projector obsolete. Presentation software makes it

possible to provide students with instructional handouts and outlines to complement classroom instruction. In some situations and in some schools, Web authoring experience and skills will prove useful.

Teachers must supplement lectures with an array of visual materials that will appeal to both visual and auditory learners. Putting words or outlines on the board or a transparency is very helpful; however, this is still basically a verbal strategy. Drawings, diagrams, cartoons, pictures, caricatures, and graphs are attention-getting visual aids for lectures. Teacher drawings need not be highly artistic, merely memorable. Often a rough or humorous sketch will be more firmly etched in students' minds than elaborate drawings. Using a very simple sketch is a better means of teaching the most critical information than is a complicated drawing. The major points stand out in a simple sketch; the teacher can add details once students understand the basic concepts.

▶ Objective 0015:

Understand and Apply Concepts and Skills Related to Rational Numbers and the Interpretation of Fractions, Decimals, Ratios, and Percentages

Solving Problems Using Integers, Fractions, Decimals, Ratios, and Percents

Most modern math programs introduce the concept of ratio and use ratio to solve various problems. Here is an example:

Candy bars are two for 25 cents. How many candy bars can Kelly buy for 50 cents?

"Two candy bars for 25 cents" suggests the fixed constant of $2/25$:

$$\frac{2 \text{ (candy bars)}}{25 \text{ (cents)}}$$

With a fixed ratio, it should be possible to figure out how many candy bars Kelly can buy for 50 cents by setting up an equivalent ratio:

$$\frac{x \text{ (number of candy bars)}}{50 \text{ (cents)}}$$

The relationship between the two ratios in the equation is one of equality; that is, they are equivalent ratios. An equation of two equivalent ratios is one of **proportion**. There are several ways to solve the equivalent ratios problem with the candy bars, but one way to do it is to use cross multiplication:

$$\frac{x}{50} \times \frac{2}{25}$$

Cross multiplication gives $25x = 100$. Solving for x requires dividing 100 by 25 to get 4. Thus, Kelly can buy four candy bars for 50 cents.

Another way to solve the problem is to set up a chart:

Candy Bars	Cost
2	25 cents
4	50 cents
6	75 cents

In solving problems involving percents, the student must always consider reasonableness in their thinking and estimating. Mathematical reasoning includes analyzing problem situations, making conjectures, organizing information, and selecting strategies to solve problems. Problem solvers must rely on both formal and informal **reasoning processes**. Consider this problem:

Center Town Middle School has an enrollment of 640 students. One day, 28 students were absent. What percent of the total number of students were absent?

A.	28%	D.	25%
B.	1%	E.	4%
C.	18%		

Even if someone forgot how to compute percents, some possible answers could be rejected through reasoning: 28 is a *small* but not *tiny* chunk of 640; 1% is too small, and 18% and 25% are too large, so those answer choices are *unreasonable*.

Ratios and Percents

Ratio notation is an alternative method for showing fractions. For example, ²/₅ can be expressed as "the ratio of 2 to 5." The use of ratio notation emphasizes the relationship of one number to another. To show ratios, one may use numbers with a colon between them; 2:5 is the same ratio as 2 to 5 and ²/₅.

To illustrate the equivalencies and conversions above, consider the fraction ¹⁹/₂₀. As a decimal, it is 0.95. As a percent, it is 95%. As a ratio, it is 19 to 20, or 19:20.

▶ Objective 0016:

Understand Concepts and Skills Related to Statistics and Probability, and Apply This Knowledge to Evaluate and Interpret Data and Solve Problems in Real-World Contexts

---

Interpreting Graphic and Nongraphic Representations of Statistical Data

Often, the impact of numbers and statistics is diminished by an overabundance of tedious numbers. A graph helps a reader rapidly visualize or organize irregular information, as well as trace long periods of decline or increase. The reader might, for instance, want to consider the terms *measures of central tendency, mean, median, mode,* and *frequency distributions.*

Measures of central tendency of a set of values include the mean, median, and mode. The **mean** is found by adding all the values and then dividing the sum by the number of values. For example, the mean of 15, 10, 25, 5, and 40 is $(15 + 10 + 25 + 5 + 40) \div 5 = 19$.

The **median** of a set is the middle number when the values are in numerical order. (If the set comprises an even number of values, and therefore no middle value, the mean of the middle two values gives the median.) To find the **median,** order a given set of numbers from smallest to largest. The **median** is the "middle" number; that is, half the numbers in the set of numbers are below the median and half the numbers in the set are above the median. For example, to find the median of the set of whole numbers 15, 10, 25, 5, 40, the first step is to order the set of numbers: 5, 10, 15, 25, 40. Because 15 is the middle number (half of the numbers are below 15, half are above 15), 15 is the median of this set of whole numbers. If the set has an even number of numbers, the median is the mean of the middle two numbers. For instance, in the set of numbers 2, 4, 6, 8, the median is the mean of 4 and 6, or 5.

The **mode** of a set is the value occurring most often. (Not all sets of values have a single mode; some sets have more than one.) The mode of the set of numbers 15, 10, 25, 10, 5, 40, 10, 15 is the number 10 because it appears most frequently (three times).

The **range** of a set of numbers is a measure of the spread of, or variation in, the numbers. The range of a set of numbers is obtained by subtracting the smallest number in the set from the largest number in the set. For example, the range of the set 15, 10, 25, 5, 40 is $40 - 5 = 35$.

Consider the following set: 6, 8, 14, 5, 6, 5, 5. The mean, median, and mode of the set are 7, 6, and 5, respectively; the range is $14 - 5$, or 9. (Note that the mean is often referred to as the *average,* but all three measures are averages of sorts.)

Frequency distributions represent the probability that a statistic of interest will fall in a certain interval; for example, the height of a person chosen at random may follow the *normal distribution.* The following are some samples of kinds of distributions, with location of the means and medians indicated:

Distribution (b) in the figure is the famous normal, or bell-shaped, curve on which tests are often said to be graded. Notice that more scores fall in the middle here than on the high or low ends. In the right-skewed distribution, shown in (a), more of the scores are low, and in (c) more of the scores are high (assuming that all of these graphs represent test scores). The distribution in (d) shows that all scores are distributed equally from high to low, and (e) shows a distribution in which most

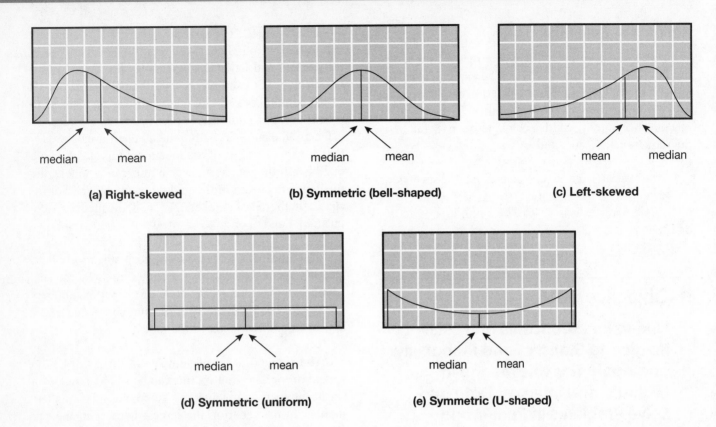

(a) Right-skewed   (b) Symmetric (bell-shaped)   (c) Left-skewed

(d) Symmetric (uniform)   (e) Symmetric (U-shaped)

scores were either high or low, with very few being average. Notice that in (a), the right-skewed distribution, the mean is higher than the median, and in (c) the median is higher than the mean.

Percentiles are the measures of where a piece of data stands in relation to the other data in its set. Perhaps best known from standardized tests, percentiles tell how many other data are lower in value. For instance, a test taker might have a raw score of 82% (that is, 82% of the answers are correct) but rank in the 91st percentile, meaning that 90% of all test takers received lower raw scores. The median occurs at the 50th percentile.

Using Statistics and Probability to Collect and Organize Data, Draw Conclusions, and Identify Trends and Patterns

Statistics is the branch of mathematics that involves collecting, analyzing, and interpreting data, organizing data to describe them usefully, and drawing conclusions and making decisions. Statistics builds on probability and typically studies "populations," meaning quantifiable groups of things. Trends and patterns not otherwise noticed may be revealed via statistics.

One key statistical concept is that of **standard deviation**. The standard deviation of a set of values tells how "tightly" all of the values are clustered around the mean of the set. When values are tightly clustered near the mean, the standard deviation is small. If values are widespread, the standard deviation is large. Here is one way to find the standard deviation of a set:

Consider the set 6, 8, 14, 5, 6, 5, 5. First find the mean (7). Next, find the difference of each value in the set and the mean (ignoring negative signs). This gives 1, 1, 7, 2, 1, 2, and 2. Now, square each of those values, giving 1, 1, 49, 4, 1, 4, and 4. Then, take the sum of those squares (64) and divide the sum by the number of values

(64 ÷ 7 = 9.14). Finally, take the square root of 9.14, giving a standard deviation of 3.02. Think of 3.02 as the amount that the values in the set "typically" vary from the center.

Probability theory provides models for chance variations. The likelihood or chance that an event will take place is called the **probability** of the event.

Making Predictions and Determining Probabilities

The probability of any event occurring is equal to the number of desired outcomes divided by the number of all possible events. Thus, the probability of blindly pulling a green ball out of a hat (in this case the desired outcome) if the hat contains two green and five yellow balls is $^2/_7$ (about 29%). In addition to expressing probability as a fraction ($^2/_7$) or as a percent (29%), one can also express the probability of a particular event occurring as the ratio of the number of ways the particular event can occur to the number of possible events (2:7). Probability is calculated mathematically as follows:

Probability of a particular event occurring =

$$\frac{\text{Number of ways the event can occur}}{\text{Total number of possible events}}$$

Odds are related to but different from probability. The odds that any given event will occur is the ratio of the probability that the event (two green balls or two chances in the previous example) will occur to the probability that the event will not occur (five chances because there are five yellow balls); this is typically expressed as a ratio. In the given example, then, the odds that a green ball will be drawn are 2:5.

Using a Variety of Methods, Models, and Materials in Mathematics Instruction

To provide for the different learning styles, teachers should use various methods, models, and materials—particularly in instructing students about statistics and probability. Kinesthetic learners may profit from actual-ly manipulating coins, colored disks, or similar objects. Auditory learners may profit from hearing the procedures for determining probability. The visual learner can often profit from charts and graphs that visually demonstrate probability and odds for and against.

For instance, human sex type is determined by the genetic material in the sperm and egg. The genetic sex code for human females is XX. The genetic sex code for human males is XY. Eggs carry only X genes. Sperm carry both X and Y genes. (Some biologists describe Y as the absence of X.) The following chart helps determine the probability of a fertilized human egg being male or female:

	Female	Female
Male	X	X
X	XX	XX
Y	XY	XY

The table shows that the probability of a female (XX) is 2 out of 4, and the probability of a male (XY) is 2 out of 4. Therefore, there is a 50% chance of a boy and a 50% chance of a girl.

► Objective 0017:
Understand and Apply Algebraic Concepts and Methods

Representing Real-World Patterns, Relationships, Verbal Expressions, Symbols, and Pictorial Information with Algebraic Expressions

An *algebraic expression* is an expression using letters, numbers, symbols, and arithmetic operations to represent a number or a relationship among numbers. Algebraic expressions are comprised of *terms*, or groupings of variables and numbers. An algebraic expression with one term is called a *monomial*; with two terms, a *binomial*; with three terms, a *trinomial*. Any algebraic expression with more than one term is called a *polynomial*.

Using Variable, Function, and Equation to Express Relationships

A *variable*, or unknown, is a letter that stands for a number in an algebraic expression. *Coefficients* are the numbers that precede the variable to give the quantity of the variable in the expression. For example, $2ab - cd$ is a binomial algebraic expression with variables a, b, c, and d, and terms $2ab$ and $(-cd)$. The number 2 is the coefficient of ab, and -1 is the coefficient of cd. $x^2 + 3y - 1$ is a trinomial algebraic expression with variables x and y and with terms x^2, $3y$, and (-1). The number 1 is the coefficient of x^2, and 3 is the coefficient of y.

Through symbols and algebraic expressions, one can express real-world patterns and relationships; these algebraic expressions and symbols can also help in translating word problems into an algebraic sentence. To make the translations, there must be a variable to represent the unknown in the problem. Key words such as *is*, *are*, and *were* represent "equals" (=); *more* and *more than* represent "plus" (+); *less*, *less than*, *fewer* indicate "minus" (−); and *of* represents ×. Consider this word problem:

> The sum of the ages of Bill and Paul is 32 years. Bill is 6 years older than Paul. Find the age of each.

If p = Paul's age, then Bill's age is $p + 6$. Therefore, $p + (p + 6) = 32$. Solve for p:

$$p + p + 6 = 32 \quad \text{(combine like terms)}$$
$$2p + 6 = 32 \quad \text{(add } -6 \text{ to both sides)}$$
$$2p = 26 \quad \text{(multiply by } \tfrac{1}{2}\text{)}$$
$$p = 13$$

Since p = Paul's age, Paul is 13 years old. Bill is $13 + 6$, which is 19 years old.

When attempting to solve one-variable equations, it is helpful to think of the task as that of producing a series of equivalent equations until, in the last equation, the variable has been *isolated* on one side. There are several ways to produce equivalent equations, but chiefly they are produced by performing identical operations on the two expressions making up the sides of equations. The equation $2x = 12$, for instance, can be solved by dividing both sides of the equation by 2, as follows:

$$\frac{2x}{2} = \frac{12}{2}$$

This then gives an equivalent equation of $x = 6$. Therefore, 6 is the solution to the original equation.

There are several caveats to observe when solving one-variable equations in that manner. One is that care must be taken to perform operations on *entire* expressions and not simply on "parts" of expressions. In the example below, the last equation fails to give a solution to the original equation because, in the second step, only *part* of the expression $2x + 8$ has been divided by 2.

$$2x + 8 = 14$$
$$\frac{2x}{2} + 8 = \frac{14}{2}$$
$$x + 8 = 7$$
$$x = -1$$

Avoid dividing by zero. That operation is considered meaningless and will not provide a solution. Also, not all single-variable equations have solutions. $0x + 3 = 9$, for instance, has no real number solutions. If the variable carries an exponent, as in $x^2 = 16$, taking the square root of each side of the equation produces the solutions. (Note that *both* 4 and −4 work.)

"Solving one variable in terms of a second" simply means rewriting multivariable equations such that the desired variable is isolated on one side of the equation. For instance, the equation $x - 3y = 5$ can be rewritten as $x = 3y + 5$. The variable x has been solved in terms of the second variable y.

Solving a *system* of two-variable linear equations (such as $y = x + 6$ and $2y = 4x$) means finding the ordered pair (or pairs) of numbers that solves (solve) both equations simultaneously. Using trial and error, we can see that (6, 12) works in both of the equations above. There are also more formal methods for solving systems of two-variable equations. If we graph each equation on the coordinate plane, the point of intersection (if any) will give the solution to the system. Another method is to literally add or subtract one equation from the other, with the intention of eliminating one variable in the process, enabling us to solve for one variable, then

the other. (One or both equations may first require multiplication in order to "line up" variables with opposite coefficients.) In the example that follows, the system of $y = x + 6$ and $2y = 4x$ has been solved using multiplication and addition.

$$
\begin{aligned}
y &= x + 6 \\
2y &= 4x \\
-2y &= -2x - 12 \\
2y &= 4x \\
0 &= 2x - 12 \\
x &= 6
\end{aligned}
$$

If $x = 6$, y must equal 12, so the solution to the system is (6, 12).

Calculators and computers are important problem-solving tools to use when teaching and learning math, but their effectiveness depends on the accuracy of the input and the ability of the user to operate the devices correctly.

Touchable, movable materials are also effective for enhancing students' understanding of a concept. Manipulatives are particularly useful in mathematics to give students a concrete way of dealing with concepts, but tangible materials are appropriate and helpful in all subject areas. Number lines, place-value cubes, and tessellation blocks can help students understand math, not only in elementary classes but also in algebra, trigonometry, and calculus. Math teachers may use wooden or plastic shapes in studying geometry.

Charts are also useful to the mathematics teacher and the students. One can represent numbers in many ways, as shown in the following chart:

Number Form	Two Wooden Blocks Can Be Represented As
Whole number	2
Integer	+2 or 2
Fraction	$^2/_1$
Decimal	2.0
Percent	200%

A real number expressed in **scientific notation** is written as the product of a real number n times an integral power of 10; the value of n is $1 \leq n \geq 10$. Some examples are shown in the following chart:

Number	Scientific Notation
1,956	1.956×10^3
0.0036	3.6×10^{-3}
59,600,000	5.96×10^7

The effective teacher uses criteria to evaluate audiovisual, multimedia, models, and computer resources. The first thing to look for is congruence with lesson goals. If the models, materials, manipulatives, and software do not reinforce student outcomes, then schools should not use them, no matter how flashy or well-made they are. A checklist for selecting the materials could include appropriate sequence of instruction, meaningful student interaction, pacing, motivation, clarity of purpose, and the potential for individual or group use.

When evaluating resources, teachers should also consider students' strengths and needs, learning styles or preferred modalities, and interests. Teachers can determine students' needs through formal or informal assessment. Most standardized tests include an indication of which objectives the student did not master. Computer or multimedia aids can assist students in mastering these objectives.

The effective teacher evaluates resources well in advance of the lesson and before purchase whenever possible. The teacher also evaluates the materials as students use them. When students have finished using the materials, the teacher can assess material usefulness by considering students' achievement levels and/ or by asking students to voice their opinions of the materials.

Exploring Relationships and Making Predictions by Using Graphs, Tables, and Charts

Teachers often use the **function machine** to encourage students to find the missing addend, factor, or operation; to make predictions; and so forth. The function machine can be an introduction to algebra for the elementary student.

For the example below, if the number 4 is inserted into the "3-Times Function Machine," the output would be 12:

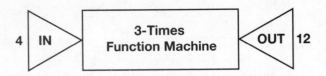

The following function machine is a subtraction machine. If the output is 12 and the input is 15, what is the value of the function machine?

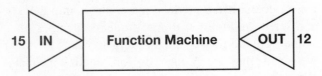

Given that 15 – 12 = 3, this is a "3-Minus Function Machine."

A key to interpretation of graphs, tables, and charts is to pay close attention to labels. One should read all labeled elements before assuming anything.

Graphs, charts, and tables may be a part of the AEPA. More than likely, you will encounter at least one passage that is accompanied by some form of graphic information. You may need to answer one or more questions based on the interpretation of the information presented in the graph, chart, or table.

Graphs are used to represent sets of information visually. Often, the impact of numbers and statistics is diminished by an overabundance of tedious numbers. A graph helps a reader rapidly visualize or organize irregular information, as well as trace long periods of decline or increase. The following is a guide to reading the three principal graphic forms that you will encounter when taking the test:

Line Graphs. Line graphs are used to track multiple elements of one or more subjects. One element is usually a time factor, over whose span the other element increases, decreases, or remains static. The lines that compose such graphs are connected points that are displayed on the chart through each integral stage. Figure 3-1 is an example of a line graph; it concisely presents immigration data for a period spanning more than 100 years.

You should approach any graphic information you encounter as a key to a larger body of information in abbreviated form. Be sure to use the visual aids of the graphics (for example, the size of slices on pie charts) as aids only; do not ignore the written information listed on the graph, table, or chart. Note especially the title and headings so that you know exactly what you are looking at. Also, be aware of the source of the information, where applicable. Know what each element of the graphic information represents; this will help you compare how drastic or subtle any changes are, and over what span of time they take place. Be sure you realize what the actual numbers represent, whether it is dollars, thousands of people, millions of shares, and so forth. Finally, note the way in which the graphic information relates to the text it seeks to illustrate; know in what ways the graphic information supports the arguments of the author of the given passage.

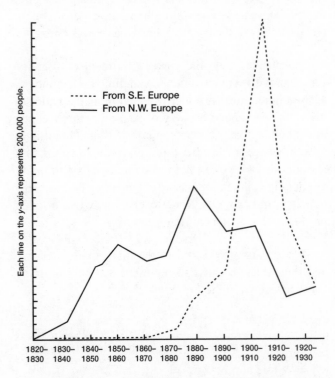

Source: *Immigration and Naturalization Service of the U.S. Dept. of Justice*

Figure 3-1. Immigration to the United States, 1820–1930

Bar Graphs. Bar graphs are also used to plot two dynamic elements of a subject. However, unlike a line graph, the bar graph usually deals with only one

subject. The exception to this is when the graph is three-dimensional, and the bars take on the dimension of depth. However, because we will only be dealing with two-dimensional graphs, we will only be working with a single subject. The other difference between a line and a bar graph is that a bar graph usually calls for a single element to be traced in terms of another, whereas a line graph usually plots either of the two elements with equal interest. For example, in the following bar graph, inflation and deflation are being marked over a span of years:

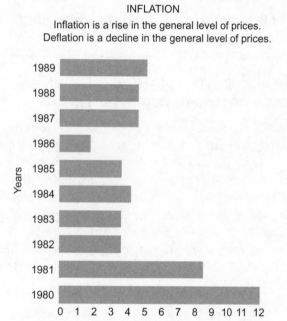

INFLATION

Inflation is a rise in the general level of prices.
Deflation is a decline in the general level of prices.

Percentage points are assigned to each year's level of prices; that percentage decreases (deflation) from 1980 to 1981 and from 1981 to 1982. The price level is static from 1982 to 1983. The price level increases (inflation) from 1983 to 1984. Therefore, it is obvious that the bar graph is read strictly in terms of the changes exhibited over a period of time or against some other element. Conversely, the line graph plots two dynamic elements of equal interest to the reader (e.g., either number of immigrants or the particular decade in question).

To read a bar graph, simply begin with the element at the base of a bar and trace the bar to its full length. Once reaching its length, cross-reference the other element of information that matches the length of the bar.

Pie Charts. Pie charts differ greatly from line or bar graphs. Pie charts help a reader visualize percentages of information with many elements to the subject. An entire "pie" represents 100% of a given quantity of information. The pie is then sliced into measurements that correspond to their respective shares of the 100%. For example, Myrna's rent occupies a slice greater than any other in the pie, because no other element equals or exceeds 25% of Myrna's monthly budget.

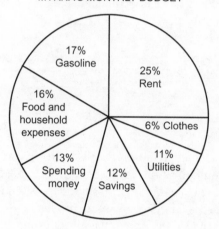

MYRNA'S MONTHLY BUDGET

Another aspect of pie charts is that the smaller percentage elements are moved consecutively to the larger elements. Therefore, the largest element in the chart will necessarily be adjacent to the smallest element in the chart, and the line that separates them is the beginning or endpoint of the chart. From that point the chart fans out to the other elements of the chart, going from the smallest percentages to the largest.

To read a pie chart, choose the element of the subject that interests you and compare its size to those of the other elements. In cases where the elements are similar in size, do not assume that they are equal. The exact percentage of the element will be listed within that slice of the chart. For example, Myrna's utilities, savings, and spending money are all similar in size, but it is clear when reading the chart that each possesses a different value.

Using Expressions and Comparing Expressions That Use Exponents and Roots

In the expression 5^3, 5 is called the *base* and 3 is called the *exponent*. The expression $5^3 = 5 \times 5 \times 5$. The base (5) represents the factor used in the expression and the exponent (3) represents the number of times the base is to be used as a factor.

> **EXAMPLE**
>
> $4^2 = 4 \times 4$
>
> $3^5 = 3 \times 3 \times 3 \times 3 \times 3$

The Basic Laws of Exponents are

1. $b^m \times b^n = b^{m+n}$
2. $b^m \div b^n = b^{m-n}$
3. $(b^m)^n = b^{m \times n}$

Roots

Consider again the expression 5^3. If we carry out the implied multiplication, we get $5^3 = 5 \times 5 \times 5 = 125$. Five is called the cube root of 125, since $5^3 = 125$. In general, when a base is raised to a power to produce a given result, the base is called the *root* of the given result.

If the power for the base is 2, the base is called the *square root*. If the power for the base is 3, the base is called the *cube root*. In general, if $b^n = p$, the b is the nth root of p.

> **EXAMPLE**
>
> Since $4^2 = 16$, 4 is the square root of 16.
>
> Since $2^3 = 8$, 2 is the cube root of 8.
>
> Since $3^5 = 253$, 3 is the fifth root of 253.

Making Use of Materials, Models, and Methods to Explore Concepts and to Solve Algebraic Problems

Materials and models can supplement the methods that the teacher uses to help students explore and solve algebraic problems. Concrete objects for models can be especially useful to the kinesthetic learners in the lower grades; for instance with a missing addend equation like $3 + \square = 7$, the student can count out seven popsicle sticks, remove three, and find the missing addend 4. Visual learners may profit particularly from charts and drawings that represent the equation, whereas auditory learners may benefit most from the teacher's verbal explanation of the procedures for solving algebraic equations. Varied methods, materials, and models can help to meet the needs of diverse learners.

▶ Objective 0018:
Understand and Apply Principles of Geometry

Identifying Types and Properties of Both Space and Plane Geometric Figures

A fundamental concept of geometry is the notion of a point. A **point** is a specific location taking up no space and having no area and is frequently represented by a dot. A point is considered one dimensional. Through any two points there is exactly one **straight line**; straight lines are one dimensional. A **plane** is a two-dimensional object; students might think of a surface without elevations or depressions. From these foundational ideas, you can move to some other important geometric terms and ideas.

A **segment** is any portion of a line between two points on the line. It has a definite start and a definite end. The notation for a segment extending from point A to point B is $\overline{AB}$.

A **ray** is similar to a straight segment, except it extends forever in one direction. The notation for a ray originating at point X (an endpoint) through point Y is $\overrightarrow{XY}$.

When two rays share their endpoints, an **angle** is formed. A degree (°) is a unit of measure of the angle created. If a circle is divided into 360 even slices, each slice has an angle measure of 1°. If an angle has exactly 90°, it is called a **right angle**. Angles of less than 90° are **acute angles**. Angles greater than 90° are **obtuse angles**. If two angles have the same size (regardless of how long their rays might be drawn), they are **congruent**.

One may represent congruence this way:

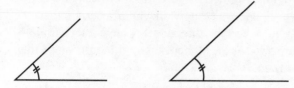

A **polygon** is a closed plane figure bounded by straight lines or a closed figure on a sphere bounded by arcs of great circles. In a plane, three-sided polygons are triangles; four-sided polygons, quadrilaterals; five-sided, pentagons; six-sided, hexagons; and eight-sided, octagons. (Note that not all quadrilaterals are squares.) If two polygons (or any figures) have exactly the same size and shape, they are congruent. If they are the same shape, but different sizes, they are similar.

The **diameter** of a circle is a straight line segment that goes from one edge of a circle to the other side, passing through the center. The **radius** of a circle is half of its diameter (from the center to an edge). A **chord** is any segment that goes from one spot on a circle to any other spot; all diameters are chords, but not all chords are diameters.

The **perimeter** of a two-dimensional (flat) shape or object is the distance around the object. **Volume** is the amount of space inside of a three-dimensional, closed container. It is useful to think of volume as how many cubic units could fit into a solid. If the container is a rectangular solid, multiplying width, length, and height together computes the volume. If all six faces (sides) of a rectangular solid are squares, then the object is a cube.

Parallel and **perpendicular** are key concepts in geometry. *Parallel* means extending in the same direction and at the same distance apart at every point, so as never to meet. *Perpendicular* means at right angles to a line or plane; exactly upright; vertical; straight up and down.

Consider the following two parallel lines that follow, and the third line (a transversal), which crosses them:

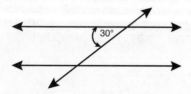

Note that among the many individual angles created, there are only two angle measures: 30° (noted in the figure) and 150° (180° − 30°).

Triangles have various properties. One is that the sum of the measures of the three angles of any triangle is 180°. If, therefore, one knows the measures of two angles, one can deduce the third using addition, then subtraction. The **Pythagorean theorem** states that in any right triangle with legs (shorter sides) a and b, and hypotenuse (longest side) c, the sum of the squares of the sides will be equal to the square of the hypotenuse. In algebraic notation the Pythagorean theorem is given as $a^2 + b^2 = c^2$.

The main topics (scope) in elementary mathematics and the sequence (order) in which the school introduces the topics is essentially the same in all states. These main topics and their introduction order are:

Grade	Colors, Geometry, Equations
Kindergarten	Recognize primary and secondary colors and black; recognize square, circle, triangle; use *up*, *down*, *top*, *next*
1	Recognize circle, square, oval, diamond, triangle, oval, cube
2	Measure area, perimeter, volume; recognize pyramid, pentagon, hexagon
3	Measure volume of cube; recognize rays, angles, congruent shapes, prisms
4	Distinguish shapes and solids; recognize obtuse, vertex, ray, diameter, radius; use operations on equations
5	Use compass, protractor; measure surface area; use operations on fractions; recognize chords; classify polygons
6	Construct a right and equilateral triangle, a parallelogram, a square; bisect an angle

Using Basic Geometric Concepts and Spatial Sense to Solve Problems

Geometric figures are similar if they have the exact same shapes, even if they do not have the same sizes. In transformational geometry, two figures are said to be similar if and only if a similarity transformation maps

one figure onto the other. In the figure that follows, triangles *A* and *B* are similar:

Remember that if two angles have the same size (regardless of how long their rays might be drawn), they are congruent.

A **tessellation** is a collection of plane figures that fill the plane with no overlaps and no gaps. The following chart provides some examples:

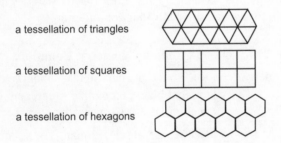

a tessellation of triangles

a tessellation of squares

a tessellation of hexagons

In solving geometry problems, students must always consider reasonableness in their thinking and estimating. Geometric reasoning requires analyzing problem situations, making conjectures, organizing information, and selecting strategies to solve problems. Problem solvers must rely on both formal and informal *reasoning processes*—and especially the use of spatial sense.

Identifying and Using Geometric Transformation

Transformations include a variety of different operations from geometry; these operations can include rotations, reflections, and translations. Students will have experiences in such transformations as flips, turns, slides, and scaling. For example, the teacher might ask students to select a shape that is a parallelogram. Then the teacher might ask the students to do the following:

- Describe the original position and size of the parallelogram. Students can use labeled sketches if necessary.

- Translate (or slide) the parallelogram several times. (A **translation** of a figure occurs if it is possible to give an object a straight shove for a certain distance and in a certain direction.) Rotate the parallelogram two times. Students should list the steps they followed.

- Challenge a friend to return the parallelogram to its original position.

- Determine if the friend used a reversal of the original steps or a different set of steps.

Scaling that is uniform is a linear transformation that enlarges or reduces an object; the scale factor is the same in all directions. The result of uniform scaling is similar (in the geometric sense) to the original. Scaling may be directional or may have a separate scale factor for each axis direction. This type of scaling may result in a change in shape.

Classifying Figures According to Symmetries

Polygons may have lines of symmetry, which can be thought of as imaginary fold lines that produce two congruent, mirror-image figures. Squares have four lines of symmetry, and nonsquare rectangles have two. Circles have an infinite number of lines of symmetry; a few are shown here:

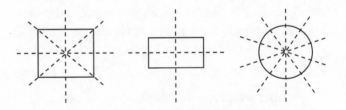

Applying Coordinate Systems on Lines and Planes to Solve Problems

Two important coordinate systems are the number line and the coordinate plane, and both systems can be used to solve certain problems. A particularly useful tool related to the coordinate plane is the **distance formula**, which allows you to compute the distance between any two points on the plane. Consider points *C* and *D* in the following:

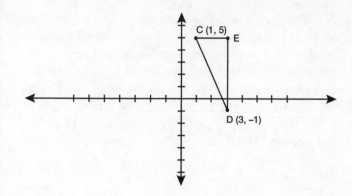

By finding the difference of the points' *x* coordinates (3 − 1, or 2) and the difference of their *y* coordinates (−1 − 5, or −6), you have found the lengths of the sides of triangle *CED* (2 units and 6 units—you can ignore the negative sign on the 6). You can now use the Pythagorean theorem to finish solving the problem.

The **coordinate plane** is useful for graphing individual ordered pairs and relationships. The coordinate plane is divided into four quadrants by an *x*-axis (horizontal) and a *y*-axis (vertical). The upper-right quadrant is quadrant I, and the others (moving counterclockwise from quadrant I) are quadrants II, III and IV.

The coordinate plane can show the graphs of functions. Such graphs always indicate a continuous (although not necessarily consistent) "movement" from left to right. Here is a graph of a function:

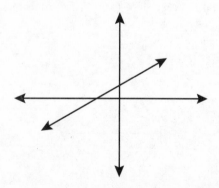

As noted earlier in the chapter, a key to interpretation of graphs, tables, and charts is to pay close attention to labels. Specific axes labels are also important. Don't assume anything about what a graph, table, or chart might be saying without carefully reading all labeled elements.

Ordered pairs indicate the locations of points on the plane. For instance, the ordered pair (−3, 4) describes a point that is three units *left* from the center of the plane (the **origin**) and four units *up*, as shown in the following diagram:

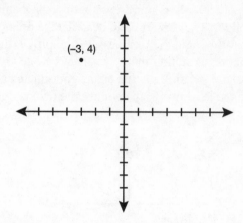

Ordered pairs are sets of data that one can display in a chart and graph on the coordinate plane. For example, the following set of data demonstrates four ordered pairs:

x	*y*
3	5
4	6
5	7
6	8

Considering each pairing individually, one produces the following ordered pairs: (3, 5), (4, 6), (5, 7), and (6, 8). Plotting each pair on the coordinate plane produces the following graph:

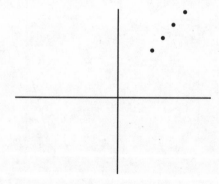

If the sets represent continuous change, the resulting graph may be a line (straight or curved in various

ways). Often, relationships between sets of data can be shown as two variable equations or inequalities. Consider the following ordered pairs:(–4, –2), (–2, –1), (0, 0), (2, 1), (4, 2). Note that the first value in each (the *x* value) is twice as big as the second (the *y* value). Assuming that the ordered pairs represent continuous change, the equation $x = 2y$ can be used to describe the relationship of the *x* values and the *y* values. It is helpful to think of the equation as stating that "*x* is always twice as big as *y*." We can show the equation on the coordinate plane by graphing at least two of the points, and then connecting them as shown below here:

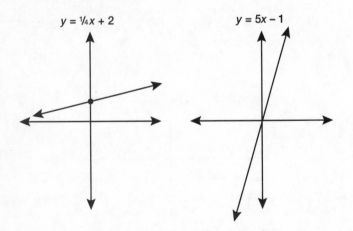

The generic equation $y = mx + b$ is a template for graphs on the plane that are straight lines. That form (sometimes called the **y-intercept** form of an equation) is especially useful because it tells two important characteristics of lines at a glance. The coefficient of *x* in the equation (or *m*) indicates the steepness, or **slope**, of the line on the plane. The larger the absolute value of *m*, the steeper the slope of the line. (A number's **absolute value** is its distance from zero, giving no regard to negative signs.) Consider the two equations that follow and their accompanying graphs:

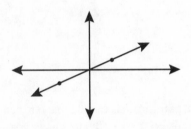

$y = \frac{1}{4}x + 2$ $y = 5x - 1$

Note that the equation on the left has a small slope ($\frac{1}{4}$); its graph is nearly horizontal. The other equation has a comparatively large slope (5), so it is steep.

If the coordinates of any two points of a straight line are known, the numerical slope of that line can easily be computed by finding the difference between the points' *y* values and dividing by the difference of the points' *x* values. For example, if (2, 5) and (4, 10) are points on a line, the slope of the line is $\frac{5}{2}$, or [(5 – 10) ÷ (2 – 4)]. Note that slopes are generally shown as fractions or whole numbers, but not as mixed fractions.

Making Use of Materials, Models, and Methods to Explore Concepts and to Solve Geometric Problems

Of course, with students in a classroom having varied learning styles (visual, auditory, kinesthetic), a teacher must use a variety of methods, models, and materials.

A **network** is a union of points (its vertices or nodes) and segments (its arcs) connecting them. Using the concrete method is an excellent way to develop geometric understanding in students; following the methods of learning mentioned earlier (concrete, semiconcrete, semiabstract, and abstract), the concrete level should come before using drawings alone to solve problems. Networks, or *nets*, can help make this understanding possible. Students can cut out the net ("pattern"), fold, and paste the appropriate tabs to construct three-dimensional figures. Here is a net for a tetrahedron—a tetranet:

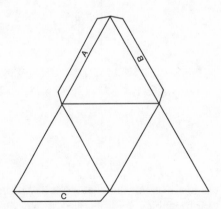

Materials and models can supplement the methods that the teacher uses to help students explore and solve geometric problems. Concrete objects for models can be especially useful to the kinesthetic learners. For ex-

ample, to help illustrate the formula for perimeter (*a* + *b* + *c* + *d*), a teacher might have kinesthetic learners measure the distance around a rectangular flower pot. The teacher whose students have difficulty with formulas at the abstract level may need to drop back to the semiconcrete level and use a drawing to help the students; visual learners may profit particularly from charts and drawings that represent the geometric shapes. Auditory learners, meanwhile, may benefit most from the teacher's verbal explanations for solving geometric formulas. As noted previously, varied methods, materials, and models can help to meet the needs of diverse learners.

▶ Objective 0019:
Understand and Apply Principles, Concepts, and Procedures Related to Measurement

Estimating and Converting Measurements within the Customary and Metric Systems

The fundamental uncertainty of the measuring device limits all measurements. The concept of **significant figures** derives from the simple assumption that calculations using measurements cannot generate results that are more precise than the measurements themselves. For example, if one pie is divided into three pieces, a calculator might report that each piece is 0.33333333 of the pie (depending on the number of digits on the calculator display). However, because crumbs will undoubtedly remain in the pan, no amount of care in dividing the pieces will result in the level of accuracy the calculator suggests.

Customary units are generally the same as **U.S. units**. Customary units of length include inches, feet, yards, and miles. Customary units of weight include ounces, pounds, and tons. Customary units of capacity (or volume) include teaspoons, tablespoons, cups, pints, quarts, and gallons.

The **metric system of measurement** relates to the base-10 place-value scheme. The following chart lists the common metric prefixes:

Prefix	Meaning	Meaning in Exponential Notation
Deci-	Tenth (0.1)	10^{-1}
Centi-	Hundredth (0.01)	10^{-2}
Milli-	Thousandth (0.001)	10^{-3}
Deca-	Ten (10)	10^{1}
Hecto-	Hundred (100)	10^{2}
Kilo-	Thousand (1,000)	10^{3}

The basic unit of linear measure in the metric system is the **meter**, represented by **m**. The relationships among the commonly used linear units of measurement in the metric system are

1 kilometer (km) = 1,000 m

1 hectometer (hm) = 100 m

1 decameter (dm) = 10 m

1 meter (m) = 1.0 m

1 decimeter (dm) = 0.1 m

1 centimeter (cm) = 0.01 m

1 millimeter (mm) = 0.001 m

The most frequently used metric units of length include millimeters, centimeters, decimeters, meters, and kilometers. The centimeter is the basic metric unit of length for short objects.

The basic unit of measurement for mass (or weight) in the metric system is the **gram**, represented by **g**. The relationships among the commonly used units of measurement for mass in the metric system include

1 kilogram (kg) = 1,000 g

1 gram (g) = 1.0 g

1 milligram (mg) = 0.001 g

A large paperclip weighs about 1 gram. It takes about 28 grams to make 1 ounce.

The basic unit of measurement for capacity (or volume) in the metric system is the **liter**, represented by **L** or **l**. The relationships among the most common metric units of capacity include

1 liter (l) = 1,000 milliliters (ml)

1 deciliter (dl) = 100 ml; 10 cl

1 centiliter (cl) = 10 ml

A liter is slightly smaller than a quart; it takes more than four liters to make a gallon.

Solving measurement problems requires first determining whether to use customary units or metric units. The next decision is whether the problem involves measurements of length, volume, mass, or temperature. The following chart summarizes the various units used in various types of measurement:

Measure	Metric Units	Customary Units
Length	Meter Centimeter Kilometer	Yard Inch Mile
Volume	Liter, decaliter Deciliter	Quart, gallon Teaspoon, table-spoon, cup
Mass	Kilogram, gram	Ounce, pound, ton
Temperature	Kelvin (not generally used in elementary schools), Celsius	Fahrenheit

The presumption is that every measuring device is accurate to the smallest of the marked subdivisions, and every measurement with such a device should include one additional estimated digit. For instance, if one is using measurements made with a ruler whose smallest divisions are 1 centimeter apart, one should record the reading to the tenth of a centimeter, the smallest measured digit plus one estimated digit. When scientists read the results of measurements made by others, they presume that the recorded values include a final digit that is an estimate based on the inherent accuracy of the instrument or device.

Making conversions between the metric system and the customary system are often more difficult for students than making conversions within the metric system.

Here are some frequently used customary-to-metric ratios (values are approximate):

1 inch = 2.54 centimeters

1 yard = 0.91 meter

1 mile = 1.61 kilometers

1 ounce = 28.35 grams

1 pound = 2.2 kilograms

1 quart = 0.94 liter

One can determine the metric-to-customary conversions by taking the reciprocals of each of the factors noted above. For instance, 1 kilometer = 0.62 mile (computed by dividing 1 by 1.61):

1 meter = 39.37 inches

1 meter = 1.09 yards

1 kilometer = .62 mile

1 kilogram = 2.2 pounds

1 liter = 1.057 quarts

2.5 centimeters = about 1 inch

1.5 kilometers = about 1 mile

Applying Procedures for Using Measurement to Describe and Compare Phenomena

From everyday life to the pencil and field notebook to modern instruments in the laboratory, the tools of observation, measurement, and computational analysis are essential. The microscope and telescope each extend the range of human observation beyond human physiology. The spectroscope separates visible light into its component colors, and the spectrophotometer measures the selective absorption of those colors as a function of some property of a solution, solid, or gas. Mathematics is a tool to evaluate the results of scientific observations, to organize large quantities of data into averages, ranges, and statistical probabilities.

An important step in solving problems involving measurement is to decide what is being measured. Generally, such problems will fall under one of these categories: length, area, angle, volume, mass, time, money, or temperature. Solving measurement problems will likely require knowledge in several other areas of mathematics, especially algebra.

The following is one example of a measurement problem that requires knowledge of several math topics (geometry, multiplication, conversions, estimation, and so on):

> Sophie's Carpet Store charges $19.40 per square yard for the type of carpeting Tony would like in his bedroom (padding and labor included). How much would Tony pay to carpet his 9-by-12-foot room?

One way to find the solution is to convert the room dimensions to yards (3 yards by 4 yards) and then multiply to get 12 square yards. The final step is to multiply 12 by the price of $19.40 per square yard, for a total price of $232.80.

Identifying Appropriate Measurement Instruments, Units, and Procedures for Measurement Problems

Each word problem requires an individual approach, but keeping in mind the reasonableness of the computational setup should be helpful.

Solving measurement problems requires first determining whether to use customary units or metric units. The next decision is whether the problem involves measurements of length, volume, mass, or temperature. Using the metric system requires also choosing the appropriate prefix to *meter*.

There are of course hybrid approaches to problem solving. Students can mix and match strategies wherever they think they are appropriate. In general, attention to *reasonableness* may be most crucial to problem-solving success, especially in real-life situations.

Applying given measurement formulas for perimeter, area, circumference, volume, and surface area in problem situations is an important skill in measurement and computation. The formulas, of course, vary.

Perimeter of Rectangles, Squares, and Triangles

Perimeter refers to the measure of the distance around a figure. Perimeter is measured in linear units (for example, inches, feet, meters).

The formula for (method of determining) the **perimeter of a rectangle** is

$$P = 2l + 2w$$

where l is the measure of the length and w is the measure of the width. For example, to determine the perimeter of a rectangle that is 10 meters long ($l = 10$ m) and 5 meters wide ($w = 5$ m), one would use the following equation:

$$2(10 \text{ m}) + 2(5 \text{ m}) = 30 \text{ m}.$$

The formula for the **perimeter of a square** is

$$P = 4s$$

where s is the measure of a side of the square. For example, if a square's sides measure 5 feet, then the equation for finding its perimeter would be

$$4(5 \text{ ft.}) = 20 \text{ ft.}$$

The formula for the **perimeter of a triangle** is

$$P = s_1 + s_2 + s_3$$

where s_1, s_2, and s_3 are the measures of the sides of the triangle. For example, if a triangle has three sides measuring 3 inches, 4 inches, and 5 inches, respectively, one would find the perimeter as follows:

$$3 \text{ in.} + 4 \text{ in.} + 5 \text{ in.} = 12 \text{ in.}$$

Area of Rectangles, Squares, and Triangles

Area refers to the measure of the interior of a figure. The measurement of area is in square units (for example, square inches, square feet, square meters). The formula for the **area of a rectangle** is

$$A = l \times w$$

where l is the measure of the length and w is the measure of the width. For example, if a rectangle is 10 meters long and 5 meters wide, the area of the rectangle is

$$10 \text{ m} \times 5 \text{ m} = 50 \text{ m}^2.$$

The formula for the **area of a square** is

$$A = s^2$$

where *s* is the measure of a side. For example, if each of a square's sides measures 5 feet, the area of the square is

$$(5 \text{ ft.})^2 = 25 \text{ ft.}^2$$

The formula for the **area of a right triangle** is

$$A = \tfrac{1}{2}bh$$

where *b* is the base and *h* is the height. For example, if a triangle has a base of 3 inches and a height of 4 inches, the area of the triangle is

$$\tfrac{1}{2}(3 \text{ in.} \times 4 \text{ in.}) = \tfrac{1}{2}(12 \text{ in.}^2) = 6 \text{ in.}^2$$

Circumference and Area of Circles

The **radius of a circle** is the distance from the center of the circle to the edge of the circle. The **diameter of a circle** is a line segment that passes through the center of the circle, the end points of which lie on the circle. The measure of the diameter of a circle is twice the measure of the radius. The number **pi**, symbolized as π and approximately equal to 3.14, is often used in computations involving circles.

The formula for the **circumference of a circle** is

$$C = \pi \times d, \text{ or}$$
$$C = 2 \times \pi \times r$$

where *d* is the diameter and *r* is the radius.

The formula for the **area of a circle** is

$$A = \pi \times r^2$$

where *r* is the radius. For example, if a circle has a radius of 5 centimeters, the circumference is

$$\pi \times 10 \text{ cm} \approx 3.14 \times 10 \text{ cm} = 31.4 \text{ cm}$$

(The symbol $\approx$ is one of several mathematical symbols meaning "close to" but not "equal to.")

and the area is

$$\pi \times (5 \text{ cm})^2 \approx 3.14 \times (5 \text{ cm})^2 = 78.50 \text{ cm}^2.$$

Volume of Cubes and Rectangular Solids

Volume refers to the measure of the interior of a three-dimensional figure. A **rectangular solid** is a rectilinear (right-angled) figure that has length, width, and height. The formula for the **volume of a rectangular solid** is

$$V = l \times w \times h$$

where *l* is length, *w* is width, and *h* is height. For example, if rectangular solid is 5 centimeters long, 4 centimeters wide, and 3 centimeters high, its volume is

$$5 \text{ cm} \times 4 \text{ cm} \times 3 \text{ cm} = 60 \text{ cm}^3.$$

A **cube** is a rectangular solid with the same measures of length, width, and height. That measure is the **edge** of the cube. The formula for the volume of a cube is

$$V = e^3$$

where *e* is the edge. For example, the volume of a cube whose edge measures 5 centimeters is

$$(5 \text{ cm})^3 = 125 \text{ cm}^3.$$

Time and Money

Work with time and money and conversions within the systems begins in first grade. The units of time include seconds, minutes, hours, days, months, years, centuries, and even millenniums. Except in school systems where there is a large number of students who do not speak English as a first language, the focus on money usually centers on United States currency.

The main topics (scope) in elementary mathematics and the sequence (order) in which the school introduces the topics are essentially the same in all states. These main topics and their introduction order are detailed in the following table:

Grade	Ratios, Measurement, Decimals
Kindergarten	Use dime, nickel, penny, dollar; tell time on hour, half hour; name days of week, seasons; identify cup, quart; read inches
1	Name months and days; tell time on quarter hour; use nickel, dime, quarter; identify pint, pound.
2	Name months and abbreviations; tell time on the five minutes; use operations with money; use $5, $10, and $20 bills; read Fahrenheit thermometer; use liquid and dry measures.

Grade	Ratios, Measurement, Decimals
3	Read Fahrenheit and Celsius; identify tenths; add and subtract dollars and cents.
4	Understand a.m. and p.m., century, time zones; use *milli-*, *centi-*, *deci-*, *deca-*, *hecto-*, *kilo*; convert fractions to decimals; use operations on decimals; identify ratios, equal ratios.
5	Measure using standard and metric systems; count change; determine ratios; calculate percentages, sales tax, discounts.
6	Cross products; divide and multiply by 10, 100, 1,000; identify equal ratios; cross products to solve for *n*.

Using a Variety of Materials, Models, and Methods to Explore Concepts and Solve Problems Involving Measurement

In teaching measurement—as in teaching any topic—a variety of methods, models, and materials can help to meet the needs of diverse learners. Providing experiences in measuring, using models, and encouraging charts and drawings when working with area and perimeter, in particular, can help students comprehend and apply principles, concepts, and procedures related to measurement.

Important in teaching measurement is encouraging thinking at all levels of Bloom's Taxonomy. Teachers should make sure that the class has an opportunity to take the work with perimeter, circumference, area, and volume to a level higher than just "plugging in" numbers to a formula. For instance, students should realize that changing even one number in a formula can affect the final result. Having the class experiment with these numbers, make predictions, and then evaluate how and why the changes happened involves thinking at the high levels of Bloom's Taxonomy. The use of estimating is at the second level of thinking (comprehension); this skill requires students to understand the meaning of the information and restate it in their own words. Predicting that a perimeter, circumference, area, or volume will increase or decrease if a dimension becomes larger or smaller involves the third level of Bloom's Taxonomy: application.

A complete chart of Bloom's Taxonomy of Educational Objectives is available earlier in this chapter (Table 3.1).

The effective teacher will select and use various age-appropriate simulations, manipulatives, materials, and technologies to explore concepts and solve real-world problems involving measurement.

▶ Objective 0020:
Understand and Apply Formal and Informal Mathematical Reasoning Processes in a Variety of Contexts

Analyzing Problem Situations, Making Conjectures, Organizing Information, and Selecting Strategies to Solve Problems

The key to solving math problems is attention to **reasonableness,** with analyzing the problem, making conjectures, organizing the available information, and choosing the operations being crucial to success. Often, individual words and phrases translate into numbers and operation symbols; making sure that the translations from words to symbols and terms are reasonable is important to successful problem solving. The "Objective 0013: Understand Mathematical Communication and Use Mathematical Terminology, Symbols, and Representations to Communicate Information" section of this chapter includes a chart with a list of words and the suggested operations that the words imply.

Each math problem requires an individual approach, but keep in mind again the reasonableness of the computational setup. Consider this word problem:

Roberto babysat for the Yagers one evening. They paid him $5 just for coming over to their house, plus $7 for every hour of sitting. How much was he paid if he babysat for four hours?

The word *plus* indicates addition, and the phrase *for every hour* suggests multiplication. Thus, the computational work can be set up like this: $5 + (7 \times 4) =$ Roberto's earnings. It would have been unreasonable to use a multiplication symbol in place of the addition sign. He earned $5 plus $7 for each of the four hours.

Evaluating Solutions to Problems

The ability to render some real-life quandaries into mathematical or logical problems—workable via established procedures—is a key to finding solutions. Each quandary will be unique; so, too, will be your problem-solving plan of attack—and the final answer.

The beginning of this chapter ("Objective 0012: Apply a Variety of Approaches to Interpret and Solve Mathematical Problems in Real-World Contexts") gives 11 suggested approaches (for example, estimation, mental mathematics, formal and informal reasoning, modeling, pattern recognition, and technology) to interpreting and solving problems. Using some of these approaches (such as estimation, charting, working backwards, and so forth) to check the final answer may give the problem solver some idea as to the reasonableness of the answer.

Constructing Arguments and Judging the Validity or Logic of Arguments

An **argument**, in the most precise sense of the word, consists of a premise or premises and a conclusion that is inferred from the premises. A **premise** is a proposition that is assumed as already proven. Normally a thesis or arguable idea is only a **hypothesis** until evidence is summoned by the writer to prove it. Effective arguments are based on serious, factual, or demonstrable evidence, not merely opinion. Mathematics helps the presenter of an argument construct and present a valid, logical argument.

Using Logical Reasoning to Draw and Justify Conclusions from Given Information

Logical reasoning is important in mathematics. With logical reasoning, one is more able to draw and justify conclusions from the given information. Each problem requires an individual approach, but keeping in mind the reasonableness of the computational setup should be helpful. There are formal reasoning processes.

When presented with math or logic problems, including geometry problems, *deductive reasoning* may be helpful. Deductive reasoning is reasoning from the general to the specific and is supported by deductive logic. Here is an example of deductive reasoning:

All humans who have walked on the moon are males (a general proposition). Neil Armstrong walked on the moon; therefore, he is a male (a specific proposition).

Note that conclusions reached via deductive reasoning are only sound if the original assumptions are actually true.

With *inductive reasoning*, a general rule is inferred from specific observations (which may be limited). Moving from the statement "All fish I have ever seen have fins" (specific but limited observations) to "All fish have fins" (a general proposition) is an example of inductive reasoning.

Conclusions arrived at via inductive reasoning are not necessarily true.

According to Jean Piaget, a Swiss developmental psychologist, logical reasoning is a result of cognitive development. He believes that there are four stages of cognitive development, beginning with the *sensorimotor* stage describing individuals from birth to around the age of two. The second stage, *preoperational* (describing cognitive behavior between the ages of two and seven), is characterized by egocentrism, rigidity of thought, semilogical reasoning, and limited social cognition; some cognitive psychologists have observed that this stage seems to describe how individuals think more in terms of what they can't do than what they can do. This stage describes the way that children in preschool and kindergarten go about problem solving; also, many children in the primary grades may be at this stage in their cognitive development.

The next two stages describe cognitive development during the times that most students are in school; these two stages may be most important for elementary and secondary school teachers. The third stage, *concrete operations*, is the beginning of operational thinking and describes the thinking of children between the ages of 7 and 11. Learners at this age begin to decenter. They are able to take into consideration viewpoints other than their own. They can perform transformations, meaning that they can understand reversibility, inversion, reciprocity, and conservation. They can group items into categories. They can make inferences about reality and engage in inductive reasoning; they increase their quantitative skills and can

manipulate symbols if given concrete examples with which to work. This stage of cognitive development is the threshold to higher-level learning for students. Finally, *formal operations,* the last stage of cognitive development, opens wide the door for higher-ordered, critical thinking. This stage describes the way of thinking for learners between the ages of 11 and 15 and, for Piaget, constitutes the ultimate stage of cognitive development (thus also describing adult thinking). Learners at this stage of cognitive development can engage in logical, abstract, and hypothetical thought; they can use the scientific method, meaning they can formulate hypotheses, isolate influences, and identify cause-and-effect relationships. They can plan and anticipate verbal cues. They can engage in both deductive and inductive reasoning, and they can operate on verbal statements exclusive of concrete experiences or examples. These cognitive abilities characterize the highest levels of thought. Teachers must consider the cognitive stages of their students when planning and structuring activities for the classroom.

Although stage theorists, such as Piaget, expect certain cognitive and psychosocial changes to occur in predictable patterns at predictable times in an individual's lifespan, there is always individual variation. That means, for example, that although most children are ready to begin learning to read around the age of six, there will be some children who start to read before that age and some who will not be ready to read until they are older. This does not mean that there is anything

wrong with those individuals who develop at a slightly different trajectory. However, when individuals advance faster than their peers or lag substantially behind them, there will be psychological and social factors for teachers to consider. In these cases, it will be important for teachers to be observant of these patterns of individual difference and to be able to tailor instructions to meet the needs of individuals who may differ from the group as a whole.

Some students, however, do have developmental problems and/or learning disabilities. A teacher must address the special needs of these students—regardless of the subject matter that he or she teaches.

▶ References

Drexel University. "Math Forum-Ask Dr. Math." *www.mathforum.org/library/drmath/view/56495.html.*

http://web.odu.edu/educ/llshult/blooms_taxonomy.htm.

Krathwohl, David R., Benjamin S. Bloom, and Bertram B. Masia. 1964. *Taxonomy of educational objectives: The classification of educational goals.* Handbook II, *Affective domain.* New York: David McKay.

U.S. Department of Justice Immigration and Naturalization Service. 2001. *Statistical yearbook of the immigration and naturalization service 2001.* Washington, DC: U.S. Government Printing Office.

Science

► **Objective 0021:**

Understand Scientific Inquiry and the Principles and Processes of Scientific Investigation

Determining the Type of Scientific Investigation That Best Addresses a Given Question or Scientific Hypothesis

The scientific method is not a specific step method that is rigorously followed whenever a question arises that one can answer by using the knowledge and techniques of science. Rather, it is a process of observation and analysis that can develop a reliable, consistent, and nonarbitrary representation and understanding of our world. We can use the scientific method (observation and description, formulation of hypotheses, prediction based on hypotheses, tests of predictions, and communication of findings) for many but not all questions. The approach suits best those situations in which the experimenter can control the variables, eliminating or accounting for all extraneous factors, and perform repeated independent tests wherein only one variable is changed at a time.

The scientific method is more than a procedure; it is a state of mind that should become a way of thought in all problem situations. The scientific method indicates

progress and a lack of finality in findings. The method emphasizes tolerance, open-mindedness, and caution in making final judgments. With the scientific method, one must exercise interest in all information obtained—through experimentation or observation, or both. The method should be useful in any field and should encourage the question: What evidence is available through experimentation or observation? (Milne 1958, 1, 4, 5)

The following terms are an indispensable part of the vocabulary of scientific experimentation:

Scientific hypothesis. This is the starting point for most scientific experimentations or observations. A hypothesis can generally be proven wrong, but it is seldom proven right.

Scientific theory. This is a unified explanation for many related hypotheses; well-substantiated explanations of some aspect of the natural world. Examples include atomic theory and cell theory. Though a theory may be generally widely accepted (for example, through much of human history people accepted a flat earth circled by a moving sun), it remains open to revision or even replacement should a better, more logical, more comprehensive or compelling explanation be found.

Scientific fact. An observation that is repeatedly confirmed. Scientific facts may change if new

observations yield new information; the development of new, more sophisticated or precise instruments leads to such new information. The scientifically literate individual will distinguish the role and value of scientific thought from other ways of knowing, while maintaining respect and appreciation for the ways of thinking and understanding practiced in disciplines outside of science.

Observation. This is the sensing of some measurable phenomenon.

Organization. This involves relating parts to a coherent whole.

Experimental. This means testing the effect of an independent variable on a dependent variable in a controlled environment. Not all issues of our human experience are subject to the analysis and rigors of scientific experimentation and validation. Our understanding of art, poetry, philosophy, and religion relies on ways of thinking and understanding that are not necessarily subject to repeated validation through the controlled scientific experiment or that may rely more on personal values or deference to authority.

Inference. This refers to deducing a conclusion from a measurement or observation that is not explicit to either. For example, you can infer that a classroom of 30 students has 16 girls if you know that there are 14 boys. Here one makes the inference by subtracting 14 from 30.

Prediction. This means stating the outcome of an experiment in advance of doing it. An example would be predicting that a plot of velocity versus time for a freely falling object will be a straight line.

The steps in the scientific method should involve the following activities:

- **Becoming aware that a problem exists and defining the question.**

- **Gathering information and resources.** The accumulated facts or observations are the **data**. Preparation for doing experimental work usually involves researching the literature to determine what may or may not have been done in a particular field of interest. Researching includes both print and electronic resources (the Internet) where various approaches and associated outcomes can be surveyed. Survey

results can be useful in (a) suggesting refinements in procedures and techniques and (b) avoiding blind alleys of inquiry.

- **Developing a hypothesis (a testable statement) to explain the data and the interrelationships among the data.**

- **Testing the hypothesis.** The scientist designs experiments and observes the results of the trials. The experiments must occur under precise conditions and should ideally consider a single factor at a time. The experimenter gains the ability to manipulate a variable if possible and appropriate. The scientist analyzes the data.

- **Interpreting the results and drawing conclusions.** Reliability of data obtained in any experiment is always a concern. At issue are reproducibility and accuracy. In general, data must be reproducible not only by the experimenter but also by others using the same apparatus. If results cannot be reproduced, then results are suspect. Accuracy is often limited by measurement instruments. Any reported numerical result must always be qualified by the uncertainty in its value. A typical example might be a voltage readout on a meter scale as 3.0 volts. If the meter has a full scale reading of 10 volts and meter accuracy is 3 percent, then the actual value could be anywhere between 2.7 volts and 3.3 volts.

- **Communicating the findings to others.** Scientific information is communicated to scientific and non-scientific audiences in many ways in order to inform, guide policy, and influence the practices that affect society.

- **Designing scientific investigations.** From the pencil and field notebook to modern instruments in the laboratory, science involves the tools of experimentation, observation, measurement, and computational analysis. The microscope and telescope extend the range of human observation beyond human physiology. The spectroscope separates visible light into its component colors, and the spectrophotometer measures the selective absorption of those colors as a function of some property of a solution, solid, or gas. Whatever the instruments used, an open mind and a willingness to consider all the information obtained through observations and experimentation are essential.

According to Jean Piaget, students must have reached a certain stage in their development before

they can adequately perform certain experiments. The stage of *formal operations* is the last stage of cognitive development and opens the door for higher-ordered, critical thinking. This stage describes the way of thinking for learners between ages 11 and 15. (It also describes adult thinking.) Learners at this stage of cognitive development can engage in logical, abstract, and hypothetical thought; they can use the scientific method, meaning they can formulate hypotheses, isolate influences, and identify cause-and-effect relationships. They can plan and anticipate verbal cues. They can engage in both deductive and inductive reasoning, and they can operate on verbal statements exclusive of concrete experiences or examples. These cognitive abilities characterize the highest levels of thought (Wadsworth 1979, 109–116).

Recognizing Safety Issues Related to Scientific Investigations

Through active, hands-on activities, the experience of science instruction is made richer and more meaningful. With simple observations and activities at early grades and detailed, controlled experiments at higher grades, students who do science to learn science understand science better.

While students are engaged in the process of discovery and exploration, the teacher must be engaged in protecting the health and safety of these students. The hazards vary with the discipline; thoughtful planning and management of the activities will significantly reduce the risks to students.

- In all cases, students must practice appropriate personal hygiene (hand washing) and wear personal protective equipment (goggles, gloves) while engaged in laboratory or field activities.
- Substitution of less hazardous materials whenever possible is a high priority. For example, in the physical sciences, replace mercury thermometers with alcohol or electronic ones, replace glass beakers and graduated cylinders with those made of durable polyethylene, and eliminate or reduce the use of hazardous chemicals.
- In the earth sciences, rocks and minerals used in class should not contain inherently hazardous materials.
- Students should not be allowed to taste the minerals.

Handling Living Organisms Safely

- Live vertebrates are not appropriate for elementary students, except for observation.
- Students should not touch or handle reptiles; the animals may carry *Salmonella* bacteria.
- Some plants may be toxic.
- Students and teachers should wash hands after handling plants and animals.
- Both students and teachers should use gloves when handling animals that might bite or scratch.
- Children should not bring pets to class. If the students do bring animals, only the owner should handle the animal.
- The teacher and students should treat animals with care and respect.
- The teacher should remember that animal hair, scales, and waste can cause allergies.
- Plant and animal specimens from ponds, ditches, canals, and other bodies of water may contain microorganisms that can cause disease. Suppliers can provide cultures that are safer.
- Set aquariums on stable furniture out of traffic ways. Be sure electrical accessories are plugged into a ground-fault interrupter (GFI) outlet.
- The teacher should ensure that thermostats and heating elements are working correctly.

- Reagents such as hydrochloric acid (HCl), which is used for identification of carbonate minerals, should be dispensed from spillproof plastic containers.
- In the life sciences, special care should be given to topics such as safe practices for sharps, the safe handling of living organisms, and the care and use of microscopes.
- Experiments or activities involving the collection or culture of human cells or fluids should be discouraged.

- Proper sterilization procedures must be followed to prevent the growth or spread of disease agents.

- When they are possible, outdoor, museum, and other field activities can bring a valuable enrichment to the science curriculum in all disciplines. They also bring additional responsibilities for the safe planning and implementation of activities that increase student learning while maintaining the health and safety of the students.

An elementary classroom usually does not contain hazardous chemicals or equipment. The following rules are necessary for high school or college classrooms where hazardous chemicals are present:

- Rooms in which students handle materials or chemicals that are harmful to human tissue must have a dousing shower, a floor drain, and an eye-washing facility.

- Rooms in which students handle harmful materials or chemicals should have emergency exhaust systems, fume hoods, and fume-hood supply fans that shut down when emergency exhaust fans are operating.

- There must be lockable cabinets for hazardous materials or hazardous chemicals.

Tables 4-1 and 4-2 are checklists for teachers to use to ensure that their classrooms are safe places for students to learn science.

Table 4-1.
Checklist for Chemical Storage in Schools

Ventilation	
Temperature	
Heat detector	
Secured	
Well illuminated	
Uncluttered floor	
Chemical inventory	
Chemicals purged annually	
Chemicals grouped correctly	
Labels on chemical containers	
Flammables cabinet	
Spill protection	
No explosives	
No carcinogens	

Safe Preparation, Use, Storage, and Disposal of Chemicals and Other Materials

- Teachers and students must wear eye-protective devices when using hazardous materials in activities such as treating materials with heat, tempering a metal, working with caustic or explosive materials, and working with hot liquids or solids.

- School boards should give out or sell safety glasses to students, visitors, and teachers.

- Fire extinguishers must be available to classrooms.

- Fire blankets must be available in each classroom where a fire hazard exists.

- Fire alarms, detector systems, lighting, and electrical outlets should be in operating condition, even in storage rooms.

- The teachers should make sure that the outlets are grounded.

- Outlets within two feet (six feet for new construction) of water supplies must have a ground fault circuit interrupt (GFCI) protection device.

- All buildings must have GFCI-protected outlets.

- The teacher should make sure that there are no stapled, spliced, or taped extension cords.

- The teacher should make sure that no extension cords run through or over doors, windows, or walls.

- Extension cords must be in only continuous lengths.

- Adapters must be approved by the Underwriters Laboratory (UL).

- Adapters must have overcurrent protection with a total rating of no more than 15 amperes.

- Every classroom with electrical receptacles at student workstations should have an emergency, unobstructed shut-off switch within 15 feet of the teacher's workstation.

Table 4-2.
Checklist for Science Classrooms

Fire extinguisher	
Fire blanket	
Gas cut-off (present and labeled)	
Water cut-off (present and labeled)	
Electrical cut-off (present and labeled)	
Dousing shower	
Floor drain	
Eye-washing facility	
Room ventilation adequate	
Fume hood	
Grounded receptacles	
Ground fault circuit interrupters within two inches of water	
No flammable storage	
Face protection that meets standards	
Face protection in sufficient numbers	
Face protection sanitized	

In summary, the teacher must assume responsibility for planning and implementing activities that not only increase students' learning but also maintain their health and safety.

Using Appropriate Methods, Tools, Technologies, and Measurement Units to Gather and Organize Data

Science is based upon experimentation, but not all knowledge is derived daily from first principles. The informed individual will consider the knowledge that exists and its sources, because not all sources are equally reliable, accurate, or valid. Classroom teachers, too, must use trusted educational sources and sites such as those sponsored by learned societies.

Students may perform their own experiments. For the youngest students, it is appropriate and useful for the focus to be upon models and demonstrations—for example, the solar system model, volcano, or clay cross section of an egg. Later the students should move to true experiments, in which the focus is on identifying a testable hypothesis

Monitoring Guide for Chemical Storage

- Secured chemical storage areas with lock and key and limited student access are necessary.
- Signs prohibiting student access are required and must be clearly posted.
- Chemical storage areas must be well lighted to avoid mix-ups.
- Floor space in chemical storage areas must not be cluttered.
- Chemical storage areas must be inventoried at least once a year. The chemical labels and the inventory list must have the name, supplier, date of purchase of mix, the concentration, and the amount available.
- Chemicals must be purged at least once a year.
- Chemical storage must use recognized storage patterns, and chemicals should be in compatible groups—not in alphabetical order.
- Chemical supplies must include materials to dilute and absorb a large-volume (one-gallon) chemical spill.
- Certain chemicals that present a potential for explosion are not permitted in science classrooms or storage areas. These chemicals include benzoyl peroxide, phosphorus, carbon disulfide, ethyl ether, disopropyl ether, picric acid, perchloric acid, potassium chlorate, and potassium metal.
- Some chemicals present a danger as human carcinogens and are not allowed in science classrooms or chemical storage areas. These include arsenic compounds, benzene, chloroform, nickel powder, asbestos, acrylonitrile, benzidine, chromium compound, ortho-toluidine, cadmium compounds, and ethylene oxide.

and on controlling all experimental variables but the one of interest. Many projects may be elevated from model or demonstration to experiment. A proposal to demonstrate how windmills work is made an experiment when the student adds quantitative measurements designed to measure one variable while varying only one other and while holding all other variables constant. For example, using

an electric fan, a student could measure the number of rotations per minute as a function of the fan setting (low, medium, or high). However, while keeping the fan setting constant, the student could conduct several different experiments by varying any one of the following variables: number of blades, size of blades, or shape of blades while in each case measuring the rotational speed.

Science relies on evidence collected in verifiable experiments, on conclusions validated by replication, and on theories that explain observations and that are capable of making testable predictions.

In planning and conducting an experiment, the scientist or student must (1) identify relevant variables, (2) identify necessary equipment and apparatus for measuring and recording the variables, (3) eliminate or suppress any other factors that could influence measured variables, and (4) decide on a means of analyzing the data obtained. For those conducting experiments, it is imperative that questions raised by the hypotheses be testable and that the data recorded be sufficiently accurate and repeatable.

An important step in solving problems is to decide what is to be measured. Generally, such problems will fall under one of these categories: length, area, angles, volume, mass, time, money, and temperature. Solving problems will likely require knowledge in several other areas—including mathematics.

Chapter 3 explores in detail measurement and measurement units. You may need to study again the section "Objective 0019: Understand and Apply Principles, Concepts, and Procedures Related to Measurement" from that chapter. Not only does this section review customary and metric units, but it also discusses the fundamental uncertainty of measuring devices, how they limit all measurements, and the necessity of choosing the correct unit of measurement.

Interpret and Evaluate Data to Make Inferences, Form Conclusions, and Solve Problems

Scientifically literate individuals must be able to critically evaluate the information and evidence they collect, and the conclusions or theories to which that information and evidence leads. Such analysis incorporates an understanding of the limitations to knowledge in general and the limitations of all measurements and information based on the quality of the experimental design.

We trust the results of experiments, both formal and informal, to help us understand our surroundings. Unfortunately, without proper control of the variables and a sound experimental design, our observations may lead us to entirely wrong-headed or incorrect conclusions.

Communicate the Results of Investigations in a Variety of Formats

Communicating scientific investigations to others is important. Scientific information is communicated to nonscientific audiences in order to inform, guide policy, and influence the practices that affect society. This information may be presented through text, tables, charts, figures, pictures, models, and other representations that require interpretation and analysis. Scientifically literate individuals can read and interpret these representations and select appropriate tools to present the information they gather.

Experimental results are usually formatted into a report of some kind. Report essentials normally include statements of purpose (objective), methods used, experimental set-up (including instrumentation), results (raw data and reduced data), error analysis, and conclusions. Such reports are logically organized and make abundant use of figures, charts, graphs, and other graphic aids to support narrative account of the accomplishments. In addition to reports, oral presentations are sometimes required to communicate results. In most cases, graphics also used in reports will form a core of visuals that are supported by oral explanatory narrative.

Students, too, may need to present data from their science fair projects, from their reading, or from their research. Their methods of presentation may vary according to what they are presenting. Chapter 3 discusses graphs, pictures, and tables and how they can help

in making predictions and in illustrating relationships. Specifically, the subsection of "Objective: 0017" titled "Exploring Relationships and Making Predictions by Using Tables and Graphs" discusses how these graphics can serve best in illustrating information, showing patterns, indicating relationships, and sharing results of the scientific method. Some of the graphics and their purposes include line graphs, bar graphs, and pie charts; a review of this section of chapter 3 can be useful for you.

▶ Objective 0022:

Understand the Nature and Historical Development of Scientific Thought and the Connections Among the Scientific Disciplines and Between the Sciences and Other Disciplines

---

Evaluating Given Information in Terms of the Criteria of Scientific Thought

An analysis of scientific thought includes a consideration of the verifiable evidence and the logical structure of the information. Such an analysis incorporates (1) an understanding of the limitations to knowledge in general and (2) the limitations of all measurements and information based on the quality of the experimental design.

The scientifically literate individual can evaluate claims for scientific merit, identify conflicting evidence, and weigh the value and credibility of conflicting information. The evaluator should also recognize that not every question can be answered through the use of scientific knowledge; an important part of analysis is valuing the contributions of other cultures and other ways of knowing, including art, philosophy, and theology.

As noted earlier, the informed individual will consider critically the existing knowledge, the sources of the information, and the accuracy and the value of the sources consulted. Not all sources are equally reliable, accurate, or valid.

Recognizing the Historical Development and Significance of Key Scientific Ideas

Modern scientific thought traces a significant portion of its development to the work of Western European scientists—much, but certainly not all. It is important to recognize the contributions made historically by all peoples and cultures to the development of scientific knowledge. Men and women from all continents and races continue to make meaningful contributions to the advancement of science in all disciplines. Examples are readily available for enrichment and instruction from online resources.

Science relies (1) on evidence collected in verifiable experiments, (2) on conclusions validated by replication, and (3) on theories that both explain observations and are capable of making testable predictions.

Key ideas that have proved themselves historically are particularly significant for scientists and the general public. For instance, atomic theory, which views atoms and molecules as the fundamental building blocks of all matter, would surely be modified or abandoned if it did not also explain other observations.

These scientific theories that have been proven over time provide key significant ideas for people everywhere. These time-tested and proven theories supply a unified explanation for diverse and varied observations.

The scientifically literate individual is one who uses time-tested scientific knowledge, constructs new scientific knowledge, and reflects on the significance of key scientific theories constructed through time. Such individuals have specific science content knowledge, they build upon that knowledge through their experiences and activities, and they can evaluate objectively and critically the value and limitations of that knowledge. These scientifically literate individuals distinguish the role and value of scientific thought from other ways of knowing while maintaining respect and appreciation for the ways of thinking and understanding practiced in disciplines outside of science. Science disciplines hold to certain central values that unify them in their philosophy and methodology. Science gives us (1) the knowledge and tools to understand nature and (2) the principles for applying that knowledge for some useful purpose.

Applying Scientific Themes to Help Explain and Make Connections Between Seemingly Diverse Natural Phenomena

Science concepts can serve as organizers, often unifying disparate topics in the process. Examples of key interdisciplinary science concepts include patterns, change, systems, model, cycle, equilibrium, population, cause-effect, and gradient.

As an example, the concept of model is among the most ubiquitous in all of science. Models are tentative schemes or structures that relate to real-world objects or phenomena. Our explanations of many phenomena—electricity, atoms, tectonics, and genetics, for example—rely on models. Like a model airplane, a scientific model will bear a certain resemblance to the real object that is useful at some level to represent but not fully replicate the real object. Models are used when the phenomenon or object of interest cannot be used directly. Models may be constructed to scale, but often are not, in order to emphasize some portion of the object. An artistic drawing is a model, as is a three-dimensional, cross-sectional plastic casting, or a computer-rendered animation. Each has its limitations and its beneficial function: to extend our understanding of the object or phenomenon. Models can limit our understanding when they are treated as statements of descriptive fact or when the limitations of the physical model are confused with the characteristics of the real object or phenomenon.

The concept of cycle appears in the discussion of the recurring patterns of weather, life, water, and the progression of the seasons. The concept of cycle again finds application in the periodic movement of the sun and planets.

The size of objects and distances between them are difficult to represent on the same scale with a model. The National Mall in Washington, D.C., contains a 1/10,000,000,000-scale solar system model in which the sun is the size of a grapefruit. The openness of space is mirrored at a much smaller scale by vast open spaces between atoms and between nuclei and their electrons. Pluto (formerly considered a planet) had been located some 650 yards away and was the size of a poppy seed.

On August 24, 2006, the International Astronomical Union voted to exclude Pluto from its rank as a planet. The primary justification was that Pluto's orbit is oblong and overlaps with that of Neptune; astronomers had long debated Pluto's inclusion as a planet because of its oblong orbit about the sun.

Recognizing Relationships Among the Sciences and Between the Sciences and Other Disciplines

The separation of the natural sciences into life, physical, and earth sciences is relatively arbitrary. There are interrelationships not only among the life, physical, and earth sciences but also among science, mathematics, and technology. Many school curricula and state-level science standards use the cross-disciplinary integration of science; they base this integration on key concepts rather than on individual disciplines.

Science knowledge is constantly developing and expanding in a continuous process; an organizing framework can make this development and expansion more meaningful. Scientific concepts, which often have application in contexts outside the laboratory, can help us see similarities and recognize patterns; this recognition of patterns and similarities may allow us to better function within society.

As noted earlier, an example of a key science concept is that of cycle. Cycle is one of many concepts that find application in many sciences and can be used to understand science content in more than one scientific discipline. This approach to science instruction is important for several reasons. It is consistent with the goals (1) of scientific literacy and (2) of developing science content knowledge upon which students build and extend their own understanding. Science knowledge is constantly developing and expanding in a continuous process; this knowledge and its expansion are more meaningful through the development of an organizing framework. Scientific concepts, which often have application in contexts outside the laboratory, help us see similarities and recognize patterns, which allow us to better function within society.

The scientific concept of cycle can describe the seasons, life, weather, and even the movement of wa-

ter through its various phases and through each part of the environment. The term *cycle* is so broad as to find application in multiple disciplines. Cycle, for example, is a powerful concept that has widespread application throughout science, useful for both explanation and prediction. Life cycles are central to the study of biology. The recurring pattern of events in the life cycle links birth, growth, reproduction, and death. The concept of a cycle is also evident in the carbon cycle, nitrogen cycle, Krebs cycle, hydrogeologic cycle, periodic table, and many other processes, including the transformations of energy needed to sustain life. The food chain represents the complex interdependency of all plants and animals on the energy from the sun, and the recycling of nutrients from simple to complex organisms.

The scientifically literate individual recognizes key themes (such as classification, change over time, cause and effect); concepts (such as cycles, energy, molecule, conservation); links among the science disciplines; interrelationships among science, mathematics, and technology; and common themes and concepts to real-world contexts.

▶ Objective 0023:
Understand the Relationships Among Science, Technology, and Human Activities

Evaluating How a Given Scientific Advance May Affect Humans

Scientific literacy helps us participate in the decision-making process of our society as well-informed and contributing members. Real-world decisions have social, political, and economic dimensions, and scientific information is often used to both support and refute these decisions. Understanding that the inherent nature of scientific information is unbiased and is based on experimental evidence that can be reproduced by any laboratory under the same conditions, can help us all make better decisions, recognize false arguments, and participate fully as active and responsible citizens.

Technology is closely related to science. **Technology** can be loosely defined as "the application of sci-

ence for the benefit of people." For both political and economic reasons, not all peoples have the same ready access to clean, safe water supplies or to adequate food supplies, in spite of the technological capabilities that basic science has provided. Science certainly can benefit our people and our world, but arguably it, too, can harm both people and our environment. Few would debate the benefits of the wheel and axle, the electric light, the polio vaccine, or plastic. The atomic bomb, however, is a debatable invention. Did the use of the bomb during World War II increase or decrease the total number of war deaths compared with those that would have occurred if the war had continued for another year? Does the possession of such technology lessen the threat of war from aggressors? Technology can be either an asset or a liability—depending on one's position.

Analyzing the Effect of Human Activities on the Environment

Human activities can affect the environment—both the immediate environment and the entire geosphere. For example, how an individual or community disposes of waste has an impact on not only the local environment but perhaps even a larger region. A decision to recycle may increase worldwide resource availability; a decision not to recycle may result in shortages and therefore increased prices. Established fuel emission standards may affect air pollution in the immediate area and in a much wider area. Fuel standards may in turn affect oil supply and gas prices.

Various factors may affect not only the environment but also personal and community health. In fact, health on an even wider scale may be affected. Pollution and epidemics could influence the entire globe.

Understanding global interdependence begins with recognition that world regions include economic, political, historical, ecological, linguistic, and cultural regions. This understanding should include knowledge of military and economic alliances—such as the North Atlantic Treaty Organization (NATO), the Group of Eight (G8) members, or cartels such as the Organization of Petroleum Exporting Countries (OPEC)—and how their existence affects political and economic policies

within regions. Knowledge of world regions and alliances leads to identification of issues that affect people in these areas.

Any studies of the physical environment in science, social studies, or other subjects should relate to health whenever possible. Examples include the effects of pollution on health, occupational-related disease (for example, black lung disease and the effects of chemicals on soldiers), and the differences in health care options available to people in different parts of the world and in different economic circumstances.

People do not live in isolation. There are many common issues that affect people around the world; these issues include food production, human rights, resource use, prejudice, poverty, and trade. Environmental health is of utmost concern. Strategies for promoting environmental health are the responsibility of people throughout the world.

Recognizing How Technology Can Create or Solve Problems

Technology is the application of knowledge—hopefully for people's benefit. Sometimes, however, technology works to the detriment of people and the environment. Technology should ideally include activities that are designed to select those traits intended to lead to healthier, stronger, and more productive crops and animals.

The benefits and liabilities of science and technology become complicated to evaluate. Technology has provided the applications of gene splicing for genetically modified foods; of cloning (1) for reproductive purposes, (2) for therapeutic purposes, and (3) for replicating genetic elements; and of nuclear energy to replace fossil fuels. Atomic energy can be used for energy purposes, but it may also be used for weapons of mass destruction—which may be difficult to evaluate with a flat "good" or "bad."

Science and technology, then, can tell us how to do something, not whether we should do it. We must make our own decisions. Ideally, we must consider history and key scientific ideas in making our decisions for to-day—which will affect tomorrow.

▶ Objective 0024:
Understand the Principles and Concepts of Science

Recognizing Basic Characteristics and Needs of Living Things and the Diversity of Life

It is not always easy to distinguish between living and nonliving things. Some of the characteristics of living things may lie dormant for a while; these living things, then, may resemble nonliving things for the moment. The following are characteristics of living things:

- **Enlargement by growth rather than by accretion or buildup.** Living things may reach a stage when growth is no longer apparent; this characteristic is not always easy to identify.

- **Movement.** Again, a hibernating snake may go several minutes without a heartbeat and still be a living thing; on the other hand, a combination of vinegar and baking powder may appear to be moving, and thus living, when it is not.

- **Cellular organization.** This is an indication of life, but when a living thing dies, the organization is still obvious for a while. Cellular organization, then, is not a foolproof way to determine living things.

- **Reproduction.** This is an indication of life, but one cannot be certain that an object is nonliving just because it does not reproduce during an hour of observation.

- **Definite form and size.** Again, this characteristic does not always distinguish between the living and the nonliving. For a short while after death, a nonliving object may still maintain the form and size it had before its death. This is not positive proof of whether an object is living or nonliving.

- **Responding to a stimulus (irritability).** This is a characteristic of a living thing, but that characteristic does not always hold true. A seed, for instance,

may not immediately respond to a stimulus, but it is a living thing.

- **A continuous need for energy.** Living things need an appropriate temperature, oxygen, food, and water. These are not requirements for nonliving things.

- **Chemical composition.** The chemical composition of living things is different from that of nonliving things. For example, the protoplasm of living things contains many large molecules of proteins, fats, and carbohydrates; the molecular weight of living things is much heavier than that of nonliving things.

Analyzing How Organisms Interact with One Another and with Their Environment

Ecosystem is the term for all the living and nonliving things in a given environment and how they interact. Scientifically literate individuals are aware of their surroundings, the interdependence of each part, and the effects that man's activities can have on those surroundings. Mutualistic and competitive relationships also exist between the organisms in an ecosystem and define how organisms rely upon each other and exist in competition and conflict with each other.

Recognizing How Nutrients and Energy Cycle Through Ecosystems and Are Used by Organisms

Energy transformations are the driving force within an ecosystem. Many organisms obtain energy from light. For example, light drives the process of photosynthesis in green plants. Solar energy also provides necessary heat for cold-blooded animals. Organisms may also derive energy from other organisms, including other plants and/or animals. When one source of energy is depleted in an ecosystem, many organisms must shift their attention to other sources of energy. For example, a bear will eat berries, fish, or nuts, depending on the season. The energy pyramid for an ecosystem illustrates these relationships and identifies those organisms that are most dependent on the other organisms in the system. Higher-order organisms cannot survive for long without the other organisms beneath them in the energy pyramid. The availability of adequate food within an ecosystem can explain the system's functioning, the size of an animal's territory, or the effects of overpredation of a single species upon those organisms above it in the food chain.

Ecosystems change over time, both from natural processes and from the activities of humans. The scientifically literate individual will be able to identify both how the environment changes and how those changes impact the organisms that live there, and recognize the differences between long-term and short-term variation. Natural succession occurs when one community replaces another—for example, the colonies of fungus that grow, thrive, and then are replaced by different colonies.

Identifying the Basic Structures and Functions of the Human Body and Comparing Them with Those of Other Organisms

Systems of the Human Body

The human body consists of several organ systems. These include the musculoskeletal system, the nervous system, the circulatory system, the immune system, the respiratory system, the digestive and excretory systems, and the reproductive system:

Musculoskeletal system. The human skeleton consists of more than 200 bones held together by connective tissues called ligaments. Movements are effected by contractions of the skeletal muscles, to which the bones are attached by tendons. Muscular contractions are controlled by the nervous system.

Nervous system. The nervous system has two divisions: the somatic, which allows voluntary control over skeletal muscle, and the autonomic, or involuntary, which controls cardiac and glandular functions. Voluntary movement is caused by nerve impulses arising in the brain and carried by cranial or spinal cord nerves connecting to skeletal muscles. Involuntary movement occurs in direct response to outside stimulation. Involuntary responses are called reflexes. Various nerve terminals called receptors constantly send impulses to the central nervous system. There are three types of receptors:

- Exteroceptors: pain, temperature, touch, and pressure receptors

- Interoceptors: internal environment receptors
- Proprioceptors: movement, position, and tension receptors

Each of the above receptors routes nerve impulses to specialized areas of the brain for processing.

Circulatory system. Circulation begins with the heart, which pumps blood throughout the body. The blood passes first through the right chambers of the heart and through the lungs, where it acquires oxygen. From there, it is pumped back into the left chambers of the heart. Next, it is pumped into the main artery, the aorta, which branches into increasingly smaller arteries. Beyond that, blood passes through tiny, thin-walled structures called capillaries. In the capillaries, the blood gives up oxygen and nutrients to tissues and absorbs from them carbon dioxide metabolic waste product. Finally, blood completes the circuit by passing through small veins, which join to form increasingly larger vessels, until it reaches the largest veins, which return it to the right side of the heart.

Immune system. The body defends itself against foreign proteins and infectious microorganisms by means of a complex dual system that depends on recognizing a portion of the surface pattern of the invader. The system generates lymphocytes and antibody molecules to destroy the invader molecules.

Respiratory system. Respiration is carried on by the expansion and contraction of the lungs. In the lungs, oxygen enters tiny capillaries, where it combines with hemoglobin in the red blood cells and is carried to the tissues. At the same time, carbon dioxide passes through capillaries into the air contained within the lungs. Inhaling draws air into the lungs; this air is higher in oxygen and lower in carbon dioxide. Exhaling forces air from the lungs; this air is high in carbon dioxide and low in oxygen.

Digestive and excretory systems. Food supplies the energy required for sustenance of the human body. Digestion begins in the mouth, where chewing fragments the food and mixes it with saliva. Chewed food passes down the gullet into the stomach, where gastric and intestinal juices continue the process. Thereafter, the mixture of food and secretions makes its way down the alimentary canal by peristalsis, rhythmic contractions of the smooth muscle of the gastrointestinal system.

Reproductive system. The reproductive system produces eggs and sperm, which can combine to create an embryo. The female reproductive system includes the ovaries, fallopian tubes, uterus, and vagina. Each month, one egg is released from the ovaries and then travels down the fallopian tubes. If it is fertilized, it becomes implanted in the lining of the uterus, where a baby begins to form. When sufficiently grown, the baby leaves the uterus and its mother's body through the vagina, or birth canal.

The male reproductive system consists of the testicles, vas deferens, urethra, and penis. Sperm are produced in the testicles. They move through the vas deferens from the testicles to the urethra. During intercourse, sperm pass through the penis and into a woman's body. In a woman's body, sperm pass through the cervix, into the uterus, and up the fallopian tubes, where fertilization of an egg may take place.

Plant and Animal Comparisons

Plants are multicellular green organisms; their cells contain eukaryotic (nucleated) protoplasm held within cell walls composed primarily of cellulose. The most important characteristic of plants is their ability to photosynthesize—that is, to make their own food by converting light energy. The animal kingdom is also multicellular and eukaryotic, but its members differ from the plants in that they derive nutrition from other organic matter, by ingesting food rather than absorbing it.

Applying the Principles of Genetics and Evolutionary Theory to Understand How Organisms Can Change over Time

Human Genetics

Each of the cells in a living thing has a specific structure and role in the organism. The structure of a cell and its function are determined to a large degree by the genes within a cell. **Genes** are code units of chromosomes within the nucleus of a cell. Genes give information about the structure and function of a cell.

A fertilized human sex cell has 46 chromosomes, 23 from the mother and 23 from the father. This fertilized sex cell will multiply to form a new organism. The process of combining genetic materials from two parent organisms to form a unique offspring is called **sexual reproduction**.

During sexual reproduction, an organism receives two genes for each trait, one from each parent. Sometimes one trait will mask another, as is the case with eye color. If a person has one gene for brown eyes and one gene for blue eyes, the person will always have brown eyes. A genetic trait that masks another, like the gene for brown eyes, is called a **dominant trait**. A gene that can be masked, like the gene for blue eyes, is called a **recessive trait**.

Understanding genetic dominance helps us to figure out the genetic configuration of an individual. An individual with blue eyes must have two genes for blue eyes, since blue eye color is a recessive trait. Recessive traits are shown by lowercase letters, so the genetic symbol for blue eyes is *bb*. An individual with brown eyes must have at least one gene for brown eyes, which is dominant. Dominant genes are shown by uppercase letters, so the genetic symbol for brown eyes could be *Bb* or *BB*.

When the genetic type of parents is known, we can use the Punnett square to calculate the probability that the offspring will show particular traits. A **Punnett square** is a large square divided into four small boxes. The genetic symbol of each parent for a particular trait is written alongside the square, one parent along the top and one parent along the left side:

Parent Aa

Each gene symbol is written in both boxes below or to the right of it so each small box has two gene symbols in

it. The genetic symbols in the boxes are all possible genetic combinations for a particular trait of the offspring of these parents. Each box has a 25 percent probability of being the actual genetic representation for a given child.

Human sex type is determined by genetic material in sperm. The genetic sex code for human females is XX. The genetic sex code for human males is XY. Eggs carry only X genes. Sperm carry X or Y genes (some biologists view the Y gene as the absence of the X gene). The probability of a fertilized human egg being male, or XY, is 50 percent.

Heredity

The discussion of life cycles brings forward the concept that an offspring of one generation bears likeness to, but also variation from, the previous generation. Some characteristics of the individual parent are passed along, whereas others appear not to be. We observe the connections between the visible traits of the parents and children; these connections are evident in all sexually reproducing organisms. It is clear that the offspring of birds are other birds, which generally look much like the parent birds. Details of how such traits are conveyed through genetics are important to understand, yet detailed instruction in these topics is allocated to the curriculum of higher grades.

Evolution

Evolution is defined as the processes by which living organisms originated on earth and have been diversified and modified through sustained changes in form and function.

Darwin reasoned that in nature, species with qualities that made them better adjusted to their environments or gave them higher reproductive capacities would tend to leave more offspring. Thus, such individuals were said to have higher fitness. Because more individuals are born than survive to breed, elimination of the less fit (natural selection) should occur, leading to a population that is well adapted to environmental habitats. According to Darwin, evolution proceeds by the natural selection of well-adapted individuals over a span of many generations.

Fundamentalist Protestants, under the leadership of William Jennings Bryan, began a campaign in 1921 to

prohibit the teaching of evolution in the schools; he saw this as protecting the belief in the literal biblical account of creation. The South was quick to endorse the idea of prohibiting the teaching of evolution.

Darwin's work preceded that of Gregor Mendel (the "father of modern genetics") and others and therefore did not benefit from the knowledge of the role genetics plays in the evolution process.

After Mendel's genetic discoveries, most geneticists believed mutations were the only source of genetic variation. Many geneticists believed that the random accumulation of favorable mutational changes drove evolution. Natural selection as previously defined was reduced to a minor role by mutationists, whose ideas held sway well into the 1930s.

Still later, in 1935, during the establishment of what has been termed the "synthetic theory of evolution," scientific understanding was greatly expanded when James Watson and Francis Crick demonstrated that genetic material is composed of two nucleic acids, deoxyribonucleic acid (DNA) and ribonucleic acid (RNA). Mutations (in light of these discoveries) were then seen to be changes in gene position that can affect the function of the protein derived from the gene. Natural selection in this view now operates to favor or suppress a particular gene according to how strongly its protein product contributes to the reproductive success of the organism.

Today evolution is a widely accepted context within which understanding in many branches of life science continues to advance. While the tenets of evolution as scientific theory are widely accepted (particularly as they apply to the short-term changes and adaptations within a species) the subject continues to generate some debate.

The goal of science education is to develop a scientifically literate public. At the elementary level, this involves an understanding of how physical traits promote the survival of a species, how environmental changes affect species that are not adapted to those new conditions, and how heredity has a role in passing and modifying the traits of successive generations. Ample examples are available to illustrate these concepts to the elementary student. A rabbit whose coat regularly turns white before the first snowfall is at a temporary

disadvantage and is therefore subject to a higher degree of predation. This rabbit may not live to produce other early-white-coated rabbits.

An example of significant evolution of modern people occurred during the Paleolithic Age, according to theorists. During this time, 1 million years ago to 12,000 B.C.E., the human brain became much larger. Theorists have suggested two reasons for the rapid evolutionary development of the human brain. First, meat eating led to big-game hunting, an activity that necessitated group planning and cooperation; second, the use of speech facilitated planning and coordination of group activities. Tool making was once thought to be a major factor in the development of a large brain for people, but it is now known that many animals use tools and even make tools. Two other factors greatly influenced the emergence of modern people. It seems that about 100,000 years ago, genetic evolution became less important than cultural evolution as man developed the ability to pass on accumulated knowledge. Also, food supplies increased significantly after the retreat of the great glaciers about 12,000 years ago. This increase in food supplies may have contributed to the ability of people to reproduce and ensure the survival of the species.

▶ Objective 0025:
Understand the Basic Principles and Concepts of Physical Science

Recognizing Basic Concepts Related to Matter and Energy

All energy is conserved. **Conservation of energy** is a fundamental law of science that means energy never disappears; it just changes its form. A good example of energy conservation is lifting a heavy object from floor to tabletop. Work is done and is stored as potential energy when the object is placed on the tabletop. However, the potential energy can be recovered by pushing the object off of the table. The potential energy is then converted to kinetic energy (energy of motion), and work that was done is recovered. For this ideal simple system, the energy recovered (kinetic) is equal to the energy stored (potential). However, for nonideal (real) systems, the recovered energy is always less than the stored en-

ergy. This is usually attributable to losses of one type or another (often friction). Nevertheless, it is always true that energy is conserved; stored or potential energy is always the sum of recovered energy plus losses, if any.

Recognizing the Composition and Structure of Matter

All matter is composed of atoms, or combinations of atoms, selected from among the more than 100 elements. The **atom** is the smallest particle of an element that retains the properties of the element; similarly, the **molecule** is the smallest particle of a compound. Molecules cannot be separated into smaller particles (atoms or smaller) without a chemical change disrupting the chemical bonds that bind the molecule together. Physical separations—through the use of filter paper, centrifuge, or magnet, for example—do not affect chemical bonds. The scientific concept of a cycle, in this case without a time dependence, is evident in the fundamental makeup of matter and is reflected in the structure of the periodic table. Dmitri Mendeleev is credited with the development of the modern periodic table, in part for his predicting the existence of then unknown elements based on the repeating trends in reactivity and physical properties. The concepts associated with atoms and molecules are not found in the elementary benchmarks, but they should be well understood by the elementary teacher nonetheless, as they provide the basis of all our understanding of matter and chemical change.

Whereas the atoms and molecules of all materials are in constant motion (vibrational energy), those in gases and liquids are also free to move about their own axes (rotational energy) and about the container (translational energy). Increasing the temperature of a solid imparts additional energy, which increases the vibrational energy. Once any particular atom or molecule gains sufficient energy to break free of the intermolecular attractions to the bulk solid or liquid, it will slip or fly away (melt or evaporate, respectively). Hotter atoms require more space in which to vibrate. For this reason, wagon-wheel rims are heated in the forge to expand the metal before slipping the rim onto the wheel; basketballs left outside on a cold night don't bounce well; the expansion of alcohol or mercury in thermometers is used to indicate temperature.

Identifying Physical and Chemical Properties of Matter

Chemical and physical properties describe and distinguish matter. Physical properties, such as color and density, are termed *intrinsic* when they do not change as the amount of the matter changes. Properties such as mass or volume do vary when matter is added or removed, and these are termed *extrinsic properties*.

Mass is the amount of matter in an object, which is sometimes measured using a lever-arm balance. Although sometimes incorrectly used interchangeably with *mass*, **weight** is a measure of the force of gravity experienced by an object, often determined using a spring scale. An electronic scale may display an object's mass in grams, but it is dependent on gravity for its operation. Such a device is accurate only after using a calibration mass to adjust the electronics for the unique local gravitational force.

Although we may say an object is "weightless" as it floats inside the space shuttle, it is still affected by the gravitational forces from both the earth and sun, which keep it in orbit around each. The force of gravity is proportional to the product of the masses of the two objects under consideration divided by the square of the distance between them. Earth, being larger and more massive than Mars, has proportionally higher gravitational forces. This is the basis of the observation in H. G. Wells's *War of the Worlds* that the Martian invaders are "the most sluggish things I ever saw crawl" (Wells 1898/2000).

Density, the ratio of mass to volume, is an intrinsic property that depends on the matter, but not the amount of matter. **Volume** is defined as the amount of space an object occupies. The density of a five-ton cube of pure copper is the same as that of a small copper penny. However, the modern penny is a thin shell of copper over a zinc plug, and the density of this coin is significantly lower than that of the older, pure copper coin. Density is related to **buoyancy**. Objects sink, in liquids or gases alike, if they are denser than the material that surrounds them. Archimedes' principle, also related to density, states that an object is buoyed by a force equal to the mass of the material the object displaces. Thus, a 160-pound concrete canoe will easily float in water if the volume of the submerged portion is equal to the volume of 20 gallons of water (water weighs approximately 8 pounds per gallon, thus 8 lb/gal $\times$ 20 gal = 160 lb). Density is not the same

as **viscosity**, a measure of thickness or flowability. The strength of intermolecular forces between molecules determines, for example, that molasses is slow in January, or that hydrogen bromide is a gas in any season.

Water is odorless, tasteless, and colorless. It is the only substance known to exist in a natural state as a solid, liquid, or gas on the surface of the earth. It is a universal solvent. Water does not corrode, rust, burn, or easily separate into its components. It is chemically indestructible. It can corrode almost any metal and erode the most solid rock. A unique property of water is that when frozen in its solid state, it expands and floats on water. Water has a freezing point of 0°C (Celsius) and a boiling point of 100°C. Water has the capacity to absorb great quantities of heat with relatively little increase in temperature. When distilled, water is a poor conductor of electricity; when salt is added, it is a good conductor of electricity.

Acid and *base* are terms used to describe solutions of differing pH. The concentration of hydrogen ion in a solution determines its **pH**, which is based on a logarithmic scale. Solutions having a pH of 0 to 7 are called acids and have hydrogen ions (H+) present. Common acids include lemon juice, vinegar, and battery acid. Acids are corrosive and taste sour. Solutions having a pH of 7 to 14 are called bases (or referred to as alkaline) and have hydroxide ions (OH–) present. Bases are caustic and feel slippery in solution. Common bases include baking soda and lye. Solutions having a pH of 7 are called neutral and have both ions present in equal but small amounts.

Identifying Different Forms of Energy

Energy is loosely defined as the ability to do work. **Kinetic energy** is the energy of motion. The formula for kinetic energy, where m is the mass and v the velocity of an object, is as follows:

$$KE = \frac{1}{2}mv^2$$

Chemical energy is stored in the bonds of our food, held for later conversion to kinetic energy and heat in our bodies. **Potential energy** is held in an icicle hanging off the roof. The formula for potential energy, where m is mass, g is the gravitational force constant, and h is the height, is as follows:

$$PE = mgh$$

When the icicle falls, its potential energy is converted first to **kinetic energy** and then to **sound energy** as it hits the pavement, and finally to additional kinetic energy as the fragments skitter off. At the elementary level, students need to be able to identify the types of energy involved in various phenomena and identify the conversions between types.

Rube Goldberg (1883–1970) was a sculptor, a writer, and a Pulitzer Prize–winning cartoonist; his name in most dictionaries is now a label for any complicated invention that arduously performs a simple operation—often in a comic way. In the popular Rube Goldberg competitions, contestants use a number of sequential energy conversions to perform a simple task like breaking a balloon or flipping a pancake. Energy is conserved in each of these normal processes, converted to less useful forms (for example, heat), but not created or destroyed. Similarly, matter is never created or destroyed in a normal chemical reaction. Nuclear fusion is an obvious exception to both rules, following Einstein's equation, but these reactions are generally not allowed in the classroom or the school laboratory.

Energy is available in many forms, including heat, light, solar radiation, chemical, electrical, magnetic, and sound. When you turn the lights on in your car, chemical energy stored in the battery is converted into electrical energy (current flowing in the circuitry), which is then converted into both heat and light in the headlight filament. Solar radiation is used in some parts of the world to heat water by flowing cold water through pipes exposed to the sun. Here solar radiation is converted to heat, which raises the water temperature. Lightning strikes produce thunder; some of the electrical energy in the lightning strike sets up vibrations in the air. Some of the vibrations are converted into sound.

Heat is a form of energy. Temperature, however, is a measure of aggregate atomic or molecular activity within an object. To illustrate the difference, consider the example of a pot of water on a stove, where heat energy is transferred to the water. The effect of heating the water is to put its molecules into ever-increasing vibratory motion. If the water is heated sufficiently, the vibratory motion is strong enough to break intermolecular bonds and the water is thereby converted into steam and boils away. Note that adding heat is the cause of increasing temperature, not the other way around.

When heated or cooled, matter undergoes phase changes, or changes to its **thermal properties**. Phase change means that a substance changes state. The most common progression of phase changes observed, when hosting a substance, is solid to liquid to gas. In the process of cooling, the reverse progression of gas to liquid to solid is ordinarily seen.

In a phase change, the chemical properties of the matter remain unchanged: the substance still has the same chemical formulation after the change. Energy (heat) is invoked in every phase change with an input of heat required to move to less-ordered states and a release of heat involved in moving to more-ordered states. An example of the former is the conversion of water to steam. An example of the latter is heat being released by snowflakes upon conversion from water vapor.

Sound is caused by the vibration of objects. This vibration creates waves of disturbance that can travel through air and most other materials. If these sound waves hit your eardrum, you perceive sound. The speed of sound waves is related to their medium. Sound travels more quickly through denser materials (solids, liquids) than through less dense materials (gases). Sound does not travel through a vacuum.

Light travels much more quickly (300,000 kilometers per second) than sound does (330 meters per second), and light can pass through a vacuum. As light passes through a material, it travels in a straight path. When light moves from one material to another, it may be transmitted, absorbed, reflected, or refracted. Transparent materials (for example, water or glass) allow light to pass directly through them. This passing through is called **transmission**. Opaque objects (for example, wood) absorb light. No light comes out of them. Mirrors reflect light. They re-emit light into the medium it came from. **Refraction** is the bending of light. Light may be refracted when it moves from one material to another (for example, air to water). Mirages are formed when light refracts as it moves from cool air to warm air.

Transfers and Transformations of Energy and Changes in Matter

Waves are one mechanism of energy transport from one location to another. We experience waves directly in the forms of light, sound, and water; we experience

sound waves indirectly through radio and TV, wireless networks, and X-rays. Waves are periodic in their nature, and the concept of periodicity (cycles) is one of the key interdisciplinary concepts that include the motions of planets, the properties of elements, life cycles of plants and animals, and many other events.

Energy is **transmitted through a material** in a translational wave when in water. For example, particles of water move perpendicularly to the direction of energy travel. A wave with greater energy has greater amplitude. *AM radio* refers to amplitude modulation of the radio signal, where the carrier wave amplitude is modified by adding the amplitudes of the voice or music waves to create a cumulative and more complex waveform. The receiver must subtract from this complex waveform the simple sinusoidal waveform of the carrier to leave the voice or music.

Compressional waves, like sound waves, are characterized by having the media move along the same axis as the direction of energy travel. The speed of sound waves is dependent on the medium through which they travel—faster in denser materials (such as railroad tracks) and faster in water than through air. Interestingly, sound moves faster in warm air than colder air; cold air is denser, but the gas molecules in warm air move faster and thus convey the sound energy more quickly. As stated earlier, sound cannot travel in a vacuum (referring to the absence of all matter in a given space); as a compressional wave, it needs to have particles to compress as it travels.

▶ Objective 0026:
Understand the Basic Principles and Concepts of Earth and Space Science

Identifying the Geological Composition and History of Earth

Earth is composed of three layers: crust, mantle, and core. Made of solid iron and nickel, the **core** is at the earth's center. It is about 7,000 kilometers in diameter. The **mantle** is the semimolten layer between crust and core, and is about 3,000 kilometers thick. The **crust**

is the solid outermost layer, ranging from 5 to 40 kilometers thick; bedrock overlaid with mineral and/or organic sediment (soil) composes the crust.

Plates, large sections of the earth's crust, move at times and create earthquakes, volcanoes, faults, and mountains. The study of these movements is called **plate tectonics**. Faults are cracks in the crust formed when plates move. **Earthquakes** occur when plates slide past one another quickly. Earthquakes also cause volcanoes. The **seismograph**, using the Richter scale, measures the intensity of earthquakes.

Scientifically literate individuals have an understanding and appreciation for the world around them. Rocks hold an early fascination, both for their utility as objects for throwing and skipping and for their beauty, texture, and diversity. Physical landforms vary considerably across the face of the earth, and are revealed to the observant and thoughtful eye in road cuts and the scenic viewpoints everywhere. Each puddle, rivulet, and mass of sand and gravel in a yard or parking lot reveals on a small scale the same actions of erosion, deposition, and graded sorting of material by size and mass that are at work on a global scale to form and reform our physical environment. The scientifically literate individual continually constructs new knowledge by study of the geosphere through direct observation; through photographs, models, and samples; and through graphical representations (maps). The geosphere is the source for many natural resources essential for modern life and the recipient of pollution caused by man's activities.

Physical changes to the geosphere are abundant and frequently newsworthy. Each landslide, earthquake, or volcanic eruption reveals something about the earth and its structures. **Fossils**, preserved remnants of or marks made by plants and animals that were once alive, are one source of evidence about changes in the environment over time. Scientists' discovery of fossils of marine organisms in what is now a desert presents teachers an opportunity to discuss with students the scientific ways of knowing, how science forms and tests hypotheses and how theories develop to explain the reasons behind observations. The scientifically literate individual understands the concepts of uncertainty in measurement and the basis of scientific theories. Such an understanding may lead the teacher in an elementary classroom to refer to fossils and rocks simply as "very old," to dinosaurs as "living long ago," and occasionally to preface statements of scientific theory with the observation that "many scientists believe . . ."

Analyzing Major Features of Earth's Surface in Terms of the Natural Processes That Shape Them

Weathering is the breaking down of rock into small pieces. Rock is weathered by acid rain, freezing, wind abrasion, glacier scouring, and running water. **Erosion** is the transportation of rock or sediment to new areas. **Agents of erosion** include wind, running water, and glaciers. **Geology** is the study of the structure and composition of the earth.

Volcanoes form where plates move away from one another to let magma reach the crust's surface. **Magma** is molten rock beneath the earth's crust. **Lava** is molten rock on the earth's surface. Mountains are formed by volcanic activity or the collision of plates, which causes the crust to buckle upward.

Recognizing Fundamental Weather Processes and Phenomena and Factors That Influence Them

Meteorology is the study of the atmosphere and its changes. The **atmosphere** is a layer of air surrounding the earth. Air is a mixture of gases, the most common being nitrogen and oxygen.

The atmosphere can be divided into several layers. The **troposphere** is the layer closest to Earth. Almost all life and most weather are found there. The **stratosphere** is the chief thermally insulating layer of the atmosphere. It contains the ozone layer and jet stream. The stratosphere is the region where ozone is produced. The **thermosphere** causes meteors to burn up by friction as they pass through. This layer reflects radio waves. The **exosphere** is the outer layer of the atmosphere. It eventually blends into the vast region we call "space."

Weather is the local, short-term condition of the atmosphere. The two factors that affect weather most are the amounts of energy and water present. Water covers about 75 percent of the earth's surface. As that water

slowly evaporates, some of the vapor is held in the atmosphere. It is the water vapor in our atmosphere that causes humidity, fog, clouds, and precipitation.

Demonstrating an Understanding of the Water Cycle

With about 75 percent of the earth's surface covered with water, the hydrosphere defines our planet and its environment. Few people have experienced the vast reaches of the world's oceans. Closer to our daily lives, and important because of the fresh water necessary to sustain life and commerce, are rivers and streams. The hydrosphere includes not just the surface waters described, but the subsurface waters of aquifers and the water vapor present in the atmosphere. People have a significant impact on the hydrosphere through activities that contaminate, divert, and attempt to control the flow of water. These activities can benefit one part of the environment or society while harming another.

The scientific concept of cycle is used to describe the movement of water through its various phases and through each part of the environment. A climate chamber formed from discarded polyethylene soda bottles can easily demonstrate these changes: when soil, plants, and small frogs are added, a nearly complete ecosystem is formed if we count the food we add for the frog each day. In this chamber, the student can observe the water cycle as liquid water evaporates and then condenses again against an ice-filled chamber to fall back to the surface. Only two phases, solid and liquid, can be observed directly, because the individual molecules of water vapor are too small to be seen by the naked eye. The white cloud visible at the tip of the teakettle, like fog or our breath when we exhale on a cold winter day, are examples of condensed water vapor (liquid water). There is a limited supply of fresh water on the earth, and water is a reusable resource that must be carefully managed. With this in mind, we are grateful for the technology to treat and purify water, which has done much to extend the human lifespan and reduce disease by providing clean and reliable sources of water in some parts of the world.

As discussed earlier, the atmosphere is the layer of gases held close to the earth by gravitational forces. It is quite thin in comparison to the stratosphere, just as the skin on an apple is thin in proportion to the rest of the apple. The atmosphere is densest close to the surface, where gravity holds the heavier gases and the pressure is greatest. The atmosphere becomes less dense and pressure decreases exponentially as altitude increases. All weather is contained within the lowest layer of the atmosphere (troposphere), and the temperature decreases as one rises through this layer. We can often observe the top of this layer as clouds form anvil-shaped tops when they cannot rise further than the height of the cold boundary between the troposphere and the overlying layer (stratosphere).

The concept of cycle reappears in the discussion of the recurring patterns of weather and the progression of the seasons. The basis of the seasons has much more to do with the angle of sunlight striking the earth and very little to do with the distance from the sun. Classroom weather stations and weather charts are useful learning tools, and projects to build thermometers, hygrometers, and barometers are popular in classrooms.

Density variations related to temperature drive the movement of air. Heat energy warms the air and increases water evaporation; warm air expands and rises above cooler surrounding air; rising air cools and water vapor condenses forming clouds and precipitation. Cold, heavy air settles over the polar caps and flows toward the equator.

Temperature gradients and the resulting air movement are readily observed at home where the basement is cool, the upstairs warmer, and a draft evident on the stairway.

Identifying the Basic Components and Structure of the Solar System

The sun is the gravitational center of the solar system. A planet's motions are defined by their path along an elliptical orbit defined by its speed and its continual gravitational attraction to the sun.

The solar system is defined as the sun and its orbiting planets. The sun is composed of essentially hydrogen and is very massive, with a mass 750 times as great as that of all the planets combined. Planet names in order from the sun are Mercury, Venus, Earth, Mars, Jupiter,

Saturn, Uranus, and Neptune (and Pluto, which is no longer considered a full-fledged planet). The innermost planets (Mercury, Venus, Earth, and Mars) are composed mostly of rocky metallic material, while the outermost planets (Neptune, Saturn, and Uranus) are composed mostly of hydrogen, helium, and ices of ammonia and methane. Pluto has a similar composition to the outer planets. Jupiter is a gas giant exception, composed largely of hydrogen, and is best thought of as a half-formed sun. Many of the planets have satellite moons, including Earth (one), Mars (two), and Jupiter (eight). The dwarf planet Pluto has two moons. Some planets have other distinguishing features, such as the rings of Saturn, the significant atmospheres of Earth and Venus, or the giant red spot on Jupiter.

Describing the Composition, Motions, and Interactions of Objects in the Universe

Because Earth rotates once upon its axis every 24 hours, the time of day varies from point to point on its surface. For example, when it is sunrise at one point on Earth, it is sunset approximately halfway around the earth. So at a given instant of time at one point on Earth, it is sunset (6:00 P.M.), at another point diametrically opposite the first point it is sunrise (6:00 A.M.), and halfway in between it is 12:00 noon or 12:00 midnight, depending on which hemisphere one chooses. To facilitate the obvious need for time zones, the earth is gridded with latitude and longitude lines. Meridians run from pole to pole, and there are 360 of these around the earth in one-degree increments. Every hour, a given location on the earth's surface rotates through 15 degrees of longitude.

For all practical purposes, the sun is fixed in position. However, the daily west-to-east rotation of the earth appears to make the sun "rise" and "fall" in the sky each day. The sun rises above the eastern horizon at dawn, when the line of sight from an observer to the sun is first made clear by the rotation of the earth. It sets below the western horizon at dusk, when the line of sight from an observer to the sun is last made clear by the rotation of the earth. Thus, throughout the day the sun "rises" steadily higher in the sky as the west-to-east rotation of the earth continually alters a viewer's line of sight.

In longer (seasonal) periods, the sun appears to change its position in another way. As winter approaches in the Northern Hemisphere, the sun "sinks" toward the southern horizon. Later, when winter wanes and summer approaches, the sun "rises" higher above the southern horizon. The low point is on the first day of winter (December 21) and the high point is on the first day of summer (June 21). (Halfway between these two dates are the equinoxes, which mark the beginning of spring and fall.) This motion, too, is apparent and results from the earth's being tilted on its axis and thereby pointing either away from or toward the sun at different times of the year (equivalently different positions along Earth's orbital path around the sun). In winter, the north pole of Earth points away from the sun and causes it to appear lower (or further south) to observers in the Northern Hemisphere. In summer, the north pole of Earth points toward the sun and causes it to appear higher (or further north) to observers in the Northern Hemisphere. Note that the tilting of Earth's axis also accounts for the difference in length of days from season to season with the effect being more pronounced at higher latitudes. Note also that for the Southern Hemisphere, the same process occurs, but with opposite seasonal phasing.

The sun of our solar system is a medium-size star and is only one of billions of stars in our Milky Way galaxy, itself a spiral galaxy. The Andromeda Nebula Galaxy, first studied in 1612, resembles the Milky Way. It is the nearest galaxy that Northern Hemisphere observers can see. Galaxies are large collections of stars and are composed not just of stars but also hydrogen, dust particles, and other gases. They are located millions to billions of light-years from Earth. Galaxies are classified as to their appearance. Irregular systems have no special form or symmetry. Spiral systems resemble a large pinwheel, with arms extending from the dense central core. Elliptical systems appear round with spiral arms. The universe itself is composed of countless galaxies; its age is about 18 billion years.

Stars are essentially large masses of hydrogen that have been pulled together under the influence of gravity. With sufficient amounts of hydrogen and gravitational pressure, fusion is initiated in the star's interior, which causes the star to glow with visible light. (Fusion is the process of liberating energy by fusing hydrogen to form helium.) As such, stars represent the most abundant type of mass in the universe: plasma. Depending on the amount of hydrogen mass involved, stars undergo an evolutionary cycle that can involve a vast army of forms, including red giants, novas, supernovas, neutron stars, white dwarfs, and others.

Distances from the sun can be expressed in terms of astronomical units (AU), with the sun-earth distance taken as AU = 1. In terms of AU, the closest planet is Mercury (AU = 0.39); Pluto's distance from the sun, by comparison, is 39.4 AU.

Other bodies much smaller than the planets also have orbits about the sun. Innumerable asteroids lie in a belt between Mars and Jupiter and orbit into the same rotational sense as the rest of the planets. Sizes of asteroids range from the largest, Cares (having a diameter of about 1,000 kilometers), to others too small to have any perceptible gravity. Their composition is generally carbonaceous or rocky metallic.

Comets differ greatly from asteroids in their composition, having significant amounts of ices and water. Also, a comet's period (time taken to orbit the sun) can vary considerably. Comets have been described by theastronomical community as "dirty snowballs." Comet orbits are generally more acutely elliptical than that of planets or asteroids. When approaching the sun, comets exhibit tails, or comas, the result of their ice's being boiled or sublimated off by heating. For purposes of analyses, comets are described in terms of their nucleus, coma, and tail. The nucleus is the small, solid body from which an extended atmosphere is developed as the comet nears the sun. The coma is the boiled-off atmosphere that surrounds the nucleus. The tail is the long streamers of gas and dust that are swept away from the sun.

▶ References

Milne, Lorus, and Marjorie J. Milne. 1958. *The biotic world and man.* Englewood Cliffs, NJ: Prentice Hall.

Wadsworth, Barry J. 1979. *Piaget's Theory of Cognitive Development.* New York: Longman.

Wells, H. G. (Herbert George). *War of the worlds.* 1898/2000, Bartleby.com, 2000. *www.bartleby.com/1002.*

Social Studies

▶ **Objective 0028:**
Understand Democratic Principles, Practices, Values, and Beliefs, as Well as the Rights and Responsibilities of Citizenship

Basic Democratic Principles and Rights and Their Significance and Current Applications for Individuals and Society

The Constitution of the United States codifies the basic democratic principles that govern the country and enumerates the rights to which its citizens are entitled. Crucial amendments—established according to the process described in Article V of the Constitution—help to lay out these basic rights of individuals.

The first 10 amendments are listed as articles and were voted on and ratified together in 1791; they are the only Constitutional amendments prior to 1808. These articles were a necessary addition in order to gain support for the Constitution among those who thought that the original document gave too much power to the federal government and did not adequately protect the rights of citizens. The first 10 articles or amendments are called the **Bill of Rights**:

Amendment I. Forbids Congress from making any law that restricts freedom of religion, freedom of speech, freedom of the press, or the right of individuals to assemble peaceably or petition the government to respond to grievances.

Amendment II. States that the government may not infringe upon the right of the people to keep and bear arms in a regulated militia. (This was not intended to guarantee an individual's right to own a gun for personal use.)

Amendment III. Restricts the government from housing or quartering soldiers in the home of a private citizen, in peace or war, without the consent of the owner.

Amendment IV. Forbids the search of property or houses of individuals except when probable cause has been established and a search warrant has been issued.

Amendment V. Guarantees that no person shall be deprived of life, limb, or property without due process of law and further stipulates that no one can be forced to testify or otherwise incriminate themselves. A person may be held or punished only if they have been indicted and tried, except for cases of military personnel during a time of war. Article V also states that no person can be tried twice for the same crime, a provision known as **double**

jeopardy. A person may, however, be tried separately on criminal and on civil charges.

Amendment VI. Guarantees the right, in criminal cases, to a speedy and public trial by an impartial jury. In addition, individuals must be informed of the charges against them, be able to confront the witnesses against them, and be provided with counsel and be able to call witnesses on their behalf.

Amendment VII. Specifically guarantees the right to a jury trial. In addition, in civil suits where the amount exceeds $20, the right to trial by jury will apply, and no decision by a jury shall be overturned by any court of the United States except according to the rules of common law.

Amendment VIII. Bans the use of excessive bails or fines and the use of cruel and unusual punishments.

Amendment IX. Establishes that citizens have rights beyond those stated in the Constitution, and states that the specific listing of certain rights in the Constitution cannot be used to deny or abridge other rights retained by the people.

Amendment X. Reserves for the states or the people any powers not directly delegated to or prohibited by the federal government. This is the source of "reserved" powers, the bulk of powers granted to the states.

Later amendments also deal particularly with individual and personal rights:

Amendment XIII. Bans slavery and involuntary servitude except as punishment for a crime for which one has been convicted (1865).

Amendment XIV. Is the first time the Constitution addresses citizenship, which it clearly defines, stating that "all persons born or naturalized in the United States, and subject to the jurisdiction thereof, are citizens of the United States and of the State wherein they reside." It is significant that this amendment confers state "citizenship" as well as national citizenship, as some Southern states were reluctant to confer all rights and privileges to recently freed slaves. This amendment repeats the Fifth Amendment's protection against the taking of "life, liberty, or property without due process of law," this time applying to the states rather than the federal government and extending "equal protection" of the laws, which becomes one of the focal points of the

modern civil rights movements in the 1960s. This amendment allows for reapportionment of the seats in the House of Representatives after a census and counting all persons, except for untaxed Native Americans. It voids the three-fifths clause in Article I regarding population (1868).

Amendment XV. States that the right of U.S. citizens to vote cannot be denied "on account of race, color, or previous condition of servitude," clearing the way for African American men (former slaves) 21 years and older to vote. Many Southern states searched for ways to get around the amendment, breaking the spirit of the law with literacy tests, poll taxes, and grandfather clauses (1870).

Amendment XIX. States that a citizen cannot be denied the right to vote based on sex, and thus grants women the right to vote (1920).

Amendment XXIV. Indicates that poll taxes cannot be used to deny the right to vote to any citizen, effectively making poll taxes illegal (1964).

Amendment XXVI. Extends the vote to individuals who are 18 years of age (thus changing the previous requirement, which was 21 years of age) (1971).

The first nine amendments spell out specific guarantees of personal freedoms. The Tenth Amendment reserved to the states all those powers not specifically withheld or granted to the federal government. Those values include life, liberty, pursuit of happiness, common good, justice, equality, truth, diversity, popular sovereignty, and patriotism. This core set of values is expressed in America's essential founding documents: the Declaration of Independence, the Articles of Confederation, and the Constitution.

Furthermore, the ideals of American democracy include the following essential Constitutional principles:

    The rule of law

    Separation of powers

    Representative government

    Checks and balances

    Individual rights

    Freedom of religion

    Federalism

    Limited government

    Civilian control of the military

Essential democratic principles include those principles fundamental to the American judicial system:

Right to due process of law

Right to a fair and speedy trial

Protection from unlawful search and seizure

Right to decline to self-incriminate

Comprehension of the rights and responsibilities of citizens of the United States involves understanding that it is essential for citizens to be active in order to maintain a democratic society. This activity includes participation in political activities such as voting, providing service to communities, and regulating oneself in accordance with the law.

Individual Responsibilities in the Classroom, School, and Community

Becoming informed; respecting the rights of others; obeying laws, rules, and regulations; voting; and expressing dissent appropriately are all responsibilities that citizens of the United States should begin at an early age. Ideally, these activities should be pursued in the classroom, in the school, and in the community. The teacher can help ensure that this is done.

The Role of Values, Attitudes, and Beliefs in Shaping Debate on National Issues

There are three domains of instruction: the cognitive domain, which deals with knowledge and learning; the psychomotor domain, which deals with skills such as keyboarding or dribbling a basketball; and the affective domain, which focuses on attitudes and feelings. One's values, attitudes, and beliefs usually shape debate on issues and how one votes.

Each school campus should have an approved approach to values education. The teacher must work within these guidelines for teaching and clarifying values. Many school boards are showing an increased acceptance of character-building strategies and expect teachers to promote the human qualities deemed admirable. Generally these qualities concern the traits of a good, law-abiding citizen and decent human being. For some students, the only worthy model of self-discipline

and hard work, traits once identified with the head of a family, will be their teacher.

The teaching of values may be best achieved as students and teachers discuss pertinent events in their everyday lives or in their reading for school. The media's tendency to provide sensational coverage of well-known sports figures, politicians, and business leaders in the news brings the ugliest of human motives and behavior to everyone's attention. Appropriate class discussion, carefully moderated and directed toward a greater depth of understanding human nature, can help students struggle with a public hero or heroine's fall from grace. The stories read in class, or the events recounted from history, offer equally valid opportunities for discussion.

The concept of censorship is another aspect of values interchange that a teacher may meet. Even if a teacher limits reading to the state-adopted textbooks, some materials or ideas within these textbooks may be challenged by some parents or community members. The district may have a committee responsible for dealing with problems of censorship, and the teacher's responsibility will end once the problem is submitted to the committee. Complaints from parents are generally sincere, directed by their concerns for their own children. Sometimes, however, organized groups exert pressure to remove certain reading from the classroom. In recent years, parents have expressed concerns with such readings as Judy Blume's *Are You There God? It's Me Margaret*, J. K. Rowling's Harry Potter books, and even the children's fairy tale "Rumpelstiltskin." Whenever a matter of censorship arises, the teacher should promptly inform the school administrator and follow the district guidelines for such matters.

▶ **Objective 0029:**

Understand Cultural Diversity and the Historical and Contemporary Role of Cultural Diversity in Shaping Arizona, the United States, and Other World Areas

To obtain a historical perspective of the role of cultural diversity in shaping the development of Arizona and the United States, one should begin by examining

the types of people present during its exploration and settlement and the people who would later come to Colonial America. Looking at the reasons that settlers came to Colonial America is important in determining the implications of commonalities and differences among groups.

The Nature and Implications of Commonalities and Differences Among Groups

"The United States is a nation of immigrants" is a frequently quoted remark. The quotation, however, may cause some to forget that the Europeans came to a country already occupied by Native Americans.

The so-called New World that Columbus and other explorers found in the late fifteenth and early sixteenth centuries was neither recently formed nor recently settled. Native Americans had actually settled the land between 15,000 and 35,000 years before. As in other areas of the world, the native peoples of the New World formed communities but did not immediately develop written languages. The lack of any kind of written record makes interpreting the prehistoric past more difficult. Archaeologists and anthropologists working in North and South America have unearthed the remains of these early communities, and it is on this evidence that anthropologists base the earliest theories about the origins, movements, and lifestyles of native people.

There is not one universally accepted theory regarding the earliest history of the people who settled North and South America. By the time Europeans came into contact with the indigenous peoples of the Americas, more than 2,000 distinct cultures and hundreds of distinct languages existed. It is therefore necessary to remember not just the origins but also the developments (affected by various factors such as the environment) that took place before and have taken place since the Europeans arrived. This will provide an understanding of the various Indian cultures and societies and the impact that contact with Europeans had on them and on the development of Arizona and the nation. For instance, Arizona had 233,370 Native Americans within its borders in 2004; this total ranked Arizona second in the nation on the number of Native Americans. Oklahoma, with 266,158 Native Americans, was ranked first.

These Native Americans contribute to the rich cultural diversity of Arizona.

Following the various migrations westward and immigrations into America can yield additional information. Studies of Old Immigration (1830–1850) and New Immigration (1900–1920) further complete the picture of the settling of America that encouraged diversity.

When considering the role of cultural diversity in shaping the state of Arizona, the United States, and the world, one should note the struggles the various groups have endured to gain equality and recognition within society. Within this historical understanding, one should be able to identify examples of how immigrants have sought to assimilate themselves into American culture, how they have contributed to American culture, and how they have been exploited.

Diverse cultural groups have shaped world history and diversity has both positive and negative results. Negative results of diversity include contributing to disputes over territories, creating alliances that eventually lead to world and regional conflicts, outsourcing of jobs, and relocating companies from the United States to foreign countries. Among the positive results are economic specialization, which enhances choice, and modern globalization, which results in economic interdependence. To explore the impact of cultural diversity on world history, one must analyze the following events, among others: the origin and spread of Christianity and Islam, colonialism and exploration, the beginning of World War I, and contemporary conflict in the Middle East.

Understanding the role of cultural diversity in shaping the state of Arizona, the United States, and the world begins with knowledge of the commonalities and differences among such groups as African Americans, Asian Americans, Hispanic Americans, and Native Americans. Commonalities and differences become more evident when one analyzes the role of language, education, religion, culture, and struggles for equality within and among groups. These understandings can help one gain an appreciation for the diversity of Arizona and the nation as a whole.

Immigration and the resulting cultural diversity continues. Arizona had a significant increase in immigrant population between 2000 and 2005; in fact, over

that five-year period, the state ranked seventeenth in the number of people who immigrated here. The number of immigrants in 2000 was 692,000; in 2005 that number had risen to 851,000—a 23 percent increase.

The state highest in an increase in the number of immigrants is Mississippi (148.7 percent); possibly Hurricane Katrina contributed to this increase from 29,000 to 72,000. The nation on a whole had a 17.2 percent increase during the same five-year period, when the number of immigrants rose from 29,987,000 to 35,156,000 (*www.cis.org/articles/2005/back1405.html*).

Immigration and the Government

Calls for immigration restriction began in the nineteenth century, but the only major restriction imposed on immigration was the Chinese Exclusion Act of 1882. Labor leaders believed that immigrants depressed wages and impeded unionization. Some progressives believed that immigrants created social problems. In June 1917, Congress, over President Wilson's veto, imposed a **literacy test for immigrants** and excluded many Asian nationalities. In 1921, Congress passed the **Emergency Quota Act**.

In practice, the law admitted almost as many immigrants as wanted to come from such nations as Britain, Ireland, and Germany but severely restricted Italians, Greeks, Poles, and eastern European Jews wanting to enter the country. The law became effective in 1922 and reduced the number of immigrants annually to about 40 percent of the 1921 total.

Congress then passed the National Origins Act of 1924, which further reduced the number of southern and eastern European immigrants and cut the annual immigration total to 20 percent of the 1921 figure. In 1927, the annual maximum number of immigrants allowed into the United States was reduced to 150,000.

In *Korematsu v. United States* (1944), the Supreme Court upheld sending the Issei (Japanese Americans from Japan) and Nisei (native-born Japanese Americans) to concentration camps, some of which were in Arizona. During World War II, Arizona was also the site of prisoner of war camps for both German and Italian prisoners. The camps closed in March 1946. (Interest-

ingly the Maytag family, which provided appliances, purchased the Phoenix site for its business.)

Since the United States first began tracking immigrant arrivals in 1820, the nation has accepted 66 million legal immigrants. Of those 11 percent arrived from Germany and 10 percent from Mexico (Martin 2002). In 2005 Mexico had the highest number of immigrants in the United States: 10,805,000 of the total number of 35,157,000; China/Hong Kong/Taiwan had the second-highest number of immigrants: 1,833,000. One million people receive permanent residency annually; there is an annual increase of 500,000 illegal immigrants (*www.cis.org/articles/2005/back1405.html*).

Recent decades have witnessed contentious debates over the place of immigrants and their children in the educational, welfare, and political systems of the United States, or more broadly, whether the immigration system serves U.S. national interests (Martin 2002). As discussed earlier, the treatment of immigrants has long been a point of debate. Two centuries of immigration and integration have not yielded consensus on the three major immigration questions: how many newcomers should be admitted, what countries should they be from, and what status should they be granted?

Martin (2002) predicts that immigration is likely to continue at current levels of 900,000 legal and at least 300,000 to 400,000 unauthorized immigrants who settle annually in the country. In the words of Kenneth Prewitt, a former director of the U.S. Census Bureau, America is "the first country in world history which is literally made up of every part of the world" (Alvarez 2001).

▶ Objective 0030:
Understand Global Interdependence and Social, Political, Economic, and Environmental Issues That Affect World Citizens

Understanding global interdependence begins with the recognition that world regions include economic, political, historical, ecological, linguistic, and cultural regions. This understanding should include knowledge of military and economic alliances such as the North

Atlantic Treaty Organization (NATO); the Group of Eight (G8 members); cartels, such as the Organization of Petroleum Exporting Countries (OPEC); and how their existence affects political and economic policies within regions. Knowledge of world regions and alliances leads to identification of issues that affect people in these areas. Common issues that affect people around the world include food production, human rights, resource use, prejudice, poverty, and trade. A true sense of global interdependence results from an understanding of the relationship between local decisions and global issues. For example, individual or community actions regarding waste disposal or recycling may affect worldwide resource availability, fuel emissions standards may affect air pollution, and fuel standards may affect oil supply and gas prices.

An understanding of the theme of human-environmental interaction involves consideration of how people rely on the environment, how they alter it, and how the environment may limit what people are able to do. For example, the Arizona tourist industry is an example of how the state uses its features and its natural resources to bring people to the state.

The Interrelatedness of Geography, Economics, Culture, Belief Systems, and Political Philosophies Throughout History

The people living in a particular area help to determine the characteristics of that area. The physical, cultural, economic, and political characteristics are important to most area residents and may affect their original decision to settle there.

If the characteristics of an area become unacceptable to residents, the inhabitants may consider moving to a different location. With the ease of transportation today, most people can move more easily than they could have a generation ago. The move may be to another region of the state, the nation, or the world. With the flooding during Hurricane Katrina (2005), many people looked for a more suitable location for a while, at least.

Economic reasons for migration include the finances of an individual considering relocating and the

economic level required to live comfortably in the area. Some residents may move to a more expensive area, but others may decide to go to a less expensive area. Many change their places of residence, therefore, to get ahead economically or to raise their standard of living.

Some people decide to relocate for **cultural reasons**. These people might consider their neighbors too similar to them and decide to move to an area with more diversity. On the other hand, some people would rather live with others who are similar to them.

Physical reasons can also affect a person's decision to relocate. Sometimes people move to a place where they can satisfy their physical wants or needs. In some cases, people can modify their environment or bring the needed goods to their area without having to relocate. For example, improvement of the roads in Arizona helped in the development of tourism within the state and increased jobs and incomes for the residents who responded to the demands of tourists and for those who moved to the state in hopes of finding jobs and improving their lot.

An understanding of the geographic themes of (1) **location** and (2) **movement and connections** involves identifying how people are connected through different forms of transportation and communication networks and how those networks have changed over time. This would include identifying the channels of movement of people, goods, and information. For example, senior citizens who wanted to escape the harsh winters of the Northeast and the Midwest found the climate of Arizona appealing. Del Webb established Sun City in 1960; this was one of the first of the special age-restricted subdivisions to spring up in Arizona. Some of the "snowbirds" came to Arizona for the winter only and illustrate perfectly location and movement, one of the themes of geography.

Political reasons also compel the movement of people. Government carries out the decisions of the political system. The organizations and processes that contribute to the decision-making process make up the political system. Individuals may move to another region or area if they are unhappy with the government and/or political systems in their area and are unable to bring about change. On the other hand, an

attractive system of government may bring people to an area.

► Objective 0031:
Understand the Basic Principles and Concepts of Economics in the United States and the World

Recognizing the Fundamental Concepts and Principles of Economics

Economic resources include the land (natural resources), labor (human resources), and entrepreneurial ability (capital) used in the production of goods and services; economic resources are also the **factors of production**: labor, capital, and land. **Wants** are those resources you would *like* to have but that you do not *have* to have. **Needs**, on the other hand, are resources you *have* to have.

An understanding of economics involves exploring the implications of **scarcity** (the concept that wants are unlimited, while resources are limited). Exploration of scarcity involves an understanding of economic principles spanning from personal finance to international trade. Economic understanding is rooted in exploring principles of choice, opportunity costs, incentives, trade, and economic systems.

Goods and services refer to anything that satisfy human needs, wants, or desires. Goods are tangible items, such as food, cars, and clothing, whereas services are intangible items, such as education and health care. A **market** is the interaction between potential buyers and sellers of goods and services. **Money** is usually the **medium of exchange**. **Supply** of a good is the quantity of that good that producers offer at a certain price. The collection of all such points for every price is called the **supply curve**. **Demand** for a good is the quantity of a good that consumers are willing and able to purchase at a certain price. The **demand curve** is the combination of quantity and price, at all price levels.

The United States does not exist in isolation. A country with a true sense of global interdependence realizes that its actions can affect the world. For instance,

continuing to allow the use of certain sprays in a country can damage the ozone layer and affect the entire world.

Major Features of Economic Systems

Command economies rely on a central authority to make decisions. The central authority may be a dictator or a democratically constituted government. The economies of many former Soviet countries rely mainly on the government to direct economic activity; there is a small market sector as well.

Market economies have no central authority, and custom plays very little role. Every consumer makes buying decisions based on his or her own needs, desires, and income; individual **self-interest** rules. Every producer decides for him- or herself what goods or services to produce, what price to charge, what resources to employ, and what production methods to use; producers are motivated solely by profit considerations. There is vigorous competition in a market economy.

Adam Smith (1723–1790) was a Scottish economist whose writing may have inaugurated the modern era of economic analysis. Published in 1776, his *Wealth of Nations* is an analysis of a market economy. According to Smith, a market economy is a superior form of organization from the standpoint of both economic progress and human liberty. Smith acknowledged that self-interest is a dominant motivating force in a market economy; this self-interest, he said, is ultimately consistent with the **public interest**. An "invisible hand" guides market participants to act in ways that promote the public interest. **Profits** may be the main concern of firms, but only firms that satisfy consumer demand and offer **suitable prices** earn profits.

Mixed economies contain elements of command economies and market economies. All real-world economies are mixed economies, but the proportions of the mixture can vary greatly.

Traditional economies largely rely on custom to determine production and distribution issues. While not static, traditional systems are slow to change and are not well equipped to propel a society into sustained growth. Many of the poorer countries of the developing world have traditional systems.

Recognizing How Different Economic Systems Influence Resource Allocation and the Production, Distribution, and Exchange of Goods and Services

Monopolies occur when one supplier dominates an industry. Monopolies arise due to conditions in the market in which a firm has complete control over its prices. A monopoly has the following properties:

- There is only one seller.
- There are no close substitutes for the company's product.
- The monopolist is the price setter.
- There are barriers to enter the monopolist's market (that is, the firm, and sometimes the government, prevents competition so as to stay the sole producer of the good).

An **oligopoly** is a market structure that is characterized by a few sellers of goods that are similar to one another. Each firm, when making pricing decisions, considers the prices charged by the other firms in the industry.

Analyzing Patterns and Results of Trade, Exchange, and Interdependence Among Individuals, Businesses, and Governments

The economy of the United States places greater emphasis on the market sector than on the private sector, although it includes a large and active government (command) sector as well. **Capitalist economies** produce resources that are owned by individuals. **Command economies** produce resources that are owned collectively by society. In a socialist economy, these resources are often under the control of the government.

▶ Objective 0032:
Understand Geographic Concepts and Issues and Analyze Interrelationships Among Geography, Culture, and Society

Understanding major geographic concepts involves comprehending both physical features of geography and the cultural aspects of geography. This would include knowledge of the five fundamental themes of geography; comprehension of the relationships within and between places; understanding of the interdependence within the local, natural, and global communities; and familiarity with global issues and events.

Applying the Five Themes of Geography to Arizona

The five themes of geography are: location; place; human-environmental interaction; movement and connections; and regions, patterns, and processes. An understanding of these themes would include the ability to use them to analyze regions within Arizona, the United States, and the world to gain a perspective about interrelationships among those regions. The use of the five themes should also result in the ability to compare regions.

Location. Absolute location is determined by longitude and latitude. Relative location deals with the interactions that occur between and among places. Relative location involves the interconnectedness among people because of land, water, and technology. For example, knowledge of the history of Arizona includes an understanding of how its location and its natural features (deserts, Grand Canyon, Painted Desert, Petrified Forest) have contributed to its economic development and vitality.

Place. This includes the characteristics of a location; characteristics define a place and make it different from other places. Both human and physical characteristics work together to describe place. Physical characteristics include such things as animal and plant life; mountains; rivers; topography; beaches; lakes; or the absence thereof. Human characteristics may include the cultural features that people designed in a particular place; these features include architecture, religion, food, transportation forms, communication networks, etc.

Human-environmental interaction. This involves consideration of how people rely on the environment, how they alter it, and how the environment may limit what people are able to do. For example, the Arizona tourist industry has made use of areas ill suited for farming or housing by establishing

parks and tourist attractions (Grand Canyon, Painted Desert, Petrified Forest, alpine peaks ski resorts). Lakes, rivers, hiking, biking, jeep tours, and 22 reservations for 17 American Indian tribes also draw visitors year round. Historical sites such as Tombstone and museums provide the traveler or the resident with some unique vacation experiences.

Movement and connections. This theme refers to identifying how people are connected through different forms of transportation and communication networks and how those networks have changed over time—including identifying channels of the movement of people, goods, and information. For example, the increased use of the automobile and the better highways in Arizona have had a profound impact on the movement patterns of ideas, fashion, and people.

Regions, patterns, and processes. Within this theme are climatic, economic, political, and cultural patterns within regions. Understanding why these patterns were created includes understanding how climatic systems, communication networks, international trade, political systems, and population changes contributed to a region's development. An understanding of regions enables a social scientist to study their uniqueness and relationship to other regions.

From the lowest point of the Sonoran Desert (the second-most-diverse ecosystem on earth) to the highest alpine peaks, visitors to Arizona can traverse over 12,600 feet in elevation and pass through all five climatic zones. With the most diverse geology in the world and vast array of natural, cultural, historical, and sports-related attractions, Arizona brings visitors from throughout the world.

Understanding global issues and events includes comprehending the interconnectedness of peoples throughout the world. For example, knowledge of the relationship between world oil consumption and oil production would result in an understanding of the impact that increased demand for oil in China would have on the price of a barrel of oil, which in turn could affect the decisions of consumers of new vehicles in the United States. Of course, the price of gasoline will affect the amount of tourism in Arizona and will impact the economy in a state that relies heavily on tourism. Global interdependence is a given.

Using Globes, Maps, and Other Resources to Interpret Geographical Information and Explore Geographical Themes

Any study of maps should begin with a study of the globe—a model of the earth with a map on its surface. A globe is more accurate than a flat map. Constantly using the globe helps bring understanding of the earth's shape and structure.

Some of the points on the globe that students should be able to locate:

- Equator
- Antarctic Circle
- Arctic Circle
- Prime Meridian
- International Date Line
- North Pole
- South Pole
- Meridians
- Parallels
- Great Circle Route
- Time zones

The use of maps requires students to identify four main types of map projections: conic, cylindrical, interrupted, and plane. Additional graphics that students use in geography include charts, graphs, and picture maps.

Geologic maps provide much information about the earth and provide a perfect opportunity to integrate social studies and science. By reading a **topographical map**, a student can find out about **altitudes** (heights above and below sea level) and landforms. **Symbols** on the map may represent rivers, lakes, rapids, and forests. Map **scales** allow the student to determine distances. The **legends** of a map furnish additional information, including the locations of mineral deposits and quarries, dams and boat ramps, fire and ranger stations, and more. Often a map displays a **compass rose**, which gives the cardinal directions: north, south, east, and west.

Parallels and meridians grid the earth. **Meridians** run from pole to pole, and 360 of them surround the earth in one-degree increments. Every hour, a given location on the earth's surface rotates through 15 degrees of longitude. Meridians help measure longitude, the distance

east and west of the prime meridian, which has a measurement of 0° E-W. **Parallels** are the lines that run in an east-west direction; parallels help measure **latitude**, the distance north and south of the equator.

Geologic maps often contain all this information. A geologic map usually differs from a political map, which shows political boundaries, counties, cities, towns, churches, schools, and other representations of government and people.

▶ Objective 0033:

Understand and Apply Knowledge of Various Political Systems and the Structures, Functions, and Principles of Local, State, and National Governments

---

The Basic Purposes and Concepts of Government

Many people equate the terms *political system* and *government*, but the two concepts are distinct. Government is the agency for regulating the activities of people. It is the system that carries out the decisions of the political system or, in some countries, the decisions of the ruler. The organizations and processes that contribute to the decision-making process comprise the political system.

The question of how to define the purpose of government has puzzled scholars from Plato's time to the present day. Although some say that government's purpose is to protect all people's rights and preserve justice, others contend that its purpose is to preserve and protect the rights of the few. From these diverging definitions, myriad ideologies—such as communism, liberalism, and conservatism—have evolved. News commentator Bob Schieffer stated boldly in 2005, after Hurricane Katrina, "There is no purpose for government except to improve the lives of its citizens" (*www.cbsnews.com/ stories/2005/09/06/opinion/schieffer/main818486.html*).

The *Merit Students Encyclopedia* (1969) notes that the **functions** of a government include the following:

1. Political functions, to maintain order within its territories and to protect its borders

2. Legal functions (in fact the word *anarchy*—lack of government—has come to mean "lawlessness")

3. Economic functions, or those concerned with the economic activity of citizens

4. Social functions, which may include civil rights, religion, and education

The Significant Features of Different Political Systems and Forms of Government

The distribution of power within the various **structures** of government is a key variable in the different political systems and forms of government. Separation of powers among branches of the federal government is another aspect of structure useful in comparing political systems. The most important political systems and forms of government and their significant features follow:

Confederation. A weak central government delegates principal authority to smaller units, such as states. The United States had this structure under the Articles of Confederation, before the Constitution was ratified in 1789.

Federal. Sovereignty is divided between a central government and a group of states. Contemporary examples of federal republics are the United States, Brazil, and India.

Unitary. The centralized government holds the concentration of power and authority. Examples are France and Japan.

Authoritarian. A government's central power is in a single or collective executive, with the legislative and judicial bodies having little input. Some examples of this are the former Soviet Union, the People's Republic of China, and Nazi Germany.

Parliamentary. The legislative and executive branches are combined, with a prime minister and cabinet selected from within the legislative body. They maintain control as long as the legislative assembly supports their major policies. Great Britain is an example of this form of government.

Presidential. The executive branch is clearly separate from the legislative and judicial branches. However, all three (particularly the executive and legislative branches) must cooperate for policy to be consistent and for smooth government operation. An example of this is the United States.

Basic Functions of the Legislative, Executive, and Judicial Branches of Government at the National, State, and Local Levels

A key principle of the U.S. Constitution is separation of powers. The national government is divided into three branches—legislative, executive, and judicial—with separate functions, but they are not entirely independent. Articles I, II, and III of the main body of the Constitution outline these functions.

The Legislative Branch

Legislative power is vested in a bicameral (two houses) Congress, which is the subject of Article I of the Constitution. The expressed or delegated powers are set forth in Section 8 and can be divided into several broad categories.

Economic powers are as follows:

1. Lay and collect taxes
2. Borrow money
3. Regulate foreign and interstate commerce
4. Coin money and regulate its value
5. Establish rules concerning bankruptcy

Judicial powers comprise the following:

1. Establish courts inferior to the Supreme Court
2. Provide punishment for counterfeiting
3. Define and punish piracies and felonies committed on the high seas

War powers of Congress include the following:

1. Declare war
2. Raise and support armies
3. Provide and maintain a navy
4. Provide for organizing, arming, and calling forth the militia

Other **general peace powers** include the following:

1. Establish uniform rules on naturalization
2. Establish post offices and post roads
3. Promote science and the arts by issuing patents and copyrights

4. Exercise jurisdiction over the seat of the federal government (District of Columbia)

The Constitution also grants Congress the power to discipline federal officials through impeachment and removal from office. The House of Representatives has the power to charge officials (impeach), and the Senate has the power to conduct the trials. The first impeachment of a president was that of Andrew Johnson.

Significant also is the Senate's power to confirm presidential appointments (to the cabinet, federal judiciary, and major bureaucracies) and to ratify treaties. Both houses are involved in choosing a president and vice president if there is no majority in the Electoral College. The House of Representatives votes for the president from among the top three electoral candidates, with each state delegation casting one vote. The Senate votes for the vice president. The Senate has exercised this power only twice, in the disputed elections of 1800 and 1824.

The Executive Branch

Article II of the Constitution deals with the powers and duties of the president. The chief executive's constitutional responsibilities include the following:

1. Serve as commander in chief
2. Negotiate treaties (with the approval of two-thirds of the Senate)
3. Appoint ambassadors, judges, and other high officials (with the consent of the Senate)
4. Grant pardons and reprieves for those convicted of federal crimes (except in impeachment cases)
5. Seek counsel of department heads (cabinet secretaries)
6. Recommend legislation
7. Meet with representatives of foreign states
8. See that federal laws are "faithfully executed"

The president's powers with respect to foreign policy are paramount. Civilian control of the military is a fundamental concept embodied in the naming of the president as commander in chief. In essence, the president is the nation's leading general. As such, the president can make battlefield decisions and shape the military policy.

The president also has broad powers in domestic policy. The most significant domestic policy tool is

the president's budget, which he or she must submit to Congress. Though Congress must approve all spending, the president has a great deal of power in budget negotiations. The president can use considerable resources in persuading Congress to enact legislation, and the president also has opportunities, such as in the "State of the Union" address, to reach out directly to the American people to convince them to support presidential policies.

The Judicial Branch

Article III of the Constitution states that "the judicial power of the United States shall be vested in one Supreme Court and in such inferior courts as the Congress may from time to time ordain and establish." The Constitution makes two references to a trial by jury in criminal cases (in Article III and in the Sixth Amendment).

Essential democratic values fundamental to the American judicial system include life, liberty, the pursuit of happiness, the common good, justice, equality, truth, diversity, popular sovereignty, and patriotism.

It is essential—indeed, a responsibility—for citizens to be active in maintaining a democratic society. As noted earlier in the chapter, active citizens participate in the political process by voting, providing services to their communities, and regulating themselves in accordance with the law. Citizens of the United States need also to assume responsibilities to their communities, their states, the nation, and the world.

The Role of Law and Its Relationship to Social and Political Systems

Understanding of the role of law in a democratic society results from a knowledge of the nature of civil, criminal, and constitutional law and how the organization of the judicial system serves to interpret and apply such laws. Essential judicial principles to know include comprehension of rights, such as the right of due process, the right to a fair and speedy trial, and the right to a hearing before a jury of one's peers. Additional judicial principles include an understanding of the protections granted in the Constitution, which include protection from self-incrimination and unlawful searches and seizures.

An understanding of various political systems involves the ability to compare different political systems, their ideologies, structures, institutions, processes, and political cultures. This requires knowledge of alternative ways of organizing constitutional governments from systems of shared power to parliamentarian systems. Systems of shared power include federal systems, in which sovereign states delegate powers to a central government; a federal system, in which a national government shares power with state and local governments; and unitary systems, in which all power is concentrated in a centralized government.

► ## Objective 0034:
Understand Major Historical Developments in the World and the United States and Analyze Their Significance

---

The Causes and Effects of Major Developments and Trends in World and U.S. History

The earth is estimated to be approximately 6 billion years old. The earliest known humans, called **hominids**, lived in Africa 3 million to 4 million years ago. Of the several species of hominids that developed, all modern humans descended from just one group, ***Homo sapiens sapiens***. *Homo sapiens sapiens* is a subspecies of *Homo sapiens* (along with Neanderthals, who became extinct) and appeared in Africa between 200,000 and 150,000 years ago.

Historians divide prehistory into three periods. The period from the emergence of the first-known hominids around 2.5 million years ago until approximately 10,000 B.C.E. is the **Paleolithic period**, or **Old Stone Age**. During that period, human beings lived in small groups of perhaps 10 to 20 nomadic people, constantly moving from place to place. Human beings had the ability to **make tools and weapons** from stone and from the

bones of animals they killed. Hunting large game such as mammoths, which were sometimes driven off cliffs in large numbers, was crucial to the survival of early humans, who used the meat, fur, and bones of the animals to survive. Early humans supplemented their diets by foraging for food. They took shelter in caves and other natural formations, and they **painted and drew on the walls of caves**. Cave paintings discovered in France and northern Spain and created during the prehistoric period depict scenes of animals such as lions, owls, and oxen. Around 500,000 years ago, humans began to use **fire**, which provided light and warmth in shelters and caves, and cooked meat and other foods. Human beings developed **means of creating fire** and improved techniques of **producing tools and weapons**.

The **Mesolithic period**, or **Middle Stone Age**, from 10,000 to 7000 B.C.E., marked the beginning of a major transformation called the **Neolithic Revolution**. Historians and archeologists previously thought this change occurred later. They called it the Neolithic Revolution, because they thought it took place entirely within the Neolithic period, or New Stone Age.

Beginning in the Mesolithic period, humans domesticated plants and began to shift away from a reliance on hunting large game and foraging. Human beings had previously relied on gathering food where they found it and had moved almost constantly in search of game and wild berries and other vegetation. During the Mesolithic period, humans were able to **plant and harvest** some crops and began to stay in one place for longer periods. Early humans also improved their tool-making techniques and developed various kinds of tools and weapons.

During the **Neolithic period**, or **New Stone Age**, this "revolution" was complete, and humans engaged in systematic agriculture and began domesticating animals. Although humans continued to hunt animals, both to supplement their diet with **meat** and to use the skins and bones to make clothing and weapons, major changes in society occurred. Human beings became settled and lived in farming villages or towns, the population increased, and people began to live in much larger communities. A more settled way of life led to a **more structured social system**; a higher level of organization within societies; the development of **crafts**, such as the

production of **pottery**; and a rise in **trade** or exchange of goods among groups.

Between 4000 and 3000 B.C.E., **writing** developed, and the towns and villages settled during the Neolithic period developed a more complex pattern of existence. The existence of written records marks the **end of the prehistoric period**. The beginning of history coincides with the emergence of the earliest societies that exhibited characteristics that enabled them to be considered as civilizations. The first civilizations emerged in Mesopotamia and Egypt.

Ancient and Medieval Times

Appearance of Civilization and Related Cultural and Technological Developments. Between 6000 and 3000 B.C.E., humans invented the **plow**, developed the **wheel**, harnessed the **wind**, discovered how to smelt **copper ores**, and began to develop accurate **solar calendars**. Small villages gradually grew into populous cities. The **invention of writing** in 3500 B.C.E. in Mesopotamia marks the beginning of civilization and divides prehistoric from historic times.

Mesopotamia. Sumer (4000–2000 B.C.E.) included the city of Ur. The Sumerians constructed **dikes and reservoirs** and established a loose confederation of **city-states**. They probably invented writing (called **cuneiform** because of its wedge-shaped letters). After 538 B.C.E., the peoples of Mesopotamia, whose natural boundaries were insufficient to thwart invaders, were absorbed into other empires and dynasties.

Egypt. During the end of the Archaic period (5000–2685 B.C.E.), in about 3200 B.C.E., Menes, or Narmer, probably unified upper and lower Egypt. The capital moved to Memphis during the Third Dynasty (circa 2650 B.C.E.). The **pyramids** were built during the Fourth Dynasty (circa 2613–2494 B.C.E.). After 1085 B.C.E., in the post-empire period, Egypt came under the successive control of the Assyrians, the Persians, Alexander the Great, and finally, in 30 B.C.E., the Roman Empire. The Egyptians developed papyrus and made many medical advances.

Palestine and the Hebrews. Phoenicians settled along the present-day Lebanon coast (Sidon, Tyre, Beirut, Byblos) and established colonies at Carthage and in Spain. They spread **Mesopotamian culture** through

their trade networks. The Hebrews probably moved to Egypt in about 1700 B.C.E. and suffered enslavement in about 1500 B.C.E. The Hebrews fled Egypt under Moses and, around 1200 B.C.E., returned to Palestine. King David (reigned circa 1012–972 B.C.E.) defeated the Philistines and established Jerusalem as a capital. The poor and less attractive state of Judah continued until 586 B.C.E., when the Chaldeans transported the Jews to Chaldea as advisers and slaves (Babylonian captivity). The Persians conquered Babylon in 539 B.C.E. and allowed the Jews to return to Palestine.

Greece. In the Archaic period (800–500 B.C.E.), the Greeks organized around the *polis*, or city-state. Oligarchs controlled most of the polis until near the end of the sixth century, when individuals holding absolute power (tyrants) replaced them. By the end of the sixth century, **democratic governments** in turn replaced many tyrants.

The Classical Age. The fifth century B.C.E. was the high point of Greek civilization. It opened with the Persian Wars (560–479 B.C.E.), after which Athens organized the Delian League. Pericles (ca. 495–429 B.C.E.) used money from the league to rebuild Athens, including construction of the Parthenon and other buildings on the Acropolis hill. Athens's dominance spurred war with Sparta. At the same time, a revolution in philosophy occurred in classical Athens. The **Sophists** emphasized the individual and the attainment of excellence through rhetoric, grammar, music, and mathematics. **Socrates** (circa 470–399 B.C.E.) criticized the Sophists' emphasis on rhetoric and emphasized a process of questioning, or dialogues, with his students. Like Socrates, **Plato** (circa 428–348 B.C.E.) emphasized ethics. Aristotle (circa 384–322 B.C.E.) was Plato's pupil. He criticized Plato and argued that ideas or forms did not exist outside of things. He contended that it was necessary, in treating any object, to examine four factors: its matter, its form, its cause of origin, and its end or purpose.

Rome. The traditional founding date for Rome is 753 B.C.E. Between 800 and 500 B.C.E., Greek tribes colonized southern Italy and brought their alphabet and religious practices to Roman tribes. In the sixth and seventh centuries B.C.E., the Etruscans expanded southward and conquered Rome. In the early republic, power was in the hands of the patricians (wealthy landowners). During the 70s and 60s, **Pompey** (106–48 B.C.E.) and **Julius Caesar** (100–44 B.C.E.) emerged as the most powerful men.

In 60 B.C.E., Caesar convinced Pompey and Crassus (circa 115–53 B.C.E.) to form the First Triumvirate. When Crassus died, Caesar and Pompey fought for leadership. In 47 B.C.E., the Senate proclaimed Caesar dictator and later named him consul for life. **Brutus** and **Cassius** believed that Caesar had destroyed the republic. They formed a conspiracy, and on March 15, 44 B.C.E. (the Ides of March), Brutus and Cassius assassinated Caesar in the Roman forum. Caesar's 18-year-old nephew and adopted son, Octavian, succeeded him.

The Roman Empire. After a period of struggle, Octavian (reigned 27 B.C.E.–14 C.E.), named as Caesar's heir, gained absolute control while maintaining the appearance of a republic. When he offered to relinquish his power in 27 B.C.E., the Senate gave him a vote of confidence and a new title, Augustus. He introduced many reforms, including new coinage, new tax collection, fire and police protection, and land for settlers in the provinces. By the first century C.E., Christianity had spread throughout the empire. Around 312 C.E., Emperor Constantine converted to Christianity and ordered toleration in the Edict of Milan (circa 313 C.E.). In 391 C.E., Emperor Theodosius I (reigned 371–395 C.E.) proclaimed Christianity the empire's official religion.

The Byzantine Empire. Emperor Theodosius II (reigned 408–450 C.E.) divided his empire between his two sons, one ruling the east and the other ruling the west. After the Vandals sacked Rome in 455 C.E., Constantinople was the undisputed leading city of the Byzantine Empire. In 1453 C.E., Constantinople fell to the Ottoman Turks.

Islamic Civilization in the Middle Ages. **Mohammed** was born about 570 C.E. In 630 C.E., he marched into Mecca. The Sharia (code of law and theology) outlines five pillars of faith for Muslims to observe:

First, there is one God, and Mohammed is his prophet.

Second, the faithful must pray five times a day.

Third, they must perform charitable acts.

Fourth, they must fast from sunrise to sunset during the holy month of Ramadan.

Finally, they must make a haj, or pilgrimage, to Mecca.

The Koran, which consists of 114 *suras* (verses), contains Mohammed's teachings.

The Omayyad caliphs, with their base in Damascus, governed from 661–750 C.E. They called themselves **Shiites** and believed they were Mohammed's true successors. (Most Muslims were **Sunnis**, from the word *sunna*, meaning "oral traditions about the prophet.")

The Abbasid caliphs ruled from 750 to 1258 C.E. They moved the capital to Baghdad and treated Arab and non-Arab Muslims as equals. Genghis (or Chingis) Khan (reigned 1206–1227 C.E.) and his army invaded the Abbasids. In 1258 C.E., they seized Baghdad and murdered the last caliph.

Feudalism in Japan. Feudalism in Japan began with the arrival of mounted nomadic warriors from throughout Asia during the Kofun Era (300–710 C.E.). Some members of the nomadic groups formed an elite class and became part of the court aristocracy in the capital city of Kyoto, in western Japan. During the Heian Era (794–1185 C.E.), a hereditary military aristocracy arose in the Japanese provinces; by the late Heian Era, many of these formerly nomadic warriors had established themselves as independent landowners, or as managers of *shoen*, landed estates owned by Kyoto aristocrats. These aristocrats depended on the warriors to defend their *shoen*, and in response to this need, the warriors organized into small groups called *bushidan*.

After victory in the Taira-Minamoto War (1180–1185 C.E.), Minamoto no Yorimoto forced the emperor to award him the title of **shogun**, which is short for "barbarian-subduing generalissimo." Yorimoto used this power to found the Kamakura Shogunate, a feudal military dictatorship that survived for 148 years.

By the fourteenth century C.E., the great military governors (*shugo*) had augmented their power enough to become a threat to the Kamakura, and in 1333 C.E. they led a rebellion that overthrew the shogunate. The Tokugawa shogunate was the final and most unified of the three shogunates. Under the Tokugawa, the *daimyo* were direct vassals of the shoguns and were under strict control. The warriors gradually became scholars and bureaucrats under the *bushido*, or code of chivalry, and the principles of neo-Confucianism. Under the Meji

Restoration of 1868, the emperor again received power and the samurai class lost its special privileges.

Chinese and Indian Empires. In the third century B.C.E., the Indian kingdoms fell under the Mauryan Empire. The grandson of the founder of this empire, named Ashoka, opened a new era in the cultural history of India by believing in the Buddhist religion.

Buddha had disregarded the Vedic gods and the institutions of caste and had preached a relatively simple ethical religion that advocated two levels of aspiration—a monastic life of renunciation of the world and a high, but not too difficult, morality for the layman. Although the two religions of Hinduism and Buddhism flourished together for centuries in a tolerant rivalry, Buddhism virtually disappeared from India by the thirteenth century C.E.

Chinese civilization originated in the Yellow River Valley and only gradually extended to the southern regions. Three dynasties ruled early China: the Xia or Hsia, the Shang (circa 1500 to 1122 B.C.E.), and the Zhou (circa 1122 to 211 B.C.E.). After the Zhou Dynasty fell, China welcomed the teachings of **Confucius**; warfare between states and philosophical speculation created circumstances ripe for such teachings. Confucius made the good order of society depend on an ethical ruler, who would receive advice from scholar-moralists like Confucius himself. In contrast to the Confucians, the Chinese Taoists professed a kind of anarchism; the best kind of government was none at all. The wise man did not concern himself with political affairs but with mystical contemplation that identified him with the forces of nature.

African Kingdoms and Cultures. The **Bantu** peoples lived across large sections of Africa. Bantu societies lived in tiny chiefdoms, starting in the third millennium B.C.E., and each group developed its own version of the original Bantu language.

The **Nok** people lived in the area now known as Nigeria. Artifacts indicate that they were peaceful farmers who built small communities consisting of houses of wattle and daub (poles and sticks). The **Ghanaians** lived about 500 miles from what is now Ghana. Their kingdom fell to a Berber group in the late eleventh century C.E., and Mali emerged as the next great kingdom

in the thirteenth century. The Malians lived in a huge kingdom that lay mostly on the savanna bordering the Sahara Desert. Timbuktu, built in the thirteenth century C.E., was a thriving city of culture where traders visited stone houses, shops, libraries, and mosques.

The Songhai lived near the Niger River and gained their independence from the Mali in the early 1400s. The major growth of the empire came after 1464 C.E., under the leadership of Sunni Ali, who devoted his reign to warfare and expansion of the empire.

Civilizations of the Americas.

The great civilizations of early America were agricultural, and the foremost civilization was the Mayan in Yucatan, Guatemala, and eastern Honduras. Farther north, in Mexico, a series of advanced cultures arose that derived much of their substance from the Maya. Peoples such as the Zapotecs, the Totonacs, the Olmecs, and the Toltecs evolved into a high level of civilization. By 500 B.C.E., agricultural peoples had begun to use a **ceremonial calendar** and had built **stone pyramids** on which they held religious observances.

The Aztecs then took over Mexican culture, and a major feature of their culture was human sacrifice in repeated propitiation of their chief god. Aztec government was centralized, with an elective king and a large army. The evolution of beautifully made pottery, intricate fabrics, and flat-topped mounds, or *huacas*, characterized Andean civilization.

In the interior of South America, the Inca, who called themselves "Children of the Sun," controlled an area stretching from Ecuador to central Chile. They were sun worshippers who believed that they were the sun god's vice regents on Earth and more powerful than any other humans. They believed that every person's place in society was fixed and immutable and that the state and the army were supreme. They were at the apex of their power just before the Spanish conquest.

In the present-day southwestern United States and northern Mexico, two varieties of ancient culture are still identifiable. The Anasazi developed **adobe architecture**, worked the land extensively, had a highly developed system of **irrigation**, and made cloth and baskets. The Hohokam built separate stone and timber houses around a central plaza.

Europe in Antiquity.

The Frankish Kingdom was the most important medieval Germanic state. Under Clovis I (reigned 481–511 C.E.), the Franks finished conquering France and the Gauls in 486 C.E. Clovis converted to Christianity and founded the Merovingian dynasty.

Charles the Great, or **Charlemagne** (reigned 768–814 C.E.), founded the Carolingian dynasty. In 800 C.E., Pope Leo III named Charlemagne Emperor of the Holy Roman Empire. In the Treaty of Aix-la-Chapelle (812 C.E.), the Byzantine emperor recognized Charles's authority in the West. The purpose of the Holy Roman Empire was to reestablish the Roman Empire in the West. Charles's son, Louis the Pious (reigned 814–840 C.E.), succeeded him. On Louis's death, his three sons vied for control of the Empire. The three eventually signed the Treaty of Verdun in 843 C.E. This gave Charles the Western Kingdom (France), Louis the Eastern Kingdom (Germany), and Lothair the Middle Kingdom, a narrow strip of land running from the North Sea to the Mediterranean.

In this period, **manorialism** developed as an economic system in which large estates, granted by the king to nobles, strove for self-sufficiency. The lord and his serfs (also called villeins) divided the ownership.

The church was the only institution to survive the Germanic invasions intact. The power of the popes grew in this period. **Gregory I** (reigned 590–604 C.E.) was the first member of a monastic order to rise to the papacy. He advanced the ideas of penance and purgatory. He centralized church administration and was the first pope to rule as the secular head of Rome. Monasteries preserved the few remnants that survived the decline of antiquity.

The year 1050 marked the beginning of the High Middle Ages. Europe was poised to emerge from five centuries of decline. Between 1000 and 1350, the population of Europe grew from 38 million to 75 million. New technologies, such as **heavy plows**, and a slight temperature rise produced a longer growing season and contributed to agricultural productivity.

The Holy Roman Empire.

Charlemagne's grandson Louis the German became Holy Roman Emperor under the Treaty of Verdun. Otto became Holy Roman

Emperor in 962. His descendants governed the empire until 1024, when the Franconian dynasty assumed power, reigning until 1125. Under the leadership of **William the Conqueror** (reigned 1066–1087), the Normans conquered England in 1066. William stripped the Anglo-Saxon nobility of its privileges and instituted feudalism. He ordered a survey of all property of the realm; the Domesday Book (1086) records the findings.

William introduced feudalism to England. **Feudalism** was the decentralized political system of personal ties and obligations that bound vassals to their lords. Serfs were peasants who were bound to the land. They worked on the *demesne*, or lord's property, three or four days a week in return for the right to work their own land.

In 1215, the English barons forced King John I to sign the **Magna Carta Libertatum**, acknowledging their "ancient" privileges. The Magna Carta established the principle of a limited English monarchy.

In 710 to 711, the Moors conquered Spain from the Visigoths. Under the Moors, Spain enjoyed a stable, prosperous government. The caliphate of Córdoba became a center of scientific and intellectual activity. The Reconquista (1085–1340) wrested control from the Moors. The fall of Córdoba in 1234 completed the Reconquista, except for the small state of Granada.

Most of eastern Europe and Russia was never under Rome's control; Germanic invasions separated the areas from Western influence. In Russia, Vladimir I converted to Orthodox Christianity in 988. He established the basis of Kievian Russia. After 1054, Russia broke into competing principalities. The **Mongols (Tartars)** invaded in 1221. They completed their conquest in 1245 and cut Russia's contact with the West for almost a century.

The **Crusades** attempted to liberate the Holy Land from so-called infidels. Seven major crusades occurred between 1096 and 1300. Urban II called Christians to the First Crusade (1096–1099) with the promise of a plenary indulgence (exemption from punishment in purgatory). Younger sons who would not inherit their fathers' lands were also attracted. The Crusades helped to renew interest in the ancient world. However, the Crusaders massacred thousands of Jews and Muslims, and relations between Europe and the Byzantine Empire collapsed.

Scholasticism. Scholasticism was an effort to reconcile reason and faith and to instruct Christians on how to make sense of the pagan tradition. The most influential proponent of this effort was Thomas Aquinas (circa 1225–1274), who believed that there were two orders of truth. The lower level, reason, could demonstrate propositions such as the existence of God, but the higher level necessitated that some of God's mysteries, such as the nature of the Trinity, be accepted on faith. Aquinas viewed the universe as a great chain of being, with humans midway on the chain, between the material and the spiritual.

Late Middle Ages and the Renaissance

The Black Death. Conditions in Europe encouraged the quick spread of disease. Refuse, excrement, and dead animals filled the streets of the cities, which lacked any form of urban sanitation. Living conditions were overcrowded, with families often sleeping in one room or one bed; poor nutrition was rampant; and there was often little personal cleanliness. Merchants helped bring the plague to Asia; carried by fleas on rats, the disease arrived in Europe in 1347. By 1350, the disease had killed 25 to 40 percent of the European population.

Literature, Art, and Scholarship. Humanists, as both orators and poets, often imitated the classical works that inspired them. The literature of the period was more secular and wide ranging than that of the Middle Ages. **Dante Alighieri** (1265–1321) was a Florentine writer whose *Divine Comedy*, describing a journey through hell, purgatory, and heaven, shows that reason can take people only so far and that attaining heaven requires God's grace and revelation. Francesco Petrarch (1304–1374) encouraged the study of ancient Rome, collected and preserved works of ancient writers, and produced a large body of work in the classical literary style.

Giovanni Boccaccio (1313–1375) wrote *The Decameron*, a collection of short stories that the Italian author meant to amuse, not edify, the reader. Artists also broke with the medieval past, in both technique and content. Renaissance art sometimes used religious topics but often dealt with secular themes or portraits of individuals. Oil paints, chiaroscuro, and linear perspectives produced works of energy in three dimensions.

Leonardo da Vinci (1452–1519) produced numerous works, including *The Last Supper* and *Mona Lisa*. Raphael Santi (1483–1520), a master of Renaissance grace and style, theory, and technique, brought all his skills to his painting *The School of Athens*. Michelangelo Buonarroti (1475–1564) produced masterpieces in architecture, sculpture (*David*), and painting (the Sistine Chapel ceiling). His work was a bridge to a new, non-Renaissance style: mannerism.

Renaissance scholars were more practical and secular than medieval ones. **Manuscript collections** enabled scholars to study the primary sources and to reject traditions established since classical times. Also, scholars participated in the lives of their cities as active politicians. Leonardo Bruni (1370–1444), a civic humanist, served as chancellor of Florence, where he used his rhetorical skills to rouse the citizens against external enemies. Niccolo **Machiavelli** (1469–1527) wrote *The Prince*, which analyzed politics from the standpoint of expedience rising above morality in the name of maintaining political power.

The Reformation. The Reformation destroyed western Europe's religious unity and introduced new ideas about the relationships among God, the individual, and society. Politics greatly influenced the course of the Reformation and led, in most areas, to the subjection of the church to the political rulers.

Martin Luther (1483–1546), to his personal distress, could not reconcile the sinfulness of humans with the justice of God. During his studies of the Bible, Luther came to believe that personal efforts— good works, such as living a Christian life and offering proper attention to the sacraments of the church— could not "earn" the sinner salvation but that belief and faith were the only way to obtain grace. By 1515, Luther believed that "justification by faith alone" was the road to salvation.

On October 31, 1517, Luther nailed 95 theses, or statements, about **indulgences** (the cancellation of a sin in return for money) to the door of the Wittenberg church and challenged the practice of selling them. At this time he was seeking to reform the church, not divide it. In 1519, Luther presented various criticisms of the church and declared that only the Bible, not religious traditions or papal statements, could determine correct religious practices and beliefs. In 1521, Pope Leo X excommunicated Luther for his beliefs.

In 1536, **John Calvin** (1509–1564), a Frenchman, arrived in Geneva, a Swiss city-state that had adopted an anti-Catholic position. In 1540, Geneva became the center of the Reformation. Calvin's *Institutes of the Christian Religion* (1536), a strictly logical analysis of Christianity, had a universal appeal. Calvin emphasized the doctrine of **predestination**, which indicated that God knew who would obtain salvation before those people were born. Calvin believed that church and state should unite. Calvinism triumphed as the majority religion in Scotland, under the leadership of John Knox (circa 1514–1572), and in the United Provinces of the Netherlands. Puritans in England and New England also accepted Calvinism.

The Thirty Years' War. Between 1618 and 1648, the European powers fought a series of wars. The reasons for the wars varied; religious, dynastic, commercial, and territorial rivalries all played a part. The battles were fought over most of Europe and ended with the Treaty of Westphalia in 1648. The Thirty Years' War changed the boundaries of most European countries.

Explorations and Conquests. Between 1394 and 1460 (Prince Henry the Navigator's lifespan) and afterward, a period of exploration and conquests characterized European history.

Revolution and the New World Order
The Scientific Revolution. For the first time in human history, the eighteenth century saw the appearance of a secular worldview: the **Age of Enlightenment**. The philosophical starting point for the Enlightenment was the belief in the autonomy of man's intellect apart from God. The most basic assumption was faith in reason rather than faith in revelation. René Descartes (1596–1650) sought a basis for logic and believed he found it in man's ability to think. "I think; therefore, I am" was his most famous statement.

Benedict de Spinoza (1632–1677) developed a rational pantheism in which he equated God and nature. He denied all free will and ended up with an impersonal, mechanical universe. Gottfried Wilhelm Leibniz (1646–1716) worked on symbolic logic and calculus and invented a calculating machine. He, too, had a mecha-

nistic view of the world and life and thought of God as a hypothetical abstraction rather than a persona.

John Locke (1632–1704) pioneered the empiricist approach to knowledge; he stressed the importance of the environment in human development. Locke classified knowledge as either (1) according to reason, (2) contrary to reason, or (3) above reason. Locke thought reason and revelation were complementary and from God.

The Enlightenment's Effect on Society.
The Enlightenment affected more than science and religion. New political and economic theories originated as well. John Locke and **Jean-Jacques Rousseau** (1712–1778) believed that people were capable of governing themselves, either through a political (Locke) or social (Rousseau) contract forming the basis of society.

Most philosophers opposed democracy and preferred a limited monarchy that shared power with the nobility. The assault on mercantilist economic theory was begun by the physiocrats in France, who proposed a laissez-faire (minimal governmental interference) attitude toward land usage that culminated in the theory of economic capitalism associated with **Adam Smith** (1723–1790) and his notions of free trade, free enterprise, and the law of supply and demand.

The French Revolution.
The increased criticism directed toward governmental inefficiency and corruption and toward the privileged classes demonstrated the rising expectations of "enlightened" society in France. The remainder of the population (called the Third Estate) consisted of the middle class, urban workers, and the mass of peasants, who bore the entire burden of taxation and the imposition of feudal obligations.

The most notorious event of the French Revolution was the so-called Reign of Terror (1793–1794), the government's campaign against its internal enemies and counterrevolutionaries. **Louis XVI** faced charges of treason, was declared guilty, and was executed on January 21, 1793. Later the same year, the queen, **Marie Antoinette**, met the same fate.

The middle class controlled the Directory (1795–1799). Members of the Directory believed that through peace they would gain more wealth and establish a society in which money and property would become the only requirements for prestige and power. Rising inflation and mass public dissatisfaction led to the downfall of the Directory.

The Era of Napoleon.
On December 25, 1799, a new government and constitution concentrated supreme power in the hands of **Napoleon**. Napoleon's domestic reforms and policies affected every aspect of society.

French-ruled peoples viewed Napoleon as a tyrant who repressed and exploited them for France's glory and advantage. Enlightened reformers believed Napoleon had betrayed the ideals of the revolution. The downfall of Napoleon resulted from his inability to conquer England, economic distress caused by the Continental System (boycott of British goods), the Peninsular War with Spain, the German War of Liberation, and the invasion of Russia. The actual defeat of Napoleon occurred at the **Battle of Waterloo** in 1815.

The Industrial Revolution.
The term *Industrial Revolution* describes a period of transition when machines began to significantly displace human and animal power in methods of producing and distributing goods and when an agricultural and commercial society became an industrial one.

Roots of the Industrial Revolution are evident in the following changes:

- The Commercial Revolution (1500–1700), which spurred the great economic growth of Europe and brought about the Age of Discovery and Exploration, which in turn helped to solidify the economic doctrines of mercantilism
- The effect of the Scientific Revolution, which produced the first wave of mechanical inventions and technological advances
- The increase in population in Europe from 140 million people in 1750 to 266 million people by the mid-nineteenth century (more producers, more consumers)
- The nineteenth-century political and social revolutions that began the rise to power of the middle class and that provided leadership for the economic revolution

A transportation revolution ensued to distribute the productivity of machinery and to deliver raw materials

to the eager factories. Industries demanded the growth of canal systems; the construction of hard-surfaced **"macadam" roads**; the commercial use of the **steamboat** that **Robert Fulton** (1765–1815) demonstrated; and the **railway locomotive** that **George Stephenson** (1781–1848) made commercially successful.

The Industrial Revolution created a unique new category of people who depended on their jobs for income and who needed job security. Until 1850, workers as a whole did not share in the general wealth produced by the Industrial Revolution. Conditions improved as the century wore on. Union action combined with general prosperity and a developing social conscience to improve the working conditions, wages, and hours of skilled labor first and unskilled labor later.

Socialism. The Utopian Socialists were the earliest writers to propose an equitable solution to improve the distribution of society's wealth. The name of this group comes from *Utopia*, the book by **Saint Thomas More** (1478–1535) on a fictional ideal society. While they endorsed the productive capacity of industrialism, the Utopian Socialists denounced its mismanagement. Human society was ideally a community rather than a mixture of competing, selfish individuals. According to them, all the goods a person needed could be produced in one community.

Scientific socialism, or Marxism, was the creation of **Karl Marx** (1818–1883), a German scholar who, with the help of **Friedrich Engels** (1820–1895), intended to replace utopian hopes and dreams with a militant blueprint for socialist working-class success. The principal works of this revolutionary school of socialism were *The Communist Manifesto* and *Das Kapital*.

Marxism has four key propositions:

1. An economic interpretation of history that asserts that economic factors (mainly centered on who controls the means of production and distribution) determines all human history

2. The belief that there has always been a class struggle between the rich and the poor (or the exploiters and the exploited)

3. The theory of surplus value, which holds that the true value of a product is labor; because workers receive a small portion of their just labor price, the difference is surplus value "stolen" from workers by capitalists

4. The belief that socialism is inevitable, because capitalism contains the seeds of its own destruction (overproduction, unemployment, and so forth). The rich grow richer and the poor grow poorer until the gap between each class (proletariat and bourgeoisie) becomes so great that the working classes rise up in revolution and overthrow the elite bourgeoisie to install a "dictatorship of the proletariat." The creation of a classless society guided by the principle "from each according to his abilities, to each according to his needs" will be the result from dismantling capitalism.

Beginnings of European Exploration

Europeans were largely unaware of the existence of the American continent, even though a Norse seaman, **Leif Eriksson**, had sailed within sight of the continent in the eleventh century. Few other explorers ventured nearly as far as America. Before the fifteenth century, Europeans had little desire to explore and were not ready to face the many challenges of a long sea voyage. Just as developments led to changes and conflict in North America and produced an increasing number of distinct cultures and systems, developments in Europe were about to make possible the great voyages that led to contact between Europe and the Americas. In the fifteenth and sixteenth centuries, technological devices such as the **compass** and **astrolabe** freed explorers from some of the constraints that had limited early voyages. Three primary factors—God, gold, and glory—led to increased interest in exploration and eventually to a desire to settle in the newly discovered lands.

Although Europeans, such as Italians, participated in overland trade with the East and sailed through the Mediterranean and beyond, it was the Arabs who played the largest part in such trade and who benefited the most economically. **Prince Henry the Navigator**, ruler of Portugal, sponsored voyages aimed at adding territory and gaining control of trading routes to increase the power and wealth of Portugal. Prince Henry also wanted to spread Christianity and prevent the further expansion of Islam in Africa. Henry the Navigator brought a number of Italian merchant traders to his court at Cape St. Vincent, and subsequently they sailed in Portuguese

ships down the western coast of Africa. The initial voyages were extremely difficult, because the explorers lacked navigational instruments and any kind of maps or charts. Europeans had charted the entire Mediterranean Sea, including harbors and the coastline, but they had no knowledge or maps of the African coast.

The first task of the explorers was to create accurate charts of the African shoreline. The crews on these initial voyages did not encounter horrible monsters or boiling water, which rumors had said existed in the ocean beyond Cape Bojador, the farthest point Europeans had previously reached. They did discover, however, that strong southward winds made it easy to sail out of the Mediterranean but difficult to return.

Most people believed that Africa and China were joined by a southern continent, eliminating any possibility of an eastern maritime route to the Indian Ocean. Prince Henry, however, sent ships along the coast of Africa, because he believed it was possible to sail east through the Atlantic and reach the Indian Ocean.

Technical Innovations Aiding Exploration

One of the reasons that the explorers sailing from Portugal traveled along the coast was to avoid losing sight of land. By the thirteenth century, explorers were using the compass, borrowed from China, to determine direction; however, they still found it difficult to determine relative position from the North and South poles and from landmasses or anything else. In the Northern Hemisphere, a navigator could determine the relative north-south position, or latitude, by calculating the height of the **Pole Star** from the horizon. South of the equator, one cannot see the Pole Star; until around 1460, captains had no way to determine their position if they sailed too far south. Although longitude (relative east-west position) remained unknown until the eighteenth century, the introduction of the **astrolabe** allowed sailors to calculate their latitude south of the equator.

Along with navigational aids, improvements in shipbuilding and in weaponry also facilitated exploration. Unlike the Mediterranean, the Atlantic Ocean was not suited for ships propelled only by oarsmen: its waves were too high, and its currents and winds were too strong. Europeans had initially used very broad sails on ships that went out into the Atlantic; the ships were heavy and often became stranded by the absence of the favorable tailwinds upon which the ships and sailors depended. The Portuguese borrowed techniques from Arab and European shipbuilding and developed the Caravela Redondo. This ship proved to be more worthy of long voyages, because it combined square rigging for speed with lateen sails, which were more responsive and easier to handle. Other European states adopted the ship and also the practice of mounting artillery and other weapons on exploration vessels.

Main Elements of European Exploration

As the Portuguese began to trade and explore along the coast of Africa, they brought back slaves, ivory, gold, and knowledge of the African coast. It looked as though the Portuguese might find a route to the Indian Ocean, and it was clear that the voyages sponsored by Prince Henry were benefiting Portugal in many ways.

Other European states wanted to increase their territory and wealth and to establish trade routes to the East. Although the desire for control of trade routes and wealth was a primary motive in launching voyages of exploration, it was not the only incentive.

Europe in the fifteenth and sixteenth centuries, despite the increase in dissenting views, was still extremely religious. The Catholic Church continued to exert a tremendous influence, and some Christians were motivated to go on voyages of discovery to conduct missionary activities and spread the word of God. After the beginning of the Reformation, many Lutherans, Calvinists, and other groups who had left the Catholic Church emigrated from Europe in the hopes of settling where they would be free from religious persecution or violent conflicts.

Other individuals sponsored or participated in voyages in the hope of gaining wealth or increased opportunities. For example, though younger sons of families in Europe were able to secure prominent positions in the church, they were often not able to find lucrative opportunities at home, because the eldest son usually inherited lands and wealth. The voyages of exploration, therefore, were a means of securing fame and fortune and of obtaining opportunities that would not be available otherwise.

Although the motivation of fame and fortune was often secondary to God and glory, many individuals were attracted to exploration by the possibility of adventure and by their desire to explore uncharted territory. Gold, God, and glory operated on both individual and state levels; kings and heads of states were as interested as the seamen were in spreading their faith and increasing the wealth and prestige of their states.

Portugal was the first European state to establish sugar plantations on an island off the west coast of Africa and to import slaves from Africa to labor there. It was the beginning of the slave trade. The level of trading was initially far less extensive and intense than during the later period of slave trade, when Spain and England became involved. In an attempt to maintain control of the slave trade and of the eastern routes to India, the Portuguese appealed to the pope; he ruled in their favor and forbade the Spanish and others to sail south and east in an attempt to reach India or Asia.

Ferdinand and Isabella married and united Castile and Aragon, the two largest provinces in Spain. The rulers not only began the process of uniting all of Spain but also agreed to sponsor **Christopher Columbus** in his voyage of exploration. Only the heads of states had the necessary resources and could afford the risk involved in sponsoring a major voyage across the oceans of the world, but most monarchs were unwilling to take such a risk. Columbus was an Italian explorer looking for a sponsor and had approached Ferdinand and Isabella after having been turned down by the English government. He convinced the Spanish monarchs that a western route to the Indian Ocean existed and that it would be possible to make the voyage.

However, Columbus had miscalculated the distance of the voyage from Europe to Asia. He greatly underestimated the circumference of the earth, and no Europeans were aware of the existence of the American continents. One of the reasons that Ferdinand and Isabella were willing to support Columbus was that the previous agreements prevented all states but Portugal from sailing east to reach India. Therefore, the only chance for Spain to launch an expedition to India and to participate in trade and exploration was in the discovery of a western route to India.

European Contact with the Americas

In 1492, Columbus sailed from Spain with 90 men on three ships, the *Niña*, the *Pinta*, and the *Santa María*. After a 10-week voyage, they landed in the Bahamas. On his second trip, Columbus reached Cuba, and then in 1498, during his third trip, he reached the mainland and sailed along the northern coast of South America. Columbus originally thought he had reached India; he referred to the people he encountered in the Bahamas and on his second landing in Cuba as Indians.

There is considerable debate over whether Columbus realized, either during his third voyage or just before his death, that he had landed not in India but on an entirely unknown continent between Europe and Asia. Another question is whether Columbus, who died in obscurity despite his fame for having discovered America, should receive credit for this discovery, in light of the fact that earlier explorers had reached the American continent.

However, because Columbus's voyages prompted extensive exploration and settlement of the Americas, it is accurate to state that he was responsible for the discovery of the New World by Europeans. Another result of Columbus's voyages was the increased focus of Spain on exploration and conquest.

Nevertheless, the New World took its name from the Florentine merchant **Amerigo Vespucci**—not Columbus. Vespucci took part in several voyages to the New World and wrote a series of descriptions that not only gave Europeans an image of this "New World" but also spread the idea that the discovered lands were not a part of Asia or India. Vespucci, then, popularized the image of the Americas and the idea that the Americas were continents separate from those previously known.

It was a Portuguese navigator, **Vasco da Gama**, who crossed the Isthmus of Panama and came to another ocean, which separates the American continents from China. The Spanish sponsored another Portuguese sailor, **Ferdinand Magellan**, who discovered at the southern end of South America a strait that provided access to the ocean west of the Americas. Magellan named this ocean the Pacific ("peaceful"), because it was much calmer than the strait through which he had sailed to reach it. Later, he reached the Philippines and met his

death in a conflict with the natives. Magellan's voyage, nevertheless, was the final stage of the process whereby Europeans completed the first-known circumnavigation of the globe. Although initially the Spanish were eager to find a route around the Americas that would enable them to sail on toward their original goal—the treasures of the Far East—they began to consider the Americas as a possible source of untapped wealth.

The Spanish claimed all the New World except Brazil, which papal decree gave to the Portuguese. The first Spanish settlements were on the islands of the Caribbean Sea. It was not until 1518 that Spain appointed Hernando Cortez as a government official in Cuba; Cortez led a small military expedition against the Aztecs in Mexico. Cortez and his men failed in their first attack on the Aztec capital city, Tenochtitlan, but were ultimately successful.

A combination of factors allowed the small force of approximately 600 Spanish soldiers to overcome the extensive Aztec Empire. The Spanish were armed with rifles and bows, which provided an advantage over Aztec fighters armed only with spears. However, weapons and armor were not the main reason that the Spanish were able to overcome the military forces of the natives.

The Aztec ruler, Montezuma, allowed a delegation, which included Cortez, into the capital city, because the description of the Spanish soldiers in their armor and with feathers in their helmets was similar to the description in Aztec legend of messengers who would be sent by the chief Aztec god, Quetzalcoatl. The members of Cortez's expedition exposed the natives to smallpox and other diseases that devastated the native population. Finally, the Spanish expedition was also able to form alliances with other native tribes that the Aztecs had conquered; these tribes were willing to cooperate to defeat the Aztecs and thus break up their empire.

Twenty years after Cortez defeated the Aztecs, another conquistador ("conqueror"), Francisco Pizarro, defeated the Incas in Peru. Pizarro's expedition enabled the Spanish to begin to explore and settle South America. Spain funded the **conquistadors,** who were the first Europeans to explore some areas of the Americas. However, the sole purpose of the conquistadors' explorations was defeating the natives to gain access to gold,

silver, and other wealth. Spain established mines in the territory it claimed and produced a tremendous amount of gold and silver. In the 300 years after the Spanish conquest of the Americas in the sixteenth century, those mines produced 10 times as much gold and silver as the total produced by all the mines in the rest of the world.

Spain had come to view the New World as more than an obstacle to voyages toward India; over time, Spain began to think that it might be possible to exploit this territory for more than just mining. It was the conquistadors who made it possible for the Spanish to settle the New World, but they were not responsible for forming settlements or for overseeing Spanish colonies in the New World. Instead, Spain sent officials and administrators from Spain to oversee settlements after their initial formation.

Spanish settlers came to the New World for various reasons: some went in search of land to settle or buy, others went looking for opportunities that were not available to them in Europe, and priests and missionaries went to spread Christianity to the natives. By the end of the sixteenth century, Spain had established firm control over not only the several islands in the Caribbean, Mexico, and southern North America but also in the territory currently within the modern states of Chile, Argentina, and Peru.

Spanish Settlements in the New World

The first permanent settlement established by the Spanish was the predominantly military fort of St. Augustine, located in Florida. In 1598, Don Juan de Onate led a group of 500 settlers north from Mexico and established a colony in what is now New Mexico.

Onate granted *encomiendas* to the most prominent Spaniards who had accompanied him. Under the *encomienda* system that the Spanish in Mexico and parts of North America established, these distinguished individuals had the right to exact tribute and/or labor from the native population, which continued to live on the land in exchange for the services it provided.

Spanish colonists founded Santa Fe in 1609, and by 1680 about 2,000 Spaniards were living in New Mexico. Most of the colonists raised sheep and cattle on large ranches and lived among approximately 30,000

Pueblo Indians. The Spanish crushed a major revolt that threatened to destroy Santa Fe in 1680. Attempts to prevent the natives—both those who had converted to Catholicism and those who had not—from performing religious rituals that predated the Spaniards' arrival provoked the revolt. The natives drove the Spanish from Santa Fe, but they returned in 1696, crushed the Pueblos, and seized the land. Although the Spanish ultimately quelled the revolt, they began to change their policies toward the natives, who still greatly outnumbered the Spanish settlers.

The Spanish continued to try to Christianize and civilize the native population, but they also began to allow the Pueblos to own land. In addition, the Spanish unofficially tolerated native religious rituals, although Catholicism officially condemned all such practices. By 1700, the Spanish population in New Mexico had increased and reached about 4,000; the native population had decreased to about 13,000, and intermarriage between natives and Spaniards increased.

Nevertheless, disease, war, and migration resulted in the steady decline in the Pueblo population. New Mexico had become a prosperous and stable region, but it was still relatively weak and, as the only major Spanish settlement in northern Mexico, was isolated.

Effects of European-American Contact

One cannot underestimate the impact of Europeans on the New World, both before and after the arrival of the English and French. The most immediate effect was the spread of disease, which decimated the native population. In some areas of Mexico, 95 percent of the native population died as a result of contact with Europeans and the subsequent outbreaks of diseases such as smallpox. In South America, the native population was devastated not only by disease but also by deliberate policies instituted to control and in some cases eliminate native peoples.

Although Europeans passed most diseases to the natives, the natives did pass syphilis to the Europeans, who carried it back to Europe.

The European and American continents exchanged plants and animals. Europeans brought over animals to the New World, and they took plants such as potatoes, corn, and squash back to Europe, where introduction of these crops led to an explosion of the European population. The decimation of the native population and the establishment of large plantations led to a shortage of workers, and Europeans began to transport slaves from Africa to the New World to fill the shortage.

European Settlement and Development in North America

In 1497, King Henry VIII of England sponsored a voyage by **John Cabot** to try to discover a northwest passage through the New World to the Orient. However, the English made no real attempt to settle in the New World until nearly a century later. By the 1600s, the English became interested in colonizing the New World for several reasons. Many people in England emigrated overseas because the country's population was increasing and because much of the land was being used for raising sheep for wool rather than for growing foodstuffs for survival. Scarce opportunities, like those for buying land, were primary motivators for emigration from England.

Some people in England left their homeland because of the religious turmoil that engulfed England after the beginning of the Protestant Reformation. In addition to converts to Lutheranism and Calvinism, a major emigrating group was the Puritans, who called for reforms to "purify" the church.

Mercantilism also provided a motive for exploration and for the establishment of colonies. According to mercantile theories, an industrialized nation needed an inexpensive source of raw materials and markets for finished products. Colonies provided a way to obtain raw materials and to guarantee a market for industrial goods.

Economic reasons, among others, motivated the French and the Dutch to explore and establish colonies in the New World. In 1609, the year after the first English settlement, the French established a colony in Quebec. Overall, far fewer French settlers traveled to the New World than did English settlers, but the French were able to exercise a tremendous influence through the establishment of strong ties with the natives. The French created trading partnerships and a vast trading network; they often intermarried with the local native population.

The Dutch financed an English explorer, **Henry Hudson**, who claimed for Holland the territory that is

now New York. The Dutch settlements along the Hudson, Delaware, and Connecticut rivers developed into the colony of New Netherlands and established a vast trading network that effectively separated the English colonies of Jamestown and Plymouth.

One reason that English settlements began to become more prominent after 1600 was the defeat of the Spanish fleet, the supposedly invincible Armada, by the English in 1588. The changing power balance on the seas encouraged the English to increase their exploration and attempted colonization of the Americas. The first few colonies founded by the English in America did not flourish.

Sir Humphrey Gilbert, who had obtained a six-year grant giving him the exclusive rights to settle any unclaimed land in America, was planning to establish a colony in Newfoundland, but a storm sank his ship. Instead, **Sir Walter Raleigh** received the six-year grant. Raleigh explored the North American coast and named the territory through which he traveled *Virginia*, in honor of the "Virgin Queen" Elizabeth I of England. In addition, Raleigh convinced his cousin Sir Grenville to establish a colony on the island of Roanoke.

Roanoke was off the coast of what later became North Carolina. The first settlers lived there for a year while Sir Grenville returned to England for supplies and additional settlers. However, when Sir Francis Drake arrived in Roanoke nearly a year later and found that Sir Grenville had not yet returned, the colonists left on his ship and abandoned the settlement. In 1587, Raleigh sent another group of colonists to Roanoke, but a war with Spain broke out in 1588 and kept him from returning until 1590. When Raleigh returned to Roanoke, the colonists had vanished. A single word, *Croatan*, carved into a tree could have referred to a nearby settlement of natives. This suggested a number of possibilities in regard to the missing settlers; conclusive proof of their fate has never been found.

Colonization: The Jamestown Settlement

In 1606, King James I of England granted to the Virginia Company a charter for exploration and colonization. This charter marked the beginning of ventures sponsored by merchants rather than directly by the Crown. The charter of the Virginia Company had two branches. James I gave one branch to the English city of

Plymouth, which had the right to the northern portion of territory on the eastern coast of North America, and he granted the London branch of the company the right to the southern portion.

Considerable difficulties prevented the English from founding and maintaining a permanent settlement in North America. The Plymouth Company failed to establish a lasting settlement. The company itself ran out of money, and the settlers who had gone to the New World gave up and abandoned their established Sagadahoc Colony, in Maine.

Having decided to colonize the Chesapeake Bay area, the London Company sent three ships with about 104 sailors to that area in 1607. The company's ships sailed up a river, which they named the James in honor of the English king, and they established the fort and permanent settlement of Jamestown. The London Company and the men who settled Jamestown were hoping to find a northwest passage to Asia, gold and silver, or lands capable of producing valuable goods such as grapes, oranges, and silk.

The colony at Jamestown did not allow the settlers to accomplish any of those things, and its location on the river, which became contaminated every spring, led to the outbreak of diseases such as typhoid, dysentery, and malaria. More than half the colonists died the first year, and by the spring of 1609, only one-third of the total number of colonists who had joined the colony were still alive.

The colony initially survived largely through the efforts of **Captain John Smith**. Smith was a soldier who turned the colony's focus from exploration to obtaining food. Initially, Smith was able to obtain corn from the local Indians led by **Powhatan** and his 12-year-old daughter, **Pocahontas**. Smith also forced all able men in the colony to work four hours a day in the wheat fields.

Attempts by the London Company to send additional settlers and supplies encountered troubles and delays. **Thomas Gates** and some 600 settlers, who left for Jamestown in 1609, ran aground on Bermuda and had to build a new ship. Although some new settlers did arrive in Jamestown, disease continued to shrink the population.

When the seriously injured Smith had to return to England, his departure deprived the colony of its most effective and resourceful leader. Not long after Smith left, the colonists provoked a war with Powhatan, who was beginning to tire of the colonists' demands for corn. Powhatan realized that the settlers intended to stay indefinitely and might challenge the Indians for control of the surrounding territory.

Gates finally arrived in June 1610, with only 175 of the original 600 settlers. He found only 60 colonists who had survived the war with the Indians and the harsh winter of 1610, during which they had minimal food and other resources. Gates decided to abandon Jamestown and was sailing down the river with the surviving colonists on board when he encountered the new governor from England, **Thomas West**, Baron de la Warr. Gates and West returned to Jamestown, imposed martial law, responded to Indian attacks, and survived a five-year war with the Indians. Although the war did not end until 1614, when the colonists were able to negotiate a settlement by holding Pocahontas hostage, the situation in Jamestown began to improve in 1610.

Some of the settlers went to healthier locations, and in 1613 one of them, **John Rolfe**, married Pocahontas. In 1614, the settlers planted a mild strain of tobacco, which gave them a crop they could sell for cash. The Crown issued two new charters that allowed Virginia to extend its borders all the way to the Pacific and made the London Company a joint-stock company. Changes in the company led to a new treasurer, **Sir Edwin Sandy**, who tried to reform Virginia.

Sandy encouraged settlers in Virginia to try to produce grapes and silkworms and to diversify the colony's economy in other ways. Sandy also replaced martial law with English common law. The colonists established a council to make laws, and settlers now had the right to own land. By 1623, about 4,000 additional settlers had arrived in Virginia. Attempts to produce and sell crops other than tobacco, however, failed, and the arrival of large numbers of new colonists provoked renewed conflict with the Indians. A major Indian attack launched in March 1622 killed 347 colonists.

Investors in the London Company withdrew their capital and appealed to the king, and a royal commission visited the colony. As a result of this investigation, the king declared the London Company bankrupt and assumed direct control of Virginia in 1624. Virginia became the first royal colony, and the Crown appointed a governor and a council to oversee its administration. Three trends continued after the Crown assumed control. The first was unrelenting conflict with the Indians. Through war and raids, by 1632 the colonists had killed or driven out most of the Indians in the area immediately around Jamestown. The other two trends were the yearly influx of thousands of new settlers and the high death rate in the colony.

Despite the high mortality rate, the population of the colony gradually began to increase. The expansion of tobacco production led to a demand for labor, and thousands of the young men who came were indentured servants. In exchange for their passage to America and food and shelter during their terms of service, these men were bound to work for their masters for four or five years. After that time, they gained their freedom and often a small payment to help them become established. Most of these men were not able to participate in the running of the colony even after they became free, but some were able to acquire land.

In 1634, the Crown divided Virginia into counties, each with appointed justices and the right to fill all other positions. Under this type of system, individuals from a few wealthy families tended to dominate the government. Most of the counties became Anglican, and the colony continued to elect representatives to its House of Burgesses, an assembly that met with the governor to discuss issues of common law. The king, however, refused to recognize the colony's House of Burgesses. After 1660, the colony became even more dominated by the wealthiest 15 percent of the population, and these individuals and their sons continued to be the only colonists to serve as justices and burgesses. Settlement of the colonies continued, primarily for religious and economic reasons. Conflict between the colonists and the natives was a constant.

Growth of the Slave Trade

The shortage of labor in the southern colonies and a drop in the number of people coming to the colonies as indentured servants forced the colonists to search for other sources of labor. Although the colonists had begun using African servants and slaves almost immediately after settling in the New World, the slave trade and

the slave population in British North America remained small in the first half of the seventeenth century. Toward the end of the seventeenth century, increasing numbers of slaves from Africa became available, and the demand for them in North America further stimulated the growth of the transatlantic slave trade.

By the nineteenth century, millions of Africans had been forcibly taken from their native lands and sold into perpetual slavery. The Europeans sold slaves at forts the slave traders had established on the African coast; the Europeans packed the slaves as closely as possible into the lower regions of ships for the long journey to the Americas. Chained slaves traveled in deplorably unsanitary conditions and received only enough food and water to keep them alive. Many slaves died during this Middle Passage voyage.

Plantation owners in the Caribbean, Brazil, or North America bought the slaves to do the work. It was only after 1697 that English colonists began to buy large numbers of slaves. By 1760, the slave population had reached approximately a quarter of a million, with most of the slaves concentrated in the southern colonies. Slave labor replaced indentured servitude, and a race-based system of perpetual slavery developed. Colonial assemblies began to pass "slave codes" in the eighteenth century. These codes identified all non-whites or dark-skinned people as slaves, made their condition permanent, and legalized slavery in British North America.

Salem Witch Trials

During this period of increasing tensions, several communities held witchcraft trials. In Salem, Massachusetts, a group of young girls accused servants from West India and older white members of the community, mostly women, of exercising powers that Satan had given to them. Other towns also experienced turmoil and charged residents with witchcraft. In Salem alone, the juries pronounced 19 people guilty; in 1692 after the execution of all 19 victims, the girls admitted their stories were not true.

The witchcraft trials illustrate the highly religious nature of the New England society, but they also suggest that individuals who did not conform to societal expectations were at risk. Most of the accused were outspoken women who were often critical of their communities, were older, and were either widows or unmarried. Some of these women had acquired property despite the accepted views and limitations regarding women's role in society.

Religion in the Colonies and the Great Awakening

The religious nature of colonial settlers did not lead to the kind of intolerance or persecution that had plagued Europe since the Reformation. Conflict among various religious groups did break out occasionally, but British North America enjoyed a far greater degree of religious toleration than anywhere else. Among the reasons this toleration existed were that several religious groups had immigrated to North America and that every colony, except Virginia and Maryland, had ignored the laws establishing the Church of England as its official faith. Even among the Puritans, differences in religious opinion led to the establishment of different denominations.

Although there was some religious toleration, Protestants still tended to view Roman Catholics as a threatening rival. In Maryland, Catholics numbered about 3,000, the largest population of all the colonies, and were the victims of persecution. Jews likewise suffered persecution; they could not vote or hold office in any of the colonies, and only in Rhode Island could they practice their religion openly.

The other main trends in addition to toleration were the westward spread of communities, the rise of cities, and a decline in religious piousness. This sense of the weakening of religious authority and faithfulness led to the Great Awakening.

The **Great Awakening** refers to a period beginning in the 1730s in which several well-known preachers traveled through British North America, gave speeches, and argued for the need to revive religious piety and closer relationships with God. The main message of the preachers was that everyone has the potential, regardless of past behavior, to reestablish his or her relationship with God. This message appealed to many women and younger sons of landowners who stood to inherit very little. The best-known preacher during this period was **Jonathan Edwards**. Edwards denounced some current beliefs as doctrines of easy salvation. At his church in Northampton, Edwards sermonized about the absolute sovereignty of God, predestination, and salvation by grace alone.

The Great Awakening further divided religion in America by creating distinctions among New Light groups (revivalists), Old Light groups (traditionalists), and new groups that incorporated elements of both. The various revivalists, or New Light groups, did not agree on every issue. Some revivalists denounced education and learning from books; others founded schools in the belief that education was a means of furthering religion. While some individuals stressed a need for renewed spiritual focus, others began to embrace the ideas of the Enlightenment.

The **Scientific Revolution** had demonstrated the existence of natural laws that operated in nature, and enlightened thinkers began to argue that people had the ability to improve their own situations through the use of rational thought and acquired knowledge. Intellectuals of the **Enlightenment** shifted the focus from God to people, introduced the idea of progress, and argued that people could improve their own situations and make decisions on how to live rather than just having faith in God and waiting for a better life after death and salvation.

Enlightenment thought had a tremendous impact on the North American colonists, who began to establish more schools, encourage the acquisition of knowledge, and become more interested in gaining scientific knowledge. The colleges founded in North America taught the scientific theories held by **Copernicus**, who argued that planets rotated around the sun, not the earth, and Newton, who introduced the key principles of physics, including gravity.

The colonists did not just learn European theories. **Benjamin Franklin** was among the colonists who began to carry out their own experiments and form their own theories. Franklin experimented with electricity and was able to demonstrate in 1752, by using a kite, that electricity and lightning were the same.

Scientific theories also led to inoculations against smallpox. The Puritan theologian **Cotton Mather** convinced the population of Boston that injections with a small amount of the smallpox virus would build up their resistance to the disease and reduce the likelihood of reinfection. Leading theologians and scientists spread European scientific ideas and developed their own theories and applications, using their acquired knowledge.

The American Revolution

The Coming of the American Revolution.

In 1764, George Grenville pushed through Parliament the **Sugar Act** (the Revenue Act), which aimed at raising revenue by taxing goods imported by Americans. The **Stamp Act** (1765) imposed a direct tax on the colonists for the first time. By requiring Americans to purchase revenue stamps on everything from newspapers to legal documents, the Stamp Act would have created an impossible drain on hard currency in the colonies.

Americans reacted first with restrained and respectful petitions and pamphlets in which they pointed out that "taxation without representation is tyranny." The colonists began to limit their purchase of imported goods. From there, resistance progressed to stronger protests, which eventually became violent. In October 1765, delegates from nine colonies met as the Stamp Act Congress, passed moderate resolutions against the act, and asserted that Americans could not be taxed without the consent of their representatives. The colonists now ceased all importation.

In March 1766, Parliament repealed the Stamp Act. At the same time, however, it passed the **Declaratory Act**, which claimed the power to tax or make laws for the Americans "in all cases whatsoever." In 1766, Parliament passed a program of taxes on items imported into the colonies. The taxes eventually were known as the Townsend duties, a name that came from Britain's chancellor of the exchequer, Charles Townsend. American reaction was at first slow, but the sending of troops aroused them to resistance.

Again, the colonies halted importation, and soon British merchants were calling on Parliament to repeal the Townsend duties. In March 1770, Parliament repealed all the taxes except that on tea; Parliament wanted to prove that it had the right to tax the colonies if it so desired. When Parliament ended the **Tea Act** in 1773, a relative peace ensued.

In desperate financial condition—partially because the Americans were buying smuggled Dutch tea rather than the taxed British product—the British East India Company sought and obtained from Parliament concessions that allowed it to ship tea directly to the colonies rather than only by way of Britain. The result would be that the East India Company tea, even with the tax,

would be cheaper than smuggled Dutch tea. The company hoped that the colonists would thus buy the tea, tax and all, save the East India Company, and tacitly accept Parliament's right to tax them.

The Americans, however, proved resistant to this approach. Rather than acknowledge Parliament's right to tax, they refused to buy the cheaper tea and resorted to various methods, including tar and feathers, to prevent the collection of the tax on tea. In most ports, Americans did not permit tea-carrying ships to dock.

In Boston, however, the pro-British governor **Thomas Hutchinson** forced a confrontation by ordering Royal Navy vessels to prevent the tea ships from leaving the harbor. After 20 days, this would, by law, result in selling the cargoes at auction and paying the tax. The night before the time was to expire, December 16, 1773, Bostonians thinly disguised as Native Americans boarded the ships and threw the tea into the harbor. This was the **Boston Tea Party**.

The British responded with four acts collectively titled the **Coercive Acts** (1774), in which they strengthened their control over the colonists. The **First Continental Congress** (1774) met in response to the acts. The Congress called for strict nonimportation and rigorous preparation of local militia companies.

The War for Independence.   British troops went to Massachusetts, which the Crown had officially declared to be in a state of rebellion. General Thomas Gage received orders to arrest the leaders of the resistance or, failing that, to provoke any sort of confrontation that would allow him to turn British military might loose on the Americans. Americans, however, detected the movement of Gage's troops toward Concord, and dispatch riders like **Paul Revere** and **William Dawes** spread the news throughout the countryside.

In Lexington, about 70 **minutemen** (trained militiamen who would respond at a moment's notice) awaited the British on the village green. A shot was fired; it is unknown which side fired first. This became "**the shot heard 'round the world.**"

The British opened fire and charged. Casualties occurred on both sides. The following month, the Americans tightened the noose around Boston by fortifying

Breed's Hill (a spur of Bunker Hill). The British determined to remove them by a frontal attack. Twice thrown back, the British finally succeeded when the Americans ran out of ammunition. There were more than 1,000 British casualties in what turned out to be the bloodiest battle of the war (June 17, 1775), yet the British had gained very little and remained "bottled up" in Boston.

Congress put **George Washington** (1732–1799) in charge of the army, called for more troops, and adopted the Olive Branch Petition, which pleaded with **King George III** to intercede with Parliament to restore peace. However, the king gave his approval to the Prohibitory Act, declaring the colonies in rebellion and no longer under his protection. Preparations began for full-scale war against America.

In 1776, the colonists formed two committees to establish independence and a national government. One was to work out a framework for a national government. The other was to draft a statement of the reasons for declaring independence. The statement, called the **Declaration of Independence**, was primarily the work of Thomas Jefferson (1743–1826) of Virginia. It was a restatement of political ideas by then commonplace in America and showed why the former colonists felt justified in separating from Great Britain. Congress formally adopted the Declaration of Independence on **July 4, 1776**.

The British landed that summer at New York City. Washington, who had anticipated the move, was waiting for them. However, the undertrained, underequipped, and badly outnumbered American army was no match for the British and had to retreat. By December, what was left of Washington's army had made it into Pennsylvania.

With his small army melting away as demoralized soldiers deserted, Washington decided on a bold stroke. On Christmas night 1776, Washington's army crossed the **Delaware River** and at Trenton, New Jersey, they struck the Hessians (German mercenaries who fought for the British). Washington's troops easily defeated the Hessians, who were still groggy from their hard-drinking Christmas party.

A few days later, Washington defeated a British force at **Princeton**, New Jersey. The Americans re-

gained much of New Jersey from the British and saved the American army from disintegration. Hoping to weaken Britain, France began making covert shipments of arms to the Americans early in the war. These French shipments were vital for the Americans. The American victory at Saratoga, New York, convinced the French to join openly in the war against England. Eventually, the Spanish (1779) and the Dutch (1780) joined as well.

The final peace agreement between the newly formed United States and Great Britain became known as the Treaty of Paris of 1783. Its terms stipulated the following:

1. The recognition by the major European powers, including Britain, of the United States as an independent nation
2. The establishment of America's western boundary at the Mississippi River
3. The establishment of America's southern boundary at latitude 31° north (the northern boundary of Florida)
4. The surrender of Florida to Spain and the retainment of Canada by Britain
5. The enablement of private British creditors to collect any debts owed by U.S. citizens
6. The recommendation of Congress that the states restore confiscated loyalist property

The Creation of New Governments

After the adoption of the Articles of Confederation, Congress adopted a new constitution and the Americans elected George Washington as president under its guidelines.

The Federalist Era.   George Washington received virtually all the votes of the presidential electors. **John Adams** (1735–1826) received the next-highest number and became the vice president. After a triumphant journey from Mount Vernon, his home in Virginia, Washington attended his inauguration in New York City, the temporary seat of government.

To appease the antifederalists, the states ratified 10 amendments—the Bill of Rights—by the end of 1791. The first nine spelled out specific guarantees of personal freedoms, and the Tenth Amendment reserved for the states all powers not specifically withheld or granted to the federal government.

Alexander Hamilton (1757–1804) interpreted the Constitution as having vested extensive powers in the federal government. This "implied powers" stance claimed that the government had all powers that the Constitution had not expressly denied it. Hamilton's was the "broad" interpretation of the Constitution.

By contrast, **Thomas Jefferson** and **James Madison** (1751–1836) held the view that the Constitution prohibited any action not specifically permitted in the Constitution. Based on this view of government, adherents of this "strict" interpretation opposed the establishment of Hamilton's national bank. The Jeffersonian supporters, primarily under the guidance of Madison, began to organize political groups in opposition to Hamilton's program. The groups opposing Hamilton's view called themselves Democratic-Republicans or Jeffersonians.

The Federalists, Hamilton's supporters, received their strongest confirmation from the business and financial groups in the commercial centers of the Northeast and from the port cities of the South. The strength of the Democratic-Republicans lay primarily in the rural and frontier areas of the South and West. Federalist candidate John Adams won the election of 1796.

The elections in 1798 increased the Federalists' majorities in both houses of Congress, which then used their "mandate" to enact legislation to stifle foreign influences. The **Alien Act** raised new hurdles in the path of immigrants trying to obtain citizenship, and the **Sedition Act** widened the powers of the Adams administration to muzzle its newspaper critics. Democratic-Republicans were convinced that the Alien and Sedition Acts were unconstitutional, but the process of deciding on the constitutionality of federal laws was as yet undefined.

The Jeffersonian Era.   **Thomas Jefferson** and **Aaron Burr** ran for the presidency on the Democratic-Republican ticket, though not together, against John Adams and Charles Pinckney for the Federalists. Both Jefferson and Burr received the same number of votes in the Electoral College, so the election went to the House of Representatives. After a lengthy deadlock, Alexander Hamilton threw his support to Jefferson. Burr had to accept the vice presidency, the result obviously intended by the electorate.

The adoption and ratification of the Twelfth Amendment in 1804 ensured that a tie vote between candidates of the same party could not again cause the confusion of the Jefferson-Burr affair. Following the constitutional mandate, an 1808 law prevented the importation of slaves. An American delegation purchased the trans-Mississippi territory from Napoleon for $15 million in April 1803 (the Louisiana Purchase), even though they had no authority to buy more than the city of New Orleans.

The War of 1812.

Democratic-Republican **James Madison** won the election of 1808 over Federalist Charles Pinckney, but the Federalists gained seats in both houses of Congress.

The Native American tribes of the Northwest and the **Mississippi Valley** were resentful of the government's policy of pressured removal to the West, and the British authorities in Canada exploited their discontent by encouraging border raids against the American settlements. At the same time, the British interfered with American transatlantic shipping, including impressing sailors and capturing ships. On June 1, 1812, President Madison asked for a declaration of war, and Congress complied. After three years of inconclusive war, the British and Americans signed the Treaty of Ghent (1815). It provided for the acceptance of the status quo that had existed at the beginning of hostilities, and both sides restored their wartime conquests to the other.

The Monroe Doctrine.

As Latin American nations began declaring independence, British and American leaders feared that European governments would try to restore the former New World colonies to their erstwhile royal owners. In December 1823, **President James Monroe** (1758–1831) included in his annual message to Congress a statement that the peoples of the American hemisphere were "henceforth not to be considered as subjects for future colonization by any European powers."

The Marshall Court.

Chief Justice **John Marshall** (1755–1835) delivered the majority opinions in several critical decisions in the formative years of the U.S. Supreme Court. These decisions served to strengthen the power of the federal government (and of the court itself) and restrict the powers of state governments. Here are two key examples:

- *Marbury v. Madison* (1803) established the Supreme Court's power of judicial review over federal legislation.
- In *Gibbons v. Ogden* (1824), a case involving competing steamboat companies, Marshall ruled that commerce includes navigation and that only Congress has the right to regulate commerce among states. Marshall's ruling voided the state-granted monopoly.

The Missouri Compromise.

The Missouri Territory, the first territory organized from the Louisiana Purchase, applied for statehood in 1819. Because the Senate membership was evenly divided between slaveholding and free states at that time, the admission of a new state would give the voting advantage to either the North or the South. As the debate dragged on, the northern territory of Massachusetts applied for admission as the state of Maine. By combining the two admission bills, the creators of the compromise legislation established Maine as a free state and Missouri as a slave state. So that the Missouri Compromise would be palatable for the House of Representatives, the bill included a provision prohibiting slavery in the remainder of the Louisiana Territory north of the southern boundary of Missouri (latitude 36°30′).

Jacksonian Democracy.

The candidate of a faction of the emerging Democratic Party, **Andrew Jackson** (1767–1845) won the election of 1828. Jackson was popular with the common man. He seemed to be the prototype of the self-made westerner: rough-hewn, violent, vindictive, with few ideas but strong convictions. He ignored his appointed cabinet officers and relied instead on the counsel of his "Kitchen Cabinet," a group of partisan supporters. He exercised his veto power more than any other president before him.

Jackson supported the removal of all Native American tribes to an area west of the Mississippi River. The **Indian Removal Act** of 1830 provided for the federal enforcement of that process. One of the results of this policy was the **Trail of Tears**, the forced march under U.S. Army escort of thousands of Cherokee Indians to the West. One-quarter or more of them, mostly women and children, perished on the journey.

The National Bank.

The Bank of the United States had operated under the direction of Nicholas Biddle

since 1823. He was a cautious man, and his conservative economic policy enforced conservatism among state and private banks—which many bankers resented. In 1832, Jackson vetoed the national bank's renewal, and it ceased being a federal institution in 1836.

The Antislavery Movement.   In 1831, William Lloyd Garrison started his newspaper the *Liberator* and began to advocate total and immediate emancipation. He founded the New England Antislavery Society in 1832 and the American Antislavery Society in 1833. Theodore Weld pursued the same goals but advocated more gradual means. Some women, such as Julia Ward Howe (author of "Battle Hymn of the Republic"), supported Garrison's work.

The movement split into two wings: Garrison's radical followers and the moderates, who favored "moral suasion" and petitions to Congress. In 1840, the Liberty Party, the first national antislavery party, fielded a presidential candidate on the platform of "free soil" (preventing the expansion of slavery into the new western territories).

The Role of Minorities.   The women's rights movement focused on social and legal discrimination, and women like Lucretia Mott and Sojourner Truth became well-known figures on the speakers' circuit. By 1850, roughly 200,000 free blacks lived in the North and West. Prejudice restricted their lives, and "Jim Crow" laws separated the races.

Manifest Destiny and Westward Expansion. The coining of the term *Manifest Destiny* did not occur until 1844, but the belief that the destiny of the American nation was expansion all the way to the **Pacific Ocean**— and possibly even to Canada and Mexico—was older than that. A common conviction was that Americans should share American liberty and ideals with everyone possible, by force if necessary. In the 1830s, American missionaries followed the traders and trappers to the Oregon country and began to publicize the richness and beauty of the land. The result was the Oregon Fever of the 1840s, as thousands of settlers trekked across the Great Plains and the Rocky Mountains to settle the new Shangri-la.

Texas had been a state in the Republic of Mexico since 1822, following the Mexican revolution against Spanish control. The new Mexican government invited immigration from the North by offering land grants to Stephen Austin and other Americans. By 1835, approximately 35,000 "gringos" were homesteading on Texas land. When the Mexican officials saw their power base eroding as the foreigners flooded in, they moved to tighten control through restrictions on immigration and through tax increases. The Texans responded in 1836 by proclaiming independence and establishing a new republic. In 1845, after a series of failed attempts at annexation, the U.S. Congress admitted Texas to the Union.

The Mexican War.   Though Mexico broke diplomatic relations with the United States immediately after Texas's admission to the Union, there was still hope of a peaceful settlement. In the fall of 1845, President **James K. Polk** (1795–1849) sent **John Slidell** to Mexico City with a proposal for a peaceful settlement, but like other attempts at negotiation, nothing came of it. Racked by coup and countercoup, the Mexican government refused even to receive Slidell. Polk responded by sending U.S. troops into the disputed territory. On April 5, 1846, Mexican troops attacked an American patrol. When news of the clash reached Washington, Polk sought and received from Congress a declaration of war against Mexico.

Negotiated peace came about with the signing of the Treaty of Guadalupe Hidalgo on February 2, 1848. Under the terms of the treaty, Mexico ceded to the United States the southwestern territory from Texas to the California coast.

Sectional Conflict and the Causes of the Civil War
The Crisis of 1850.   The Mexican War had barely started when, on August 8, 1846, a freshman Democratic congressman, **David Wilmot** of Pennsylvania, introduced his **Wilmot Proviso** as a proposed amendment to a war appropriations bill. It stipulated that "neither slavery nor involuntary servitude shall ever exist" in any territory to be acquired from Mexico. The House passed the proviso, but the Senate did not; Wilmot introduced his provision again amid increasingly acrimonious debate.

One compromise proposal called for the extension of the 36°30′ line of the Missouri Compromise westward through the Mexican cession to the Pacific, with territory north of the line closed to slavery. Another

compromise solution was "popular sovereignty," which held that the residents of each territory should decide for themselves whether to allow slavery.

Having more than the requisite population and being in need of better government, California petitioned in September 1849 for admission to the Union as a free state. Southerners were furious. Long outnumbered in the House of Representatives, the South would find itself, should Congress admit California as a free state, similarly outnumbered in the Senate. At this point, the aged **Henry Clay** proposed a compromise. For the North, Congress would admit California as a free state; the land in dispute between Texas and New Mexico would go to New Mexico; popular sovereignty would decide the issue of slavery in the New Mexico and Utah territories (all of the Mexican cession outside of California); and there would be no slave trade in the District of Columbia. For the South, Congress would enact a tougher Fugitive Slave Law, promise not to abolish slavery in the District of Columbia, and declare that it did not have jurisdiction over the interstate slave trade; the federal government would pay Texas's $10 million preannexation debt.

The Kansas-Nebraska Act. All illusion of sectional peace ended abruptly in 1854 when Senator **Stephen A. Douglas** of Illinois introduced a bill in Congress to organize the area west of Missouri and Iowa as the territories of Kansas and Nebraska on the basis of popular sovereignty. The **Kansas-Nebraska Act** aroused a storm of outrage in the North, which viewed the repeal of the Missouri Compromise as the breaking of a solemn agreement, hastened the disintegration of the Whig Party, and divided the Democratic Party along North-South lines.

Springing to life almost overnight as a result of northern fury at the Kansas-Nebraska Act was the Republican Party. This party included diverse elements whose sole unifying principle was banning slavery from all the nation's territories, confining slavery to the states in which it already existed, and preventing the further spread of slavery.

The *Dred Scott* Decision. In *Dred Scott v. Sanford* (1857), the Supreme Court attempted to settle the slavery question. The case involved a Missouri slave, **Dred Scott**, whom the abolitionists had encouraged to

sue for his freedom on the basis that his owner had taken him to a free state, Illinois, for several years and then to a free territory, Wisconsin.

The Court attempted to read the extreme Southern position on slavery into the Constitution. The Court ruled not only that Scott had no standing to sue in federal court but also that temporary residence in a free state, even for several years, did not make a slave free. In addition, the Court ruling signified that the Missouri Compromise (already a dead letter by that time) had been unconstitutional all along; Congress did not have the authority to exclude slavery from a territory, nor did territorial governments have the right to prohibit slavery.

The Election of 1860. As the 1860 presidential election approached, the Republicans met in Chicago, confident of victory and determined to do nothing to jeopardize their favorable position. Accordingly, they rejected as too radical the front-running candidate, New York Senator **William H. Seward**, in favor of Illinois's favorite son, **Abraham Lincoln** (1809–1865). The platform called for federal support of a transcontinental railroad and for the containment of slavery. On election day, the voting went along strictly sectional lines. Lincoln led in popular votes; though he was short of a majority of popular votes, he did have the needed majority in Electoral College votes and was elected.

The Secession Crisis. On December 20, 1860, South Carolina, by vote of a special convention, seceded from the Union. By February 1, 1861, six more states (Alabama, Georgia, Florida, Mississippi, Louisiana, and Texas) had followed suit.

Representatives of the seceded states met in Montgomery, Alabama, in February 1861 and declared themselves to be the Confederate States of America. They elected former secretary of war and U.S. senator **Jefferson Davis** (1808–1889) of Mississippi as president and Alexander Stephens (1812–1883) of Georgia as vice president.

Civil War and Reconstruction
Hostilities Begin. In his inaugural address, Lincoln urged Southerners to reconsider their actions but warned that the Union was perpetual, that states could not secede, and that he would therefore hold the federal

forts and installations in the South. Only two remained in federal hands: Fort Pickens, off Pensacola, Florida; and Fort Sumter, in the harbor of Charleston, South Carolina.

From **Major Robert Anderson**, commander of the small garrison at Sumter, Lincoln soon received word that supplies were running low. Desiring to send in the needed supplies, Lincoln informed the governor of South Carolina of his intention but promised that no attempt would be made to send arms, ammunition, or reinforcements unless Southerners initiated hostilities.

Confederate **General P. G. T. Beauregard**, acting on orders from President Davis, demanded Anderson's surrender. Anderson said he would surrender if not re-supplied. Knowing supplies were on the way, the Con-federates opened fire at 4:30 A.M. on April 12, 1861. The next day, the fort surrendered. The day following Sumter's surrender, Lincoln declared an insurrection and called for the states to provide 75,000 volunteers to put it down. In response, Virginia, Tennessee, North Carolina, and Arkansas declared their secession. The re-maining slave states—Delaware, Kentucky, Maryland, and Missouri—wavered but stayed with the Union.

The North enjoyed many advantages over the South. It had the majority of wealth and was vastly su-perior in industry. The North also had an advantage of almost three to one in manpower; more than one-third of the South's population was slaves, whom Southerners would not use as soldiers. Unlike the South, the North received large numbers of **immigrants** during the war. The North retained control of the U.S. Navy; it could command the sea and blockade the South. Finally, the North enjoyed a much superior system of railroads.

The South did, however, have some advantages. It was vast in size and difficult to conquer. In addition, its troops would be fighting on their own ground, a fact that would give them the advantage of familiarity with the terrain and the added motivation of defending their homes and families.

The Homestead Act and the Morrill Land Grant Act.

In 1862, Congress passed two highly important acts dealing with domestic affairs in the North. The Homestead Act granted 160 acres of government land free of charge to any person who would farm it for at least five years. Many of the settlers of the West used the provisions of this act. The Morrill Land Grant Act offered large amounts of the federal government's land to states that would establish "agricultural and mechanical" colleges. Many of the nation's large state universi-ties were founded under the provisions of this act.

The Emancipation Proclamation.

By mid-1862, Lincoln, under pressure from radical elements of his own party and hoping to create a favorable impression on foreign public opinion, determined to issue the **Eman-cipation Proclamation**, which declared free all slaves in areas still in rebellion as of January 1, 1863. At the recommendation of William Seward, now his secretary of state, Lincoln waited to announce the proclamation until the North won some sort of victory. The Battle of Antietam (September 17, 1862) provided this victory.

Northern Victory.

Lincoln ran on the ticket of the National Union Party—essentially, the Republican Party with the addition of loyal or "war" Democrats. His vice presidential candidate was **Andrew Johnson** (1808–1875), a loyal Democrat from Tennessee.

In September 1864, word came that **General William Sherman** (1820–1891) had taken Atlanta. The capture of this vital southern rail and manufacturing center brought an enormous boost to northern morale. Along with other northern victories that summer and fall, it ensured a re-sounding election victory for Lincoln and the continua-tion of the war to complete victory for the North.

General Robert E. Lee (1807–1870) abandoned Richmond, Virginia, on April 3, 1865, and attempted to escape with what was left of his army. Under the command of **Ulysses S. Grant** (1822–1885), Northern forces pursued and cornered Lee's troops. Lee surren-dered at Appomattox, Virginia, on April 9, 1865. Other Confederate troops still holding out in various parts of the South surrendered over the next few weeks.

Lincoln did not live to receive news of the final sur-renders. On April 14, 1865, **John Wilkes Booth** shot Lincoln in the back of the head while the president was watching a play in Ford's Theater in Washington, D.C.

Reconstruction.

In 1865, Congress created the **Freedman's Bureau** to provide food, clothing, and education and generally to look after the interests of

former slaves. To restore legal governments in the se- ceded states, Lincoln had developed a policy that made it relatively easy for Southern states to enter the col- lateral process.

Congress passed a **Civil Rights Act** in 1866, de- claring that all citizens born in the United States are, regardless of race, equal citizens under the law. This act became the model of the Fourteenth Amendment to the Constitution.

President Andrew Johnson obeyed the letter but not the spirit of the Reconstruction acts. Congress, angry at his refusal to cooperate, searched in vain for grounds to impeach him. In August 1867, Johnson violated the Ten- ure of Office Act, which forbade the president from re- moving from office those who had been approved by the Senate. This test of the act's constitutionality took place not in the courts but in Congress. The House of Repre- sentatives impeached Johnson, who then came within one vote of being removed from office by the Senate.

The Fifteenth Amendment. In 1868, the Repub- licans nominated **Ulysses S. Grant** for president. His narrow victory prompted Republican leaders to decide that it would be politically expedient to give the vote to all blacks, Northern as well as Southern. For this pur- pose, leaders of the North drew up and submitted to the states the Fifteenth Amendment. Ironically, the idea was so unpopular in the North that it won the necessary three-fourths approval only because Congress required the Southern states to ratify it.

Industrialism, War, and the Progressive Era

The Economy. Captains of industry—such as **John D. Rockefeller** in oil, **J. P. Morgan** in banking, **Gustavus Swift** in meat processing, **Andrew Carne- gie** in steel, and **E. H. Harriman** in railroads—created major industrial empires. In 1886, **Samuel Gompers** and **Adolph Strasser** put together a combination of national craft unions, the **American Federation of La- bor (AFL)**, to represent labor's concerns about wages, hours, and safety conditions. Although militant in its use of the strike and in its demand for collective bar- gaining in labor contracts with large corporations, the AFL did not promote violence or radicalism.

The Spanish-American War. The Cuban revolt against Spain in 1895 threatened American business interests in Cuba. Sensational "yellow" journalism and nationalistic statements from officials such as Assistant Secretary of the Navy **Theodore Roosevelt** (1858–1919) encouraged popular support for direct American mili- tary intervention on behalf of Cuban independence.

On March 27, 1897, President **William McKinley** (1843–1901) asked Spain to call an armistice, accept American mediation to end the war, and stop using concentration camps in Cuba. Spain refused to comply. On April 21, Congress declared war on Spain with the objective of establishing Cuban independence (Teller Amendment). The first U.S. forces landed in Cuba on June 22, 1898, and by July 17 had defeated the Spanish forces. Spain ceded the Philippines, Puerto Rico, and Guam to the United States in return for a payment of $20 million to Spain for the Philippines.

Theodore Roosevelt and Progressive Reforms. On September 6, 1901, while attending the Pan Ameri- can Exposition in Buffalo, New York, President McKin- ley was shot by Leon Czolgosz, an anarchist. The president died on September 14. Theodore Roosevelt, at age 42, became the nation's twenty-fifth president and its youngest president to date.

In accordance with the Antitrust Policy (1902), President Theodore Roosevelt ordered the Justice De- partment to prosecute corporations pursuing monopolis- tic practices. Attorney General P. C. Knox first brought suit against the Northern Securities Company, a railroad holding corporation put together by J. P. Morgan, and then moved against John D. Rockefeller's Standard Oil Company. By the time he left office in 1909, Roosevelt had indictments against 25 monopolies.

Roosevelt engineered the separation of Panama from Colombia and the recognition of Panama as an independent country. The **Hay-Bunau-Varilla Treaty** of 1903 granted the United States control of the Ca- nal Zone in Panama for $10 million and an annual fee of $250,000; the control would begin nine years after ratification of the treaty by both parties. Construction of the **Panama Canal** began in 1904 and was completed in 1914.

In 1905, the African American intellectual and mili- tant **W.E.B. DuBois** founded the **Niagara Movement**, which called for federal legislation to protect racial

equality and to grant full citizenship rights. Formed in 1909, the **National Association for the Advancement of Colored People** (NAACP) pressed actively for the rights of the African Americans.

A third organization of the time, the radical labor organization called the **Industrial Workers of the World** (IWW, or Wobblies; 1905–1924), promoted violence and revolution. The IWW organized effective strikes in the textile industry in 1912 and among a few western miners' groups, but it had little appeal to the average American worker. After the Red Scare of 1919, the government worked to smash the IWW and deported many of its immigrant leaders and members.

The Wilson Presidency. The nation elected Democratic candidate **Woodrow Wilson** (1856–1924) as president in 1912. Before the outbreak of World War I in 1914, Wilson, working with cooperative majorities in both houses of Congress, achieved much of the remaining progressive agenda, including lower tariff reform (Underwood-Simmons Act, 1913); the Sixteenth Amendment (graduated income tax, 1913); the Seventeenth Amendment (direct election of senators, 1913); the Federal Reserve banking system (which provided regulation and flexibility to monetary policy, 1913); the Federal Trade Commission (to investigate unfair business practices, 1914); and the Clayton Antitrust Act (improving the old Sherman Act and protecting labor unions and farm cooperatives from prosecution, 1914).

Wilson's Fourteen Points. When America entered World War I in 1917, President Wilson maintained that the war would make the world safe for democracy. In an address to Congress on January 8, 1918, he presented his specific peace plan in the form of the Fourteen Points. The first five points called for open rather than secret peace treaties, freedom of the seas, free trade, arms reduction, and a fair adjustment of co_____ claims. The next eight points addressed national a_____ tions of various European peoples and the adjustm_____ boundaries. The fourteenth point, which he consi_____ the most important and which he had espoused as _____ as 1916, called for a "general association of natio_____ preserve the peace.

Social Conflicts. Although many Americans _____ called for immigration restriction since the late _____ teenth century, the only major restriction impose_____

immigration by 1920 had been the Chinese Exclusion Act of 1882. Labor leaders believed that immigrants depressed wages and impeded unionization. Some progressives believed that immigrants created social problems. In June 1917, Congress, over Wilson's veto, imposed a **literacy test for immigrants** and **excluded many Asian nationalities**.

In 1921, Congress passed the **Emergency Quota Act**. In practice, the law admitted almost as many immigrants as the nation wanted from such nations as Britain, Ireland, and Germany but severely restricted Italians, Greeks, Poles, and eastern European Jews hoping to enter the country. The law became effective in 1922 and reduced the number of immigrants annually to about 40 percent of the 1921 total. Congress then passed the National Origins Act of 1924, which further reduced the number of southern and eastern European immigrants and cut the annual immigration total to 20 percent of the 1921 figure. In 1927, the nation set at 150,000 the annual maximum number of immigrants allowed into the United States.

On Thanksgiving Day in 1915, **William J. Simmons** founded the **Knights of the Ku Klux Klan**. Its purpose was to intimidate African Americans, who were experiencing an apparent rise in status during World War I. The Klan's methods of repression included cross burnings, tar and featherings, kidnappings, lynchings, and burnings. The Klan was not a political party, but it endorsed and opposed candidates and exerted considerable control over elections and politicians in at least nine states.

Fundamentalist Protestants, under the leadership of **William Jennings Bryan**, began a campaign in 1921 to prohibit the teaching of evolution in the schools and protect the belief in the literal biblical account of c____

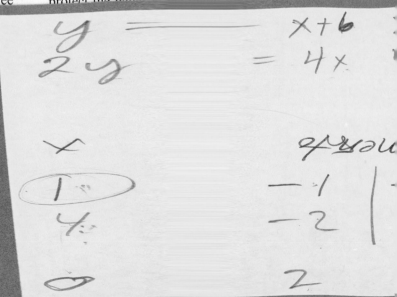

the crash of 1929. Stock prices increased throughout the decade. The boom in prices and volume of sales was especially active after 1925 and was intensive from 1928 to 1929. Careful investors recognized the overpricing of stocks and began to sell to take their profits.

During October 1929, prices declined as more people began to sell their stock. **Black Thursday**, October 24, 1929, saw the trading of almost 13 million shares; this was a large number for that time, and prices fell precipitously. Investment banks tried to boost the market by buying, but on October 29, **Black Tuesday**, the market fell about 40 points, with 16.5 million shares traded.

Hoover's Depression Policies. The nation had elected **Herbert Hoover** (1874–1964) to the presidency in 1928. In June 1929, Congress passed the Agricultural Marketing Act, which created the Federal Farm Board. The board had a revolving fund of $500 million to lend agricultural cooperatives to buy commodities, such as wheat and cotton, and hold them for higher prices.

The Hawley-Smoot Tariff of June 1930 raised duties on both agricultural and manufactured imports. Chartered by Congress in 1932, the Reconstruction Finance Corporation lent money to railroads, banks, and other financial institutions. It prevented the failure of basic firms, on which many other elements of the economy depended, but many people criticized it as relief for the rich.

The Federal Home Loan Bank Act, passed in July 1932, created home loan banks, which made loans to building and loan associations, savings banks, and insurance companies. Its purpose was to help avoid foreclosures on homes.

The First New Deal. Franklin D. Roosevelt (1882–1945), governor of New York, easily defeated Hoover in the election of 1932. By the time of Roosevelt's inauguration on March 4, 1933, the American economic system seemed to be on the verge of collapse. In his inaugural address, Roosevelt assured the nation that "the only thing we have to fear is fear itself," called for a special session of Congress to convene on March 9, and asked for "broad executive powers to wage war against the emergency." Two days later, he closed all banks for a brief time and forbade the export of gold

or the redemption of currency in gold. A special session of Congress from March 9 to June 16, 1933 ("The Hundred Days") passed a great body of legislation that has left a lasting mark on the nation. Historians have divided Roosevelt's legislation into the First New Deal (1933–1935) and a new wave of programs beginning in 1935 called the Second New Deal.

Passed on March 9, the first day of the special session, the Emergency Banking Relief Act provided additional funds for banks from the Reconstruction Finance Corporation and the Federal Reserve, allowed the Treasury to open sound banks after 10 days and to merge or liquidate unsound ones, and forbade the hoarding or exporting of gold. Roosevelt, on March 12, assured the public of the soundness of the banks in the first of many **"fireside chats,"** or radio addresses. People believed him, and most banks were soon open, with deposits outnumbering withdrawals.

The Banking Act of 1933, or the Glass-Steagall Act, established the Federal Deposit Insurance Corporation to insure individual deposits in commercial banks and to separate commercial banking from the more speculative activity of investment banking. The Federal Emergency Relief Act appropriated $500 million for state and local governments to distribute to aid the poor. The act also established the Federal Emergency Relief Administration under **Harry Hopkins** (1890–1946).

The **Civilian Conservation Corps** enrolled 250,000 young men ages 18 to 24 from families on relief to go to camps where they worked on flood control, soil conservation, and forest projects under the direction of the War Department. The **Public Works Administration** had $3.3 billion to distribute to state and local governments for building projects such as schools, highways,

which established the National Recovery Administration (NRA); the goal was the self-regulation of business and the development of fair prices, wages, hours, and working conditions. Section 7-a of the NRA permitted collective bargaining for workers; laborers would test the federal support for their bargaining in the days to come. The slogan of the NRA was "We do our part." The economy improved but did not recover.

The Second New Deal. The **Works Progress Administration (WPA)** began in May 1935, following the passage of the Emergency Relief Appropriations Act of April 1935. The WPA employed people from the relief rolls for 30 hours of work a week at pay double that of the relief payment but less than private employment.

Created in May 1935, the **Rural Electrification Administration** provided loans and WPA labor to electric cooperatives so they could build lines into rural areas that the private companies did not serve. Passed in August of 1935, the **Social Security Act** established for persons over age 65 a retirement plan to be funded by a tax on wages paid equally by employee and employer. The government paid the first benefits, ranging from $10 to $85 per month in 1942. Another provision of the act forced states to initiate unemployment insurance programs.

Labor Unions. The 1935 passage of the National Labor Relations Act, or the **Wagner Act**, resulted in a massive growth of union membership but at the expense of bitter conflict within the labor movement. Primarily craft unions made up the **American Federation of Labor (AFL)**, formed in 1886. Some leaders wanted to unionize the mass-production industries, such as automobiles and rubber, with industrial unions.

In November 1935, **John L. Lewis** formed the Committee for Industrial Organization (CIO) to unionize basic industries, presumably within the AFL. **President William Green** of the AFL ordered the CIO to disband in January 1936. When the rebels refused, the AFL expelled them. The insurgents then reorganized the CIO as the independent Congress of Industrial Organizations. Labor strikes, particularly in the textile mills, marked the end of the 1930s. Soon the nation would receive another test.

World War II

The American Response to the War in Europe. In August 1939, Roosevelt created the War Resources Board to develop a plan for industrial mobilization in the event of war. The next month, he established the Office of Emergency Management in the White House to centralize mobilization activities.

Roosevelt officially proclaimed the neutrality of the United States on September 5, 1939. The Democratic Congress, in a vote that followed party lines, passed a new Neutrality Act in November. It allowed the cash-and-carry sale of arms and short-term loans to belligerents but forbade American ships to trade with belligerents or Americans to travel on belligerent ships.

Roosevelt determined that to aid Britain in every way possible was the best way to avoid war with Germany. In September 1940, he signed an agreement to give Britain 50 American destroyers in return for a 99-year lease on air and naval bases in British territories in Newfoundland, Bermuda, and the Caribbean.

The Road to Pearl Harbor. In late July 1941, the United States placed an embargo on the export of aviation gasoline, lubricants, and scrap iron and steel to Japan and granted an additional loan to China. In December, additional articles—iron ore and pig iron, some chemicals, machine tools, and other products—fell under the embargo.

In October 1941, a new military cabinet headed by **General Hideki Tojo** took control of Japan. The Japanese secretly decided to make a final effort to negotiate with the United States and to go to war if there was no solution by November 25. A new round of talks followed in Washington, but neither side would make a substantive change in its position. The Japanese gave final approval on December 1 for an attack on the United States.

The Japanese planned a major offensive to take the Dutch East Indies, Malaya, and the Philippines and to obtain the oil, metals, and other raw materials they needed. At the same time, they would attack Pearl Harbor in Hawaii to destroy the American Pacific fleet to keep it from interfering with their plans.

At 7:55 A.M. on Sunday, December 7, 1941, the first wave of Japanese carrier-based planes attacked the American fleet in **Pearl Harbor**. A second wave followed at 8:50 A.M. The United States suffered the loss of two battleships sunk, six damaged and out of action, three cruisers and three destroyers sunk or damaged, several lesser vessels destroyed or damaged, and the destruction of all the 150 aircraft on the ground at Pearl Harbor. Worst of all, 2,323 American servicemen were killed and about 1,100 were wounded. The Japanese lost 29 planes, five midget submarines, and one fleet submarine.

Declared War Begins. On December 8, 1941, Congress declared war on Japan, with one dissenting vote—Representative Jeanette Rankin of Montana. On December 11, Germany and Italy declared war on the United States. Great Britain and the United States then established the Combined Chiefs of Staff, headquartered in Washington, to direct Anglo-American military operations.

On January 1, 1942, representatives of 26 nations met in Washington, D.C., and signed the Declaration of the United Nations, pledged themselves to the principles of the Atlantic Charter, and promised not to make a separate peace with their common enemies.

The Home Front. In *Korematsu v. United States* (1944), the Supreme Court upheld sending the Issei (Japanese Americans from Japan) and Nisei (native-born Japanese Americans) to concentration camps. The camps did not close until March 1946. Roosevelt died on April 12, 1945, at Warm Springs, Georgia. **Harry S Truman** (1884–1972), formerly a senator from Missouri and vice president of the United States, became president on April 12, 1945. (Harry Truman did not have a middle name; he used only the letter *S*, which he did not follow with a period.)

The Atomic Bomb. The Army Corps of Engineers established the Manhattan Engineering District in August 1942 for the purpose of developing an atomic bomb; the program eventually took the name the **Manhattan Project**. Physicist **J. Robert Oppenheimer** directed the design and construction of a transportable atomic bomb at Los Alamos, New Mexico. On July 16,

1945, the Manhattan Project exploded the first atomic bomb at Alamogordo, New Mexico.

The *Enola Gay* dropped an atomic bomb on Hiroshima, Japan, on August 6, 1945, killing about 78,000 people and injuring 100,000. On August 9, the United States dropped a second bomb on Nagasaki, Japan. Japan surrendered on August 14, 1945, and signed the formal surrender on September 2.

The Postwar Era
The Cold War and Containment. In February 1947, Great Britain notified the United States that it could no longer aid the Greek government in its war against Communist insurgents. The next month, President Truman asked Congress for $400 million in military and economic aid for Greece and Turkey. In his **Truman Doctrine**, Truman argued that the United States must support free peoples who were resisting Communist domination.

Secretary of State George C. Marshall proposed in June 1947 that the United States provide economic aid to help rebuild Europe. The following March, Congress passed the European Recovery Program; popularly known as the **Marshall Plan**, the program provided more than $12 billion in aid.

Anticommunism. On February 9, 1950, Senator **Joseph R. McCarthy** of Wisconsin stated that he had a list of known Communists who were working in the State Department. He later expanded his attacks. After McCarthy made charges against the army, the Senate censured and discredited him in 1954.

Korean War. On June 25, 1950, North Korea invaded South Korea. President Truman committed U.S. forces to the United Nations (UN) auspices; **General Douglas MacArthur** would command the troops. By October, UN forces (mostly American) had driven north of the 38th parallel, which divided North and South Korea.

Chinese troops attacked MacArthur's forces on November 26, pushing them south of the 38th parallel, but by spring 1951, UN forces had recovered their offensive. The armistice of June 1953 left Korea divided

along virtually the same boundary that had existed before the war.

Eisenhower-Dulles Foreign Policy. Dwight D. Eisenhower (1890–1969), elected president in 1952, chose **John Foster Dulles** as secretary of state. Dulles talked of a more aggressive foreign policy, calling for "massive retaliation" and "liberation" rather than containment. He wished to emphasize nuclear deterrents rather than conventional armed forces.

After several years of nationalist war against French occupation, in July 1954 France, Great Britain, the Soviet Union, and China signed the Geneva Accords, which divided Vietnam along the 17th parallel. The North would be under the leadership of **Ho Chi Minh** and the South under **Emperor Bao Dai**. The purpose of the scheduled elections was to unify the country, but **Ngo Dinh Diem** overthrew Bao Dai and prevented the elections from taking place. The United States supplied economic aid to **South Vietnam**.

In January 1959, **Fidel Castro** overthrew the dictator of Cuba. Castro criticized the United States, moved closer to the Soviet Union, and signed a trade agreement with the Soviets in February 1960. The United States prohibited the importation of Cuban sugar in October 1960 and broke off diplomatic relations in January 1961.

Space Exploration.   The launching of the Soviet space satellite *Sputnik* on October 4, 1957, created fear that America was falling behind technologically. Although the United States launched *Explorer I* on January 31, 1958, the concern continued. In 1958, Congress established the **National Aeronautics and Space Administration** to coordinate research and development and passed the National Defense Education Act to provide grants and loans for education.

Civil Rights.   Eisenhower completed the formal integration of the armed forces; desegregated public services in Washington, D.C., naval yards, and veterans' hospitals; and appointed a civil rights commission. In *Brown v. Board of Education of Topeka* (1954), **Thurgood Marshall**, lawyer for the National Association for the Advancement of Colored People, challenged the doctrine of "separate but equal" (*Plessy v. Ferguson*, 1896). The Court declared that separate educational facilities were inherently unequal. In 1955, the Court ordered states to integrate "with all deliberate speed."

On December 11, 1955, in Montgomery, Alabama, **Rosa Parks** refused to give up her seat on a city bus to a white man and faced arrest. Under the leadership of **Martin Luther King Jr.** (1929–1968), an African American pastor, African Americans of Montgomery organized a bus boycott that lasted for a year until, in December 1956, the Supreme Court refused to review a lower-court ruling that stated that separate but equal was no longer legal.

In February 1960, a segregated lunch counter in Greensboro, North Carolina, denied four African American students service; the students staged a sit-in. This inspired sit-ins elsewhere in the South and led to the formation of the Student Nonviolent Coordinating Committee, which had a chief aim of ending segregation in public accommodations.

The New Frontier, Vietnam, and Social Upheaval

Kennedy's "New Frontier."   Democratic Senator **John F. Kennedy** (1917–1963) won the presidential election of 1960. The Justice Department, under Attorney General **Robert F. Kennedy**, began to push for civil rights, including desegregation of interstate transportation in the South, integration of schools, and supervision of elections. President Kennedy presented a comprehensive civil rights bill to Congress in 1963. With the bill held up in Congress, 200,000 people marched and demonstrated on its behalf, and Martin Luther King Jr. gave his "I Have a Dream" speech.

Cuban Missile Crisis.   Under Eisenhower, the **Central Intelligence Agency** had begun training some 2,000 men to invade Cuba and to overthrow Fidel Castro. On April 19, 1961, this force invaded at the **Bay of Pigs**; opposing forces pinned them down, demanded their surrender, and captured some 1,200 men.

On October 14, 1962, a U-2 reconnaissance plane brought photographic evidence of the construction of missile sites in Cuba. Kennedy, on October 22, announced a blockade of Cuba and called on the Soviet premier, **Nikita Khrushchev** (1894–1971), to dismantle the missile bases and remove all weapons capable of attacking the United States from Cuba. Six days later,

Khrushchev backed down and withdrew the missiles. Kennedy lifted the blockade.

Johnson and the Great Society. On November 22, 1963, **Lee Harvey Oswald** assassinated President Kennedy in Dallas, Texas; **Jack Ruby** killed Oswald two days later. Debate still continues as to whether the assassination was a conspiracy. **Lyndon B. Johnson** (1908–1973) succeeded John Kennedy as president of the United States.

The **1964 Civil Rights Act** outlawed racial discrimination by employers and unions, created the Equal Employment Opportunity Commission to enforce the law, and eliminated the remaining restrictions on black voting.

In 1959 the poverty rate in the United States was 22.4 percent. Michael Harrington, author of *The Other America: Poverty in the United States* (1962), frequently referred to the 20 to 25 percent of American families living below the governmentally defined poverty line as "the invisible poor." The book was a best-seller, and even presidents John F. Kennedy and Lyndon B. Johnson used that phrase.

The Economic Opportunity Act of 1964 sought to address the problem by establishing a job corps, community action programs, educational programs, work-study programs, job training, loans for small businesses and farmers, and a "domestic peace corps" called Volunteers in Service to America. The Office of Economic Opportunity administered many of these programs. By 1969 the country's proportion of "invisible poor" had dropped to 12.1 percent.

Emergence of Black Power. In 1965, Martin Luther King Jr. announced a voter registration drive. With help from the federal courts, he dramatized his effort by leading a march from Selma, Alabama, to Montgomery, Alabama, between March 21 and 25. The Voting Rights Act of 1965 authorized the attorney general to appoint officials to register voters.

Seventy percent of African Americans lived in city ghettos. In 1966, New York and Chicago experienced riots, and the following year riots broke out in Newark and Detroit. The Kerner Commission, appointed to investigate the riots, concluded that the focus of the riots was a social system that prevented African Americans from getting good jobs and crowded them into ghettos.

On April 4, 1968, **James Earl Ray** assassinated Martin Luther King Jr. in Memphis, Tennessee. Ray was an escaped convict; he pled guilty to the murder and received a sentence of 99 years in prison. Riots in more than 100 cities followed.

Vietnam. After the defeat of the French in Vietnam in 1954, the United States sent military advisers to South Vietnam to aid the government of **Ngo Dinh Diem**. Gradually, the pro-Communist Vietcong forces grew in strength, because Diem failed to follow through on promised reforms and because of the support from North Vietnam, the Soviet Union, and China.

"Hawks" in the Congress defended President Johnson's policy and, drawing on the containment theory, said that the nation had the responsibility to resist aggression. The claim was if Vietnam should fall, all Southeast Asia would eventually go. Antiwar demonstrations were attracting large crowds by 1967. "Doves" argued that the war was a civil war in which the United States should not meddle.

On January 31, 1968, the first day of the Vietnamese new year (Tet), the Vietcong attacked numerous cities and towns, American bases, and even Saigon, the South Vietnamese capital. Although they suffered large losses, the Vietcong won a psychological victory as American opinion began turning against the war.

The Nixon Conservative Reaction. Republican **Richard M. Nixon** (1913–1994), emphasizing stability and order, defeated Democratic nominee Hubert Humphrey by a margin of one percentage point. The Nixon administration sought to block renewal of the Voting Rights Act and delay implementation of court-ordered school desegregation in Mississippi. In 1969, Nixon appointed **Warren E. Burger**, a conservative, as chief justice. Although more conservative than the previous court (of Earl Warren, appointed by Eisenhower), the Burger court did declare in 1972 that the death penalty in use at the time was unconstitutional; it also struck down state antiabortion legislation in 1973.

The president turned to "Vietnamization," the effort to build up South Vietnamese forces while with-

drawing American troops. In 1969, Nixon reduced American troop strength by 60,000 but at the same time ordered the bombing of Cambodia, a neutral country. In the summer of 1972, negotiations between the United States and North Vietnam began in Paris. A few days before the 1972 presidential election, **Henry Kissinger**, the president's national security adviser, announced that "peace was at hand."

Nixon resumed the bombing of North Vietnam in December 1972; he claimed that the North Vietnamese were not bargaining in good faith. In January 1973, the two sides reached a settlement in which the North Vietnamese retained control over large areas of the south and agreed to release American prisoners of war within 60 days. Nearly 60,000 Americans had been killed and 300,000 wounded, and the war had cost American taxpayers $109 billion. On March 29, 1973, the last American combat troops left South Vietnam. The North Vietnamese forces continued to push back the South Vietnamese, and in April 1975, Saigon fell to the North.

Watergate, Carter, and the New Conservatism
Watergate. The Republicans renominated Nixon, who won a landslide victory over the Democratic nominee, Senator **George McGovern**. What later became known as the Watergate crisis began during the 1972 presidential campaign. Early on the morning of June 17, a security officer for the Committee for the Reelection of the President, along with four other men, broke into Democratic headquarters at the Watergate apartment complex in Washington, D.C. The authorities caught the men going through files and installing electronic eavesdropping devices.

In March 1974, a grand jury indicted some of Nixon's top aides and named Nixon an unindicted co-conspirator. Meanwhile, the House Judiciary Committee televised its debate over impeachment. The committee charged the president with obstructing justice, misusing presidential power, and failing to obey the committee's subpoenas. Before the House began to debate impeachment, Nixon announced his resignation on August 8, 1974, to take effect at noon the following day.

Gerald Ford (born in 1913) then became president. Ford was in many respects the opposite of Nixon.

Although a partisan Republican, he was well liked and was free of any hint of scandal. Ford encountered controversy almost immediately when in September 1974 he offered to pardon Nixon. Nixon accepted the offer, although he admitted no wrongdoing and had not yet received any charges of crime.

Carter's Moderate Liberalism. In 1976, the Democrats nominated **James Earl Carter** (born in 1924), formerly governor of Georgia, who ran on the basis of his integrity and lack of Washington connections. Carter narrowly defeated Ford in the election.

Carter offered amnesty to Americans who had fled the draft and gone to other countries during the Vietnam War. He established the departments of Energy and Education and placed the civil service on a merit basis. He created a "superfund" for cleanup of chemical waste dumps, established controls over strip-mining, and protected 100 million acres of Alaskan wilderness from development.

Carter's Foreign Policy. Carter negotiated a controversial treaty with Panama, affirmed by the Senate in 1978, that provided for the transfer of ownership of the canal to Panama in 1999 and guaranteed its neutrality. In 1978, Carter negotiated the Camp David Accords between Israel and Egypt. Israel promised to return occupied land in the Sinai to Egypt in exchange for Egyptian recognition, a process completed in 1982. An agreement to negotiate the Palestinian refugee problem proved ineffective.

The Iranian Crisis. In 1978, a revolution forced the **shah of Iran** to flee the country and replaced him with a religious leader, **Ayatollah Ruhollah Khomeini** (circa 1900–1989). Because the United States had supported the shah with arms and money, the revolutionaries were strongly anti-American, calling the United States the "Great Satan."

After Carter allowed the exiled shah to come to the United States for medical treatment in October 1979, some 400 Iranians broke into the American embassy in Teheran on November 4 and took the occupants captive. They demanded the return of the shah to Iran for trial, the confiscation of his wealth, and the presentation of his wealth to Iran. Carter rejected these demands; in-

stead, he froze Iranian assets in the United States and established a trade embargo against Iran. After extensive negotiations with Iran, in which Algeria acted as an intermediary, the Iranians freed the American hostages on January 20, 1981.

Attacking Big Government. Republican **Ronald Reagan** (1911–2004) defeated Carter by a large electoral majority in 1980. Reagan placed priority on cutting taxes. He based his approach on "supply-side" economics, the idea that if government left more money in the hands of the people, they would invest, rather then spend the excess on consumer goods. The results would be greater production, more jobs, and greater prosperity, resulting in more income for the government despite lower tax rates. However, the federal budget deficit ballooned from $59 billion in 1980 to $195 billion by 1983. Reagan ended ongoing antitrust suits against IBM and AT&T and fulfilled his promise to reduce government interference with business.

Iran-Contra. In 1985 and 1986, several Reagan officials sold arms to the Iranians in hopes of encouraging them to use their influence in obtaining the release of American hostages being held in Lebanon. Profits from these sales went to the Nicaraguan contras—a militant group opposed to the left-leaning elected government—thus circumventing congressional restrictions on funding the contras. The attorney general appointed a special prosecutor, and Congress held hearings on the affair in May 1987.

The Election of 1988. Vice President George H. W. Bush (born in 1924) won the Republican nomination. Bush defeated Democrat **Michael Dukakis**, but the Republicans were unable to make any inroads in Congress.

Operation Just Cause. Since coming to office, the Bush administration had been concerned that Panamanian dictator **Manuel Noriega** was providing an important link in the drug traffic between South America and the United States. After economic sanctions, diplomatic efforts, and an October 1989 coup failed to oust Noriega, Bush ordered 12,000 troops into Panama on December 20 for what became known as **Operation Just Cause**.

On January 3, 1990, Noriega surrendered to the Americans and faced drug-trafficking charges in the United State. Found guilty in 1992, his sentence was 40 years.

Persian Gulf Crisis. On August 2, 1990, Iraq invaded Kuwait, an act that Bush denounced as "naked aggression." The United States quickly banned most trade with Iraq, froze Iraq's and Kuwait's assets in the United States, and sent aircraft carriers to the Persian Gulf. On August 6, after the UN Security Council condemned the invasion, Bush ordered the deployment of air, sea, and land forces to Saudi Arabia and dubbed the operation Desert Shield.

On February 23, the allied air assault began. Four days later, Bush announced the liberation of Kuwait, and ordered offensive operations to cease. The UN established the terms for the cease-fire, which Iraq accepted on April 6.

The Road to the Twenty-First Century
The Election of 1992. William Jefferson Clinton (born in 1946) won 43 percent of the popular vote and 370 electoral votes; President Bush won 37 percent of the popular vote and 168 electoral votes. Although he won no electoral votes, the Independent Party candidate Ross Perot (born in 1930) gained 19 percent of the popular vote.

Domestic Affairs. The **North American Free Trade Agreement (NAFTA)**, negotiated by the Bush administration, eliminated most tariffs and other trade barriers between the United States, Canada, and Mexico. Passed by Congress and signed by Clinton in 1993, NAFTA became law in January 1994.

In October 1993, the Clinton administration proposed legislation to reform the health care system, which included universal coverage with a guaranteed benefits package, managed competition through health care alliances that would bargain with insurance companies, and employer mandates to provide health insurance for employees. With most Republicans and small business, insurance, and medical business interests opposed to the legislation, the Democrats dropped their attempt at a compromise package in September 1994.

Impeachment and Acquittal. Clinton received criticism for alleged wrongdoing in connection with a

real estate development called Whitewater. While governor of Arkansas, Clinton had invested in Whitewater, along with **James B. and Susan McDougal**, owners of a failed savings and loan institution. After Congress renewed the independent counsel law, a three-judge panel appointed **Kenneth W. Starr** to the new role of independent prosecutor.

The Starr investigation yielded massive findings in late 1998, roughly midway into Clinton's second term, including information on an adulterous affair that Clinton was said to have had with Monica Lewinsky while she was an intern at the White House. It was on charges stemming from this report that the House of Representatives impeached Clinton in December 1998 for perjury and obstruction of justice. The Senate acquitted him of all charges in February 1999.

Continuing Crisis in the Balkans.   During Clinton's second term, ongoing political unrest abroad and civil war in the Balkans continued to be a major foreign policy challenge. In 1999, the Serbian government attacked ethnic Albanians in Kosovo, a province of Serbia. In response, North Atlantic Treaty Organization (NATO) forces, led by the United States, bombed Serbia. Several weeks of bombing forced Serbian forces to withdraw from Kosovo.

The Election of 2000.   Preelection polls indicated that the election would be close, and few ventured to predict the outcome. Indeed, the election outcome was much in doubt for several weeks after the election. Though Clinton's vice president, **Al Gore** (born in 1948), won the popular vote, the Electoral College was very close, and Florida (the state governed by George W. Bush's brother) was pivotal in deciding the election.

George W. Bush (born in 1946), son of former President George H. W. Bush, appeared to win Florida by a very small margin; a recount began. Then controversy over how to conduct the recount led to a series of court challenges, with the matter ultimately decided by the U.S. Supreme Court, which ruled in favor of Bush. George W. Bush thus became the 43rd president of the United States.

Terrorism Hits Home.   The new president would soon face the grim task of dealing with a massive ter-

rorist attack on major symbols of U.S. economic and military might. On the morning of September 11, 2001, hijackers deliberately crashed two U.S. commercial jetliners into the World Trade Center in New York City; the impact toppled the 110-story twin towers. A third hijacked plane crashed into the Pentagon, just outside Washington, D.C. A fourth airliner (hijacked the same day) crashed in a field outside Shanksville, Pennsylvania, when passengers attempted to retake it. More than 2,900 died in these deadliest acts of terrorism in American history.

The United States had earlier seen terrorism on its home soil; the 1993 bombing of the World Trade Center seemed the work of Islamic militants. A member of the American militia movement was responsible in the bombing of the Oklahoma City federal building in 1995. Alhough the person behind the 9/11 attacks was not immediately known, President Bush cast prime suspicion on the Saudi exile Osama bin Laden, the alleged mastermind of the bombings of two U.S. embassies in 1998 and of a U.S. naval destroyer in 2000.

Afghanistan, Osama bin Laden, and the United States.   On October 7, 2001, the United States and British forces began air strikes against Afghanistan; these strikes came after the Taliban refused to hand over Osama bin Laden, whom the Bush administration blamed for the September 11 attacks against the United States. The October 7 air strikes were not the first attempts that the United States had made to obtain Osama bin Laden. In 1998 the United States had fired missiles at suspected bases of al-Qaida leader Osama bin Laden. The United Nations had imposed sanctions on Afghanistan to try to obtain Osama bin Laden from the Taliban.

Like the other attempts, the October 2001 air strikes were not successful in obtaining Osama bin Laden. On December 7, 2001, bin Laden and Taliban leader Mullah Mohammed Omar escaped after Kandahar (the Taliban stronghold) fell. The hunt for Osama bin Laden continued in 2006.

Hamid Karzai took the oath of office (December 2002) as head of an interim government of Afghanistan. In June of 2002 Karzai received election to head

the state. August 2003 marked the deployment of troops to Kabul for peacekeeping; during the next year the force expanded to Afghanistan areas in addition to Kabul and numbered over 9,000. In October 2004 Afghanistan held its first presidential election. Karzai won the election and named three women as ministers in his cabinet.

As of 2006, Afghanistan had the support of many members of the international community; Operation Enduring Freedom and the International security Assistance Force led by NATO are helping to secure Afghanistan's borders to promote internal order. Coalition forces work closely with the government to seek out remaining forces of al-Qaida and the Taliban.

Iraq and the United States in the Period After September 11, 2001.   After the end of the 1991 Gulf War, periodic newspaper articles and "witnesses" suggested that Iraq (led by Saddam Hussein) was in violation of the agreements that limited armaments in Iraq. After the terrorist attacks on September 11, 2001, President George Bush and his administration indicated (based on intelligence reports) that Saddam Hussein and Iraq were almost certainly in possession of weapons of mass destruction; they insisted that the occupation of Iraq was an important part of the Global War on Terrorism. The United States and the United Kingdom invaded Iraq in March 2003; they had the support of military aid from other nations. A preponderance of weapons of mass destruction was not evident. The coalition is still in Iraq. Warfare between the insurgency and the coalition continues, as does violence between the Sunni and the Shia populations in Iraq.

Both criticism of and support for (1) the reasons for the invasion and (2) the handling of the continuing conflict remain. The outcome of sending troops to Iraq is as yet undetermined as this book goes to press.

▶ References

Alvarez, Lizette. 2001. Census director marvels at the new portrait of America. *New York Times*. January 1.

AZGuide.com. "Arizona's travel network." *www. azguide.com/travelpagetext.htm*.

Cayne, Bernard S., ed. 1969. *Merit students encyclopedia*. Chicago: Crowell-Collier.

"Congress for Kids." *http://congressforkids.net/ Constitution_amendments.htm*.

Davis, Anita Price. 2003. *North Carolina during the Great Depression: A documentary portrait of a decade*. Jefferson, NC: McFarland.

Harrington, Michael. 1962. *The other America: Poverty in the United States*. New York: Macmillan.

Huitt, W. 1998. Critical thinking: An overview. *Educational psychology interactive*. Valdosta, GA: Valdosta State University. *http://chiron.valdosta.edu*.

Martin, Philip L. 2002. Immigration in the United States. *www.cis.org/articles/2005/back1405.html*.

Research Center of the Church of the Nazarene. "Native American Population Density, U. S. Census 2000." *www.nazarene.org*.

Schieffer, Bob. 2005 (September 4). Government failed the people. *CBS news. www.cbsnews.com/stories/ 2005/09/06/opinion/schieffer/main818486.html*.

Schug, Mark C., and R. Beery. 1987. *Teaching social studies in the elementary school*. Prospect Heights, IL: Waveland Press.

Schuncke, George M. 1988. *Elementary social studies: Knowing, doing, caring*. New York: Macmillan.

Woolever, Roberta, and Kathryn P. Scott. 1988. *Active learning in social studies: promoting cognitive and social growth*. Glenview, IL: Scott, Foresman and Company.

The Arts

6

▶ **Objective 0035:**
Understand Basic Principles and Skills Related to Music

Recognizing Common Musical Terms and Concepts

Music is the arrangement of sounds for voice and musical instruments and, like dance and visual art, requires training and repetitive practice. For most of history, music has been an outgrowth of a community's or an ethnic group's need to celebrate. It has often been linked to storytelling or poetry. In Europe, a system of musical notation developed during the Middle Ages, and the use of notation (written symbolic indications of pitch and duration of tones) is a convenient way to distinguish "art" (or classical, or complexly composed) music from folk and ethnic music.

Music notation is a way of writing music. Teaching students to use, read, and interpret music notation will heighten their enjoyment of music. Students can begin with **simple music notation**. For example, students might try listening to a simple melody and making dashes on the board or on their papers to indicate the length the notes are held. As they sing "Three Blind Mice," for instance, they would mark dashes of similar length for the words/notes *three* and *blind*.

With **traditional music notation**, the students use the lines and spaces on the staff. They observe that the staff has four spaces and five lines, for instance. They also notice that the appearance of the notes indicates their length and the placement of the notes on the staff indicates their various tones.

Nontraditional music notation is something that many students in the upper grades may have noticed in their books. In the South, for example, many of the hymnals use a nontraditional type of music notation called shape notes. Instead of the elliptical note head in the traditional notation, the heads of the notes are in various shapes to show the position of the notes on the major scale. Another nontraditional music notation is Braille notation.

Music has several elements:

Rhythm. The contrast among the various lengths of musical tones. For instance, in "The Star-Spangled Banner," the rhythm is short, short, medium, medium, medium, long.

Harmony. The sounding of more than one tone at a time, or the vertical aspect of the groups of notes. The sheet music uses simultaneous combinations of musical tones to indicate harmony.

Melody. The succession of the notes or, in other words, the horizontal aspect of the notes. Some-

times the teacher may refer to the melody as the *tune*.

Form. The structure of the song, or the way that it is put together. Sometimes, a refrain is repeated; sometimes, a chorus is used after each verse.

Texture. The context in which simultaneous sounds occur. The sounds can be chords (harmony) or even counterpoint (concurrent melodies of equal importance).

Dynamics. Refers to the volume or the loudness of the sound or the note. The two basic dynamic indications are *p* (for *piano*, meaning softly or quietly) and *f* (for *forte*, meaning loudly or strong).

Tone or timbre. The musical sound of the instrument or voice; it may describe the quality of the musical sound. For instance, one might say that someone sings with a "nasal tone," a "thin tone," or a "full tone."

All the above elements work together to express a text, ideas, certain emotions, settings, time, and place through music.

The materials used for a quality music program in any grade should reflect various musical periods and styles, cultural and ethnic diversity, and a gender balance. The goal of a quality music program is to make students aware that music is both a part of and a reflection of many cultures and many ethnic groups. The teacher should provide and encourage students to sing, play, and listen to music of many cultural and ethnic groups.

The teacher should include diverse **styles** (basic musical languages) and **genres** (categories). Dividing music into categories is difficult. Styles are constantly emerging. Many songs include multiple genres. Nevertheless, the main groupings are classical, gospel, jazz, Latin American, blues, rhythm and blues, rock, country, electronic, electronic dance, electronica, melodic music, hip-hop, rap, punk, reggae, contemporary African music, and dub.

Identifying Types and Characteristics of Musical Instruments

Traditional instruments have been indigenous variations on drums, horns, pipes (such as flutes), and hol-

low boxes fitted with vibrating strings (such as lyres or lutes). Since the seventeenth century, orchestral instruments of the West have multiplied to include pianos, saxophones, clarinets, cellos, and, in our own era, electronic synthesizers.

The instruments that the classroom teacher normally teaches include the **rhythmic instruments** (for example, triangle, tambourine, blocks, and sticks), **melodic instruments** (for example, melody bells and simple flutes), and **harmonic instruments** (for example, chording instruments, like the autoharp).

Rhythmic Instruments

After the students have had a chance to move with the music in the manner that the music suggests, and after singing games and action songs, they may be ready to try rhythmic instruments. The students will need opportunities to experiment with triangles, tambourines, sticks, and blocks, among others, to experience the sounds they make; students might try striking the tambourine with the hand to get one sound and with the knee to get another, for instance. After this experimentation, the teacher and class will be ready to try something new.

If the teacher decides on the instruments the class will use, who will use them, and when, music instruction becomes a teacher-directed activity that can stifle the children's creativity. Allowing the students to make decisions about what and when to play is a more engaging technique than the teacher-directed approach. For example, the teacher might write out a piece of music on a large sheet of paper and allow the students to draw pictures where they should play their instruments. Another student-directed approach to music instruction is having students first listen to a piece of music and then allowing them to decide on the instruments they want to play and when it seems right to play them. This more creative approach is appropriate for young children who cannot read music or even for music readers who want to produce their own performance techniques. Upper-grade students can even try making their own instruments.

Melodic Instruments

Melodic bells are melodic instruments that the child strikes with a mallet. The child may use the bells before the flutes. The simple flutes include the trade

names of Flutophone, Song Flute, and Tonette. Teachers usually include these melodic instruments with the music instruction at about the fifth grade. For most of these instruments, the student supports the flute by using the right thumb and plays the notes by covering the various holes with the fingers. The use of the fingers to help attain the sounds varies from one instrument to the other. The melodic instruments are helpful to use as the children are learning to read music.

Harmonic Instruments

The wooden base of an autoharp (which is approximately rectangular in shape) has wire strings stretched across it. The child can press the wooden bars attached at right angles; when the child presses the bars and strums the wires, the instrument produces chords. Students can experiment with harmony by using the autoharp. They will find that sometimes a variety of choices of chords "sound right" but that at other times only one choice works.

The study of simple instruments differs from the study of orchestral instruments. The child does not usually begin the study of orchestral instruments until the fourth or fifth grade; a music teacher—not the classroom teacher—gives instruction in orchestral instruments.

Evaluating Activities Intended to Foster Skills in Participating in, Listening to, and Responding to Music

Making music is a basic experience. Mothers sing to their babies. Children beat sticks together, make drums, and sing during their play. Adults whistle or sing along with tunes on the radio. Sound and music naturally draw people; music is an important part of culture, religious practice, and personal experience for all people. Some people become professional musicians, whereas others whistle, sing, or play for their own enjoyment and nothing more. Only a very small segment of society does not make music. These people would likely choose to make music if they could but are unable as a result of a physical impairment or personal choice (for example, a vow of silence). Music making is a natural part of human experience.

It is important that students have the opportunity to experience as many ways as possible to make music.

It is through the acquisition of basic skills in singing and playing instruments that people grow in their ability to express themselves through music. As students develop skills, they are also exposed to basic musical concepts such as melody, harmony, rhythm, pitch, and timbre. With experience, students come to make decisions about what is acceptable or not acceptable within a given cultural or historical context and thereby develop their own aesthetic awareness.

Any work to encourage the thinking skills of children can help develop the analytical skills needed to evaluate musical performance. The thinking skills, according to Benjamin Bloom's Taxonomy, proceed from knowledge, comprehension, application, analysis, and synthesis to evaluation. The skill of **analysis** requires looking at the parts that make up the whole.

For example, a teacher might ask young children, after they played "Here We Go 'Round the Mulberry Bush," some questions requiring them to perform some very basic analysis of the music. A simple question might be "Do you think this song would be good to march to on the playground?" Upper-elementary students might listen to *Peter and the Wolf*, by Sergei Prokofiev, and try to identify the instruments in the recording. The students might talk about why the composer used certain instruments for a character, suggest other instrument sounds for the characters, and give their justifications for the new instrument. Because these activities involve analysis, they help develop the upper-level thinking skills needed to evaluate musical performance.

The overall goals of music education include the following:

- Encouraging responsiveness to music
- Increasing involvement in music
- Aiding in music discrimination
- Promoting understanding of music and music structure
- Increasing listening awareness
- Developing sensitivity to the expressive qualities of music

Table 6-1 describes the elements of an elementary school music curriculum.

Table 6-1. Music Strategies, Materials, Skills, Techniques, Creativity, and Communication

Grades	Strategies	Materials	Skills	Techniques	Creativity	Communication
Kindergarten–2	Provide exposure to a wide variety of sounds: recorded music, sheet music, live performances. Experiment with ways to change sounds. Use simple instruments in the classroom.	Simple instruments. Compact discs (CDs), tapes, records. Written programs from musical events.	Classify sounds as high and low; use body to show high and low. Play simple rhythm instruments.	Play simple rhythm instruments. Sing, especially rote songs. Move in time with the music.	Walk, run, jump to music. Create simple songs.	Create symbols to notate sounds of music. Use musical terms and concepts to express thoughts about music.
3–5	Provide experiences with music of many periods and many cultures. Experiment with ways to change sounds. Use simple instruments in the classroom. Move to music.	Simple instruments. CDs, tapes, records. Written programs.	Sing rounds. Sing by rote songs in two-part harmony. Conduct simple songs. Move to music. Distinguish between classical and popular music.	Play music. Dance to music. Conduct duple and triple meter.	Encourage students to express themselves through music. Encourage students to create sounds. Encourage students to improvise.	Sing and play instruments from written notation. Create notation system. Hear, read, and learn about careers in music. Notate a simple phrase. Create a simple phrase. Practice basic etiquette for performing and as audience. Read music notation. Express ideas about origin, culture, and so forth, of music listened to in class.
6–8	Provide occasions to listen to music of many cultures and many periods. Encourage students to respond to music and create their own music. Provide opportunities for students to communicate with notation. Use a range of instruments and types of music.	Simple instruments. CDs, tapes, records. Musical programs. Autoharp and/or guitar.	Sing rounds. Sing three-part songs by rote. Conduct simple songs. Move to music. Identify major and minor scales. Dance.	Play simple accompaniment on autoharp, guitar, and so forth. Read some music. Use correct terminology. Perform dance steps.	Create simple songs. Create an accompaniment. Create a dance.	Write notation for original song. Write own idea of notation for song heard. Read notation.

Although students can experience music and find it satisfying, challenging, or beautiful without prior knowledge of a piece or an understanding of its form, cultural significance, and so forth, those things can enrich the experience. People respond to music naturally. They do not need prompting or help to respond. However, to share their thoughts and feelings about music, students must learn how to put their responses into musical terminology. Some people call music a language, but it does not function as a spoken language. It does not provide specific information, instructions, or reactions.

Rather, music sparks thoughts, feelings, and emotions. To put their experiences into words, musicians and artists have developed vocabularies and approaches to discussing music and art. This does not mean there is only one way to respond to or talk about music or art. However, students will find it easier to understand music and musicians, art and artists if they understand and can use the kind of vocabulary and approaches that musicians or artists use to discuss their work. This includes terms as basic as *melody* and *harmony* and as profound as *the aesthetic experience.*

People cannot express themselves or effectively communicate if they do not understand the structures and rules that underlie the "language" that they are trying to use. Although music does not provide the kind of specific communication that spoken language does, it has structures. When students are able to think about and discuss music, they gain a deeper understanding of the music and can better express their responses to it.

The aesthetic experience is what draws people to music. The experience is one that most people have had but one that some people cannot describe. In fact, words seem clumsy when it comes to describing something that can be so profound and wonderful.

The type of music, the period, or the performer does not necessarily limit the aesthetic experience. It is just as possible to have an aesthetic experience when listening to a child sing a simple melody as it is when listening to a professional orchestra performing a symphony by Beethoven. The important thing is to share that aesthetic experience. It is part of what makes music and art special.

Teachers can use a variety of methods to encourage exploration of and growth through aesthetic responsiveness. A common experience is a crucial starting point. After students listen attentively to several pieces of music, the teacher might ask them to describe how each piece made them feel. It is often best for students to write their responses down before starting a discussion. Then the teacher might ask them to explain why each piece of music made them feel the way they indicated. Young students will likely provide simple, straightforward emotional responses to music (for example, "It made me feel happy!"). Older students should explore why the music affected them the way it did and use both musical concepts (for example, "It made me feel happy because it was in a major key") and nonmusical associations (for example, "It made me feel happy because it sounded like a circus, and I like to go to the circus"). Through this kind of sharing, along with teacher insights and readings about how other people have responded to music, students can explore and come to a deeper understanding of their personal responses to music, other art forms, and possibly the world. In addition, it should provide them with practical ways to express their responses or reactions to what they experience in life.

In addition to having aesthetic experiences, recognizing their value, and being able to grapple with discussing or sharing those experiences, teachers and students must attempt to foster an appreciation for the arts and their ability to create meaning. The arts provide an opportunity to explore and express ideas and emotions through a unique view of life experiences. It is through the experience of music, or any art form, that people begin to transcend the mundane day-to-day experience and reach beyond to a richer life experience.

When preparing for this part of the exam, remember that the primary objectives of music education are teaching the contexts of music, the concepts and skills involved in experiencing music, and the aesthetic and personal dimensions of music. These constitute a broad overview of the field of music and the musical experience.

▶ Objective 0036:
Understand Basic Principles and Skills Related to Creating, Viewing, and Responding to Works of Visual Art

Recognizing the Basic Terms and Concepts of Visual Art

Ideas, meanings, and human emotions are varied and numerous. To respond to these many stimulations, students must have knowledge of and be able to use many of the elements of art (the things that make up a painting, drawing, or design) and the basic principles of design (what one does with the elements of design). The basic principles follow:

Line. Linear mark from a pen or brush the edge created where two shapes meet.

Color. Hue. There are three primary colors (red, yellow, blue) and three secondary colors (green, orange, violet); tertiary colors are those that fall between primary and secondary colors, and compound colors are those containing a mixture of the three primary colors. Complementary colors are those that lie opposite each other on the color wheel, and saturated colors are those that lie around the outside of the color wheel.

Shape. A self-contained, defined area of a form (geometric or organic). A positive shape in a painting (for instance, a yellow ball) automatically results in a negative shape (the background around the ball).

Form. A total structure; a synthesis of all the visible aspects of a structure or design; all the elements of a work of art independent of their meaning.

Texture. The surface quality of a shape. Quality types include rough, smooth, soft, hard, and glossy. Texture can be physical (felt with the hand; for example, a buildup of paint, layering, and so on) or visual (giving the illusion of texture; for example, the paint gives the impression of texture, but the surface remains smooth and flat).

Balance. A way of creating visual weight. Balance may be symmetrical, asymmetrical, or radial. Symmetrical (formal) balance indicates that both sides of an imaginary line are the same. Asymmetrical (informal) balance indicates that each side of an imaginary line is different and yet both sides are equal. Radial balance indicates that lines or shapes grow from a center point, like spokes on a wheel.

Movement. A way of combining elements of art to produce the appearance of action; a representation of or suggestion of motion; implied motion.

Identifying Types and Characteristics of Visual Arts Materials, Techniques, and Processes

Throughout the lower elementary grades, students should engage in drawing, painting, designing, constructing, making crafts, sculpting, weaving, finger painting, and Styrofoam carving. In grades 3 through 5, students should continue to work with drawing, painting, designing, constructing, making crafts, and sculpting and should start new techniques, such as printmaking, sponge painting, graphics, film animation, and environmental design. In the upper elementary grades, students should continue with the earlier activities and add jewelry making and intaglio, a special printmaking technique.

Both large and small motor skills are involved in art activities. For example, students would likely use large motor skills in painting a mural on a cement-block fence but small motor skills in painting a tiny clay figure.

Art materials for the elementary art program include scissors, wet and dry brushes, fabrics, wrapping papers, film, computers, clay, glue, Styrofoam, construction paper, crayons, beads, and much more (South Carolina Visual and Performing Arts Curriculum Framework Writing Team 1993).

The overall goals of art education include the following:

- Developing aesthetic perception
- Providing opportunities to examine many art forms of both natural and human in form
- Providing opportunities to reflect on and discuss observations and reactions
- Providing opportunities to develop and extend the students' own art abilities
- Providing opportunities to identify symbols and characteristics of art, objects of art, and natural art forms
- Increasing awareness of tactile art
- Fostering the ability to select and enjoy arts (natural and human made)
- Promoting the ability to analyze and enjoy forms bases on informed judgments

Evaluating Activities Intended to Foster Skills in Creating, Viewing, and Responding to Works of Visual Art

Students should be able to describe a work of art using terms such as *line*, *color*, *value*, *shape*, *balance*, *texture*, *repetition*, and *rhythm*. Students should be able to discuss some of the major periods in the history of the visual arts. It is important that students be able to confront a work and judge its aesthetic merits, regardless of their ability to recognize it from memory. Analytical questions a teacher might ask include the following:

- What is the purpose of the work? Religious? Entertainment? Philosophical? Emotional? Didactic? Pure form? Social or political commentary?
- To what culture does it belong, and to what geographical region and period? How does it reflect that context?
- Is its origin and/or function popular or commercial?
- Does it derive organically from the needs or celebratory functions of a community, or is it a self-conscious artistic creation of one individual?

Often after answering such questions, some students might be able to determine the specific artist by putting all the clues together, as in a detective story.

Table 6-2 summarizes an elementary school art curriculum.

Understanding How Visual Art Can Be Used as a Form of Communication, Self-Expression, and Social Expression

At its most fundamental level, art—be it opera, ballet, painting, or pantomime—is a form of communication. The realm of visual art encompasses many forms of communication, including sculpture, painting and drawing, ceramics, performance art, printmaking, jewelry, fiber art, photography, and film and video. Each medium or field of specialization communicates differently than the others. Take, for instance, the difference between viewing a sculpture and a tapestry. Sculpture (in the round) requires the viewer to move around in space to comprehend the work, whereas one can view a tapestry from a stationary position. Sculpture is three-dimensional, encompassing height, width, and depth, whereas a tapestry is two-dimensional, encompassing only height and width. Although each of these art forms can have a strong visual presence, sculpture is unique in that it has the capacity to be fully physically engaging in actual space. Artists choose different disciplines and media because each method and medium has its own communicative potential.

Visual art can affect viewers in ways that are difficult to define. The powerful experience of encountering, for example, a huge carved Olmec head sculpture in an outdoor garden in Villahermosa, Mexico, or contemplating a quiet, delicate Vermeer painting in The Hague, Netherlands, is sometimes termed an aesthetic moment or experience. We may try to put into words the experience of these moments—beautiful, colossal, overwhelming, transcendental—but the words often seem inadequate. What the art is communicating is perhaps hard to verbalize, but the feeling is undeniable. As viewers, we are momentarily transported so that we are no longer aware of our surroundings or ourselves. When art communicates to us in such a direct and forceful way, we consider it an aesthetic experience.

Although aesthetics has long been recognized as the branch of philosophy pertaining to beauty, it is impossible to find agreement on what is beautiful. In keeping with the Greek root (*aisthetikos*, which means perceptive by feeling) aesthetics can be understood more as a study of sensation or feeling than one of beauty alone. This broader understanding of aesthetics has the ability to encompass the range of sensations that one can expe-

Table 6-2. Art Strategies, Materials, Skills, Techniques, Creativity, and Communication

Grade	Strategies	Materials	Skills	Techniques	Creativity	Communication
Kindergarten–2	Provide a wide variety of art, including both natural and human-made forms. Experiment with art materials. Provide opportunities to view art in the classroom, the art room, and elsewhere.	Art materials to use in the art room and classroom. Art forms from nature and humans, slides, art shows, visiting guests, trips, the computer, and so forth. Written programs for art exhibit.	Use terms like *line, color, value, shape, balance, texture, repetition, rhythm,* and *shape.* Respond to art. Describe feelings and ideas while viewing art. Use various art materials to produce art in the art room and classroom. Use a program from an art exhibit. Practice acceptable behavior at an art exhibit or as a member of an audience.	Try various art media and produce art forms. Behave as a responsible member of an audience. Use an art program to locate exhibits at an art show.	Experiment with various art supplies. Create simple art projects. Respond to art in an individual way.	Create feelings, ideas, and impressions through art products. Use art terms and concepts to express thoughts about art.
3–5	Experience art of many periods and many cultures through exhibits, computer, slides, speakers, and so on. Experiment with ways to produce art by using many media.	Actual art materials to use in the classroom and art room. Actual art forms from speakers and teacher. Slides, computer programs, and so on. Attend programs and study written programs.	Continue to use terms such as *line, color, value, shape, balance, texture, repetition, rhythm,* and *shape.* Continue to respond to art. Become more adept at describing feelings and ideas while producing and viewing art. Continue to use various art materials to produce art in the art room and classroom. Use a program from an art exhibit. Practice acceptable behavior at an art exhibit or as a member of an audience. Distinguish between classical and popular art.	Try various art media and produce art forms. Behave as a responsible member of an audience. Use an art program to locate exhibits at an art show. Describe feelings about own art and the art of others.	Express self through art. Create art. Improvise. Respond to art.	Create art by using various materials to express self. Create original art. Hear, read, and learn about careers in art. Practice basic etiquette for showing own art and for participating as audience member. Read art programs. Express ideas about art's origin, culture, and so on.
6–8	Provide occasions to view art of many cultures and many periods through exhibits, slides, books, computer searches, speakers, and so forth. Encourage students to respond to art and create own art. Give chances to communicate orally and in written form. Use a range of types of art.	Many art media, including weaving, film, crafts, and so forth. CDs, Internet searches, slides, books. Programs for art shows. Exhibits and guest speakers.	Use art to express self. Use many different art media to produce many art forms. Identify major artists, media, and periods.	Produce simple art products. Demonstrate understanding of terms when others use them. Use correct terminology. Read about art.	Create simple art. Explain the art and the feelings it produces.	Realize that art can be a career. Produce an original art piece for display. Express a feeling for an event by producing art. Analyze art. Talk about ways that art can be used as a career.

rience in viewing a work of art. Art is not always beautiful in the traditional sense of the word, and our aesthetic philosophies must be able to encompass this reality.

From the earliest cave paintings to the most recent art installations, visual art has functioned as a form of commentary on the society from which it springs; consequently, visual art is continually changing. Over the millennia, visual art has played (and continues to play) a key role in the dissemination of aesthetic tendencies, political ideas, religious and spiritual doctrines, cultural beliefs and critiques, and societal norms and trends. Conversely, visual art has changed and adapted to the same influences. In essence, visual art has the capacity to both shape and be shaped by the society in which it exists.

Visual art has also served the vital role of empowering the artist in his or her subject matter. For example, there has been broad speculation about the functions of the animal imagery that adorns the caves of France and Spain. Some suggest that the act of representing the animals gave the creator power over the creature or the creature's soul; others postulate that these artistic gestures were an early form of inventory: a means to count, organize, and track the myriad animals that existed in the outside world. The function of art as an empowering tool is as vital today as it was in past millennia. Much like the cave painters of the past, contemporary artists often use their art as a means to chart and order the complexities, wonders, and inspirations of the present-day world.

▶ Objective 0037:
Understand Basic Principles and Skills Related to Theater and Dance

Recognizing Various Forms Associated with Theater and Dance

Drama means "to do, act." Drama/theater is an experiential way to connect to content. Students are engaged physically, mentally, and emotionally. In today's classroom, infusing these techniques into the curriculum allows for hands-on learning that is meaningful and lasting. Young people can learn not only *about* drama/theater but also *through* the art form if it is partnered with another subject. Using these techniques helps children to understand both artistic and paired subject content.

At one end of the drama/theater spectrum is **creative drama**. In this format, process is more important than product; the benefit to the participant is paramount. Creative drama is frequently used in classrooms, because it is informal drama that can work in any setting and with any number of children. Scenery, costumes, and/or props are not required. These activities move from teacher centered to student centered, from shorter to longer activities and sessions, from unison play to individual play, and from simple beginning activities to more complex story work. Participants need little, if any, previous experience with this approach to curriculum. Once they are introduced to this pedagogy, however, both their interests and their skills will grow. The following are definitions for the many types of activities that are components of creative drama:

Beginning activities. These are warmup activities such as name games, chants, listening games, and other simple exercises designed to relax and motivate participants.

Games. These are more challenging than beginning activities and often focus on developing players' concentration, imagination, and teamwork skills. Frequently, they are played with students seated or standing in a circle.

Sequence games. The teacher takes a story or similar material, divides it into particular events or scenes, and places each on an index card. These are randomly distributed to players. When a student recognizes his or her cue, that student goes next. Index cards should have the cue at the top and the new action at the bottom, preferably in a different font or color. The teacher should keep a master list, in order, of cues. This helps students if the correct sequence is interrupted or lost.

Pantomime. Players use their bodies, rather than their voices, to communicate. Pantomime sentences and stories, creative movement exercises, and miming games are common examples.

Improvisations. These are spontaneously created performances based upon at least two of the following: who (characters), what (conflict), where (setting), when (time), and how (specifics of interpretation).

Performed either in pantomime or with dialogue, improvisations should not be planned or rehearsed. Interesting episodes that emerge may be further developed through story creation. Role-playing improvisations deal with problem solving. Replaying and switching roles exposes students to differing points of view. Role-playing is not the same as playing in-role, which is when the teacher enters the dramatization as a character.

Stories. A number of activities can be based upon stories and can range from simple to complex. In the former category, for example, are noisy stories. These are simple stories that players help to tell by making sounds or saying words associated with characters. Story creation activities require that players develop stories, and these activities can be stimulated by various items, including props, titles, students' own writing, or true events. Open-ended stories are those from which students build stories given only a beginning and then share their creations either orally, in writing, or through performance. Story dramatization is the most complex informal dramatic activity; it utilizes players' previously developed skills in service to playing stories. Once proficient here, students move naturally to formal theatrical endeavors. Several types of activities bridge the gap between creative drama and theater for youth. These include theater-in-education (TIE), readers' theater, and puppetry. Each can be integrated into classroom practice.

Theater-in-education (TIE). Originating in Britain, theater-in-education is performed by actor-teachers and students. Using material based upon curriculum or social issues, players assume roles and, through these, explore and problem solve. TIE's structure is flexible, and its focus is educational.

Puppetry. Puppets can range from simple paper bag or sock creations to elaborately constructed marionettes. Puppets can be used for creative drama and theater activities. Likewise, puppet stages can be as simple as a desktop or table, or they can be intricately constructed and have artistically designed settings and theatrical trappings.

Readers theater. Called "theater of the imagination," readers theater offers performance opportunities without elaborate staging. Traditionally, this type of performance has players sitting on stools, using onstage and/or offstage focus, and employing notebooks or music stands to hold scripts. A narrator may be used, and readers may or may not play multiple roles. This type of performance is wedded to literature. A common misconception, however, is that this is simply expressive reading. To impact an audience, readers theater must be more than that. Rich characterization, suggested movement, and clear interpretation of the literature are necessary. In their minds' eyes, audience members complete the stage pictures suggested by the interpreters.

Children's theater. Children's theater is product oriented and audience centered. This theater for young people can be performed by and for children, by adults for youth, or with a combined cast of adults and young people. In addition, actors can be either amateurs or professionals. Here, dialogue is memorized, the number of characters in the play determines the cast size, and scenery and costumes are generally expected production elements. Educators may take their students to see plays, or they may wish to stage plays in their classrooms or other school facilities. In addition to the familiar format, plays for young people can also be done as participation plays and as story theater. The last two are especially adaptable to educational venues.

Traditional theater. In this most commonly used form of theater, performers and audience are separate entities. Actors use character and story to communicate, and the audience responds with feedback (for example, laughing, applauding). Typically, actors perform on a stage and are supported by others who contribute the technical elements of theater.

Participation theater. Children have opportunities to use their voices and bodies within the context of the play. They might be asked for their ideas, invited to join the actors, or given chances to contribute to the play in meaningful ways.

Story theater. In this format, actors can function as both characters and narrators, sometimes commenting upon their own actions in role. They can play one role or multiple parts. Scenery, if used, is minimal, and costume pieces can suggest a character. Story theater is classroom friendly and closely linked to literature. Because story theater uses live actors performing for an audience that is "in the moment" with them, it can be repeated, but it will never be exactly the same.

Young people benefit from exposure to theater, whether as participant or audience member. Opportunities abound for developing vocal skills, vocabulary, imagination, understanding of dramatic structure and types of conflict, physical skills, and empathy. Theater offers innovative instructional options. Theater is not a new art form; it emerged in ancient Greece as a part of religious celebrations. The fact that theater has evolved over centuries is a testament to its nature; it is both experimental and transitional, allowing innovative elements to be absorbed into the mainstream while continuing to look for new artistic inventions. This is not its only dichotomy. Theater is a profession for some and an avocation for others. It is a communal and a collective art form. Regardless of its structure, theater engages through both visual and auditory stimulation.

Evaluating Activities Intended to Foster Skills in Creating, Viewing, and Responding to Works of Theater and Dance

Some of the benefits inherent in using dance and theater in the classroom include developing concentration skills, analyzing content, demonstrating artistic discipline, improving listening, learning to apply research, communicating information, and making and justifying artistic choices. These are important to a student's educational growth, regardless of the individual's future career. Students who have a chance to learn about and through drama are motivated; their imaginations are engaged and their work is often quite focused. There are also more specific aesthetic benefits.

By participating in these activities, students learn about dramatic process and product. They acquire knowledge of theater artists and their responsibilities. They engage in making artistic choices and learn about the personal discipline that the arts demand. Furthermore, students develop personal aesthetics that are based on informed judgments. They develop insight into cultures and communities and better understand how this art form is manifest in both their artistic and their everyday lives.

Dance, drama, and theater offer multiple approaches to gaining knowledge. Whether a student's preferred learning style is visual (verbal or nonverbal), aural, or tactile/kinesthetic, infusing lessons with drama/theater expands ways of knowing, especially because of the variety of activities available. Multiple approaches to knowledge acquisition and retention help to ensure that all children learn. It should be no surprise, then, that in addition to students who regularly achieve in their studies, even those students who generally are less successful may thrive in classrooms in which drama/theater is a regular part of their learning environment.

Teaching and learning through and with dramatic art is a unique and effective approach to instruction at all educational levels and with students of varying degrees of academic achievement. Educators teaching elementary school age children will find that understanding child drama and the continuum of activities that defines it will help determine what type of activity is best to use at any given time. While the following comparison helps to distinguish the two major components of this progression, it is important to recognize that one is not better than the other; they are simply different in composition and purpose. Creative drama, children's theater, and the activities between them offer ample opportunities for integration and demonstrate that the arts are powerful partners for learning.

Understanding How Drama and Dance Can Be Used as a Form of Communication, Self-Expression, and Social Expression

Plays reflect culture. They hold up a mirror that allows us to travel to different places and time periods to learn about the conditions, people, and viewpoints that have shaped the world of the play. They challenge learners to explore and to deepen their understanding. Theater introduces children to some characters who are like them and to some who are not. It enriches and broadens a child's way of knowing.

Using drama/theater in the classroom may result in a lively educational environment. Teachers should welcome the energetic chatter and movement that indicate students are learning. Educator should recognize that in this type of experience, there might be more than one correct answer or interpretation. Part of the joy and challenge of using drama in the classroom is that it pushes students to think creatively and independently. If teachers view themselves as coexplorers in this process,

the journey they take with their students is both productive and fun!

The arts are a part of the core curriculum, in terms of state standards, learned profession standards, and the No Child Left Behind federal mandate. Dance, music, theater, and the visual arts are essential parts of a complete education. Study of one or more art forms develops the intellect, provides unique access to meaning, and connects individuals with works of genius, multiple cultures, and contributions to history.

Drama and theater activities offer learners opportunities to experience an art form in many different ways. Whether students study a play, mount a production, attend a performance, or engage in creative drama in the classroom, such activities help them to learn about themselves and their world, develop social skills, strengthen both their verbal and nonverbal communication skills, and creatively solve problems, analyze, and collaborate.

▶ Objective 0038:
Understand Connections Among the Arts, the Connections Between the Arts and Other Disciplines, and the Relationship of the Arts to Their Historical and Cultural Context

Understanding the Role and Function of the Arts in Various Cultures and Historical Periods

According to the objective, merely experiencing the music or art is not enough. The students must be able to recognize the music or art as part of its historical context and then, through discussion or written exercises that emphasize higher-order thinking, they must be able to note things that are common and things that are different between one context and another—period to period, culture to culture, and so forth—appropriate to their age and level of development.

For example, Franz Joseph Haydn, Wolfgang Amadeus Mozart, and William Billings used simple melodies in their compositions. Haydn and Mozart wrote mostly large works, like symphonies and operas. Billings wrote mostly psalms and songs. Students must be aware of these facts and then consider why more highly developed forms were preferred in the "old world," while basic psalms and songs were more common in the American colonies. The obvious answer is that colonists did not have the time or the resources to encourage or produce larger musical works. However, the discussion could go beyond that basic step, depending on the sophistication of the students.

Recognizing Ways in Which the Arts Can Be Used to Explore Other Aspects of Various Cultures and Historical Periods

Throughout history, the fine arts have been rich with meaning and passion. They express the depths of humanness across all cultures. The fine arts mirror culture of a particular historical period. When we consider why people draw, paint, or sculpt, we learn that they portray what is important to them, what their community or culture values at a particular time. When a culture values strength and power, the arts will show it. When a culture values the community over the individual, it is clear in the fine arts. When a culture values order and hierarchy in social structure, the fine arts will give evidence of the same structure. With an observant eye, then, one can learn a great deal about a culture by studying its fine arts.

All cultures define beauty in their own way. The fine arts of a particular time and place reflect that culture's idea of beauty at the historical period. Dances, for instance, clearly reflect that ideal (aesthetic) of beauty. Some African dances, for example, feature plump and fleshy female dancers, who embody health, fertility, the earth, and beauty to their people. In the European traditional form of ballet, however, the skeletal ballerina is spotlighted to reflect the fragile, ethereal, romantic ideal of female beauty; other visual arts of that culture, too, may also portray a thin maiden on the canvas and on the stage.

Recognizing the Connections Among the Arts

Visual art, like other forms of communication, has the capacity to convey the complexity of issues, ideas,

and feelings. What generally (and traditionally) distinguishes visual art from the other disciplines in the arts is the emphasis on the visual. However, numerous visual artists work entirely in sound. In such cases, what is the factor that distinguishes visual artists from experimental sound artists, video artists from cinematographers, and performance artists from actors or dancers? The categories that distinguish one discipline from another are becoming increasingly blurred. While the traditional areas of fine art study (namely, music, theater, dance, and visual art) still exist, many artists today are what we term *interdisciplinary*. These artists are often conversant with different art disciplines while maintaining an identity in their primary field of study. The interdisciplinary crossover of art forms has opened up many exciting possibilities for music, theater, dance, and visual art. Indeed, interdisciplinary art has the potential to capture the complexities of our present world differently than was previously possible.

Understanding the Connections Between the Arts and Other Disciplines

This objective suggests an integration of subject matter that is an opportunity for teachers and students to make connections between social studies, reading or language arts, mathematics (time signatures, note values, etc.), science (sound, pitch, and vibrations, etc.), health, physical education, and the fine arts. For example, when students are reading stories about the American Revolution, they should be aware that it occurred during the era in music history known as the Classical Period. Listening to a work by Haydn or Mozart and talking about how that composer reflected the "old world" and then comparing the work to a Colonial American tune of the time such as Billings's "Chester" is a great exercise. Similarly, the visual art of Andy Warhol, the music of the Beatles, the assassination of John F. Kennedy, and the war in Vietnam all share the same approximate time frame. In these and the virtually infinite number of other cases or combinations, the students can be asked to find contrasts and similarities, or they can attempt to find ways that historical context affected art and ways that art affected and reflected history.

These examples from American history are easy for most to grasp quickly. However, the objective seeks to have teachers and students consider the role of the

arts in history and culture beyond the American experience. Listening to music, reading plays in translation, viewing films of performances, and observing art works from China, Japan, Germany, Australia, or Africa when studying those cultures can enrich the experience and make it more memorable for students. It is even more valuable to experience live or videotaped performances of the music and dance of these cultures, because often the music is performed in traditional costume with traditional instruments (which are sometimes very different from modern instruments); seeing the costumes and the movement is an important part of understanding the culture.

Understanding concepts and skills suggests more than an appreciation of these concepts and skills. The students ought to experience, respond to, and express what they have experienced in the arts in accepted terminology. For instance, the students can readily see a contrast between the traditional court dances of Bali and American modern dance. In Bali, the court dances have existed for centuries. Dancers train for many years to perform with great serenity, balance, and symmetry. They embody the ideal beauty of Balinese culture. In contemporary America, modern dance can express the very different aesthetic of a driving, off-balance asymmetry. Each image mirrors a cultural definition of what is beautiful. We can all discover many different kinds of beauty through experiencing the fine arts of various cultures at different historical periods.

Dance can be, as the topics of the two section titles imply, an example of an art form through which one can readily view a connection with other subjects and an example of an art form relating to the other fine arts. Dance plays important roles among the peoples of the world and thus acts as a mirror of culture. Whether as a social activity, a performing art, or a creative pursuit, dance is important enough to be represented in the art of most cultures from antiquity to today.

This section speaks to many dance-evident cultural values such as gender roles, sexuality, concepts of beauty and aesthetics, community solidarity, and creativity.

Most cultural dances are historically connected to religion. All over the world, one can observe dances of devotion and worship in which participants bow in reverence to their deities, lift their arms to the heavens, or

gesture to receive divine benefits. Some cultural dances (for example, those of Egypt, Greece, India, and Japan) tell stories of the power and conquests of deities. Movements may include a wide, strong stance with fisted hands and stamping feet. Other cultures use dance and sometimes mime to appeal to the gods for survival. For example, a dance for hunting success (like those of the Native American and Inuit people) may include pantomime of the animal and hunter and the inevitable killing of the animal. A dance for fertile fields and lavish harvest (common among Hebrew, Egyptian, and European cultures) may include pantomime of the planting, tending, and harvesting, as well as lifting or expanding actions that suggest crop growth. Some dances (like those of the Chinese, Roman, and African cultures) seek victory in war and include the use of swords, spears, or shields, and the miming of conflict and victory.

Still other dances are intended to ask for divine blessings on life events. For the birth of a child, African and Polynesian dances, among others, include childbearing, cradling and offering the child up to the deity, and crawling, walking, and running to indicate growth of the child. For rituals of initiation into adulthood (such as those of Native American and African cultures), dance movements may include shows of strength and manhood for the male and swaying and nurturing gestures for the female. For marriage (in most cultures), dance movements are jubilant, reflect traditional gender roles for men and women, and may include movements that suggest sexuality and fertility. Funeral dances (for example, those of Egypt, Cambodia, and Zimbabwe) often include movements that reenact the life story of the deceased and may include grieving as well as celebration of an afterlife.

For many cultures, dance is the primary connection between people and their gods. And in most cultures, the power of the dance to elicit the gods' positive response is unquestioned.

It is readily apparent that the arts can relate to one another and to other disciplines. Teachers should provide experiences and materials to ensure that students can experience the arts, respond to the arts, and express their reactions in appropriate terminology—objectives for proficient Arizona elementary education teachers.

▶ References

South Carolina visual and performing arts curriculum framework writing team. South Carolina visual and performing arts curriculum framework. 1993. Columbia, SC: South Carolina Department of Education.

Elementary Education

Practice Test 1

Answer Sheet

1. Ⓐ Ⓑ Ⓒ Ⓓ
2. Ⓐ Ⓑ Ⓒ Ⓓ
3. Ⓐ Ⓑ Ⓒ Ⓓ
4. Ⓐ Ⓑ Ⓒ Ⓓ
5. Ⓐ Ⓑ Ⓒ Ⓓ
6. Ⓐ Ⓑ Ⓒ Ⓓ
7. Ⓐ Ⓑ Ⓒ Ⓓ
8. Ⓐ Ⓑ Ⓒ Ⓓ
9. Ⓐ Ⓑ Ⓒ Ⓓ
10. Ⓐ Ⓑ Ⓒ Ⓓ
11. Ⓐ Ⓑ Ⓒ Ⓓ
12. Ⓐ Ⓑ Ⓒ Ⓓ
13. Ⓐ Ⓑ Ⓒ Ⓓ
14. Ⓐ Ⓑ Ⓒ Ⓓ
15. Ⓐ Ⓑ Ⓒ Ⓓ
16. Ⓐ Ⓑ Ⓒ Ⓓ
17. Ⓐ Ⓑ Ⓒ Ⓓ
18. Ⓐ Ⓑ Ⓒ Ⓓ
19. Ⓐ Ⓑ Ⓒ Ⓓ
20. Ⓐ Ⓑ Ⓒ Ⓓ
21. Ⓐ Ⓑ Ⓒ Ⓓ
22. Ⓐ Ⓑ Ⓒ Ⓓ
23. Ⓐ Ⓑ Ⓒ Ⓓ
24. Ⓐ Ⓑ Ⓒ Ⓓ
25. Ⓐ Ⓑ Ⓒ Ⓓ

26. Ⓐ Ⓑ Ⓒ Ⓓ
27. Ⓐ Ⓑ Ⓒ Ⓓ
28. Ⓐ Ⓑ Ⓒ Ⓓ
29. Ⓐ Ⓑ Ⓒ Ⓓ
30. Ⓐ Ⓑ Ⓒ Ⓓ
31. Ⓐ Ⓑ Ⓒ Ⓓ
32. Ⓐ Ⓑ Ⓒ Ⓓ
33. Ⓐ Ⓑ Ⓒ Ⓓ
34. Ⓐ Ⓑ Ⓒ Ⓓ
35. Ⓐ Ⓑ Ⓒ Ⓓ
36. Ⓐ Ⓑ Ⓒ Ⓓ
37. Ⓐ Ⓑ Ⓒ Ⓓ
38. Ⓐ Ⓑ Ⓒ Ⓓ
39. Ⓐ Ⓑ Ⓒ Ⓓ
40. Ⓐ Ⓑ Ⓒ Ⓓ
41. Ⓐ Ⓑ Ⓒ Ⓓ
42. Ⓐ Ⓑ Ⓒ Ⓓ
43. Ⓐ Ⓑ Ⓒ Ⓓ
44. Ⓐ Ⓑ Ⓒ Ⓓ
45. Ⓐ Ⓑ Ⓒ Ⓓ
46. Ⓐ Ⓑ Ⓒ Ⓓ
47. Ⓐ Ⓑ Ⓒ Ⓓ
48. Ⓐ Ⓑ Ⓒ Ⓓ
49. Ⓐ Ⓑ Ⓒ Ⓓ
50. Ⓐ Ⓑ Ⓒ Ⓓ

51. Ⓐ Ⓑ Ⓒ Ⓓ
52. Ⓐ Ⓑ Ⓒ Ⓓ
53. Ⓐ Ⓑ Ⓒ Ⓓ
54. Ⓐ Ⓑ Ⓒ Ⓓ
55. Ⓐ Ⓑ Ⓒ Ⓓ
56. Ⓐ Ⓑ Ⓒ Ⓓ
57. Ⓐ Ⓑ Ⓒ Ⓓ
58. Ⓐ Ⓑ Ⓒ Ⓓ
59. Ⓐ Ⓑ Ⓒ Ⓓ
60. Ⓐ Ⓑ Ⓒ Ⓓ
61. Ⓐ Ⓑ Ⓒ Ⓓ
62. Ⓐ Ⓑ Ⓒ Ⓓ
63. Ⓐ Ⓑ Ⓒ Ⓓ
64. Ⓐ Ⓑ Ⓒ Ⓓ
65. Ⓐ Ⓑ Ⓒ Ⓓ
66. Ⓐ Ⓑ Ⓒ Ⓓ
67. Ⓐ Ⓑ Ⓒ Ⓓ
68. Ⓐ Ⓑ Ⓒ Ⓓ
69. Ⓐ Ⓑ Ⓒ Ⓓ
70. Ⓐ Ⓑ Ⓒ Ⓓ
71. Ⓐ Ⓑ Ⓒ Ⓓ
72. Ⓐ Ⓑ Ⓒ Ⓓ
73. Ⓐ Ⓑ Ⓒ Ⓓ
74. Ⓐ Ⓑ Ⓒ Ⓓ
75. Ⓐ Ⓑ Ⓒ Ⓓ

76. Ⓐ Ⓑ Ⓒ Ⓓ
77. Ⓐ Ⓑ Ⓒ Ⓓ
78. Ⓐ Ⓑ Ⓒ Ⓓ
79. Ⓐ Ⓑ Ⓒ Ⓓ
80. Ⓐ Ⓑ Ⓒ Ⓓ
81. Ⓐ Ⓑ Ⓒ Ⓓ
82. Ⓐ Ⓑ Ⓒ Ⓓ
83. Ⓐ Ⓑ Ⓒ Ⓓ
84. Ⓐ Ⓑ Ⓒ Ⓓ
85. Ⓐ Ⓑ Ⓒ Ⓓ
86. Ⓐ Ⓑ Ⓒ Ⓓ
87. Ⓐ Ⓑ Ⓒ Ⓓ
88. Ⓐ Ⓑ Ⓒ Ⓓ
89. Ⓐ Ⓑ Ⓒ Ⓓ
90. Ⓐ Ⓑ Ⓒ Ⓓ
91. Ⓐ Ⓑ Ⓒ Ⓓ
92. Ⓐ Ⓑ Ⓒ Ⓓ
93. Ⓐ Ⓑ Ⓒ Ⓓ
94. Ⓐ Ⓑ Ⓒ Ⓓ
95. Ⓐ Ⓑ Ⓒ Ⓓ
96. Ⓐ Ⓑ Ⓒ Ⓓ
97. Ⓐ Ⓑ Ⓒ Ⓓ
98. Ⓐ Ⓑ Ⓒ Ⓓ
99. Ⓐ Ⓑ Ⓒ Ⓓ
100. Ⓐ Ⓑ Ⓒ Ⓓ

Practice Test 1

TIME: Four hours for total test.
100 multiple-choice questions.
1 performance assignment.

Directions: Read each item and select the best answer.

---

1. Which of the following describes best practice in writing instruction?

   A. Instruct students in writing, and give them time to write.
   B. Have students complete worksheets about writing.
   C. Have students copy famous speeches.
   D. Have students create a mural of the story so far and label all of the characters.

2. Each month the teacher kept track of the number of books as well as the genre of the books the students read during free-reading time in school. Here is the graph constructed from the data from October and May of the same school year:

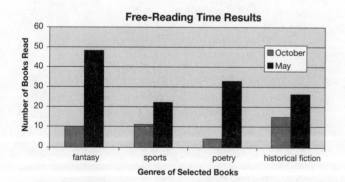

Free-Reading Time Results

This teacher completed a unit on fairy tales in May. What conclusions could be reached?

I. These children are reading more titles during free-reading time.
II. Completing a fairy-tale unit created interest in the fantasy genre.
III. These children need to complete more worksheets.
IV. These children are participating in an Accelerated Reader Program.

   A. I and III only.
   B. IV and III only.
   C. I, II, III only.
   D. I and II only.

3. If you were developing a pyramid that represents the pattern of progression from simple to complex activities in creative drama and were using the base of the pyramid for the simplest activities and the tip for the most complex, which of the following patterns correctly represents this progression?

   A. story dramatization, story creation, improvisation, pantomime, beginning activities
   B. improvisation, pantomime, beginning activities, story dramatization, story creation
   C. beginning activities, improvisation, pantomime, story dramatization, story creation
   D. beginning activities, pantomime, improvisation, story creation, story dramatization

4. Ms. Smith has decided to stage three different versions of *Cinderella* with her students. Knowing that this is one of the world's most famous fairy tales, she has located Chinese, Native American, and Russian versions of the story. She has found age-appropriate plays of each that can be staged in her classroom. In addition to acting in these plays, her students are creating scenery, costumes, and props to use in their performances.

Which of the following best describes what Ms. Smith primarily expects her students to achieve through these activities?

I. understanding cultural similarities and differences through dramatic literature
II. understanding theatrical practices
III. gaining experience with creative drama practices
IV. gaining experience with adapting stories into plays

A. I only
B. I and II only
C. III and IV only
D. I, II, and IV only

5. Which of the following characteristics are correctly matched to the dramatic activity?

A. children's theater—process-oriented and audience-centered
B. reader's theater—*A Theater of the Imagination* characterized by full-scale productions
C. creative drama—student-centered, informal drama activities
D. puppetry plays—done with elaborate dolls

6. In selecting or creating material for students to pantomime, a teacher should look for which of the following?

A. content rich with active verbs
B. content rich with descriptive narrative
C. content rich with inactive verbs
D. content rich with dialogue

7. Mr. Nelson's class has just returned from seeing a children's theater production at a nearby university. Now, Mr. Nelson plans to ask his students to discuss what they have seen. In preparation for this, he plans to model the types of responses desired.

Which of the following should he use as examples?

I. I liked the play.
II. I liked the play because the characters reminded me of people I know.
III. I liked the play because the theater was big.
IV. I liked the play because sometimes the story was funny and sometimes it was sad.

A. I only
B. II and IV only
C. I and III only
D. IV only only

8. Reading and then dramatizing a story, using that story as the basis of a puppet play, scripting that story and performing it in the classroom, and then attending a performance of that story done as a play by a theater company illustrates which of the following concepts?

A. Teachers should work with material until they find the correct way to use it with students.
B. There are multiple ways to express and interpret the same material.
C. Plays are more interesting than classroom dramatizations.
D. Students learn less as audience members than as participants in drama activities.

9. A lesson where students are given a tankful of water and various objects and are asked to order the objects by weight would be considered a(n)

A. science lesson.
B. discovery-learning lesson.
C. inductive-reasoning lesson.
D. eg-rule lesson.

10. Mr. Drake wants to ensure that the class will have a quality discussion on the needs of house pets. In response to a student who said that her family abandoned their cat in a field because it ate too much, Mr. Drake asks, "What is one way to save pets that are no longer wanted?"

    This exercise involves what level of questioning?

    A. evaluation
    B. analysis
    C. comprehension
    D. synthesis

11. Mr. Drake has a heterogeneously grouped reading class. He has the students in groups of two—one skilled reader and one remedial reader—reading selected stories to one another. The students read the story and question each other until they feel that they both understand the story.

    By planning the lesson this way, Mr. Drake has

    A. set a goal for his students.
    B. condensed the number of observations necessary, thereby creating more time for class instruction.
    C. made it possible for another teacher to utilize the limited materials.
    D. utilized the students' strengths and weaknesses to maximize time, materials, and the learning environment.

12. Mr. Drake is continuing his lesson on the animal kingdom. He wants to ensure that the students learn as much as they can about animals, so he incorporates information they are familiar with into the new information.

    Knowing that these are first-grade learners, what should Mr. Drake consider when contemplating their learning experience?

    A. The students will know how much information they can retrieve from memory.
    B. The students will overestimate how much information they can retrieve from memory.

C. The students will be able to pick out the information they need to study and the information they do not need to study due to prior mastery.
D. The students will estimate how much they can learn in one time period.

13. Before reading a story about a veterinary hospital, Mr. Drake constructs a semantic map of related words and terms using the students' input. What is his main intention for doing this?

    A. to demonstrate a meaningful relationship between the concepts of the story and the prior knowledge of the students
    B. to serve as a visual means of learning
    C. to determine the level of understanding the students will have at the conclusion of the topic being covered
    D. to model proper writing using whole words

14. Student data such as scores on tests and assignments would be the best criteria for determining which of the following?

    A. only the students' academic grades
    B. behavior assessment
    C. students' grades and the teacher's quality of instruction
    D. students' grades and behavior assessment

15. Results of a standardized test indicate that a teacher's students did poorly on the mathematics problem-solving section; students in another classroom in the same school did much better. What would be the best action for the teacher of the students who did poorly to take?

    A. Look at her students' scores from last year to justify their poor achievement.
    B. Tell future students to study harder because that section is hard.
    C. Suggest that parents hire a math tutor.
    D. Ask the other teacher to share strategies that she used to help make her students successful.

16. Mr. Joseph is a fifth-grade math and science teacher working in a large suburban middle school. At the beginning of each of his classes, he stands outside of his classroom and greets his students as they walk into his classroom. Mr. Joseph notices students coming into his class who appear upset or angry and show signs of poor self-esteem. Sometimes, he overhears his students arguing with other students before class. Often, these students seem to "shut down" during class and do not follow along with the work. He knows this is a problem, but he is not sure what he should do to solve it. He wants to keep these students from getting behind in their learning.

To reduce this problem, Mr. Joseph should

A. inform the school counselor of the problem and send each student with these symptoms to see the counselor as soon as class starts.

B. call the parents of students who seem upset or angry and try to persuade them to fix the problem.

C. send students with these kinds of problems out in the hall so they can get themselves together and learn.

D. create an environment in his classroom where students feel safe and let them know he is aware of their problems and will do all he can to help them learn.

17. The question "What was the name of Hamlet's father?" is

A. a high-order question of evaluation.

B. a low-order question that can be used to begin a discussion.

C. a transition.

D. questioning a skill.

18. Piaget's theory of cognitive development states that

A. children should be able to understand complex directions.

B. younger children are unable to understand complex language.

C. younger children will be unable to understand directions, even in simple language.

D. directions should not be given to young children.

19. Children under the age of eight

A. are unable to answer questions.

B. process information more slowly than older children.

C. can answer the same questions as slightly older children.

D. cannot learn in a cooperative environment.

20. Inductive thinking can be fostered through which activity?

A. choral chanting of skill tables

B. computer experience

C. multiple-choice questions

D. personal-discovery activities

21. Mr. Owen, a third-grade teacher, has been teaching in a small rural district for three years. He enjoys the slow pace of the community and the fact that he knows most of his students' families relatively well. He is a member of the Evening Lions Club, plays on the church basketball team, and volunteers at the animal shelter.

His class this year is made up of 21 eight- and nine-year-olds. Most of the students are of average ability, two receive special services for learning disabilities, and one receives speech therapy. Mr. Owen works hard at making his classroom an exciting place to learn with lots of hands-on, problem-based cooperative group projects. In the past, students have had difficulty grasping relationships between math concepts and economics. Mr. Owen has decided to offer a savings program with the help of local banks. Once a week, students will make deposits into their savings accounts. Periodically, they will use their accounts to figure interest at different rates, class totals saved, and so on. As part of the social studies, he encourages them to do chores at home and in their neighborhoods to earn the money for their savings.

This approach is evidence that Mr. Owen understands the importance of

A. the relevance and authenticity in planning instructional activities for students.
B. integrating curriculum concepts across disciplines that support learning.
C. saving money.
D. all of the above.

22. Students are presented with the following problem: "Bill is taller than Ann, but Ann is taller than Grace. Is Ann the tallest child or is Bill the tallest?" This question requires students to use

A. inductive reasoning.
B. deductive reasoning.
C. hypothesis formation.
D. pattern identification.

23. Which answer choice lists the following historical events in correct chronological order?

I.   Puritans arrive in New England.
II. Protestant Reformation begins.
III. Columbus sets sail across the Atlantic.
IV. Magna Carta is signed in England.

A. IV, III, II, I
B. IV, III, I, II
C. III, IV, II, I
D. III, II, I, IV

24. The intellectual movement that encouraged the use of reason and science and anticipated human progress was called

A. the American System.
B. mercantilism.
C. the Enlightenment.
D. the Age of Belief.

25. In American government, "checks and balances" were developed to

A. regulate the amount of control each branch of government would have.
B. make each branch of government independent from one another.

C. give the president control.
D. give the Supreme Court control.

26. Which of the following groups did not play a role in the settlement of the English colonies in America?

A. Roman Catholics
B. Puritans
C. Mormons
D. Quakers

27. On the following map, which letter represents the Philippines?

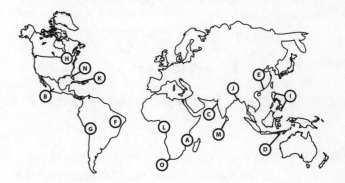

A. K
B. D
C. I
D. M

28. The Bill of Rights

A. listed the grievances of the colonists against the British.
B. forbade the federal government from encroaching on the rights of citizens.
C. gave all white males the right to vote.
D. specified the rights of slaves.

29. A teacher asks her sixth-grade English students to select a career they would enjoy when they grow up and then find three sources on the World Wide Web with information about that career. She tells the students that they must find out how much education is required for this career. If the career requires postsecondary education, then the student must find a school or college that provides this education and find out how long it will take to be educated or trained for this career.

   Through this assignment, the teacher is helping her students to

   A. explore short-term personal and academic goals.

   B. explore long-term personal and academic goals.

   C. evaluate short-term personal and academic goals.

   D. synthesize long-term personal and academic goals.

30. A teacher asks a student, "When you were studying for your spelling test, did you remember the mnemonic we talked about in class for spelling *principal*, that 'a principal is your pal'?" The teacher is

   A. leading the student in a divergent thinking exercise.

   B. teaching the student mnemonics, or memory devices.

   C. asking questions to guide the student in correcting an error.

   D. modeling inductive reasoning skills for the student.

31. When working with students enrolled in an English as a Second Language (ESL) program, the teacher should be aware that

   A. students should speak only English in class.

   B. an accepting classroom and encouraging lessons will foster learning.

   C. the student should be referred to a specialist.

   D. limiting the number of resources available is beneficial to the students.

32. Ms. Borders, a second-year, third-grade teacher, is preparing a theme study on water and the related concepts of conservation, ecology, and human needs. One of her instructional outcomes deals with students' abilities to demonstrate their new learning in a variety of ways. As she plans her unit of study, Ms. Borders first needs to consider

   A. the strengths and needs of the diverse learners in her classroom.

   B. the amount of reading material she assigns.

   C. how the theme connects to other academic disciplines.

   D. inviting guest speakers to the classroom.

33. Sequential language acquisition occurs when students

   A. learn a second language after mastery of the first.

   B. learn a second language at the same time as the first.

   C. learn two languages in parts.

   D. develop language skills.

34. Teachers should provide a variety of experiences and concrete examples for children with reading difficulties because some children

   A. come from environments with limited language exposure.

   B. have poor learning habits.

   C. have trouble distinguishing letters.

   D. can speak well but have difficulty reading.

35. A teacher writes on the board, "All men are created equal," and asks each student to explain the meaning of the statement. One student says that it means that all people are equal; another student says that it just applies to men. A third student says that it is a lie because not all people are equally good at all things; for example, some people can run faster than others and some can sing better than others.

   The teacher's instructional aim is to

   A. see if students can reach a consensus on the meaning of the statement.

B. see how well students can defend their beliefs.

C. provoke the students to disagree with the statement.

D. engage the students in critical thinking and to allow them to express their opinions.

36. If the other students laugh when a first-grade girl says, "I want to be a truck driver when I grow up" and tell her that "girls can't drive big trucks," what should the teacher do?

A. Tell the class to quiet down, that the student can be whatever she wants to be when she grows up.

B. Tell the class that most truck drivers are men.

C. Tell the class that women and men can both be truck drivers, depending on their skills.

D. Ask the class to vote on whether women should be truck drivers.

Questions 37 and 38 refer to the bar graph below.

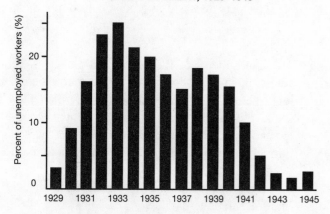

UNEMPLOYMENT, 1929–1945

37. According to the bar graph, the unemployment rate was highest in

A. 1929.
B. 1933.
C. 1938.
D. 1944.

38. According to the graph, the unemployment rate was lowest in

A. 1929.
B. 1933.
C. 1938.
D. 1944.

39. According to the graph below, "Household by Income Class," which one of the following statements is true?

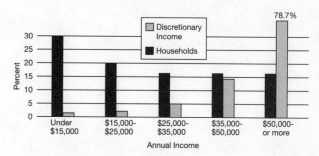

Households by Income Class

Percentage Distribution of Households and Discretionary Income

(Total U.S. = 100 percent)

A. About 50 percent of households had under $15,000 in annual income.

B. Almost 75 percent of households had $50,000 or more in annual income.

C. About 78 percent of households had $50,000 or more in annual income.

D. About 20 percent of households had between $15,000 and $25,000 in annual income.

40. According to the graph below, which one of the following statements is true?

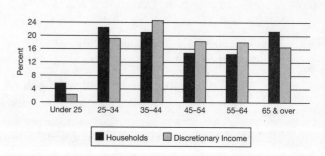

Households by Income Class

Percentage Distribution of Households and Discretionary Income

(Total U.S. = 100 percent)

A. Middle-age households tend to have greater discretionary income.

B. The youngest have the most discretionary income.

C. The oldest have the most discretionary income.

D. The older one gets, the least discretionary income one has.

41. When a student writes about attempting suicide in a journal, the best way for the teacher to deal with the situation is to

A. write encouraging notes to the student in the margins of the journal.

B. ask the student to come over to his or her house after school to spend some time together.

C. suggest that the student read some inspirational and motivational books.

D. take the student's threats of suicide seriously and report the situation to the appropriate school authorities.

42. While the teacher is reading aloud to the class, Linda is telling jokes to get her peers to laugh. According to behavioral theory, what is a possible hypothesis for the function of Linda's behavior?

A. Linda tells jokes to make her peers laugh, which may serve to gain attention for Linda or may serve to distract the teacher from the lesson, which allows Linda to escape academic tasks.

B. Linda tells jokes to make the teacher angry.

C. Linda obviously has trouble at home and therefore this is an issue her parents need to deal with.

D. Linda enjoys the performing arts.

43. Which sequence is most appropriate for an elementary school music program?

A. provide opportunities for students to use notation, create a dance, and read music notation

B. classify sounds as high and low, walk to music, and sing simple songs

C. play the guitar, identify major and minor scales, and conduct duple and triple meter

D. learn to play the autoharp, play rhythm instruments, and conduct simple songs

44. A student in a program for English for Speakers of Other Languages (ESOL) is proficient in oral language; however, he continues to experience difficulty with academic language used in science and social studies classes. The teacher believes academic proficiency correlates with oral language proficiency.

What has the teacher failed to acknowledge in her analysis of the student's language proficiency?

A. Both basic interpersonal communication skills and cognitive academic language proficiency are needed for successful academic performance.

B. Basic interpersonal communication skills develop equally with cognitive academic language proficiency.

C. Basic interpersonal communication skills are criteria for successful academic performance.

D. Cognitive academic language proficiency is primary to basic interpersonal communication skills.

45. The atmospheres of the Moon and planets were studied using telescopes and spectrophotometers long before the deployment of interplanetary space probes. In these studies, scientists studied the spectral patterns of sunlight that passed through the atmosphere of distant objects to learn what elements make up those atmospheres. Which of the following explains the source of the black-line spectral patterns?

A. When an element is excited, it gives off light in a characteristic spectral pattern.

B. When light strikes an object, some wavelengths of light are absorbed by the surface and others are reflected to give the object its color.

C. When light passes through a gas, light is absorbed at wavelengths characteristic of the elements in the gas.

D. The black lines are the spectra of ultraviolet light, which is called black light because it cannot be seen with human eyes.

46. A student making top grades in class has received a percentile score of 63 on a nationally standardized math test. Which of the following best explains the student's score?

    A. A percentile score of 63 means that on a scale of 1 to l00, the student is 37 points from the top.
    B. A percentile score of 63 means that out of a group of 100 students, 37 would score higher and 62 would score lower, meaning that the student has done well by scoring in the top half of all students taking the test.
    C. A percentile score of 63 is just like a grade of 63 on a test; it means that the student earned a low D on the test.
    D. A percentile score of 63 means that out of a group of 100 students, 37 would score higher and 62 would score lower, showing a big difference between the student's performance on the standardized test and in class.

47. The launching of *Sputnik* by the Soviet Union in 1957 triggered increased emphasis on all of the following areas of study EXCEPT

    A. world history.
    B. math.
    C. science.
    D. foreign language.

48. The ruling of the Supreme Court in *Brown v. Board of Education of Topeka, Kansas* (1954) found that

    A. separate educational facilities could offer equal educational opportunities to students.
    B. students could be placed in segregated tracks within desegregated schools.
    C. segregated schools resulted in unequal educational opportunity but caused no psychological effects.
    D. separate educational facilities were inherently unequal and violated the equal protection clause of the Fourteenth Amendment.

49. President Lyndon B. Johnson's "War on Poverty" resulted in all of the following EXCEPT

    A. the Peace Corps.
    B. Head Start.
    C. Volunteers in Service to America (VISTA).
    D. the Elementary and Secondary Education Act.

50. The Education for All Handicapped Children Act of 1975 mandates that schools provide free and appropriate education for all of the following EXCEPT

    A. mentally handicapped children.
    B. physically handicapped children.
    C. socially-emotionally handicapped children.
    D. learning disabled children.

51. The pose of the horse in the sculpture pictured below serves to express

Flying Horse. Second-century Han. Wuwie Tomb, Gansu

    A. physical aging and decay.
    B. massiveness and stability.
    C. lightness and motion.
    D. military prowess.

52. Rueben Stein is a middle school teacher who wants to teach his class about the classification system in the animal kingdom. He decides to introduce this unit to his class by having the students engage in general classification activities. He brings to class a paper bag filled with 30 household items. He dumps the contents of the bag onto a table and then asks the students, in groups of three or four, to put like items into piles and then to justify or explain why they placed certain items into a particular pile.

By assigning this task to his students, Mr. Stein is providing his students with a developmentally appropriate task because

A. middle school students like to work in groups.
B. the items in the bag are household items with which most students will be familiar.
C. the assignment gives students the opportunity to practice their skills at categorizing.
D. the assignment will give students a task to perform while the teacher finishes grading papers.

53. Elva Rodriguez teaches fourth grade. She has structured her class so that students can spend 30 minutes daily, after lunch, in sustained, silent reading activities with books and reading materials of their own choosing. In order to maximize this reading opportunity and to recognize differences among learners, Ms. Rodriguez

A. allows some students to sit quietly at their desks while others are allowed to move to a reading area where they sit on floor cushions or recline on floor mats.
B. makes sure that all students have selected appropriate reading materials.
C. plays classical music to enhance student learning.
D. dims the lights in the classroom in order to increase students' reading comprehension.

54. Karla Dixon is a second-grade teacher who has selected a book to read to her class after lunch. She shows the students the picture on the cover of the book and reads the title of the book to them. She then asks, "What do you think this book is about?"

By asking this question, Ms. Dixon is

A. learning which students are interested in reading strategies.
B. trying to keep the students awake since she knows they usually get sleepy after lunch.
C. encouraging students to make a prediction, a precursor of hypothetical thinking.
D. finding out which students are good readers.

55. Mrs. Johnson teaches middle school reading. She teaches reading skills and comprehension through workbooks and through reading and class discussion of specific plays, short stories, and novels. She also allows students to make some selections according to their own interests. Because she believes there is a strong connection between reading and writing, her students are required to write their responses to literature in a variety of ways. Some of her students have heard their high school brothers and sisters discuss portfolios, and they have asked Mrs. Johnson if they can use them, also.

Which of the following statements are appropriate for Mrs. Johnson to consider in deciding whether to agree to the students' request?

I. Portfolios will develop skills her students can use in high school.
II. Portfolios will make Mrs. Johnson's students feel more mature because they will be making the same product as their older brothers and sisters.
III. Portfolios will assist her students in meeting course outcomes relating to reading and writing.
IV. Portfolios will make grading easier because there will be fewer papers and projects to evaluate.

A. I, II, and IV only
B. I and III only
C. II and III only
D. II and IV only

56. Miss Bailey teaches fifth-grade social studies in a self-contained classroom with 25 students of various achievement levels. She is starting a unit on the history of their local community and wants to stimulate the students' thinking. She also wants to encourage students to develop a project as a result of their study.

Which type of project would encourage the highest level of thinking by the students?

A. giving students a list of questions about people, dates, and events, then having them put the answers on a poster, with appropriate pictures, to display in class

B. giving students questions to use to interview older members of the community, then having them write articles based on the interviews and publish them in a booklet

C. discussing the influence of the past on the present community, then asking students to project what the community might be like in 100 years

D. using archived newspapers to collect data, then having them draw a timeline that includes the major events of the community from its beginning to the current date

57. Mr. Roberts' sixth-grade social studies class has developed a research project to survey student use of various types of video games. They designed a questionnaire and then administered it to all fourth-, fifth-, and sixth-grade students on their campus. The students plan to analyze their data, then develop a presentation to show at the next parent-teacher meeting.

Which types of computer software would be helpful during this class project?

I. word processing
II. database
III. simulation
IV. graph/chart

A. I, II, III, and IV
B. I, II, and IV only
C. I and III only
D. III and IV only

58. Kate Tillerson is an art teacher at McGregor High School, where she has taught successfully for several years. She is respected by her students as well as her fellow teachers. This year, the new director of instruction for the McGregor Independent School District has introduced several curriculum ideas, one of which is the concept of authentic assessment. All curriculum areas have had one or more staff development sessions on this concept. The idea will be incorporated into the curriculum as one of the strategies for assessment in each discipline and at each grade level. Kate has just received a request from the Fine Arts Department chairperson to submit an example of a lesson involving authentic assessment. A central office form to complete the example accompanies the request, along with a review of the authentic assessment concept, a model of a completed example, and a deadline for submitting teachers' samples. Kate's general response to the entire focus on authentic assessment has been that all she does in her classroom is based upon authentic assessment philosophy. She really sees no need for making any changes in the curriculum guide or for preparing the assignment sent to her. On the other hand, Kate is an excellent teacher and generally cooperates in the various curriculum tasks requested of her. She has been a leader of staff development sessions within the district and has shared her innovative ideas with fellow professionals at both regional and state meetings of art educators.

Which of the following responses should Kate make to her departmental chairperson's request?

A. Kate files the request under things to do and forgets about it.

B. Kate writes a passionate letter in response to the Fine Arts Department chairperson's request, explaining how she feels about the proposed example of an authentic assessment in art. She sends a copy of this letter to her chairperson and also to the director of curriculum and takes no further action.

C. Kate writes a passionate letter in response to the Fine Arts Department chairperson's request, explaining how she feels about the proposed example of an authentic assessment in art. Attached to the letter is a model unit of study Kate has used in her classes, including an authentic assessment project described in detail but not submitted on the form provided by the director of curriculum. Kate sends copies of these items to both her chairperson and the director of instruction.

D. Kate completes an authentic assessment project idea on the form provided by her chairperson. She submits this idea with supplementary photographs of students' projects and a copy of the grading rubric returned to the students for each project photographed. She also sends a videotape of a student discussing the project he has submitted for the unit of study.

59. The diagram below shows a path for electric flow. As the electrically charged particle flow moves through one complete circuit, it would NOT have to go through

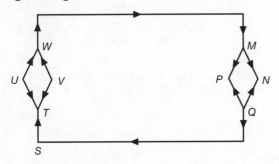

A. *V* to get to *W*.
B. *W* to get to *M*.
C. *Q* to get to *T*.
D. *T* to get to *S*.

60. The floor of a rectangular room is to be covered in two different types of material. The total cost of covering the entire room is $136. The cost of covering the inner rectangle is $80. The cost of covering the shaded area is $56.

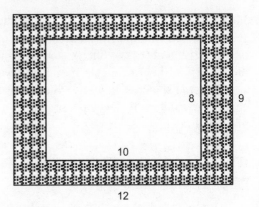

We wish to determine the cost of material per square foot used to cover the shaded area. What information given below is unnecessary for this computation?

I. the total cost of covering the entire room
II. the cost of covering the inner rectangle
III. the cost of covering the shaded area

A. I only
B. II only
C. I and II only
D. I and III only

61. Who is the central focus in the picture below and why?

Jacques-Louis David. 1789.
The Metropolitan Museum of Art, New York

A. the man on the left, with his hands and face pressed against the wall, because he is separate and thus draws attention
B. the man sitting at the foot of the bed, because he is at the lowest elevation

C. the man standing beside the bed, because he is standing alone

D. the man sitting on the bed, because the other men are focused on him

62. The drop in temperature that occurs when sugar is added to coffee is the result of

I. sugar passing from a solid to a liquid state.
II. sugar absorbing caloric from the water.
III. heat becoming latent when it was sensible.

A. I only
B. I and II only
C. I, II, and III
D. I and III only

63. Ms. Thompson wants to teach her students about methods of collecting data in science. This is a skill required by the state curriculum. Which of the following describes the most appropriate method of teaching students about collecting data in science?

A. Ms. Thompson should arrange the students into groups of four. She should then have each group observe while she gently touches the class's pet mouse with a feather. The students should record how many times out of 10 the pet mouse moves away from the feather. Then, she should gently touch the class's philodendron 10 times with a feather. The students should record how many out of 10 times the philodendron moves away from the feather.

B. Ms. Thompson should arrange the students into groups of four. She should give each group five solid balls made of materials that will float and five solid balls made of materials that will not float. She should have the students drop the balls into a bowl of water and record how many float and how many do not.

C. Ms. Thompson should show the students a video about scientific methods of gathering data.

D. Ms. Thompson should have a scientist come and talk to the class about methods of col-

lecting data. If she cannot get a scientist, she should have a science teacher from the high school come and speak about scientific methods of data collection.

64. Which of the following seems most true of the sculpture pictured below?

Gianlorenzo Bernini. *David.* 1623.
Galleria Borghese, Rome

A. The statue is conceived as a decorative work without a narrative function.

B. The figure seems to be static, passive, and introverted.

C. The figure is depicted as though frozen in a moment of action.

D. The figure's garments indicate that he is a soldier or warrior.

65. A positive condition depending on the absence of cold is

A. Fahrenheit.
B. intense artificial cold.
C. heat.
D. Celsius.

Questions 66 to 68 refer to the following short passages.

A. Once upon a time and a very good time it was there was a moocow coming down along the road and this moocow that was coming down along the road met a nicens little boy named baby tuckoo . . .

B. And thus have these naked Nantucketers, these sea hermits, issuing from their ant-hill in the sea, overrun and conquered the watery world like so many Alexanders . . .

C. A large rose tree stood near the entrance of the garden: the roses growing on it were white, but there were three gardeners at it, busily painting them red. Alice thought this a very curious thing, and she went nearer to watch them, and, just as she came up to them, she heard one of them say "Look out now, Five!"

D. Emma was not required, by any subsequent discovery, to retract her ill opinion of Mrs. Elton. Her observation had been pretty correct. Such as Mrs. Elton appeared to her on this second interview, such she appeared whenever they met again: self-important, presuming, familiar, ignorant, and ill-bred. She had a little beauty and a little accomplishment, but so little judgment that she thought herself coming with superior knowledge of the world, to enliven and improve a country neighborhood . . .

66. Which passage makes use of allusion?

67. Which passage employs a distinct voice to imitate the speech of a character?

68. Which passage is most likely taken from a nineteenth-century novel of manners?

Questions 69 to 72 refer to the following passage.

The issue of adult literacy has finally received recognition in the media as a major social problem. It is more important that the politicians themselves recognize the seriousness of the problem and support increased funding for literacy programs.

Literacy education programs need to be directed at two different groups of people with very different needs. The first group is composed of people who have very limited reading and writing skills. These people are complete illiterates. A second group is composed of people who can read and write but whose skills are not sufficient to meet their needs. This second group is called functionally illiterate. Successful literacy programs must meet the needs of both groups.

Instructors in literacy programs have three main responsibilities. First, the educational needs of the illiterates and functional illiterates must be met. Second, the instructors must approach the participants in the program with empathy, not sympathy. Third, all participants must experience success in the program and must perceive their efforts as worthwhile.

69. What is the difference between illiteracy and functional illiteracy?

A. There is no difference.
B. A functional illiterate is enrolled in a literacy education program but an illiterate is not.
C. An illiterate cannot read or write; a functional illiterate can read and write but not at a very high skill level.
D. There are more illiterates than functional illiterates in the United States today.

70. What is the purpose of the passage?

A. to discuss the characteristics of successful literacy programs

B. to discuss the manner in which literacy programs are viewed by the media
C. to discuss some of the reasons for increased attention to literacy as a social issue
D. all of the above

71. According to the passage, which of the following is NOT a characteristic of successful literacy programs?

   A. Participants should receive free transportation.
   B. Participants should experience success in the program.
   C. Instructors must have empathy, not sympathy.
   D. Programs must meet the educational needs of illiterates.

72. What is the author's opinion of the funding for literacy programs?

   A. too much
   B. too little
   C. about right
   D. too much for illiterates and not enough for functional illiterates

73. Mr. Dobson teaches fifth-grade mathematics at Valverde Elementary. He encourages students to work in groups of two or three as they begin homework assignments so they can answer questions for each other. Mr. Dobson notices immediately that some of his students choose to work alone even though they had been asked to work in groups. He also notices that some students are easily distracted even though the other members of their group are working on the assignment as directed.

   Which of the following is the most likely explanation for the students' different types of behavior?

   A. Fifth-grade students are not physically or mentally capable of working in small groups; small groups are more suitable for older students.
   B. Fifth-grade students vary greatly in their physical development and maturity; this variance influences the students' interests and attitudes.

C. Fifth-grade students lack the ability for internal control and therefore learn best in structured settings. It is usually best to seat fifth-graders in single rows.
D. Mr. Dobson needs to be more specific in his expectations for student behavior.

74. Mr. Dobson wants to encourage all of his students to participate in discussions related to the use of math in the real world. Five students in one class are very shy and introverted. Which of the following would most likely be the best way to encourage these students to participate in the discussion?

   A. Mr. Dobson should call on these students by name at least once each day and give participation grades.
   B. Mr. Dobson should not be concerned about these students because they will become less shy and introverted as they mature during the year.
   C. Mr. Dobson should divide the class into small groups for discussion so these students will not be overwhelmed by speaking in front of the whole class.
   D. Mr. Dobson should speak with these students individually and encourage them to participate more in class discussions.

75. Mrs. Kresmeier teaches sixth-grade language arts classes. One of her curriculum goals is to help students improve their spelling. As one of her techniques, she has developed a number of special mnemonic devices that she uses with the students, getting the idea from the old teaching rhymes like "*I* before *E* except after *C* or when sounding like *A* as in *neighbor* or *weigh*." Her own memory tricks—"The moose can't get loose from the noose" or "Spell rhyme? Why me?"—have caught the interest of her students. Now, besides Mrs. Kresmeier's memory tricks for better spelling, her students are developing and sharing their own creative ways to memorize more effectively.

To improve her students' spelling, Mrs. Kresmeier's method has been successful primarily because of which of the following factors related to student achievement?

A. The students are not relying on phonics or sight words to spell difficult words.
B. Mrs. Kresmeier has impressed her students with the need to learn to spell.
C. The ideas are effective with many students and help to create a learning environment that is open to student interaction.
D. Mrs. Kresmeier teaches spelling using only words that can be adapted to mnemonic clues.

76. Which of the following is incorrectly punctuated?

A. The book "Marching to the Beat" is actually an autobiography of the author.
B. Billy and Joe ran and jumped; they were happy because they were on their way to their first day of school.
C. Sally's walking to school was a new experience for her.
D. The dog shook free of its collar.

77. Choose the best-written sentence.

A. Sheena encountered many adventures walking to school.
B. Serpes served sandwiches to the men on his best china dishes.
C. The dog won the contest by posing during examination, jumping through the hoops, and coming on command.
D. The pioneer saw a new world looking through the flap of the wagon.

78. Which is not a goal of music education in the lower grades?

A. encouraging responsiveness to music
B. creating patriotism by emphasizing the music of America
C. increasing listening awareness
D. increasing involvement in music

79. Mr. Dobson and Mr. Lowery, fifth-grade science teachers, are planning a celebration of Galileo's birthday. The students will research Galileo's discoveries, draw posters of those discoveries, and prepare short plays depicting important events in his life. They will present the plays and display the posters for grades 1 to 4.

This is an example of

A. an end-of-the-year project.
B. problem solving and inquiry teaching.
C. working with other teachers to plan instructions.
D. teachers preparing to ask the Parent Teacher Association for science lab equipment.

80. Mr. Dobson wants to use a variety of grouping strategies during the year. Sometimes he groups students with others of similar ability; sometimes he groups students with varying ability. Sometimes he permits students to choose their own groupings. Sometimes he suggests that students work with a particular partner; sometimes he assigns a partner. Sometimes he allows students to elect to work individually.

This flexibility in grouping strategies indicates Mr. Dobson recognizes that

A. fifth graders like surprises and unpredictable teacher behavior.
B. grouping patterns affect students' perceptions of self-esteem and competence.
C. frequent changes in the classroom keep students alert and interested.
D. it is not fair to place the worst students in the same group consistently.

81. Which of the following is the equivalent of 6^6?

A. 36
B. 66
C. 46,656
D. 7,776

Questions 82 and 83 refer to the following scenario.

The social studies teachers of an inner-city school wanted to change to a more relevant curriculum. The department wanted to have units on economics throughout the world instead of only regions of the United States. Mrs. Dunn was asked to submit a proposal for the new curriculum, related activities, sequencing, themes, and materials. In consultation with the other teachers in the department, a needs assessment was planned.

82. The group felt that the needs assessment would

    A. help the students make a connection between their current skills and those that will be new to them.
    B. reveal community problems that may affect the students' lives and their performance in school.
    C. foster a view of learning as a purposeful pursuit, promoting a sense of responsibility for one's own learning.
    D. engage students in learning activities and help them to develop the motivation to achieve.

83. When the needs assessment was evaluated, it revealed an ethnically diverse community. Student interests and parental expectations varied, different language backgrounds existed, student exceptionalities were common, and academic motivation was low. The question confronting the teachers was how to bridge the gap from where the students are to where they should be. The most effective way to do this would be to

    A. change the text only.
    B. relate the lessons to the students' personal interests.
    C. create a positive environment to minimize the effects of the negative external factors.
    D. help students to learn and to monitor their own performance.

84. During a period of community-involvement field experiences, Ms. Parks continually directs her students' attention to the fact that science is a way of solving problems. Following the period of field experiences, Ms. Parks asks her students to identify a problem in their school and to devise a scientific way of studying and solving that problem. The students work in groups for two class periods and select the following problem for investigation: It is late spring, and the classroom gets so hot during the afternoon that the majority of the students are uncomfortable. Their research question becomes "Why is it hotter in our classroom than in the music room, art room, or library? How can we make our classroom cooler?"

    Of the following choices, what is the most important benefit of allowing the students to select their own problem to investigate, rather than having the teacher assign a problem?

    A. Students become self-directed problem solvers who can structure their own learning experiences.
    B. The teacher can best assess each student's academic and affective needs in a naturalistic setting.
    C. Students will have the opportunity to work with a wide variety of instructional materials.
    D. Students will learn to appreciate opposing viewpoints.

85. Which of the following is the most important force at work when students are allowed to select their own problem for investigation?

    A. increased student motivation
    B. increased student diversity
    C. increased structure of student groups
    D. increased use of self-assessment

86. Mrs. Jones, the economics teacher, hoped that at the end of the question-and-answer period, the students would have an <u>awareness of the correlation between skills or lack of skills and salaries</u>. A parent/guardian support group would be established to enhance the students' motivation to master new skills. Strategies for use at home and in the classroom would be developed. Mrs. Jones felt that with the aid of parents

    A. she could promote her own professional growth as she worked cooperatively with professionals to create a school culture that would enhance learning and result in positive change.
    B. she would be meeting the expectations associated with teaching.
    C. she would be fostering strong home relationships that support student achievement of desired outcomes.
    D. she would be exhibiting her understanding of the principles of conducting parent-teacher conferences and working cooperatively with parents.

87. What might Mrs. Walker, a sixth-grade teacher of world history, include in her planning to keep gifted students challenged?

    A. Assign an extra report on the history of the Greeks.
    B. Let them tutor the students who are unmotivated.
    C. Encourage students to plan learning activities of their own.
    D. Create for the student a tightly organized and well-designed unit.

88. Ms. Carter is a second-grade social studies teacher at a small rural school in southern Florida. Several times during the semester, she has found herself in conversations with colleagues in the school and various community members regarding concerns about a program initiated by the school librarian who is active in the wildlife refuge program in the county. The librarian often brings hurt or orphaned animals to the library to care for them during the day. Several parents are concerned about issues of hygiene and students with allergies.

    As a member of the site-based decision-making (SBDM) committee, Ms. Carter's best course of action is to

    A. tell the librarian to remove the animals at once.
    B. submit an agenda item to the principal to discuss the concerns at the next meeting.
    C. call the Health Department for a surprise inspection.
    D. take up for the librarian and praise her efforts to expose students to the issues of wildlife preservation.

89. When a member of the House of Representatives helps a citizen from his or her district receive federal aid to which that citizen is entitled, the representative's action is referred to as

    A. casework.
    B. pork barrel legislation.
    C. lobbying.
    D. logrolling.

90. The probability of parents' offspring showing particular traits can be predicted by using

    A. the Linnaean system.
    B. DNA tests.
    C. the Punnett square.
    D. none of the above.

91. Which of the following is a cone-shaped formation one might find on the floor of a cave?

    A. stalactite
    B. stalagmite
    C. graphite
    D. limestone

92. Use the pie chart below to answer the question that follows.

Votes for City Council

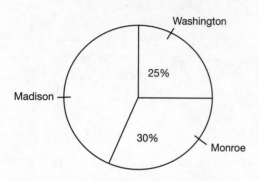

If the total number of people voting was 600, which of the following statements are true?

I.   Madison received more votes than Monroe and Washington combined.
II. Madison received 45 percent of the votes.
III. Monroe received 180 votes.
IV. Madison received 330 votes.

A.   I and II only
B.   I and IV only
C.   II and III only
D.   II and IV only

93. Use the graph below to answer the question that follows.

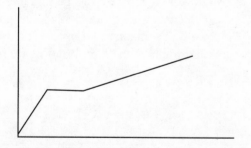

Which of the following scenarios could be represented by the graph above?

A.   Mr. Cain mowed grass at a steady rate for a while, then took a short break, and then finished the job at a steady but slower rate.

B.   Mr. Cain mowed grass at a steady rate for a while, then mowed at a steady slower rate, and then he took a break.

C.   Mr. Cain mowed grass at a variable rate for a while, then took a short break, and then finished the job at a variable rate.

D.   Mr. Cain mowed grass at a steady rate for a while, then took a short break, and then finished the job at a steady but faster pace.

94. Use the bar graph below to answer the question that follows.

MS. PATTON'S EARNINGS, 1998–2002

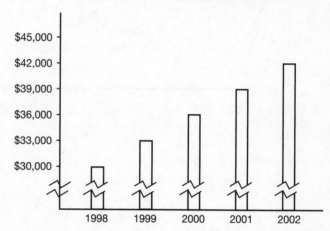

Only one of the following statements is necessarily true. Which one?

A.   The range of Ms. Patton's earnings for the years shown is $15,000.

B.   Ms. Patton's annual pay increases were consistent over the years shown.

C.   Ms. Patton earned $45,000 in 2003.

D.   Ms. Patton's average income for the years shown was $38,000.

95. The following graph shows the distribution of test scores in Ms. Alvarez's class.

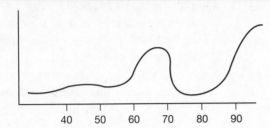

Which of the following statements do you know to be true?

I.   The majority of students scored higher than 60.
II. The test was a fair measure of ability.
III. The mean score is probably higher than the median.
IV. The test divided the class into distinct groups.

A. I and II only
B. I and IV only
C. I, III, and IV only
D. IV only

96. Which of the following is not the direct result of volcanic activity?

A. sedimentary rock
B. igneous rock
C. magma
D. lava

97. Round the following number to the nearest hundredths place: 287.416.

A. 300
B. 290
C. 287.42
D. 287.4139

98. Translate the following problem into a one-variable equation, and then solve the equation.

"There are 10 vehicles in a parking lot. Each is either a car with four tires or a motorcycle with two tires. (Do not count any spare tires.) There are 26 wheels in the lot. How many cars are there in the lot?"

A. 8
B. 6
C. 5
D. 3

99. Which equation could be used to solve the following problem?

"Three consecutive odd numbers add up to 117. What are they?"

A. $x + (x + 2) + (x + 4) = 117$
B. $1x + 3x + 5x = 117$
C. $x + x + x = 117$
D. $x + (x + 1) + (x + 3) = 117$

100. Which equation could be used to solve the following problem?

"Here is how the Acme Taxicab Company computes fares for riders: People are charged $3 for just getting into the cab, then they are charged $2 more for every mile or fraction of a mile of the ride. What would be the fare for a ride of 10.2 miles?"

A. $3 \times (2 \times 10.2) = y$
B. $3 + (2 + 11) = y$
C. $.3 \times (2 + 10.2) = y$
D. $3 + (2 \times 11) = y$

DIRECTIONS FOR THE PERFORMANCE ASSIGNMENT

This section of the test consists of a performance assignment. **The assignment can be found on the next page.** You are asked to prepare a written response of approximately 2–3 pages on the assigned topic. You should use your time to plan, write, review, and edit your response for the assignment.

Read the assignment carefully before you begin to work. Think about how you will organize your response. You may use any blank space in this test booklet to make notes, write an outline, or otherwise prepare your response. **(On the actual test, your score will be based solely on the version of your response written in the response booklet.)**

As a whole, your response must demonstrate an understanding of the knowledge and skills of the field. In your response to the assignment, you are expected to demonstrate the depth of your understanding of the content area through your ability to apply your knowledge and skills rather than merely to recite factual information.

Your response will be evaluated based on the following criteria:

- Purpose: the extent to which the response achieves the purpose of the assignment
- Subject matter knowledge: accuracy and appropriateness in the application of subject matter knowledge
- Support: quality and relevance of supporting details
- Rationale: soundness of argument and degree of understanding of the subject matter

The performance assignment is intended to assess subject knowledge content and skills, not writing ability. However, you must communicate clearly enough to permit scorers to make a valid evaluation according to the criteria listed above. Your response should be written for an audience of educators in this field. The final version of your response should conform to the conventions of edited American English. This should be your original work, written in your own words, and not copied or paraphrased from some other work.

Practice Test 1 Performance Assignment

101. Read the paragraph below; then complete the exercise that follows.

> Lecturing is an important component in day-to-day teaching. Some critics see lecturing as far too passive a student activity. Others suggest it promotes student nonparticipation and inactivity, while some teachers say it is just plain obsolete. Then there are those who claim that lecturing is the most efficient way of communicating. Mrs. Adams does not plan a lot of lectures during the unit on Colonial America.

Discuss your philosophy on lecturing and its pedagogical values. What are the elements that Mrs. Adams should use to ensure a good lecture? What alternative methods could take the place of lecturing?

Practice Test 1 Answer Key

1. (A)	26. (C)	51. (C)	76. (A)
2. (D)	27. (C)	52. (C)	77. (C)
3. (D)	28. (B)	53. (A)	78. (B)
4. (B)	29. (B)	54. (C)	79. (C)
5. (C)	30. (C)	55. (B)	80. (B)
6. (A)	31. (B)	56. (C)	81. (C)
7. (B)	32. (A)	57. (B)	82. (A)
8. (B)	33. (A)	58. (D)	83. (C)
9. (B)	34. (A)	59. (A)	84. (A)
10. (D)	35. (D)	60. (C)	85. (A)
11. (D)	36. (C)	61. (D)	86. (C)
12. (B)	37. (B)	62. (C)	87. (C)
13. (A)	38. (D)	63. (B)	88. (B)
14. (C)	39. (D)	64. (C)	89. (A)
15. (D)	40. (A)	65. (C)	90. (C)
16. (D)	41. (D)	66. (B)	91. (B)
17. (B)	42. (A)	67. (A)	92. (C)
18. (B)	43. (B)	68. (D)	93. (A)
19. (B)	44. (D)	69. (C)	94. (B)
20. (D)	45. (C)	70. (D)	95. (B)
21. (D)	46. (D)	71. (A)	96. (A)
22. (B)	47. (A)	72. (B)	97. (C)
23. (A)	48. (D)	73. (B)	98. (D)
24. (C)	49. (A)	74. (C)	99. (A)
25. (A)	50. (C)	75. (C)	100. (D)

AEPA Elementary Education Practice Test 1
Answers Sorted by Competency

Question	Objective	Answer	Did you answer correctly?
16	Objective 0001	D	
31	Objective 0001	B	
13	Objective 0002	A	
30	Objective 0002	C	
34	Objective 0002	A	
75	Objective 0002	C	
10	Objective 0003	D	
12	Objective 0003	B	
54	Objective 0003	C	
56	Objective 0003	C	
17	Objective 0004	B	
53	Objective 0004	A	
66	Objective 0005	B	
67	Objective 0005	A	
68	Objective 0005	D	
55	Objective 0006	B	
11	Objective 0007	D	
41	Objective 0007	D	
69	Objective 0007	C	
70	Objective 0007	D	
71	Objective 0007	A	
72	Objective 0007	B	
76	Objective 0008	A	
77	Objective 0008	C	
42	Objective 0009	A	
44	Objective 0009	D	
7	Objective 0010	B	
33	Objective 0010	A	
8	Objective 0011	B	
2	Objective 0012	D	

Question	Objective	Answer	Did you answer correctly?
73	Objective 0012	B	
74	Objective 0012	C	
22	Objective 0013	B	
81	Objective 0014	C	
97	Objective 0014	C	
94	Objective 0015	B	
95	Objective 0015	B	
15	Objective 0016	D	
46	Objective 0016	D	
37	Objective 0017	B	
38	Objective 0017	D	
39	Objective 0017	D	
40	Objective 0017	A	
98	Objective 0017	D	
99	Objective 0017	A	
100	Objective 0017	D	
92	Objective 0018	C	
60	Objective 0019	C	
93	Objective 0019	A	
14	Objective 0020	C	
18	Objective 0020	B	
19	Objective 0020	B	
20	Objective 0020	D	
80	Objective 0020	B	
9	Objective 0021	B	
84	Objective 0021	A	
85	Objective 0021	A	
32	Objective 0022	A	
52	Objective 0023	C	
57	Objective 0023	B	

Question	Objective	Answer	Did you answer correctly?
16	Objective 0001	D	
31	Objective 0001	B	
13	Objective 0002	A	
30	Objective 0002	C	
34	Objective 0002	A	
75	Objective 0002	C	
10	Objective 0003	D	
12	Objective 0003	B	
54	Objective 0003	C	
56	Objective 0003	C	
17	Objective 0004	B	
53	Objective 0004	A	
66	Objective 0005	B	
67	Objective 0005	A	
68	Objective 0005	D	
55	Objective 0006	B	
11	Objective 0007	D	
41	Objective 0007	D	
69	Objective 0007	C	
70	Objective 0007	D	

Question	Objective	Answer	Did you answer correctly?
71	Objective 0007	A	
72	Objective 0007	B	
76	Objective 0008	A	
77	Objective 0008	C	
42	Objective 0009	A	
44	Objective 0009	D	
7	Objective 0010	B	
33	Objective 0010	A	
8	Objective 0011	B	
2	Objective 0012	D	
73	Objective 0012	B	
74	Objective 0012	C	
22	Objective 0013	B	
81	Objective 0014	C	
97	Objective 0014	C	
94	Objective 0015	B	
95	Objective 0015	B	
15	Objective 0016	D	
46	Objective 0016	D	
37	Objective 0017	B	

Practice Test 1
Explanations of Answers

1. A

There is a direct relationship between what is taught in school and what is learned in school. Also, if you want children to improve in writing, they need time to write. Creating murals (D), doing worksheets (B), and copying speeches (C) do not improve writing.

2. D

This teacher is doing a good thing by collecting data and displaying the data. I hope this teacher also shared the findings with the children, their parents, and anybody else who would look at it. Look how successful the literacy program is! Notice the interest in fantasy works and in reading increased after the unit.

3. D

In creative drama, activities build upon one another and establishing a foundation of skill-building activities is the norm. Beginning activities are warm-ups. These are used to introduce a session and to help players become comfortable with one another. Pantomime activities are next, as these help children to develop nonverbal communication abilities and to clearly express ideas without speaking. Without these experiences, players too often rely only upon voice for sharing ideas and for characterization. Because improvisations can be done with or without speaking, they follow pantomimes. When students incorporate dialogue into their improvisations, they have a better understanding of how an actor uses voice and body as artistic tools. Improvisations also help students learn to think quickly and creatively. Story creation is next. There are multiple ways of creating stories. These can be done using unison or individual play and in pantomime or with dialogue. The result can be simple or complex stories. In order to successfully engage in story creation, students should understand characterization and plot. They should be experienced at using imagination and ensemble play. Story dramatization is the most complex creative drama activity, as it incorporates skills developed at lower levels. Here, players engage in individual rather than unison play. Story dramatizations are often student-directed activities based upon original stories or stories from literature. These require an investment of time if believable characterizations are to result. Engaging in story dramatizations encourages an understanding of both drama and literature. If one were to construct a hierarchy of creative drama activities, story dramatization would be at the top.

4. B

In using three different versions of this well-known story, Ms. Smith is creating an opportunity to bring a multicultural perspective to the drama activity. In versions of *Cinderella* from around the world, the story of the mistreated but kindhearted protagonist is basically the same, but the characters, settings, and ways in which the plot unfolds are culturally centered. Furthermore, because Ms. Smith is using scripted versions of the story and staging these plays with costumes, scenery, and props, she is making theatrical elements integral to the performances. As the students are engaging in formal dramatic activity that will result in a theatrical product, rather than informal, process-centered drama, item III is incorrect. Item IV is incorrect because the students are not the ones who have adapted the stories, and therefore, they are not experiencing that process firsthand.

5. C

Of the choices offered, only creative drama meets specified criteria. Although children's theatre is audience centered, it is product oriented, rather than process oriented. The product is the play and assuring that the audience sees a quality production overrides benefits to individual children who are cast in it. Readers' theatre productions do not require elaborate staging. Elements such as movement are suggested to the audience who then complete the picture in their minds. Readers often sit on stools or use music stands to hold notebooks housing their scripts. Puppetry may describe plays done with elaborate dolls, but it can also describe creative drama or theatre activities done with very simple puppets.

6. A

In pantomime, there always needs to be something for the player to do or to express. Because the means of expression is physical, content with a lot of dialogue would prove a hindrance to interpretation. Likewise, inactive verbs give the player little to show or do. Descriptive narrative also limits action. The correct answer is choice A, because active verbs assure that players will be able to express actions, emotions, and ideas.

7. B

In offering criticism of the play, students should give opinions that not only reveal how they feel about what they saw but also the reasons for their opinions. In other words, they should be able to support their judgments based upon their personal aesthetic. Both statements II and IV are supported opinions that show an appreciation for the theatrical elements of character and plot. These also reveal connections to the viewer's emotions and life experiences. Statement I is an unsupported opinion and is, therefore, incorrect. Statement III is a response to the theatre building in which the play was presented rather than a response to the play, and it is the latter that Mr. Nelson wants his students to give.

8. B

One of the virtues of using drama/theatre with young people is that it challenges them to think independently and creatively. Often, there is not one right answer or interpretation. Using the same material in a variety of ways offers the following advantages: (1) information is presented through multiple channels, thereby increasing opportunities for knowing; (2) using different types of dramatic activities broadens both the appeal of and the learning opportunities inherent in the material; (3) multiple formats increase opportunities to engage students and to address their learning styles; and (4) students can see that there are various ways of creating meaning and expressing ideas. Answer choice A is incorrect because there may not be only one correct way to use material. As the rationale for the correct answer implies, exploring content is one way to move students beyond the obvious and encourage them to use higher-level thinking skills. Choice C is incorrect because it requires a value judgment based upon personal preference; it is not grounded in fact. Likewise, choice D is incorrect because it reflects a value judgment that is without substance. Some students may learn more by directly participating in activities; some may learn more by watching a performance. Both creative drama activities and theatre performances are educationally sound undertakings.

9. B

A discovery-learning lesson is one in which the class is organized to learn through their own active involvement in the lesson. In inductive-reasoning lessons (choice C), the students are provided with the examples and nonexamples and are expected to derive definitions from this information. The eg-rule method (choice D) moves from specific examples to general rules or definitions. The lesson may take place in a science class (choice A) but is still a discovery-learning lesson.

10. D

A question testing whether or not a student can synthesize information will include the need to make predictions or solve problems. An evaluation question (choice A) will require a judgment of the quality of an idea or solution. In order to be real analysis (choice B), the question would have to ask students to analyze given information to draw a conclusion or find support for a given idea. Comprehension questions (choice C)

require the rephrasing of an idea in the students' own words, and then using this for comparison. Choice D involves "putting together" a plan; this is an example of synethesizing.

11. D

Having a mixed-level pair read together enables the remedial student to receive instruction while the skilled student receives reinforcement. Thus, Mr. Drake is using alternate teaching resources, the students themselves, to enhance the learning environment. Mr. Drake has set a certain goal (choice A), comprehension, but this is not the most important outcome. The teacher will need to observe fewer groups (choice B), but it is unlikely that this will change the amount of time needed to work with all groups if quality is to be maintained. Although reading in pairs, each student should have a book, and it would be impractical to permit another teacher to utilize the books while one teacher is using them (choice C).

12. B

Students at this age do not have the cognitive skills to realize how much they have actually learned, or how much they will actually be able to retain. For this reason, choice A must be incorrect. Students cannot differentiate material that is completely understood and that which they have not completely comprehended at this stage in their intellectual development; this eliminates choice C. Students will generally feel that they are capable of learning much more than they will actually retain; therefore, choice D is also incorrect.

13. A

Mapping out previous knowledge makes students aware that they can use information they already know to support new information. Although words on the board are visual (choice B), this is not the underlying motive. Semantic mapping done at the beginning of a story tests how much knowledge the students have about the topic at the outset, not the conclusion (choice C). Semantic mapping does model proper use of words (choice D), but this is not the main intent of the exercise.

14. C

Data gathered within the learning environment resulting from day-to-day activities provide a means for reflection and discussion. This includes not only using students' in-class scores for their most recognized use, student academic grades, but also using the success of students to guide a teacher's professional development plan. Looking for inconsistencies in grading can be a basis for teachers to explore their teaching practices while looking for new and more effective methods. In considering answer choices B and D, remember that student academic grades should never be used in behavior assessment.

15. D

All teachers have different strengths and weaknesses. By working collaboratively, they can share their strengths to create more strengths and fewer weaknesses. If a teacher has found a method of teaching a concept that is successful, it is worth trying. Viewing the students' scores from the previous year would assist in seeing if they had made any progress since their last test but should not be used to justify their poor scores (choice A). This does nothing to assist students in improving their academic achievement. Telling future students to study harder (choice B) or suggesting math tutors (choice C) is always good advice but should not be the only course for helping students improve in a certain area.

16. D

During late childhood and early adolescence, students often exhibit problems with self-image, physical appearance, eating disorders, feelings of rebelliousness, and other similar problems. Teachers of these students should be aware of these developmental problems and do all they can to minimize them in their classrooms. Providing a safe learning environment and letting students know that the teacher is aware of these issues will assist in keeping these students on task. Choice A is incorrect. Many students at this age exhibit these kinds of problems. The counselors do not have time to address all of them, and this reaction would cause a major disruption in the learning process. Choice B is also incorrect. Although parents can sometimes help, this solution

should be used only for the most severe cases. Choice C is incorrect because calling students' attention to these kinds of problems in this way often only makes the problems worse by isolating and ostracizing individuals.

17. B

A high-order question (choice A) tests the student's ability to apply information, evaluate information, create new information, and so on, rather than to recall simple content. Transitions (choice C) are used to connect different ideas and tasks. The information that the question is looking for is one of content, not skill (choice D). The question presented here is a low-order question that ensures that a student focuses on the task at hand and may develop into higher questioning.

18. B

Piaget developed four stages of cognitive development. As children go through each stage, they develop new abilities particular to that stage. Children under the age of eight do not yet have the understanding of language that grasps complexities, as choice B correctly indicates. Accordingly, teachers should use simple language when working with these children.

19. B

When designing learning activities, teachers should be aware that younger students process information more slowly than their older counterparts. Activities for younger children should be simple and short in duration.

20. D

In inductive thinking, students derive concepts and definitions based upon the information provided to them; personal-discovery activities (choice D) in which students try to determine the relationships between the objects given to them foster inductive-thinking skills. Choral chanting (choice A) practices skills, multiple-choice questions (choice C) test objective knowledge,

and general computer experience (choice B) fosters computer knowledge.

21. D

The integrated, real-life nature of this project builds deeper understandings of the economic concept of work and wages, saving versus spending, and banking. While providing the authentic experience of working and saving, the project also builds children's capacity to complete mathematical functions like figuring interest rates and compounding interest. In addition, the project illustrates the importance of saving money.

22. B

The example illustrates a deductive reasoning task. One is drawing from the information already given; one does not have to form the rule or generalization as with inductive reasoning. An inductive reasoning problem (choice A) would ask the class to form a rule or generalization based on some given information. Choices C and D are both examples of inductive tasks.

23. A

The Magna Carta was signed in 1215. Columbus's voyages began in the fifteenth century. The Protestant Reformation occurred in the sixteenth century. The Puritans came to America in the seventeenth century. Therefore, choice A is correct.

24. C

The American System (choice A), as conceived by Henry Clay, referred to the nationalist policy of uniting the three economic sections of the United States in the time following the War of 1812. Mercantilism (choice B) is an economic theory whose principal doctrine was the belief that the wealth of nations was based on the possession of gold. The Enlightenment movement was characterized by an impetus toward learning, a spirit of skepticism in social and political thought, and rational-

ism. The Age of Belief (choice D) is tied to tradition and emotion.

25. A

Checks and balances provide each of the branches with the ability to limit the actions of the other branches. Choice B is incorrect; branches of the federal government do not achieve independence from each other due to checks and balances. Choices C and D are also incorrect because they deal with only one branch, whereas the system of checks and balances involves the manner in which the three branches are interrelated.

26. C

Choices A, B, and D all played a role in the early settlements of the English colonies in America. The correct response is choice C; Mormonism was founded at Fayette, New York, in 1830, by Joseph Smith. The Book of Mormon was published in 1830, and it described the establishment of an American colony from the Tower of Babel.

27. C

The letter *K* represents Cuba, letter *D* represents Indonesia, and letter *M* represents Sri Lanka. The letter *I*, choice C, correctly represents the Philippine Islands.

28. B

The Bill of Rights clearly states that Congress may not make laws abridging citizens' rights and liberties. Choices C and D are incorrect because the Bill of Rights does not talk about voting rights or slaves. A list of grievances (choice A) is contained in the Declaration of Independence.

29. B

This assignment asks students to gather information or explore long-term goals, goals many years in the future. Short-term goals (choices A and C) are those that can be achieved in days, weeks, or maybe months. Synthesizing long-term goals (choice D) is a more complicated process than merely gathering information.

30. C

The teacher is asking the student questions to allow the student to correct a spelling error. Spelling does not allow for divergent or creative thinking (choice A). Although the teacher reminds the student of a mnemonic, the teacher is not teaching the mnemonic (choice B); finally, applying spelling rules or guides to improve spelling would be an example of deductive reasoning, not inductive reasoning (choice D).

31. B

It is very important that all students feel welcome, but it is especially effective for English as a Second Language (ESL) students to feel comfortable and welcomed in the classroom.

32. A

Ms. Borders must consider the learning preferences and emotional factors of her learners as she constructs learning activities for the study. To consider cooperative group projects versus independent work is one aspect of her preparation. Another would be the range of products deemed acceptable as demonstrations of knowledge (written or spoken, visual or performed art, technology based, and so forth). Choices B, C, and D might be considered once she plans the study, but they are unrelated to the issue of preparing for the stated instructional outcomes.

33. A

Students speaking two languages learn one of two ways: sequentially, in which one language is mastered before the study of the second language has begun (choice A), and simultaneously, in which both languages are learned concurrently (choice B). Sequential lan-

guage acquisition does not mean a student learns two languages in parts (choice C) or develops language skills (choice D).

34. A

Some students may not speak English at home or may have limited exposure to the vocabulary of the classroom. It is important to be aware of these factors and provide the materials appropriate to help guide mastery.

35. D

The teacher, realizing that students will have different interpretations of the statement, hopes to engage the students in critical thinking and allow them to express their opinions. Choices A, B, and C are possible outcomes, but choice D is the best answer because it relates specifically to the teacher's aim.

36. C

The best response is to emphasize that occupations are open to both men and women and that most people make career choices based on their abilities and their preferences. Choices A and B fail to take advantage of the opportunity to teach the class about equal opportunity in career choices, and choice D implies that popular opinion determines career choices.

37. B

The 1933 bar is highest, and the graph measures the percent of unemployment by the height of the bars. The bars for 1929 (choice A), 1938 (choice C), and 1944 (choice D) are all lower than the bar for 1933, the year in which unemployment was the highest.

38. D

The bar representing 1944 (that is, the bar between 1943 and 1945) is the lowest on the graph. As previously mentioned, the graph measures the percent-age of unemployment by the length of the bars. The bars for 1929 (choice A), 1933 (choice B), and 1938 (choice C) are all higher than the bar for 1944.

39. D

Choice A is wrong because about 30 percent of households had under $15,000. Choices B and C are also incorrect, since slightly more than 15 percent of households fell into the $50,000 or more category.

40. A

Graph reading and interpretation is the primary focus of this question. Choice B is obviously wrong because the bar representing the discretionary income of the youngest households ("Under 25") is the shortest bar on the chart, indicating that this group has the least discretionary income. Choices C and D are also incorrect. The oldest group has less discretionary income than those between 25 and 65, but more than those under 25.

41. D

Students' threats of suicide must be taken seriously and teachers must refer to trained professionals to take action in the face of such threats. Choices A, B, and C are inadequate responses to threats of suicide.

42. A

Linda's behavior serves a purpose or function. To assess the purpose or function of a behavior, teachers can use a functional behavioral assessment. Students normally do not exhibit behaviors for the purpose of making others angry (choice B). The behavior does not necessarily mean that Linda obviously has trouble at home; the behavior occurs at school, and the teacher needs first to determine if the behavior is something that the teacher can handle. Although it is possible that Linda just simply enjoys telling jokes, it is unlikely that she chooses to do so in the midst of a class lesson for the sheer enjoyment of performing (choice D). Hypotheses

about the functions of behaviors address why the person might be exhibiting the behavior and what they are accomplishing or avoiding by exhibiting it.

43. B

Even in kindergarten, students begin to classify sounds as high and low, walk to the music, and sing simple songs. Choice B is the best answer. Using notation, creating dance, and reading music notation (A) are activities for grades 6–8. Choice A is incorrect. Conducting duple and triple meter is an activity for grades 3–5; playing the guitar and identifying major and minor scales are activities for grades 6–8. Choice C is incorrect because the upper-grade activities are listed before the activities for lower grades. Playing the autoharp (grades 6–8), playing rhythmic instruments (K–2), and conducting simple songs (grades 3–5) are not listed in an orderly sequence; answer D is inappropriate.

44. D

In general, teachers believe that oral language proficiency correlates with academic proficiency. However, research indicates that oral language proficiency is easily acquired through daily living experiences, whereas academic language proficiency requires an academic setting with context-reduced activities.

45. C

Black-line spectra are formed when the continuous spectra of the Sun passes through the atmosphere. The elements in the atmosphere absorb wavelengths of light characteristic of their spectra (these are the same wavelengths given off when the element is excited, for example the red color of a neon light). By examining the line spectral gaps, scientists can deduce the elements that make up the distant atmosphere. Choice A is true, but it explains the source of a line spectrum. Choice B is true, and it explains why a blue shirt is blue when placed under a white or blue light source. Recall that a blue shirt under a red light source will appear black because there are no blue wavelengths to be reflected. Choice D

is a partial truth: black lights do give off ultraviolet light that the human eye cannot see.

46. D

Choice D is the best answer because it contains information that is technically correct and that expresses a concern about the difference in the student's standardized test score and usual performance in math class. Choice A is technically correct; however, it does not really provide as much complete information as choice D. Choice B tends to provide the student with a false impression; although it is true that the student scored in the top half, as one of the best students in class, the student could have expected to have scored perhaps in the top 10 percent or at least the top quartile. Choice C is a false statement.

47. A

The United States was shocked when the Soviet Union launched *Sputnik* in 1957. Comparisons between Soviet education and that available in U.S. public schools indicated a need to emphasize math (choice B), science (choice C), and foreign language (choice D) for the United States to compete with other countries and to remain a world power.

48. D

In handing down its decision in *Brown v. Board of Education of Topeka, Kansas*, in 1954, the Supreme Court stated that "Separate but equal has no place ... Separate educational facilities are inherently unequal and violate the equal protection clause of the Fourteenth Amendment."

49. A

The Peace Corps was established by President John F. Kennedy. Johnson's VISTA program (choice C) was modeled after it. Head Start (choice B) and the Elementary and Secondary Education Act (choice D) were also put into effect as part of Johnson's "War on Poverty."

50. C

The Education for All Handicapped Children Act of 1975 provides for mentally (choice A) and physically (choice B) handicapped as well as learning disabled children (choice D). It does not include socially emotionally handicapped youngsters.

51. C

The horse shows motion and lightness. Notice, for instance, the tail and feet, which seem to imply movement. The horse is young and spry so choice A could not be true. The horse does not suggest warlike attitudes so choice D is not appropriate. The horse appears light on its feet so massiveness (choice B) is not acceptable. Choice C is the best answer.

52. C

According to Piaget's theory of cognitive development, students in middle school are at the stage of concrete operational thought. Students at this stage of cognitive development are able to categorize items. Choice A is a false statement. Although some students will like to work in groups, some students will prefer to work alone—at this and at any age group or cognitive stage. Preferring to learn in groups (socially) or to learn alone (independently) is a characteristic of learning style or preference, not a characteristic of cognitive or affective development. Choice B is irrelevant to the teacher's intent in assigning the task. Students could just as easily work with unfamiliar items, grouping them by observable features independent of their use or function. Choice D is not a good choice under any circumstances. Teachers should assiduously avoid giving students any assignments merely to keep them busy while the teacher does something else. All assignments should have an instructional purpose.

53. A

Only choice A takes into account differences among learners by giving them options as to how and where they will read. Choice B violates the students' freedom to select reading materials that they find interesting and wish to read. When students are allowed to choose their own reading materials, it may seem that some students select materials beyond their present reading comprehension. However, reading research indicates that students can comprehend more difficult material when their interest level is high. Therefore, any efforts by the teacher to interfere with students' selection of their own reading material would be ill-advised. Choices C and D are equally poor in that they both describe a concession to only one group of learners. For example, some students may prefer to read with background music playing, as suggested by choice C, whereas other students will find music distracting. The best action for the teacher to take would be to allow some students to listen to music with earphones while others read in quiet. In regard to choice D, some students will prefer bright illumination just as some students will read better with the lights dimmed. Ms. Rodriguez would do well to attempt to accommodate various learner needs by having one area of the room more brightly illuminated than the other.

54. C

The teacher is encouraging students to become actively engaged in the learning process by making a prediction based on limited information given in the book title and cover illustration. When students can generate their own predictions or formulate hypotheses about possible outcomes on the basis of available (although limited) data, they are gaining preparatory skills for formal operations (or abstract thinking). Although second-grade students would not be expected to be at the level of cognitive development characterized by formal operations, Piagetian theory would indicate that teachers who model appropriate behaviors and who give students opportunities to reach or stretch for new cognitive skills are fostering students' cognitive growth. Choice A is a poor choice because students' responses to this one question posed by the teacher cannot be used to assess adequately their interest in reading activities. Choice B, likewise, is a poor choice in that it implies no instructional intent for asking the question. Choice D is incorrect because students' responses to a single question cannot allow the instruc-

tor to determine which students are good readers and which ones are not.

depth of the study, a teacher may want to include several of these activities.

55. B

The question asks which statements are appropriate for Mrs. Johnson to consider in making an instructional decision. Statement I is a valid reason for teaching students how to develop portfolios. Teachers constantly teach students the skills that will be useful in school and in their careers. Although statement II may produce positive affective results, feeling mature because students are imitating older siblings is not a sufficient reason to choose portfolios. Statement III is the most appropriate reason to decide whether to use portfolios. Most activities and projects that promote achievement of course outcomes would be considered appropriate strategies. Statement IV is not necessarily true; portfolio assessment can result in more written work, which can be more time consuming. Even if it were true, emphasizing student achievement is more important than easing the workload of teachers. Statements I and III are appropriate; therefore, the correct answer is choice B.

56. C

The question asks for work on the analysis, synthesis, or evaluation level. Choice C is the best choice because it asks the students to analyze how past causes have produced current effects, then to predict what future effects might be based on what they have learned about cause-effect relationships. It requires students to put information together in a new way. Choice A may involve some creativity in putting the information on a poster, but in general, answering factual questions calls for lower-level (knowledge or comprehension) thinking. Choice B may involve some degree of creativity, but giving students prepared questions requires them to use a lower level of thinking than would having students develop their own questions and then determine which answers to write about. Choice D is a lower-level activity, although there may be a great deal of research for factual information. All options may be good learning activities, but choices A, B, and D do not require as much deep thinking as choice C. Depending on the

57. B

This question asks for an evaluation of which software programs will help the students achieve their goals of analyzing data and presenting the results. Item I, word processing, would be used in developing and printing the questionnaire, as well as writing a report on the results. Item II, a database, would be used to sort and print out information in various categories so students could organize and analyze their data. Item III, a simulation, would not be appropriate here because the students' basic purpose is to collect data and analyze it. The project does not call for a program to simulate a situation or event. Item IV, graph or chart, would be very useful in analyzing information and in presenting it to others.

58. D

Kate, as an effective teacher and respected professional in her school as well as beyond her district, realizes the intent of central-office curriculum efforts is to raise the standards of instruction throughout the district. While Kate, as a team player in the educational process, may be performing at the highest level, other teachers need boosting. The work that Kate submits will probably be used as a model for other teachers throughout the district. The thoroughness of her response indicates that she will be invited to make other presentations at area and state professional meetings, perhaps on the topic of authentic assessment.

Choice A is an unprofessional action by Kate. Perhaps she is forgetful or lazy; she is certainly expressing rudeness and lack of cooperation by ignoring the request made of her and all teachers in the district. None of these characteristics represents a teacher who is effective in the classroom and highly respected by her students and peers.

Choice B indicates that Kate, not forgetful or lazy, is unaware of or resentful of the role she plays as a curriculum developer within her teaching assignment. Her

decision to write a "passionate letter in response" to the request is somewhat immature. The professional teacher who seriously questions a curricular approach from central office would discuss the situation reasonably, calmly, and privately with the new director of instruction. Of course, the very fact that Kate feels she has been incorporating authentic assessment ideas in her teaching for some time indicates her valuing the concept. Should her role not be one of support to get other teachers to value authentic assessment as well?

Choice C is incorrect because Kate, although showing support for the concept of authentic assessment, is still blocking the central-office efforts to get some degree of uniformity in preparation of curriculum material. Again, her "passionate letter in response" to the request for an authentic assessment sample indicates poor judgment on Kate's part. Does the strong expression of her feelings indicate an independent nature or a rebel in regards to teamwork? Is her refusal to rewrite her model unit of study to conform to the district format laziness, a rejection of authority, or some other indicator of malcontent? The effective professional would find some other way to communicate her concerns if the provided format for the model of authentic assessment could be improved.

59. A

You should note that the particle flow divides at two points, T and M. At these points, the flow has two paths to reach either point W or point Q. Thus, the correct choice is A. Particle flow can reach point W by going through point U, rather than V. It would have to flow through all other points listed in order to make a complete circuit or total clockwise path.

60. C

The total area of the larger rectangle is base $\times$ height, or $12 \times 9 = 108$ square feet. Next we must determine the area of the inner rectangle and subtract this inner area from the entire area to get the shaded portion.

Therefore, the area of the shaded portion surrounding the inner rectangle is

108 square feet $-$ 80 square feet $=$ 28 square feet.

If the total cost of material used to cover the shaded area is $56 and we have 28 square feet, the cost per square foot is

$$\frac{\$56}{28 \text{ square feet}} = \$2 \text{ per square foot.}$$

Choices A, B, and D are incorrect. Neither I nor II is necessary to determine the cost per square foot of the shaded area. Choice D is incorrect because III *is* needed to determine the cost per square foot.

61. D

This question tests your ability to determine the central focus in a staged dramatic production and to explain why there is such a focus. The central attraction in this picture is the man on the bed (choice D). Many eyes are turned to him, and he appears to be speaking. The other men in the picture are turned away from the viewers, and many are directing their attention toward the man on the bed. Because this character is in a full front position, he will draw more attention than those in profile or full back, which are weaker positions.

62. C

The best answer is choice C because it includes three correct statements. The sugar does pass from a solid to a liquid state, the sugar does absorb caloric from the water, and the heat does become latent when it is sensible. Since statements I, II, and III are all causes of the drop of temperature when sugar is added to coffee, all three must be included when choosing an answer. Although choices A, B, and D each contain one or more of these statements, none contains all three; subsequently, each of these choices is incorrect.

63. B

A hands-on activity will best help the students learn about data collection. Choice B is the only one that employs a hands-on activity, thus it is the best answer. The students would learn about direct observation by watching Ms. Thompson tickle the mouse and the philodendron (choice A); however, this method would not be as effec-

tive as allowing the students to conduct their own data collection. Research suggests that viewing a video is an inefficient method of learning (choice C). Having a guest speaker tell the students about data collection (choice D) is not a good choice for first-graders.

64. (C)

Gianlorenzo Bernini's *David* of 1623 is a perfect example of the Baroque sculptor's wish to express movement and action and to capture a fleeting moment of time. Here, the figure's twisting posture and intense facial expression create a dynamic, not a static, character (B), as David begins the violent twisting motion with which he will hurl the stone from his sling. His gaze is directed outward at an unseen adversary, implying interaction with another character and denying any purely ornamental conception behind this work (A). The figure's meager garments, far from identifying him as a warrior (D), emphasize both his physical vulnerability and his idealized, heroic beauty.

65. C

Because heat is a positive condition depending on the absence of cold, choice C is the best answer. Fahrenheit is a measure of temperature, not a condition; therefore, choice A is incorrect. Heat, or the absence of cold, is the opposite of intense artificial cold, so choice B is not acceptable. Like Fahrenheit, Celsius is a measure of temperature and is not a condition, thus choice D is incorrect.

66. B

This passage from Herman Melville's *Moby Dick* contains an allusion in the phrase "like so many Alexanders." Melville is illustrating the strength and power of whalers ("naked Nantucketers") by alluding and comparing them to Alexander the Great, the famous conqueror who died in 323 B.C.E.

67. A

This passage, which opens James Joyce's *A Portrait of the Artist as a Young Man*, is written in "baby talk" ("moocow," "nicens," "baby tuckoo") to convey to readers the age, speech, and mental state of the narrator.

68. D

Nineteenth-century novels of manners employed such themes as the importance (or unimportance) of "good breeding," the elation (and suffocation) caused by society, and the interaction of individuals within the confines of a closed country community (to name just a few). This passage, taken from Jane Austen's *Emma*, mentions "opinions" of other characters, the importance of "beauty" and "accomplishment" (note how Emma sees them as almost saving graces for Mrs. Elton), and the "improvement" of a "country neighborhood."

69. C

Choice C accurately restates the definition of *illiterate* and *functional illiterate* provided in the second paragraph of the passage. Choice A cannot be correct because the passage clearly distinguishes between illiterates and functional illiterates. As mentioned in the passage's third paragraph, participation in a literacy program is open to both illiterates and functional illiterates, so Choice B is incorrect. The relative number of illiterates and functional illiterates is not discussed, thus eliminating choice D.

70. D

This passage has several purposes. First, the author presents some complaints concerning the way literacy issues are presented in the media (choice B). The author also discusses the increased attention given to literacy by society (choice C). Third, the author discusses many aspects of successful literacy programs (choice A). Therefore, choice D, which includes all of these purposes, is correct.

71. A

This question must be answered using the process of elimination. You are asked to select a statement that names a possible program component that is not characteristic of successful literacy programs. Choice A is

correct because choices B, C, and D are specifically mentioned in the passage.

72. B

The author specifically states that politicians should support increased funding for literacy programs. Choices A and C are incorrect because the author states that funding should be increased. The author does not discuss funding for different programs, so choice D is incorrect.

73. B

The variance in fifth-graders' physical size and development has a direct influence on their interests and attitudes, including their willingness to work with others and a possible preference for working alone. Choice A is incorrect because fifth-graders do have the physical and mental maturity to work in small groups. Choice C is incorrect because not all fifth-grade students lack the ability for internal control. Choice D is also incorrect; although Mr. Dobson might need to be more specific in his directions to the students, this is not the main reason for their behavior.

74. C

Students who are shy are usually more willing to participate in small groups than in discussions involving the entire class. Choice A is incorrect because calling on each student once per day will not necessarily assist shy students to participate in class discussions, even if participation grades are assigned. Choice B is incorrect because although students may become less shy as the year progresses, the teacher still has a responsibility to encourage students to participate. Choice D is incorrect because although speaking to each student individually may help some students participate, the procedure outlined in choice C is a more effective way of encouraging shy students to participate.

75. C

Mrs. Kresmeier uses effective communication strategies to teach students and encourages them to interact for the same purposes. Mnemonic devices are apparently a new technique for most of the students; the teacher's own creative spelling clues are often new ones matching the age level, interests, and patterns of humor enjoyed by her students. The most success is probably derived from her encouragement to examine the words to find a feature that can be turned into a mnemonic device. Choice A is incorrect because Mrs. Kresmeier has not attempted to rule out other techniques of learning to spell. Choice B is incorrect because certainly other teachers have also impressed upon the students that spelling is important. The creative methodology is probably the major difference between Mrs. Kresmeier's method and those that students have encountered in the past. Choice D is incorrect because no evidence exists to show that Mrs. Kresmeier is especially selective in choosing her spelling lessons.

76. A

The book title is incorrectly shown. Titles of books are correctly italicized or underlined. Short stories and articles usually have quotation marks to show the title.

77. C

Choice C is the best answer. The sentence has correct punctuation and parallel structure. Choice A is incorrect because there is a misplaced modifier; the *adventures* were not *walking to school*. Choice B is incorrect because the men were not sitting on the china dishes; the sentence has a misplaced modifier. Choice D also employs a misplaced modifier; the *world* was not *looking through the flap of the wagon*.

78. B

A high-quality music program includes music from many cultures and time periods; "American" music is a vague, limiting term. Choice B is the answer to choose. Important goals of music include responding to music (A), listening to music (C), and becoming involved in music (D); therefore, none of those choices is incorrect.

79. C

This is an example of working with other teachers to plan instruction. Choice A is incorrect because it is incomplete. This activity may complete the school year, but it is not necessarily an end-of-the-year project. Choice B is incorrect because problem solving and inquiry teaching are only small components of the activity. Choice D is incorrect because asking students to research Galileo and asking the Parent Teacher Association to buy science equipment are not necessarily related.

80. B

Grouping patterns affect a student's perceptions of self-esteem and competence. Maintaining the same groups throughout the year encourages students in the average group to view themselves as average, students in the above-average group to view themselves as above average, and students in the below-average group to view themselves as below average. Choice A is incorrect because most students do not like unpredictable teacher behavior. Choice C is incorrect because changes in the classroom often create an atmosphere of mistrust and uneasiness, and do not cause students to be more alert. Choice D is incorrect because although the explanation is correct, it is incomplete when compared to choice B.

81. C

$6 \times 6 \times 6 \times 6 \times 6 \times 6$, or 46,656. Choice C is the correct answer. It is not 36, which would be only 6×6, or 6^2. Choice C, 66, would represent placing the 6 beside another 6; that is not the correct answer. The answer 7,776 represents only 6^5.

82. A

A needs assessment will help students make the connection between their current skills and those that will be new to them. Choice B is wrong because a needs assessment focuses on the skills a student currently possesses, not the problems the community faces. Choice C is incorrect because the needs assessment is designed to determine what needs to be taught that is not currently in the curriculum. Choice D is a false statement: a needs assessment is not designed to motivate students.

83. C

A positive environment must be created to minimize the effects of negative external factors. Choice A is inappropriate because changing the text but allowing the environment to remain the same serves only to maintain the status quo. Choice B is incorrect because relating the students' personal interests to the new material is only a part of creating a positive environment. Choice D is wrong because allowing students to monitor their own performance is, again, only a small part of maximizing the effects of a positive learning environment.

84. A

When students are allowed to select their own problems for study, they become self-directed problem solvers. As such, they have the opportunity to structure their own learning experiences. Assessing students' needs in a naturalistic setting (choice B) is highly time consuming and not an important benefit of having students select their own problem to investigate. There may or may not be a wide variety of instructional materials (choice C) available to the students as they engage in studying the temperature problem; this is not likely to be a major benefit. Learning to appreciate opposing viewpoints (choice D) is a competency that would be better addressed in social studies and language arts rather than in an activity that deals with a natural empirical science.

85. A

Students are more highly motivated to solve problems that they choose, rather than problems that are chosen for them. Choosing a problem for investigation does not increase student diversity (choice B). Problem selection has nothing to do with the structure of student groups (choice C). Although students may engage in more self-assessment (choice D), this is not the most important force at work.

86. C

The teacher would be fostering strong home relationships that support student achievement of desired outcomes. Choice A would result from choice C. As the teacher interacts with professionals in the community, her own professional growth would be promoted. Choice B would also result from choice C. All teachers are expected to interact with the community to help meet the expectations associated with teaching. Choice D is incomplete because strong home relationships are developed through the principles of conferences, trust, and cooperation.

87. C

This question relates to human diversity and the knowledge that each student brings to the classroom a constellation of personal and social characteristics related to a variety of factors such as exceptionality. Choice A is simply more of the same kind of schoolwork and not an acceptable answer. Being intrinsically motivated, exceptional students often find unmotivated students difficult to tutor, making choice B incorrect. Teacher-made, tightly organized units do not allow the exceptional student the opportunity to experience the learning situation, so choice D is incorrect.

88. B

This is the procedure in place at the campus level to deal with this type of issue. It respects the processes and oversight authority of the SBDM while addressing the concern of faculty and community. Choice A is incorrect because Ms. Carter does not have the authority to enforce the removal of the animals. Choice C is incorrect because the issue should remain at the campus level until the SBDM and the principal have an opportunity to consider the concerns. Choice D is incorrect because even though Ms. Carter may appreciate the librarian's efforts, the health concerns are legitimate. Ms. Carter should remain neutral until the campus can act on the issue.

89. A

The term *casework* is used by political scientists to describe the activities of congressional representatives on behalf of individual constituents. These activities might include helping an elderly person secure Social Security benefits, or helping a veteran obtain medical services. Most casework is actually done by congressional staff and may take as much as a third of the staff's time. Congressional representatives supply this type of assistance for the good public relations it provides. Choice B fails because pork barrel legislation is rarely if ever intended to help individual citizens. Pork barrel legislation authorizes federal spending for special projects, such as airports, roads, or dams, in the home state or district of a representative. It is meant to help the entire district or state. Also, there is no legal entitlement on the part of a citizen to a pork barrel project, such as there is with Social Security benefits. Choice C is not the answer because lobbying is an activity directed toward, not done by, representatives in Congress. A lobbyist attempts to get representatives to support legislation that will benefit the group that the lobbyist represents. Logrolling, choice D, is incorrect, because it does not refer to a congressional service for constituents. It refers instead to the congressional practice of trading votes on different bills. Congresswoman X will vote for Congressman Y's pork barrel project, and in return Congressman Y will vote for Congresswoman X's pork barrel project.

90. C

When the genetic type of the parents is known, the probability of the offspring showing particular traits can be predicted using the Punnett square. A Punnett square is a large square divided into four small boxes. The genetic symbol of each parent for a particular trait is written alongside the square, one parent along the top and one parent along the left side:

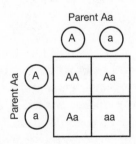

Each gene symbol is written in both boxes below or to the right of it. This results in each box having two gene symbols in it. The genetic symbols in the boxes

are all the possible genetic combinations for a particular trait of the offspring of these parents. Each box has a 25 percent probability of being the actual genetic representation for a given child.

The Linnaean system (choice A) is the system used in biology today by which all known living things are grouped in categories according to shared physical traits. This process of grouping organisms is called classification. Devised by Carl Linné, also known as Linnaeus, the Linnaean system gives all organisms a two-word name (binomial). The name consists of a genus (e.g., *Canis*) and a specific epithet (e.g., *lupus*).

DNA (choice B) holds the genetic materials of a cell, but is not the correct answer. Because two of the previous three answers are incorrect, choice D is eliminated.

91. B

A stalactite is an icicle-shaped lime deposit hanging from the roof or sides of a cave. A stalagmite is a cone-shaped deposit formed on the floor of a cave; B is the correct answer. Graphite (C) is the material found in a pencil. None of the above (D) is an inappropriate choice.

92. C

The chart shows that Madison received fewer than half of the votes. (His slice takes up less than half of the pie.) Statement I cannot be true. Washington and Monroe together received 55 percent of the votes, and everyone else voted for Madison, so Madison must have received 45 percent of the votes (all of the candidates' percents must add up to 100 percent). Statement II is therefore true.

Monroe received 30 percent of the 600 votes; $0.30 \times 600 = 180$, so statement III is true.

Madison received 45 percent of the vote, and 45 percent of 600 is 270, so statement IV is false.

93. A

The somewhat steep straight line to the left tells you that Mr. Cain worked at a steady rate for a while.

The completely flat line in the middle tells you he stopped for a while—the line doesn't go up because no grass was cut then. Finally, the line continues upward (after his break) less steeply (and therefore more flatly), indicating that he was working at a slower rate.

94. B

Because Ms. Patton's increases were consistent ($3,000 annually), and because the directions tell you that only one statement is true, choice B must be correct. To be more confident, however, you can examine the other statements:

The range of Ms. Patton's earning is $12,000 (the jump from $30,000 to $42,000), not $15,000, so choice A cannot be correct.

Although Ms. Patton may have earned $45,000 in 2003, you don't know that, so choice C cannot be correct.

Choice D gives the incorrect earnings average; it was $36,000, not $38,000.

95. B

Just from looking at the graph, it's clear that most of the space under the curve is past the 60 mark on the *x*-axis, so choice D is eliminated because it doesn't include statement I.

Statement II can't be answered by what the graph shows. It appears possible that certain questions were too hard for many in the class and that there weren't enough questions to differentiate B students from C students, but perhaps the class performed exactly as it should have, given the students' ability and Ms. Alvarez's teaching. The distribution can give a teacher many clues about the test and the students and even herself, but by itself tells us nothing about the fairness of the test. Thus, choice A can be eliminated.

Statement III is also false; in left-skewed distributions such as this one, the median is higher than the mean. This is true because the mean is lowered by the lowest score while the median is relatively unaffected by it.

Statement IV is true: one fairly large group has scored in the high 80s and 90s and another discernible group in the low to mid 60s, whereas few students fall outside these two groups. Thus, the answer has to be choice B.

96. A

Sedimentary rock may be formed by pressure over a period of time; it is not always the direct result of volcanic activity. Choice A is the correct answer. Igneous rock (B) is formed from heat and can be the result of volcanic activity. Magma (C) is molten rock within the earth; it may pour forth during a volcanic eruption; answer C is not the right choice. Lava (D) is a product of a volcanic eruption.

97. C

The 1 is in the hundredths place. If the number to the immediate right of the 1 (i.e., the number in the thousandths place) is greater than or equal to 5, we increase 1 to 2; otherwise, we do not change the 1. Then we leave off all the numbers to the right of the 1. In our problem, 6 is in the thousandths place, so we change the 1 to a 2 to get 287.42 as our answer.

98. D

One way to solve the problem is by writing a one-variable equation that matches the information given:

$$4x + 2(10 - x) = 26.$$

The $4x$ represents four tires for each car. You use x for the number of cars because at first you don't know how many cars there are.

The $(10 - x)$ represents the number of motorcycle tires in the lot. (If there are 10 vehicles total, and x of them are cars, you subtract x from 10 to get the number of "leftover" motorcycles.) Then $2(10 - x)$ stands for the number of motorcycles tires in the lot.

You know that the sum of the values of $4x$ and $2(10 - x)$ is 26, and that gives you your equation. Using the standard rules for solving a one-variable equation, you find that x (the number of cars in the lot) equals 3.

Another approach to the problem when given multiple answer choices is to try substituting each answer choice for the unknown variable in the problem to see which one makes sense.

99. A

You know that the correct equation must show three consecutive numbers being added to give 117. Odd numbers (just like even numbers) are each two apart. Only the three values given in choice A are each two apart.

Because the numbers being sought are odd, one might be tempted to choose choice D. However, the second value in choice D ($x + 1$) is *not* two numbers apart from the first value (x); it's different by only *one*.

100. D

All riders must pay at least $3, so 3 will be added to something else in the correct equation. Only choices B and D meet that requirement. The additional fare of $2 "for every mile or fraction of a mile" tells you that you will need to multiply the number of miles driven (you use 11 because of the extra two-tenths of a mile in 10.2) by 2, leading you to choice D.

101.

Essay 1

With today's economic climate forcing classroom sizes to become even bigger, the need for efficient verbal communication—that is, the complete and complex exchange of information and ideas—is more important than ever.

Some might argue that technology is the economic answer. However, the cost in actual learning capacity is too great. While technology certainly has its purpose, it can never fully replace the value of human interplay. It can never respond to a group of people the way a teacher can.

A lecture is an academic performance, and as any good dramatist knows, the audience drives

the performance. Thus, lecturing—that is, a series of academic talks—is the most comprehensive way a teacher can present the amalgamation of course theory and content.

Additionally, the intrinsic value of a lecture is the inherent flexibility it offers. Students are not excluded from an engaging lecture; it is quite the opposite. Teachers can speed up, slow down, or explore alternative avenues of explanation during an engaging lecture.

Essay 1 Analysis

This essay is well structured and well organized. It addresses the assignment by answering the questions asked of it. It has a clearly formulated, precise, specific, and focused thesis. It defines terms and uses them accurately. It also addresses opposing viewpoints and acknowledges alternative ideas. It has a well-developed introduction, body, and conclusion. It remains focused and unified throughout. It attempts to develop a thesis, and it flows logically from one concept to another. That is, it builds upon the thesis statement rather than simply restating it. The essay's use of diction and terminology is both accurate and clear. In places the writer provides definitions.

This essay, then, meets the requirements for a good essay.

Essay 2

Today's students can't relate to lectures. Lectures are boring. When students do wrong, they get lectured. It's like scolding. Who wants to come to school and get scolded? No one.

Students aren't going to respond well to that. Besides, lectures are long and monotonous to students who are used to the fast paced action of TV shows and video games. You can't expect young people to sit still while someone lectures at them.

Maybe in the old days things were different. Maybe then students were easier to control, their attention spans were more longer, or they

just didn't care. Whoever says that lectures are obsolete knew exactly what they were talking about; lectures are antiquated, and they don't involve the students. They just alienate the students because they are not personal.

I wouldn't lecture to my class. I would have them make videos, create computer programs, have discussion groups, field trips, and watch the Discovery Channel. There are lots of alternatives but lecturing to your students is just not a good thing to do anymore.

Essay 2 Analysis

While the writer of this essay has made several major flaws, its most pronounced one would have to be in its diction. The writer defines "lecture" as "scolding." Thus, from its inception the writer confuses the use of vocabulary. The writer further complicates the essay by then implying that all lecturing must be monotonous and mundane. Thus, the writer responds in an emotional way to an erroneous assumption. The resulting language and assertions are incorrect.

This writer totally neglects one of the parts of the question: What are the elements that Mrs. Adams should use to ensure a good lecture? Because of its errors in terminology, its invalid assumptions, and its failure to address all parts of the question, this essay is weak.

Essay 3

Lecturing is only passive if the teacher is passive. Lecturing can be as energetic and animated as the teacher wants it to be. There is no one saying that lectures have to be dull. I would bring props and dress in costumes and make my lectures entertaining.

I would lecture to my class because that's the way I was taught. I don't think there is anything wrong with lecturing in school. That's what they do in school. I think that lecturing is an important part of school. Besides, what other ways are there to teach certain things?

If one wants students to learn the periodic tables then a lecture on the subject is in order.

The students should be able to follow it. They are pretty smart and capable of understanding information like that. I don't think that there is any other way of dealing with certain topics but to lecture. So that is what I would do.

Essay 3 Analysis

This essay lacks a thesis. It does not develop or expand an idea. Rather, it simply states several assumptions without drawing any thoughtful conclusion. Because of its lack of structure, it fails to address the assignment. Without a thesis that is clearly formulated, precise, specific, and focused, the essay's central termi-nology cannot be well defined nor accurately employed. Additionally, the paper fails to acknowledge and/or address opposing viewpoints and alternative ideas.

Essentially this essay reads as though it were mainly filling paper rather than actually saying something. The lack of a thesis leads to the rambling, haphazard nature of the essay. The essay is hard to follow because there is no subject to develop. The insufficient use of details and lack of supporting examples only augment the lack of thesis development. Ultimately, the essay's thesis is predicated on a false assumption. This, coupled with a lack of supporting evidence, ideas, or examples, simply voids the essay of any viable credibility.

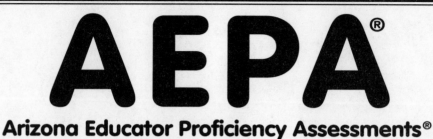

AEPA®
Arizona Educator Proficiency Assessments®

Elementary Education

Practice Test 2

Answer Sheet

1. Ⓐ Ⓑ Ⓒ Ⓓ
2. Ⓐ Ⓑ Ⓒ Ⓓ
3. Ⓐ Ⓑ Ⓒ Ⓓ
4. Ⓐ Ⓑ Ⓒ Ⓓ
5. Ⓐ Ⓑ Ⓒ Ⓓ
6. Ⓐ Ⓑ Ⓒ Ⓓ
7. Ⓐ Ⓑ Ⓒ Ⓓ
8. Ⓐ Ⓑ Ⓒ Ⓓ
9. Ⓐ Ⓑ Ⓒ Ⓓ
10. Ⓐ Ⓑ Ⓒ Ⓓ
11. Ⓐ Ⓑ Ⓒ Ⓓ
12. Ⓐ Ⓑ Ⓒ Ⓓ
13. Ⓐ Ⓑ Ⓒ Ⓓ
14. Ⓐ Ⓑ Ⓒ Ⓓ
15. Ⓐ Ⓑ Ⓒ Ⓓ
16. Ⓐ Ⓑ Ⓒ Ⓓ
17. Ⓐ Ⓑ Ⓒ Ⓓ
18. Ⓐ Ⓑ Ⓒ Ⓓ
19. Ⓐ Ⓑ Ⓒ Ⓓ
20. Ⓐ Ⓑ Ⓒ Ⓓ
21. Ⓐ Ⓑ Ⓒ Ⓓ
22. Ⓐ Ⓑ Ⓒ Ⓓ
23. Ⓐ Ⓑ Ⓒ Ⓓ
24. Ⓐ Ⓑ Ⓒ Ⓓ
25. Ⓐ Ⓑ Ⓒ Ⓓ

26. Ⓐ Ⓑ Ⓒ Ⓓ
27. Ⓐ Ⓑ Ⓒ Ⓓ
28. Ⓐ Ⓑ Ⓒ Ⓓ
29. Ⓐ Ⓑ Ⓒ Ⓓ
30. Ⓐ Ⓑ Ⓒ Ⓓ
31. Ⓐ Ⓑ Ⓒ Ⓓ
32. Ⓐ Ⓑ Ⓒ Ⓓ
33. Ⓐ Ⓑ Ⓒ Ⓓ
34. Ⓐ Ⓑ Ⓒ Ⓓ
35. Ⓐ Ⓑ Ⓒ Ⓓ
36. Ⓐ Ⓑ Ⓒ Ⓓ
37. Ⓐ Ⓑ Ⓒ Ⓓ
38. Ⓐ Ⓑ Ⓒ Ⓓ
39. Ⓐ Ⓑ Ⓒ Ⓓ
40. Ⓐ Ⓑ Ⓒ Ⓓ
41. Ⓐ Ⓑ Ⓒ Ⓓ
42. Ⓐ Ⓑ Ⓒ Ⓓ
43. Ⓐ Ⓑ Ⓒ Ⓓ
44. Ⓐ Ⓑ Ⓒ Ⓓ
45. Ⓐ Ⓑ Ⓒ Ⓓ
46. Ⓐ Ⓑ Ⓒ Ⓓ
47. Ⓐ Ⓑ Ⓒ Ⓓ
48. Ⓐ Ⓑ Ⓒ Ⓓ
49. Ⓐ Ⓑ Ⓒ Ⓓ
50. Ⓐ Ⓑ Ⓒ Ⓓ

51. Ⓐ Ⓑ Ⓒ Ⓓ
52. Ⓐ Ⓑ Ⓒ Ⓓ
53. Ⓐ Ⓑ Ⓒ Ⓓ
54. Ⓐ Ⓑ Ⓒ Ⓓ
55. Ⓐ Ⓑ Ⓒ Ⓓ
56. Ⓐ Ⓑ Ⓒ Ⓓ
57. Ⓐ Ⓑ Ⓒ Ⓓ
58. Ⓐ Ⓑ Ⓒ Ⓓ
59. Ⓐ Ⓑ Ⓒ Ⓓ
60. Ⓐ Ⓑ Ⓒ Ⓓ
61. Ⓐ Ⓑ Ⓒ Ⓓ
62. Ⓐ Ⓑ Ⓒ Ⓓ
63. Ⓐ Ⓑ Ⓒ Ⓓ
64. Ⓐ Ⓑ Ⓒ Ⓓ
65. Ⓐ Ⓑ Ⓒ Ⓓ
66. Ⓐ Ⓑ Ⓒ Ⓓ
67. Ⓐ Ⓑ Ⓒ Ⓓ
68. Ⓐ Ⓑ Ⓒ Ⓓ
69. Ⓐ Ⓑ Ⓒ Ⓓ
70. Ⓐ Ⓑ Ⓒ Ⓓ
71. Ⓐ Ⓑ Ⓒ Ⓓ
72. Ⓐ Ⓑ Ⓒ Ⓓ
73. Ⓐ Ⓑ Ⓒ Ⓓ
74. Ⓐ Ⓑ Ⓒ Ⓓ
75. Ⓐ Ⓑ Ⓒ Ⓓ

76. Ⓐ Ⓑ Ⓒ Ⓓ
77. Ⓐ Ⓑ Ⓒ Ⓓ
78. Ⓐ Ⓑ Ⓒ Ⓓ
79. Ⓐ Ⓑ Ⓒ Ⓓ
80. Ⓐ Ⓑ Ⓒ Ⓓ
81. Ⓐ Ⓑ Ⓒ Ⓓ
82. Ⓐ Ⓑ Ⓒ Ⓓ
83. Ⓐ Ⓑ Ⓒ Ⓓ
84. Ⓐ Ⓑ Ⓒ Ⓓ
85. Ⓐ Ⓑ Ⓒ Ⓓ
86. Ⓐ Ⓑ Ⓒ Ⓓ
87. Ⓐ Ⓑ Ⓒ Ⓓ
88. Ⓐ Ⓑ Ⓒ Ⓓ
89. Ⓐ Ⓑ Ⓒ Ⓓ
90. Ⓐ Ⓑ Ⓒ Ⓓ
91. Ⓐ Ⓑ Ⓒ Ⓓ
92. Ⓐ Ⓑ Ⓒ Ⓓ
93. Ⓐ Ⓑ Ⓒ Ⓓ
94. Ⓐ Ⓑ Ⓒ Ⓓ
95. Ⓐ Ⓑ Ⓒ Ⓓ
96. Ⓐ Ⓑ Ⓒ Ⓓ
97. Ⓐ Ⓑ Ⓒ Ⓓ
98. Ⓐ Ⓑ Ⓒ Ⓓ
99. Ⓐ Ⓑ Ⓒ Ⓓ
100. Ⓐ Ⓑ Ⓒ Ⓓ

Practice Test 2

TIME: Four hours for total test.
100 multiple-choice questions.
1 performance assignment.

> **Directions:** Read each item and select the best answer.

1. An acidic solution can have a pH of

    A. 20.
    B. 10.
    C. 8.
    D. 5.

2. A material with definite volume but no definite shape is called a

    A. titanium.
    B. gas.
    C. liquid.
    D. solid.

3. Simplify the following expression:

    $$\frac{2}{3x^2} + 7x + 9 + \frac{1}{3x^2} - 12x + 1$$

    A. $x^2 - 5x + 10$
    B. $6x^3 + 10$
    C. $6x^2 + 10$
    D. $x^4 - 5x + 10$

4. Use the Pythagorean theorem to answer this question: Which answer comes closest to the actual length of side x in the triangle below?

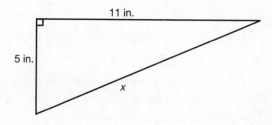

A. 14 in.
B. 12 in.
C. 11 in.
D. 13 in.

5. Use the figures given to answer the question that follows.

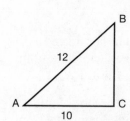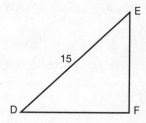

If the two triangles are similar, what is the length of side *DF*?

A. 12.5 units
B. 13 units
C. 12 units
D. 13.5 units

235

6. What does it mean that multiplication and division are inverse operations?

    A. Multiplication is commutative, whereas division is not. For example, 4×2 gives the same product as 2×4, but $4 \div 2$ is not the same as $2 \div 4$.
    B. Whether multiplying or dividing a value by 1, the value remains the same. For example, $9 \times 1 = 9$ and $9 \div 1 = 9$.
    C. When performing complex calculations involving several operations, all multiplication must be completed before completing any division, as in $8 \div 2 \times 4 + 7 - 1$.
    D. The operations "undo" each other. For example, multiplying 11 by 3 gives 33. Diving 33 by 3 then takes you back to 11.

7. The drought of the 1930s that spanned from Texas to North Dakota was caused by

    I.   overgrazing overuse of farmland.
    II.   natural phenomena, such as below-average rainfall and wind erosion.
    III. environmental factors, such as changes in the jet stream.
    IV.   the lack of government subsidies for new irrigation technology.

    A. I and II only
    B. II and III only
    C. I and III only
    D. II and IV only

8. Which of the following would be considered a primary source in researching the factors that influenced U.S. involvement in the Korean War?

    I.   the personal correspondence of a military man stationed with the 5th Regimental Combat Team (RCT) in Korea
    II.   a biography of Harry S Truman by David McCullough, published in 1993
    III. a journal article by a noted scholar about the beginning of the Korean War IV.
    IV.   an interview with Secretary of Defense George Marshall

    A. I and II only
    B. II and IV only
    C. II and III only

    D. I and IV only

9. Which of the following best describes a major difference between a state government and the federal government?

    A. State governments have more responsibility for public education than the federal government.
    B. State governments are more dependent upon the personal income tax for revenue than the federal government.
    C. State governments are more dependent upon the system of checks and balances than the federal government.
    D. State governments are subject to term limits, whereas federal representatives serve unlimited terms.

10. The intensity of an earthquake is measured by

    A. a thermograph.
    B. a seismograph.
    C. a telegraph.
    D. an odometer.

11. _____ is the ability to do work.

    A. Force
    B. Energy
    C. Distance
    D. Speed

12. Use the figure below to answer the question that follows.

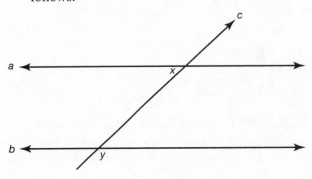

Given:
1. Lines a and b are parallel,
2. c is a line, and
3. the measure of the angle x is 50°.

What is the measure of angle *y*?

A. 50°
B. 100°
C. 130°
D. 80°

13. Use the figure below to answer the question that follows. Assume that *AD* is a line.

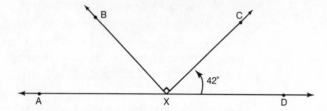

What is the measure of angle *AXB*?

A. 48°
B. 90°
C. 42°
D. There is not enough information to answer the question.

14. Which of the following statements is NOT true?

A. Infectious diseases are caused by viruses, bacteria, or protists.
B. Cancers and hereditary diseases can be infectious.
C. Environmental hazards can cause disease.
D. The immune system protects the body from disease.

15. Dance can be a mirror of culture. Which of the following is NOT an illustration of this statement?

A. Women in the Cook Islands dance with their feet together and sway while the men take a wide stance and flap their knees.
B. Movement basics include body, space, time, and relationship.
C. In Africa, the birth of a child is an occasion for a dance that asks for divine blessings.
D. The court dancers of Bali study for many years to achieve the balance, beauty, and serenity of their dance.

16. Flying buttresses, pointed arches, and stained glass windows are characteristic of which historic style of architecture?

A. Romanesque
B. Byzantine
C. Renaissance
D. Gothic

17. Mrs. Doe began planning a two-week unit of study of the Native Americans for her fifth-grade class. To begin the unit, she chose a movie on the twenty-first century Native Americans. As Mrs. Doe reflectively listened, key questions were asked.

The following day, Mrs. Doe reviewed the use of encyclopedias, indexes, and atlases. The students were divided into groups and taken to the library. Each group was responsible for locating information on their topic. The topics were maps showing the topography of the land; charts illustrating the climate, plants, and animals; a map showing migration routes; and a map showing the general areas where the Native Americans settled.

The students' involvement in the unit of study is a result of

I. the teacher's reflective listening during the discussion.
II. the available resources and materials.
III. careful planning and its relationship to success in the classroom.
IV. the students' personal acquaintance with Native Americans.

A. I only
B. I and II only
C. II and III only
D. I and IV only

18. Days 3 and 4 were spent with each group being involved in library research. The students wrote information on index cards. Each group prepared a presentation that included a written explanation of an assigned topic, a shadow box, and a sawdust map or models of Native American clothing. A pictograph was to be used in the telling of a legend or folk story. The presentation was concluded with a collage depicting the Native American way of life.

Multiple strategies and techniques were used for

I. motivation of the group and its effects on individual behavior and learning.
II. allowing each student regardless of ability to participate in the project.
III. integrating the project with other subjects.
IV. developing a foundation for teaching American history.

A. I, II, and III only
B. I and II only
C. III only
D. IV only

19. On Day 8, Mrs. Doe arranged a display of Native American artifacts and crafts in the hallway. Having collaborated with the music teacher at the onset of her planning and arranging for a general assembly of the entire student body, she took her students to the auditorium. The general assembly consisted of Native American poetry read by Fawn Lonewolf with Native American music and dance by the school chorus. At the conclusion of the assembly, the class was invited to view the video *The Trail of Tears*. Native American refreshments, including fried bread, were served to the students. As the students ate, *Knots on a Counting Rope* was read orally by the reading teacher. Following the reading, the physical education teacher taught the students several games that had been played by Native American children.

The planning of the assembly and the following activities required

I. the taking of risks by both the teacher and the students.
II. stimulating the curiosity of the student body.
III. recognizing individual talents among the students.
IV. using the collaborative process of working with other teachers.

A. I only
B. II only
C. II and III only
D. II, III, and IV only

20. Day 10 of the unit was Field Trip Day. The students were given a choice of visiting museums. Whatever the student's choice, he or she was to take notes of what was seen, heard, and experienced. These would be shared with the remainder of the class on the following day.

Field Trip Day and its experiences

I. allowed the student to make connections between their current skills and those that were new to them.
II. allowed external factors to create a learning environment that would take advantage of positive factors.
III. allowed a sense of community to be nurtured.
IV. allowed the students to take responsibility for their own learning.

A. I and II only
B. III only
C. IV only
D. III and IV only

21. The purpose of giving students a choice of field trip locations

I. was to enhance the students' self-concept.
II. was to respect differences and enhance the students' understanding of the society in which they live.
III. was to foster the view of learning as a purposeful pursuit.
IV. was an example of using an array of instructional strategies.

A. II only
B. II and IV only
C. I and II only
D. III only

22. Listening is a process students use to extract meaning out of oral speech. Activities teachers can engage in to assist students in becoming more effective listeners include

I. clearly setting a purpose for listening.
II. allowing children to relax by chewing gum during listening.
III. asking questions about the selection.

IV. encouraging students to forge links between the new information and knowledge already in place.

A. I and II only
B. II, III, and IV only
C. I, III, and IV only
D. I, II, III, and IV

23. Why should students be encouraged to figure out the structure and the features of the text they are attempting to comprehend and remember?

I. It helps the students to understand the way the author organized the material to be presented.
II. It helps the students to really look at the features of the text.
III. Talking about the structure of the text provides an opportunity for the teacher to point out the most salient features to the students.
IV. The discussions may help the students make connections between the new material in the chapter and what they already know about the topic.

A. I and III only
B. II and IV only
C. I and IV only
D. I, II, III, and IV

24. Ms. Smith's students come from a very conservative community. Which play for presentation might cause the least controversy within the small town?

A. *Harry Potter*
B. *Martha and George Washington*
C. *A Night in Las Vegas*
D. *Tom Sawyer and Huckleberry Finn*

25. When developing a unit about the Erie Canal for elementary-age students, what would you include as an assessment tool?

A. Explain to the students that the unit will cover a variety of projects; therefore, you will be using different assessment tools.
B. Explain to the students each project in the unit, then describe what they will be asked to do.

C. Give a list of new vocabulary words that they will need to know for the final test.
D. Explain to the students that they will need to hand in their notebooks at the end of the unit.

26. Rubrics are used by many teachers in elementary schools for the purposes of assessment. What criteria should be used when creating a rubric?

I. Set clearly defined criteria for each assessment.
II. Include a rating scale.
III. Use only one idea at a time so that students are not confused.
IV. Tell students that they can rate themselves.

A. III and IV only
B. II and III only
C. I and II only
D. None of the above

27. Mr. O'Brien ends the class by telling students that over the next few weeks they will be required to keep a communications journal. Every time they have an eventful exchange—either positive or negative—they are to record the details of the exchange in their journal. This assignment is given as

A. a way to help students improve their composition and rhetorical skills.
B. a way of understanding individual students, monitoring instructional effectiveness, and shaping instruction.
C. a way of helping students become more accountable for the way they manage their time.
D. the basis for giving daily grades to students.

28. Ms. Johnson requires her students to write about themselves. In doing so, Ms. Johnson is

A. fulfilling her responsibilities as an English teacher.
B. preparing her class to create autobiographies.
C. relying on the Language Experience Approach (LEA) for instruction.
D. preparing her class to read biographies about great Americans from diverse cultural backgrounds.

29. Mrs. Gettler teaches 26 third graders in a large inner-city school. About one-third of her students participate in the English as a Second Language (ESL) program at the school. Mrs. Gettler suspects that some of the students' parents are unable to read or write in English. Four of the students receive services from the learning resource teacher. At the beginning of the year, none of the students read above 2.0 grade level, and some of the students did not know all the letters of the alphabet.

    Which of the following describes the instructional strategy that is most likely to improve the reading levels of Mrs. Gettler's students?

    A. an intensive phonics program that includes drill and practice work on basic sight words
    B. an emergent literacy program emphasizing pattern books and journal writing using invented spelling
    C. an instructional program that closely follows the third-grade basal reader
    D. participation by all students in the school's ESL program so they can receive services from the learning resource center

30. Ms. Johnson collects the students' papers at the end of class. As she reads the papers, she decides that the best way to give her students positive feedback is

    A. not to mark errors on the paper so as not to discourage or inhibit their creativity.
    B. to make at least one positive comment about each paragraph.
    C. to begin with one or two positive comments about the paper and then suggest how students could improve their writing.
    D. give everyone a high grade on the paper for participating in the assignment.

31. After Ms. Johnson finishes reading all the students' papers, she observes that some of the students had difficulty identifying and describing their strengths, whether in class or outside class. She believes that all of her students have strengths and she wants to help them see the assets they possess. She decides that in the next class, students will

    A. take a learning-style assessment to uncover their particular learning strengths and characteristics.
    B. listen to a lecture about how everyone possesses special skills and strengths.
    C. read a chapter from a book about Guilford's Structure of Intellect, as a precursor to a discussion about how intelligence is specialized and diverse.
    D. rewrite their papers, correcting their errors and revising their paragraphs to name at least two additional classroom strengths they possess and at least two additional interpersonal skills they possess.

32. Which of the following statements best defines the role of the World Trade Organization?

    A. It resolves trade disputes and attempts to formulate policy to open world markets to free trade through monetary policy and regulation of corruption.
    B. It is an advocate for human rights and democracy by regulating child labor and providing economic aid to poor countries.
    C. It establishes alliances to regulate disputes and polices ethnic intimidation.
    D. It regulates trade within the United States in order to eliminate monopolistic trade practices.

33. The characteristics of fascism include all of the following EXCEPT

    A. totalitarianism.
    B. democracy.
    C. romanticism.
    D. militarism.

34. The industrial economy of the nineteenth century was based upon all of the following EXCEPT

    A. the availability of raw materials.
    B. an equitable distribution of profits among those involved in production.
    C. the availability of capital.
    D. a distribution system to market finished products.

35. "Jim Crow" laws were laws that

    A. effectively prohibited blacks from voting in state and local elections.

    B. restricted American Indians to U.S. government reservations.

    C. restricted open-range ranching in the Great Plains.

    D. established separate segregated facilities for blacks and whites.

36. Which of the following is used to effect the release of a person from improper imprisonment?

    A. a writ of mandamus

    B. a writ of habeas corpus

    C. the Fourth Amendment requirement that police have probable cause in order to obtain a search warrant

    D. the Supreme Court's decision in *Roe v. Wade*

37. Which of the following defines a salt?

    A. one of the reactant products of an acid and a base

    B. one of the reactant products of a base and water

    C. one of the reactant products of an acid and water

    D. reactant product of a phase transformation

38. The atomic number for neutral (un-ionized) atoms as listed in the periodic table refers to

    A. the number of neutrons in an atom.

    B. the number of protons in an atom.

    C. the number of electrons in an atom.

    D. both B and C.

39. Which of the following is a phenomenon involving the physical properties of a substance?

    A. corrosion of iron

    B. burning of wood

    C. rocket engine ignition

    D. melting of ice

40. Isotopes of a given element contain

    A. more electrons than protons with equal numbers of neutrons.

    B. more protons than electrons with equal numbers of neutrons.

    C. equal numbers of protons and electrons with differing numbers of neutrons.

    D. unequal numbers of protons and electrons with differing numbers of neutrons.

41. Newton's second law of motion states that "the summation of forces acting on a body is equal to the product of mass and acceleration." Which of the following is a good example of the law's application?

    A. decreased friction between surfaces by means of lubrication

    B. potential energy stored in a compressed spring

    C. a rocket lifting off at Cape Canaveral with increasing speed

    D. using a claw hammer to pull a nail out with multiplied force

42. Which of the following is considered to be evidence for plate tectonics?

    A. continental coastline "fit"

    B. identical fossil evidence at fit locations

    C. intense geological activity in mountainous regions

    D. all of the above

43. Humans have 46 chromosomes in their body cells. How many chromosomes are found in the zygote?

    A. 2

    B. 10

    C. 23

    D. 46

44. Human body-temperature regulation via the skin involves

    A. respiration.   C. perspiration.

    B. transpiration.   D. sensation.

45. Darwin's original theory of natural selection asserts that

    A. all organisms have descended with modification from a common ancestor.
    B. random genetic drift plays a major role in speciation.
    C. species characteristics are inherited by means of genes.
    D. speciation is usually due to gradual accumulation of small genetic changes.

46. Mr. Swenson teaches mathematics in high school. He is planning a unit on fractal geometry, using the computer lab for demonstrations and for exploration for his advanced math students. The students have used various computer programs to solve algebra and calculus problems. As Mr. Swenson plans a unit of study, he determines that a cognitive outcome will be that students will design and produce fractals, using a computer program. An affective outcome will be that students will become excited about investigating a new field of mathematics and will show this interest by choosing to develop a math project relating to fractals.

    The most appropriate strategy to use first would be

    A. explaining the exciting development of fractal geometry over the past 10 to 15 years.
    B. demonstrating on the computer the way to input values into formulas to produce fractal designs.
    C. giving students a few simple fractal designs and asking them to figure out the formulas for producing them.
    D. showing students color pictures of complex fractals and asking them for ideas about how they could be drawn mathematically.

47. $\sqrt{100} =$

    A. 10   C. 200
    B. 50   D. 500

48. $(2^2)^4 =$

    A. $\sqrt{2}$ C. 2^7
    B. 2^6 D. 2^8

49. $\dfrac{3}{4} \times \dfrac{8}{9} =$

    A. $^{24}/_9$ C. $^2/_3$
    B. $^{32}/_3$ D. $^{11}/_{13}$

50. Change the fraction $^7/_8$ to a decimal.

    A. .666   C. .777
    B. .75   D. .875

51. $7.04 \times 2.5 =$

    A. 17.6   C. 9.25
    B. 176   D. 1.76

52. A marble and a feather are released at the same time inside a tube that is held at very low pressure (a near vacuum). Which of the following correctly links the observation to explanation?

    A. The marble falls faster because it is heavier.
    B. The marble falls faster because is has less air resistance.
    C. Both fall at the same rate because there is no air resistance in a vacuum.
    D. Both fall at the same rate because the forces of gravity are different in a vacuum.

53. The Pacific Northwest receives the greatest annual precipitation in the United States. Which of the following statements best identifies the reason that this occurs?

    A. The jet stream moving south from Canada pushes storms through the region.
    B. The region's mountains along the coast cause air masses to rise and cool, thereby reducing their moisture-carrying capacity.
    C. Numerous storms originating in Asia build in intensity as they move across the Pacific Ocean and then dup their precipitation upon reaching land.
    D. The ocean breezes push moisture-laden clouds and fog into the coastal region, producing humid, moist conditions that result in precipitation.

54. The United States has a two-party system, while several European governments have multiparty systems. Which of the following statements is true about political parties in the United States but not true about political parties in multiparty European governments?

    A. Political parties form coalitions in order to advance their policy initiatives through Congress.

    B. Single member district voting patterns clearly identify candidates for seats in political offices.

    C. Parties provide candidates for office and organize campaigns to get the candidates elected.

    D. Political parties are linked to religious, regional, or social class groupings.

55. Use the figure below to answer the question that follows.

    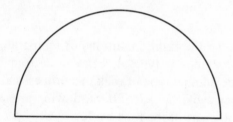

    Which formula can be used to find the area of the figure? (Assume the curve is *half* of a circle.)

    A. $A = \pi r$

    B. $A = 2\pi r^2$

    C. $A = \pi r^2$

    D. $A = \dfrac{\pi r^2}{2}$

56. Until recently, a very quiet, reserved student had completed all her work on time and was making satisfactory progress. Lately, however, she has been erratic in her school attendance, and when she comes to school, she appears distracted. She is having trouble staying on task and finishing her work. She has failed to turn in several recent assignments. On the last writing assignment, she wrote a very graphic poem about a girl who is sexually assaulted. The level of details used in the poem was shocking to the teacher.

Her teacher should

    A. ignore the topic of the poem, grade it on its poetic merit only, and return it to the student, waiting to see what will happen with the next assignment.

    B. grade the poem on its poetic merit and return it to the student with a written comment that she would like to talk to her about the poem.

    C. ask the student to stay after class, return the poem, and ask the student about it.

    D. make a copy of the poem and distribute it to other teachers to solicit their opinions about the poem.

57. Ms. Aldridge is a fifth-grade social studies teacher. Which of the following statements is most true for Ms. Aldridge's teaching?

    A. Ms. Aldridge's main responsibility is teaching social studies content to her students; she should not have to teach reading skills to them.

    B. Ms. Aldridge must teach the book parts and graphic materials specific to the social studies texts; these parts may differ from those in a regular reading basal text.

    C. Ms. Aldridge should stick closely with the textbook to ensure that the students cover the main facts; supplementing the text with other materials may distract the students and prevent proper coverage of the material.

    D. Ms. Aldridge can rest assured that her students can read the textbook by locating the grade level of the book in the teacher's manual.

58. Mr. Jones analyzes the test results and finds that many of the students in Mrs. Ratu's class have average scores in the areas of art, math, and music. He concludes that, with the exception of reading, most are average-ability students and will be successful when their remediation is complete. Mr. Jones makes several decisions: (1) the students will be evaluated annually with an achievement test; (2) reading materials of interest to teenagers will be substituted for elementary materials; (3) each student will be encouraged to read about the subject of his or her choice; and (4) roundtable discussions will be developed for each "favorite subject."

Having reviewed the students' scores in other classes, Mr. Jones can justify his decisions with all of the following reasons EXCEPT

A. development in one area can foster development in another area.

B. using a variety of techniques helps develop intrinsic and extrinsic motivation.

C. allowing students to have choices in their learning will create camaraderie.

D. roundtable discussions will increase student interactions and help develop oral language skills.

59. A music teacher plays several recordings. Which would NOT be an appropriate follow-up activity?

A. Ask students to guess the decade that the music reflects and continue the guessing until a student gives the correct decade; justification of the guess is not necessary.

B. Ask students to predict how music will sound in the year 2050.

C. Have students use tempra paint to show the mood and feelings that they believe the music is expressing.

D. Relate the music to the historical period that the composer reflects in the composition.

60. Certain rules and regulations must accompany the use of Internet in the schools and libraries. These rules and regulations do NOT include

A. using blocking or filtering technology to protect students against access to certain visual depictions on all school/library computers with Internet access.

B. filtering text.

C. forbidding disclosure of personal identification information about minors.

D. prohibiting unauthorized access, including so-called "hacking," by minors online.

61. Certain copyright laws govern the use of materials in the classroom. Which of the following is NOT true?

A. The "fair use" doctrine prohibits even limited reproduction of copyrighted works for educational and research purposes.

B. A teacher can copy a chapter from a book; an article from a periodical or newspaper; and/or a chart, graph, diagram, drawing, cartoon, or picture from a book, periodical, or newspaper.

C. A teacher can make copies of a short story, a short essay, or a short poem, whether or not from a collective work.

D. For a classroom, a teacher can make multiple copies (not to exceed the number of students in the class) as long as the copying meets the tests of brevity and spontaneity, meets the cumulative effect test, and each copy includes a notice of copyright.

62. Under the right conditions of temperature and pressure, any type of rock can be transformed into another type of rock in a process called the rock cycle. Which of the following processes is not a part of the rock cycle?

A. the drifting and encroachment of sand at the edge of a desert

B. the melting of rock beneath the surface to form magma

C. the erosion of sedimentary rocks to form sand

D. the eruption of a cinder cone volcano

63. Earth's Moon is

A. generally closer to the Sun than it is to Earth.

B. generally closer to Earth than to the Sun.

C. generally equidistant between Earth and the Sun.

D. closer to Earth during part of the year, and closer to the Sun for the rest of the year.

64. Which of the following observations explains the geologic instability surrounding the Pacific Ocean known as the "Ring of Fire"?

   A. Similarities in rock formations and continental coastlines suggest that Earth's continents were once one landmass.
   B. Earth's plates collide at convergent margins, separate at divergent margins, and move laterally at transform-fault boundaries.
   C. Earthquakes produce waves that travel through the Earth in all directions.
   D. Volcanoes form when lava accumulates and hardens.

65. In the example pictured below, which of the following contributes most to an effect of stability and changeless grandeur?

Pylon Temple of Horus, Edfu

   A. the strong horizontal thrust of the architecture
   B. the wealth of elaborate ornamental detail
   C. the vast open courtyard with its surrounding columns
   D. the simplified geometry of the massive forms and the sloping diagonal walls

66. Which of the following best describes the example pictured below?

Portrait of a Roman. ca. 80 B.C.E. Palazzo Torlonia, Rome

   A. The subject appears to be poetic, dreamy, and aristocratic.
   B. The sculptor was not concerned with descriptive detail.
   C. The hard material counteracts the effect desired by the sculptor.
   D. The subject appears to be hard-bitten, pragmatic, and realistic.

67. Which of the following is the most important artistic device in the example shown below?

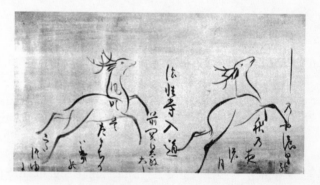

Tawaraya Sotatsu and Hon-Ami Koetsu. *Deer Scroll.*
Early Edo period. Seattle Art Museum, Seattle

   A. line   C. color
   B. tone   D. volume

Questions 68 to 70 refer to the following passages.

A. Once upon a time and a very good time it was there was a moocow coming down along the road and this moocow that was coming down along the road met a nicens little boy named baby tuckoo . . .

B. And thus have these naked Nantucketers, these sea hermits, issuing from their ant-hill in the sea, overrun and conquered the watery world like so many Alexanders . . .

C. A large rose tree stood near the entrance of the garden: the roses growing on it were white, but there were three gardeners at it, busily painting them red. Alice thought this a very curious thing, and she went nearer to watch them, and, just as she came up to them, she heard one of them say "Look out now, Five!"

D. Emma was not required, by any subsequent discovery, to retract her ill opinion of Mrs. Elton. Her observation had been pretty correct. Such as Mrs. Elton appeared to her on this second interview, such she appeared whenever they met again: self-important, presuming, familiar, ignorant, and ill-bred. She had a little beauty and a little accomplishment, but so little judgment that she thought herself coming with superior knowledge of the world, to enliven and improve a country neighborhood . . .

68. Which passage employs a metaphor?

69. Which passage employs fanciful actions of the characters?

70. Which passage employs extensive characterization?

71. Which is the national professional organization that represents teachers of students who speak another language?

A. IRA   C. NASDTEC
B. NATM   D. TESOL

72. In a barn there were lambs and people. If we counted 30 heads and 104 legs in the barn, how many lambs and how many people were in the barn?

A. 10 lambs and 20 people
B. 16 lambs and 14 people
C. 18 lambs and 16 people
D. 22 lambs and 8 people

73. Round the following number to the nearest hundreds place: 287.416.

A. 300
B. 290
C. 287.42
D. 287.4139

74. In the number 72104.58, what is the place value of the 2?

A. thousands
B. millions
C. ten-thousands
D. tenths

75. Mr. Stephens, a science teacher, has the students in Ms. Allen's second-period social studies class during first-period physical science. He tells Ms. Allen and Mr. Ramirez, the other social studies teacher, that he would like to collaborate with them by integrating some science topics into their unit on the American Revolution.

This will most likely

A. frustrate Ms. Allen and Mr. Ramirez because they will now have to discuss science.
B. cause the students to develop a broader view of the Revolutionary time period.
C. irritate the school librarian, who must put all the books related to the American Revolution on reserve.
D. cause the students to do English homework in science class and science homework in history class.

76. Which of the following is a power reserved for the federal government?

    A. ratify proposed amendments to the Constitution
    B. provide for the local governments
    C. regulate contracts and wills
    D. mint money

77. In the following lines, what does the stage direction "*(Aside)*" mean?

    King: Take thy fair hour, Laertes; time be thine,
    And thy best graces spend it at thy will!
    But now, my cousin Hamlet, and my son,—

    Hamlet: *(Aside)* A little more than kin, and less than kind.

    A. The actor steps aside to make room for other action on stage.
    B. The actor directly addresses only one particular actor on stage.
    C. The actor directly addresses the audience, while out of hearing of the other actors.
    D. The previous speaker steps aside to make room for this actor.

78. Ms. Carter, a math teacher, feels very uncomfortable when she has to make decisions about the assessment of students. She has had some difficulty with various types of assessment. She decides it is time to talk to Mr. Williams, the principal.

    Which of the following would be the most effective way for Ms. Carter to document her teaching in an authentic setting and to be aware of students' efforts, progress, and achievements in one or more areas?

    A. standardized tests
    B. teacher-made tests
    C. observation
    D. portfolio

79. Which would be the most effective way to evaluate specific objectives and specific content in Ms. Carter's course?

    A. self- and peer evaluation
    B. portfolio
    C. teacher-made test
    D. observation

80. Mr. Williams asks Ms. Carter what type of test scores are rated against the performance of other students and are reported in terms of percentiles, stanines, and scaled scores. Ms. Carter should give which response?

    A. portfolio
    B. teacher-made test
    C. observation
    D. standardized test

81. Dominique Woods has two years of teaching experience at a large urban high school. This is her first year teaching at a small, suburban, ethnically mixed elementary school.

    Ms. Woods wants to take advantage of the week of faculty meetings before school opens to become better acquainted with the school grounds, faculty, curriculum, and available materials. How could she best utilize her time?

    A. tour the school while noting the teacher's room, materials room, and other important rooms
    B. talk to the principal about what materials are available
    C. talk with a willing teacher who has spent several years at the school about community characteristics and available materials as they apply to the curriculum
    D. obtain a copy of the curriculum to take to the materials room, where she can determine what materials are available for classroom use

82. Three months have passed and Ms. Woods is preparing to submit grades and conference request forms. Although students have done well in reading, writing grades seem to be low. Ms. Woods has come to the conclusion that her students are having trouble assessing their own writing strengths and weaknesses.

Which of the following would be appropriate ways of monitoring and improving the students' writing?

I.   Have students submit an original work every day on a topic they choose; the work will then be graded.

II. Have students identify, with the help of the teacher, one area of writing in which they feel they need improvement; they will then focus on this area until they have reached their goal and are ready to identify a new area.

III. Keep all draft and final copies in a portfolio; the student will pick a piece to discuss with the teacher at a teacher-student conference.

IV. Once a week the teacher will read a quality composition written by a class member.

A.   II and III only
B.   I and III only
C.   I, III, and IV only
D.   II, III, and IV only

83. Use the figure below to answer the question that follows.

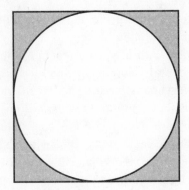

What is the approximate area of the shaded region, given the following?

The radius of the circle is 6 units.

The square inscribes the circle.

A.   106 square units
B.   31 square units
C.   77 square units
D.   125 square units

84. How many lines of symmetry do all nonsquare rectangles have?

A.   0
B.   2
C.   4
D.   8

85. Use the figure below to answer the question that follows.

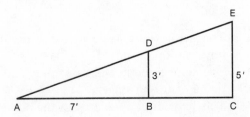

The figure is a sketch of a ramp. Given that the two ramp supports (*DB* and *EC*) are perpendicular to the ground and the dimensions of the various parts are as noted, what is the approximate distance from point *B* to point *C*?

A.   4.7 feet
B.   4.5 feet
C.   4.3 feet
D.   4.1 feet

86. Bemus School is conducting a lottery to raise funds for new band uniforms. Exactly 1,000 tickets will be printed and sold. Only one ticket stub will be drawn from a drum to determine the single winner of a big-screen television. All tickets have equal chances of winning. The first 700 tickets are sold to 700 different individuals. The remaining 300 tickets are sold to Mr. Greenfield. Given this information, which of the following statements are true?

I.   It is impossible to tell in advance who will win.

II. Mr. Greenfield will probably win.

III. Someone other than Mr. Greenfield will probably win.

IV. The likelihood that Mr. Greenfield will win is the same as the likelihood that someone else will win.

A. I and II
B. I and III
C. II and IV
D. III and IV

87. Which line on the following chart best matches the source of information with the historical question being asked?

Line	Historical Research Question	Source of Information
1	How many people were living in Boston during the time of the American Revolution?	Historical atlas
2	What role did Fort Mackinac fulfill during the American Revolution?	Encyclopedia article
3	How did the average temperatures and snowfall during the winter of 1775–1776 compare with previous winters?	Historical almanac
4	When was the first U.S. treaty signed, and what were the terms of the treaty?	Government publication

A. line 1
B. line 2
C. line 3
D. line 4

88. Which of the following is an example of a question or task requiring synthesis, according to Bloom's Taxonomy?

A. Here are five words. Write a sentence using these five words and adding any other words you might need.
B. Describe how Columbus, in his search for the New World, ended his journey in the Caribbean islands.

C. Compare Freud's theory of psychosexual development to Erikson's theory of psycho-social development.
D. Diagram the sentence written on the board.

89. A teacher plays a piece of music for her music appreciation class, telling the students that it is an example from the Romantic period. She plays the piece again and asks the students to describe the piece. After students describe the music, she asks them to define *romantic*. The teacher is engaging her students in

A. inductive reasoning.
B. deductive reasoning.
C. oral interpretation.
D. evaluation.

90. To help a student who has very creative and sophisticated ideas improve his or her spelling (and thus his or her grades in history class), a teacher might suggest that

A. the student try typing the next paper on a word processor, using a spell-checker.
B. the student use simpler words that are easier to spell.
C. the student write each misspelled word on the last paper 20 times.
D. spelling errors not count against the student on papers.

91. An English teacher wants to challenge his students to think critically. He has been teaching about the parts of speech. He writes the following sentence on the board: "The man ran down the street." He asks a student to identify the part of speech of the word *down*. The student says that *down* is an adverb telling where the man ran. The teacher should respond

A. "No, *down* is not an adverb."
B. "Yes, *down* does tell where the man ran."
C. "*Down* is a preposition, and 'down the street' is a prepositional phrase."
D. "Well, *down* does tell where the man ran, which is what adverbs do. But in this case, *down* is part of the phrase 'down the street.' Do you want to change your answer?"

92. A teacher writes this question on the board: "How do you know if someone is intelligent or not?" The class then is assigned to research the question and develop a list of all the traits and characteristics that define or describe someone who is intelligent. Through this exercise, the teacher has

    A. led her students through an activity of developing criteria against which a judgment can be made.
    B. led her students through an activity of gathering examples.
    C. led her students through an activity of testing if someone is intelligent or not.
    D. engaged her students in a creative-thinking activity.

93. Which of the following were major causes of the Great Depression?

    I. Hoarding money greatly reduced the money supply, resulting in higher prices on consumer goods.
    II. The gold standard limited the amount of money in supply, reducing money circulation and causing a drop in prices and wages.
    III. The Smoot-Hawley Tariff Act increased tariffs, which resulted in increased prices for consumer goods.
    IV. The stock market crash reduced the value of companies, causing them to raise prices of consumer goods.

    A. I and II only   C. III and IV only
    B. II and III only   D. I, II, and III

94. Why is it a good idea for a teacher to give students options and allow them to make choices?

    A. Some teachers dislike telling students what to do.
    B. Some teachers like to give students various options so they can exercise their decision-making skills.
    C. Teachers know that different students are motivated and stimulated by different tasks.
    D. Students deserve a break from all the rules and regulations in most classes.

95. Which of the following requires the higher-order thinking skill, according to Bloom's *Taxonomy*?

    A. Demonstrate how to change the printer cartridge.
    B. State what kind of cartridge the printer needs.
    C. Describe how to change the printer cartridge.
    D. If the printer does not print after the cartridge has been changed, figure out what the problem is.

96. Harmony results when a melody is accompanied by

    I. a rhythm instrument.
    II. a guitar.
    III. another instrument or singer playing or singing the melody.
    IV. another instrument playing chords.

    A. I and II only   C. II and III only
    B. I and III only   D. II and IV only

97. Ms. Gitler is selecting books for the classroom library. In addition to student interest, which of the following would be the most important considerations?

    A. The books should be at reading levels that match the students' independent reading abilities.
    B. All books should have a reading level that is challenging to the students.
    C. The books should include separate word lists for student practice.
    D. A classroom library is not appropriate for students at such a low reading level.

98. Matt earned the following scores on his first six weekly mathematics tests: 91 percent, 89 percent, 82 percent, 95 percent, 86 percent, and 79 percent. He had hoped for an average (mean) of 90 percent at this point, which would just barely give him an A− in math on his first report card. How many more total percentage points should Matt have earned over the course of those six weeks to qualify for an A− ?

A. 87
B. 3
C. 90
D. 18

99. Literacy is a person's ability to

A. perform mathematics and simple oral reading skills.
B. read and write.
C. encode and be pragmatic.
D. comprehend and engage.

100. Dr. Kenneth Goodman developed the notion of miscue analysis. This is a system for examining how a child's oral reading of a passage varies from

A. that of his or her peers.
B. encoding the passage from a dictation.
C. the printed text.
D. diagrams of the sentences.

DIRECTIONS FOR THE PERFORMANCE ASSIGNMENT

This section of the test consists of a performance assignment. **The assignment can be found on the next page.** You are asked to prepare a written response of approximately 2–3 pages on the assigned topic. You should use your time to plan, write, review, and edit your response for the assignment.

Read the assignment carefully before you begin to work. Think about how you will organize your response. You may use any blank space in this test booklet to make notes, write an outline, or otherwise prepare your response. **(On the actual test, your score will be based solely on the version of your response written in the response booklet.)**

As a whole, your response must demonstrate an understanding of the knowledge and skills of the field. In your response to the assignment, you are expected to demonstrate the depth of your understanding of the content area through your ability to apply your knowledge and skills rather than merely to recite factual information.

Your response will be evaluated based on the following criteria:

- Purpose: the extent to which the response achieves the purpose of the assignment
- Subject matter knowledge: accuracy and appropriateness in the application of subject matter knowledge
- Support: quality and relevance of supporting details
- Rationale: soundness of argument and degree of understanding of the subject matter

The performance assignment is intended to assess subject knowledge content and skills, not writing ability. However, you must communicate clearly enough to permit scorers to make a valid evaluation according to the criteria listed above. Your response should be written for an audience of educators in this field. The final version of your response should conform to the conventions of edited American English. This should be your original work, written in your own words, and not copied or paraphrased from some other work.

Practice Test 2 Performance Assignment

101. Read the paragraph below; then complete the exercise that follows.

Ms. Treen is aware that most of the homes of her Hispanic students do not have printed material in the English language. Most of the Hispanic families watch TV on a local channel, WHIS-TV, which uses only Spanish.

The families of most of the children in the class do not use the library much. In fact, only about 10 percent of all the families visit the library regularly. Fewer than half of the homes subscribe to the local newspaper or take a magazine. Ms. Treen finds, however, that most of families make regular use of the shopping malls and the video stores.

How can Ms. Treen (1) encourage reading in the home, (2) stress the importance of using the local library, which is within a block of the school, and (3) help make sure that the students have access to educational materials?

Practice Test 2 Answer Key

1. (D)	26. (C)	51. (A)	76. (D)
2. (C)	27. (B)	52. (C)	77. (C)
3. (A)	28. (C)	53. (B)	78. (D)
4. (B)	29. (B)	54. (B)	79. (C)
5. (A)	30. (C)	55. (D)	80. (D)
6. (D)	31. (A)	56. (C)	81. (C)
7. (A)	32. (A)	57. (B)	82. (D)
8. (D)	33. (B)	58. (C)	83. (B)
9. (A)	34. (B)	59. (A)	84. (B)
10. (B)	35. (D)	60. (B)	85. (A)
11. (B)	36. (B)	61. (A)	86. (B)
12. (C)	37. (A)	62. (A)	87. (C)
13. (A)	38. (D)	63. (B)	88. (A)
14. (B)	39. (D)	64. (B)	89. (A)
15. (B)	40. (C)	65. (D)	90. (A)
16. (D)	41. (C)	66. (D)	91. (D)
17. (C)	42. (D)	67. (A)	92. (A)
18. (A)	43. (D)	68. (B)	93. (B)
19. (D)	44. (C)	69. (C)	94. (C)
20. (A)	45. (A)	70. (D)	95. (D)
21. (B)	46. (D)	71. (D)	96. (D)
22. (C)	47. (A)	72. (D)	97. (A)
23. (D)	48. (D)	73. (A)	98. (D)
24. (B)	49. (C)	74. (A)	99. (B)
25. (B)	50. (D)	75. (B)	100. (C)

AEPA Elementary Education Practice Test 2
Answers Sorted by Competency

Question	Competency	Answer	Did you answer correctly?
1	Competency 0024	D	
2	Competency 0025	C	
3	Competency 0017	A	
4	Competency 0019	B	
5	Competency 0018	A	
6	Competency 0013	D	
7	Competency 0032	A	
8	Competency 0034	D	
9	Competency 0033	A	
10	Competency 0025	B	
11	Competency 0025	B	
12	Competency 0018	C	
13	Competency 0018	A	
14	Competency 0023	B	
15	Competency 0037	B	
16	Competency 0036	D	
17	Competency 0029	C	
18	Competency 0029	A	
19	Competency 0034	D	
20	Competency 0030	A	
21	Competency 0011	B	
22	Competency 0009	C	
23	Competency 0004	D	
24	Competency 0038	B	
25	Competency 0032	B	
26	Competency 0007	C	
27	Competency 0008	B	
28	Competency 0006	C	
29	Competency 0010	B	
30	Competency 0002	C	

Question	Competency	Answer	Did you answer correctly?
31	Competency 0001	A	
32	Competency 0029	A	
33	Competency 0033	B	
34	Competency 0031	B	
35	Competency 0029	D	
36	Competency 0028	B	
37	Competency 0024	A	
38	Competency 0024	D	
39	Competency 0021	D	
40	Competency 0024	C	
41	Competency 0023	C	
42	Competency 0023	D	
43	Competency 0023	D	
44	Competency 0023	C	
45	Competency 0023	A	
46	Competency 0018	D	
47	Competency 0014	A	
48	Competency 0014	D	
49	Competency 0015	C	
50	Competency 0015	D	
51	Competency 0015	A	
52	Competency 0026	C	
53	Competency 0030	B	
54	Competency 0033	B	
55	Competency 0018	D	
56	Competency 006	C	
57	Competency 0005	B	
58	Competency 0001	C	
59	Competency 0035	A	
60	Competency 0004	B	

Question	Competency	Answer	Did you answer correctly?
61	Competency 0004	A	
62	Competency 0026	A	
63	Competency 0026	B	
64	Competency 0032	B	
65	Competency 0036	D	
66	Competency 0036	D	
67	Competency 0036	A	
68	Competency 0005	B	
69	Competency 0005	C	
70	Competency 0005	D	
71	Competency 0010	D	
72	Competency 0012	D	
73	Competency 0013	A	
74	Competency 0014	A	
75	Competency 0022	B	
76	Competency 0033	D	
77	Competency 0037	C	
78	Competency 0016	D	
79	Competency 0016	C	
80	Competency 0016	D	

Question	Competency	Answer	Did you answer correctly?
81	Competency 0011	C	
82	Competency 0008	D	
83	Competency 0020	B	
84	Competency 0020	B	
85	Competency 0018	A	
86	Competency 0016	B	
87	Competency 0005	C	
88	Competency 0003	A	
89	Competency 0035	A	
90	Competency 0033	A	
91	Competency 0008	D	
92	Competency 0003	A	
93	Competency 0032	B	
94	Competency 0003	C	
95	Competency 0003	D	
96	Competency 0035	D	
97	Competency 0011	A	
98	Competency 0012	D	
99	Competency 0001	B	
100	Competency 0001	C	

Explanations of Answers

1. D

Acid and *base* are terms used to describe solutions of differing pH. The concentration of hydrogen ion in a solution determines its pH. Solutions having pH 0–7 are called acids and have hydrogen ions (H^+) present. Common acids include lemon juice, vinegar, and battery acid. Acids are corrosive and taste sour. Solutions having pH 7–14 are called bases (or alkaline) and have hydroxide ions (OH^-) present. Bases are caustic and feel slippery in solution. Common bases include baking soda and lye. Solutions of pH 7 are called neutral and have both ions present in equal but small amounts. Among the answer choices, only choice D—5—was a number between 0 and 7, indicating an acid.

2. C

A liquid has a definite volume, but it molds to the shape of the container holding it. Titanium (choice A) is a solid (choice D); solids have a definite shape and volume. A gas (choice B) will expand to fit the container in both volume and shape.

3. A

The key to simplifying expressions such as this one is to combine only *like terms*. Like terms are those with identical bases. For instance, $\frac{3}{5x^2}$ have like bases. So do $9x$ and $\frac{1}{5x}$. Real numbers without attached variables are their own like terms: 4, –21, 0.12, and $\frac{5}{8}$ are all like terms. In the expression given in this problem, $\frac{2}{3x^2}$ and $\frac{1}{3x^2}$ are like terms, and their sum is $\frac{3}{3x^2}$, or $1x^2$, or just x^2; –12x and 7x are also like terms, adding

up to –5x; and finally, 9 and 1 are like terms, with a sum of 10. Those three terms—x^2, –5, and 10—are then separated by the addition symbols to give the simplified version of the original expression.

4. B

You can use the Pythagorean theorem to compute the length of any side of any right triangle, as long as you know the lengths of the other two sides. Here is the theorem:

> For any right triangle with side lengths a, b, and c, and where c is the length of the hypotenuse (the longest side, and the one opposite the right angle), $a^2 + b^2 = c^2$.

Substituting the real values for a and b from the triangle given in question 4, you get

$$c^2 = 11^2 + 5^2$$

or

$$c^2 = 146.$$

To complete the work, you take the positive square root of 146, which is slightly over 12 ($12 \times 12 = 144$).

5. A

If two triangles are *similar*, that means they have the exact same *shape* (although not necessarily the same *size*). It also means that corresponding angles of the two triangles have the same measure, and that corresponding sides are *proportionate*.

One way then to find the solution to this problem is to set up a proportion with one corner the unknown value (x) and then solve the proportion:

$$\frac{12}{10} = \frac{15}{x}$$

This can be read as "12 is to 10 as 15 is to x." The problem can then be solved using cross-multiplication. Thus, $12x = 150$, leading to the solution $x = 12.5$.

6.   D

The operations undo each other. It is true that multiplication is commutative and division isn't, but that's not relevant to their being inverse operations. Choice A doesn't address the property of being inverse. Answer B also contains a true statement, but the statement is not about inverse operations. Answer C gives a false statement. In the example shown in choice C, the order of operations tells you to compute the first operations first, so $8 \div 2$ should be computed before 2×4. As noted in answer choice D, the inverseness of two operations indeed depends upon their ability to undo each other.

7.   A

Overgrazing, overuse, and a lack of rainfall caused the drought of the 1930s.

8.   D

Both the personal correspondence of a military man stationed with the 5th RCT in Korean and an interview with Secretary of Defense George Marshall are primary sources, because they involve correspondence or testimony from individuals who were actually involved with the Korean War.

9.   A

The responsibility for public education belongs to the state governments. The federal government has often passed legislation to regulate and provide funds for public education, but the main responsibility for establishing and regulating education resides with the state governments.

10.   B

The instrument for measuring the intensity of an earthquake is a seismograph. A thermograph (choice A) measures temperature. A telegraph (choice C) is a communication device, not a measuring device. An odometer (choice D) measures distance traveled.

11.   B

Energy is the ability to do work. Work occurs when a force (push or pull) is applied to an object, resulting in movement. The corresponding formula is work = force $\times$ distance. The greater the force (choice A) applied, or the longer the distance traveled, the greater the work done. *Distance* (choice C) is the interval between two points, and *speed* (choice D) is rate of movement.

12.   C

When two parallel lines are crossed by another line (called a *transversal*), eight angles are formed. There are, however, only two angle measures among the eight angles, and the sum of the measures is 180°. All of the smaller angles will have the same measures, and all of the larger angles will have the same measures. In this case, the smaller angles all measure 50°, so the larger angles (including angle y) all measure 130°.

13.   A

There are two things you must know in order to answer this question. One is the meaning of the small square at the vertex of angle *BXC*. That symbol tells you that angle *BXC* is a right angle (one that measures 90°). You must also understand that a straight line can be thought of as an angle that measures 180°. This is a *straight angle*. Therefore, the sum of the angles *DXC* (42°) and *BXC* (90°) is 132°. This means that the remaining angle on the line, *AXB*, must have the measure 48° (180° − 132°).

14.   B

Cancers and hereditary diseases are not infectious. Answer choices A, C, and D are all true statements: dis-

eases caused by viruses, bacteria, or protists—collectively referred to as germs—that invade the body are called infectious diseases; environmental hazards can cause diseases; and the immune system does protect the body from disease.

15. B

The statement "Movement basics include body, space, time, and relationship" is the correct answer because this describes only the dimensions of dance movement; in no way does it speak to how dance reflects the culture of which it is a part.

16. D

Flying buttresses, pointed arches, and stained glass windows appear together only on Gothic-style buildings, most of which were built between 1150 and 1500. Buildings of the Romanesque period (circa 1050–1150) usually employ wall buttresses and rounded arches; only a few employ pointed arches. The flying buttress was a device invented specifically to support the high vaults of Gothic churches. Byzantine buildings, like the famous Hagia Sophia in Istanbul, are characterized by domes and rounded arches, among other things. The same is true for Renaissance and Baroque architecture.

17. C

Choice C is correct because careful planning (item III) includes checking on the availability of resources and materials (item II). Although Mrs. Doe did reflective thinking during the discussion (item I), reflective thinking is only one component of communication and is included in careful planning and its correlation to success in the classroom. Thus, item I is incorrect, eliminating choices A, B, and D. Personal acquaintance with a Native American (item IV) would have helped shape the students' attitudes, but it is not necessary for student involvement.

18. A

Multiple strategies were planned for the motivation of the students (item I), but a result of the strategies was that each student participated in some way regardless of ability (item II) and the unit was integrated into other subjects (item III) through library assignments, reading, writing, and so forth. Only choice A includes all of these factors and is therefore correct. Developing a foundation for teaching American history (item IV, choice D) is not even a long-range goal, although the attitudes and beliefs developed in the project may become the foundation upon which the students will build their philosophy of American history.

19. D

Working collaboratively with other teachers (item IV) was the avenue through which the talents of the students were identified (item III) and the students' curiosity was stimulated (item II); only choice D encompasses all of these factors and is therefore the answer. Item I is a false statement—no risks were taken—so choice A is incorrect. Choices B and C each include only one of the correct items; thus they are also incorrect.

20. A

Only choice A includes the two correct items. The external factors of the field trip could create a positive motivation (item II) and would allow the students to make the connection between their old skills and the new skills they were learning (item I). Mrs. Doe instructed each student to take notes on what he or she saw, heard, and experienced. The skill of note taking was founded upon the library assignment that had preceded the field trip. The students were to make the connection. No mention is made of community involvement in the field trip, so item III is irrelevant, which eliminates choices B and D. The students did not take responsibility for their own learning (item IV): they were given instructions concerning what they were to do before they left for the field trip. Thus, choice C is also incorrect.

21. B

Giving the children a choice of field trips showed respect for the students' differences (item II) and is an example of the array of instructional strategies (item

IV) used by Mrs. Doe. Choice B correctly includes both these factors. Choice A is incomplete and therefore incorrect. Enhancing students' self-concept (item I) and fostering the view of learning as a purposeful pursuit (item III) are both incorporated in item II, respecting differences and understanding the society in which we live; thus choices C and D are also incorrect.

22. C

Clearly setting a purpose for listening (item I), asking questions about the selection (item III), and encouraging students to forge links between the new information and knowledge already in place (item IV) are all supported by research as effective strategies.

23. D

Children learn more from a text if the teacher helps them figure out how the book was put together. It makes the text more understandable. It also helps them to read the text critically, as part of the conversation can address the issue of what is missing in the text.

24. B

The magic in *Harry Potter* (A), the night life in Las Vegas (C), and the frequently controversial books by Mark Twain about Tom Sawyer and Huckleberry Finn may cause problems in the community. Mrs. Smith should probably select *Martha and George Washington* after careful review—and with principal approval.

25. B

This question is designed to demonstrate an understanding that the performance objective should directly tie into the assessment. Students need to know what the expectation is for them to complete the necessary assignments. Students do not understand what assessment tools are (choice A); they need clear directions and a list of explanations. Although the unit may have many new vocabulary words, students need to learn them within the context of the unit rather than from a random list (choice C); they should not feel threatened when learning to prepare for a test. There is no connection between notebooks and learning (choice D).

26. C

Rubrics are designed to help teachers assess each student's achievement and the quality of his or her responses. Therefore, criteria must be clearly defined (item I) and each criterion needs to have a quality point (item II): Outstanding (5–4), Good (3–2), and/or Fair (1–0). Rubrics need to cover a number of subject areas to allow for a fair assessment of the student's work, so item III is incorrect. Item IV is incomplete: students may rate themselves; however, the teacher needs to work with them as they complete the ratings.

27. B

Students often disclose more personal information in journals than when speaking in class. The teacher can also check for comprehension of content and the success or failure of class objectives. Journals typically are not graded with consideration to standard usage or grammatical constructions; therefore, choice A is incorrect. The assignment has no direct bearing on time-management skills; therefore, choice C is incorrect. Choice D is irrelevant: no mention is made of giving daily grades on the journal writing.

28. C

The Language Experience Approach (LEA) is a proven method of increasing students' reading and writing proficiency and their overall language competency. It requires that students write about what they know. Choices A, B, and D are irrelevant. Choice A superficially addresses that Ms. Johnson is an English teacher, and choice B refers to autobiographies, something that is not mentioned in the preceding information. Choice D foreshadows the library project, but it

has not yet been introduced into the context of these questions.

29. B

The best way to teach children to read, regardless of grade level, is to use a program of emergent literacy that includes pattern books and journal writing with invented spelling. Choice A is incorrect because although an intensive phonics program that includes drill and practice work may be effective with some students, it is not the most effective way to teach all students to read. Choice C is incorrect because these children are not expected to be exactly on grade level and should not be expected to adhere exactly to an instructional program that closely follows the third-grade basal reader; some are ESL, all are inner-city, and none were on grade level at the beginning of the year. Following a third-grade program is unrealistic. Choice D is incorrect because an English as a Second Language (ESL) program is intended to provide assistance to only those students who are, in fact, learning English as a second language. In addition, the learning resource teacher should provide assistance to only those students who have been identified as having a learning disability that qualifies them to receive services.

30. C

A basic principle in providing students with appropriate feedback is to first note the student's strengths (or positive aspects of the student's work and/or performance) and then to note specific ways the student can improve his or her work and/or performance. Therefore, the best approach for a teacher to take in providing students with feedback on written work is to first note the good things about students' writing and then to suggest ways to improve. Choices A and B are in essence the same; both choices indicate that only students' strengths would be acknowledged, omitting the important aspect of addressing ways students can improve. Neither action would enhance students' cognitive skills or their metacognitive skills (or self-awareness). Choice D is unacceptable because it denigrates the teacher's responsibility to evaluate students' performance on the basis of individual merit against the standards established by particular disciplines.

31. A

Choice A is the best answer of the four options for the following reasons. First, learning-style information acknowledges that although learners acquire knowledge in different ways, those differences can lead to effective learning when students are taught cognitive strategies that complement their natural learning tendencies; basically, teaching students about learning styles (and especially about their own learning style) is a recognition of human diversity. Second, beyond mere recognition of human diversity is the legitimacy of different approaches to learning. Every student can perform at a level of proficiency although not every student will attain that level in the same manner; in other words, learning styles validate students as learners and promote high standards for academic achievement. Third, when students are taught not only about learning styles in general but also about their own learning style specifically, they are empowered to take responsibility for their own learning. Fourth, of the four options, only choices A and D are tasks actively engaging the student. Both choices B and C are passive activities, and are therefore poor choices. Choice D requires that students perform a task without any help (direct instruction) for accomplishing the task; simply asking students to name additional strengths without giving them an opportunity to self-examine, to self-assess, and to explore their strengths will not produce the desired outcome. Only choice A gives students the information they need in order to accomplish the task the teacher has identified as being important.

32. A

The main purpose of the WTO is to open world markets to all countries to promote economic development and to regulate the economic affairs between member states.

33. B

Democracy is the correct response because it is the antithesis of the authoritarianism of fascism. Indeed, the totalitarian, romantic, militaristic, and nationalistic characteristics of fascism were, in large part, a reaction against the perceived inadequacies of democracy.

34. B

The industrial economy of the nineteenth century was not based upon an equitable distribution of profits among all those who were involved in production. Marxists and other critics of capitalism condemned the greed of capitalists and the abhorrent conditions of the industrial proletariat. Raw materials, a constant labor supply, capital, and an expanding marketplace were critical elements in the development of the industrial economy.

35. D

In the 1880s and 1890s, the U.S. Supreme Court struck down desegregation laws and upheld the doctrine of segregated "separate but equal" facilities for blacks and whites. These laws became known as "Jim Crow" laws. Their impact was to allow racist governments in the South to set up "separate but unequal" facilities in which blacks were forced to sit in the rear of streetcars and buses and in the back rooms of restaurants, or were excluded completely from white businesses, and had to use separate and usually inferior public restroom facilities. These laws allowed white supremacists to "put blacks in their place" and effectively kept blacks from achieving anything near equal status. It wasn't until the 1950s and 1960s that new Supreme Court decisions finally forced the repeal of these laws.

36. B

A writ of habeas corpus is a court order that directs an official who is detaining someone to produce the person before the court so that the legality of the detention may be determined. The primary function of the writ is to effect the release of someone who has been imprisoned without due process of law. For example, if the police detained a suspect for an unreasonable time without officially charging the person with a crime, the person could seek relief from a court in the form of a writ of habeas corpus. A writ of mandamus (choice A) is a court order commanding an official to perform a legal duty of his or her office. It is not used to prevent persons from being improperly imprisoned. The Fourth Amendment requirement that police have probable cause in order to obtain a search warrant (choice C) regulates police procedure. It is not itself a mechanism for affecting release of a person for improper imprisonment. The decision in *Roe v. Wade* (choice D) dealt with a woman's right to have an abortion. It had nothing to do with improper imprisonment.

37. A

By definition, acids and bases combine to produce a salt and water. An example would be HCI (hydrochloric acid) and NaOH (sodium hydroxide) reacting to form NaCI (salt) and water.

38. D

Atoms are neutral so the net charge must be zero, requiring that the number of negative particles (electrons) equals the number of positive particles (protons).

39. D

Choices A, B, and C all involve chemical changes, where iron, wood, and rocket fuel, respectively, are reacting with other substances to produce a reactant product with different chemical properties. Melted ice in the form of water still has the same chemical formula.

40. C

Isotopes for a given element all have the same chemical properties, differing only in their atomic weight (e.g., number of neutrons).

41. C

Newton's second law states that an unbalanced force acting on a mass will cause the mass to accelerate. In equation form, $F = ma$, where F is force, m is mass, and a is acceleration. Only C involves a mass that is being accelerated by an unbalanced force.

42. D

The east coast of South America and the west coast of Africa fit together like pieces of a jigsaw puzzle. Fossil remains in locations where "fit" is observed are too well matched to be coincidental. Earthquakes and volcanism are more prevalent in mountainous regions, where plates collided, than in other regions. Thus, all support the theory of plate tectonics.

43. D

The zygote of a human is a cell derived from a sperm containing 23 chromosomes and an egg containing 23 chromosomes. Choices A and B cannot be correct since they each represent too few chromosomes for either a haploid sex cell or a diploid body cell. Choice C represents the number of chromosomes in a sperm or an egg, and thus is also incorrect.

44. C

The body regulates water and heat through perspiration. Transpiration (choice B) describes a process not involving humans. Respiration (choice A) is breathing in humans and will cause some water loss. However, the question asks how the body regulates substances through the skin. Sensation (choice D) is the ability to process or perceive. The skin does have nerve endings that can sense, but this does not involve temperature or water regulation.

45. A

B, C, and D can be ruled out because Darwin was unaware of the genetic work that was later done by Mendel. Darwin and most other nineteenth-century biologists never knew of Mendel and his research. It was not until the beginning of the twentieth century that Mendel's pioneer research into genetic inheritance was rediscovered.

46. D

The question relates to appropriate sequencing of activities. Choice D is the best introductory activity in order to generate student interest in this new field of mathematics and to get students thinking about how to produce fractals. This activity would stimulate students to use higher-level thinking skills to make predictions by drawing on their knowledge of how to solve problems mathematically. Choice A would be the least appropriate to begin the study. Students who want to learn more could research this topic after they have developed an interest in fractals. Choice B would be appropriate as a later step, after students are interested in the process and are ready to learn how to produce fractals. Choice C would be appropriate as a subsequent step in the process of learning how to produce fractals. Choice B requires students to use preplanned formulas; choice C allows them to develop their own formulas, a very high-level activity.

47. A

The problem requires you to find the square root of 100, or to find the number that when multiplied by itself gives 100. Because $10 \times 10 = 100$, choice A is the only right answer.

48. D

The superscript 4 on the outside of the parenthesis indicates multiplication. Because $4 \times 2 = 8$, the answer is D.

49. C

To solve the multiplication problem, you must multiply the 3 times the 8 and the 4 times the 9. The answer is $^{24}/_{36}$. To simplify, divide by 12. The answer is $^{2}/_{3}$, choice C.

50. D

To change the fraction to a decimal, you must divide the 7 by 8. The answer is the decimal .875, choice D.

51. A

One can easily estimate to choose the answer: $7 \times 2 = 14$. The answer choice closest to 14 is 17.6, choice A.

52. C

The upward force of air resistance partially counteracts the force of gravity when a feather falls in air. In a vacuum or a near vacuum, this force is dramatically reduced for the feather, and both objects will fall at the same rate. The effect can be modeled without a vacuum pump by comparing the falling of two papers, one crumpled to reduce air resistance and the other flat.

53. B

The region's mountain ranges are the main reason for both the high precipitation and the varied climate.

54. B

Multiparty systems use an electoral system based on proportional representation. Therefore, each party gets legislative seats in proportion to the votes it receives. In the United States, the candidate who receives a plurality of the votes is declared the winner.

55. D

The formula for finding the area of any circle is $A = \pi r^2$ (about 3.14 times the length of the radius times itself). In this case, you need to take half of πr^2; hence the answer is choice D.

56. C

There is sufficient evidence to suggest that the student is a victim of sexual abuse. The situation is too serious to delay action (choice A) or to remain passive (choice B). In no case would it be appropriate to copy and distribute the poem to other teachers (choice D).

57. B

Ms. Aldridge may have to teach the parts of the social studies textbook to her students because a social studies text may differ significantly from a traditional basal reader. Bold print, map reading, the index, list of illustrations, and charts are some of the parts that may not be a part of a reading textbook. The other answer choices are incorrect. Teachers of content subjects may have to teach some reading skills and book parts, should use supplementary materials for the auditory and kinesthetic learners in particular, and must not always trust the grade level of the textbook and should not assume that all students are reading on grade level in the class. Only (B) is the correct answer.

58. C

Camaraderie cannot be fostered by choice alone. However, roundtable discussions (choice D) will increase student interaction and help each student develop oral language skills. A variety of techniques (choice B) can promote student motivation, and the finding that students have average scores in many areas emphasizes the importance of development in one area transferring to another (choice A).

59. A

Just guessing the decade that the composition reflects does not require the students to use their knowledge of music and the time periods. Choice A, therefore, is *not* a good choice; choices B, C, and D are all appropriate follow-up activities.

60. B

Rules and regulations for schools and libraries that make the use of the Internet available to students do NOT currently include the filtering of text. On the other hand, these computers must use blocking or filtering technology to protect students against access to certain visual depictions (choice A). The rules also mandate that no personal information about the students be disclosed (choice C) and that minors be

prohibited from using the computers for "hacking" (choice D).

61. A

Choice A is not true; the "fair use" doctrine does allow limited reproduction of copyrighted works for educational and research purposes. Choices B, C, and D are all true. Teachers can copy chapters, articles, as well as charts, graphs, diagrams, and cartoons for the classroom (choice B). Regardless of whether the copy is from a collective work, an educator may make copies of a short story, essay, or poem for the classroom (choice C). In addition, teachers can make multiple copies (not to exceed the number of students in the class) for the class—as long as the copying meets the tests of brevity and spontaneity (choice D).

62. A

The physical movement and accumulation of sand is not part of the rock cycle, because no transformation of rock type is involved.

63. B

The Moon is much closer to Earth than to any other planet or the Sun.

64. B

Expansion occurring on the ocean floor along the mid-Atlantic ridge presses creates pressure around the edges of the Pacific Plate, creating geologic instability where the Pacific Plate collides with the continental plates on all sides.

65. D

The Pylon Temple of Horus, circa 212 B.C.E., pictured in the example displays elements typical of the monumental architecture that developed during Egypt's Old Kingdom period (circa 2600–2100 B.C.E.) and continued until Egypt became a province of the Roman Empire (circa 31 B.C.E.). This architecture achieved an effect of imposing grandeur and durability through the use of simple, solid geometric forms, constructed on an overwhelming scale and laid out with exacting symmetry. The Temple of Horus avoids any emphasis on horizontal lines (choice A) and relies instead on the sloping outer walls to visually "pull" the massive building to the ground and make it seem immovable and eternal. In addition, although the temple carries minor ornamental detail (choice B), displays huge reliefs of figures, and is set within a large open courtyard (choice C), all of these elements are secondary to the massive character of the building itself.

66. D

This marble portrait bust of the first century B.C.E. is typical of a style that flourished during the late Roman Republic and that aimed for a literal, super-realistic depiction of a certain type of individual. The sculptor here avoided any tendency to idealize his subject and pursued instead an expressive, realistic depiction in which each particular feature of his subject's face and expression was painstakingly recorded; choice B, therefore, is false. The choice of hard, chiseled marble, rather than modeled clay or incised relief, helped to accentuate the craggy details of his subject's face; thus choice C is also false. The sitter here represents not the jaded, effete aristocracy of the later Roman Empire, as choice A wrongly suggests, but rather the simple, unsophisticated citizen-farmer of the earlier Republic, whose labor and determination helped to build the Roman state.

67. A

The seventeenth-century Japanese ink-on-paper scroll painting shown in the example relies almost exclusively on the qualities of line to convey the graceful forms of two leaping deer. In this painting, called *Deer Scroll*, both the animals and the scripted characters share the same quality of fluid, rhythmic, spontaneous "writing." Gradations of tone (choice B) and color (choice C) are unimportant here, since the images are defined by black line on white, and volume (choice D), too, is absent, since these forms show no shading or modulation of tone.

68. B

This passage from Herman Melville's *Moby Dick* contains a metaphor when it calls the Nantucketers "sea hermits."

69. C

The passage from Lewis Carroll's *Alice in Wonderland* suggests fantasy as the gardeners paint roses.

70. D

This passage from Jane Austen's *Emma* describes in detail the appearance and actions of Mrs. Elton. This is characterization.

71. D

Among all of the nationally recognized professional organizations, Teachers of English to Speakers of Other Languages (TESOL) is identified as the organization that provides professional support for educators. IRA (choice A) stands for the International Reading Association. The NATM (choice B) is the National Association of Teachers of Mathematics. NASDTEC (choice C) is the abbreviation for the National Association of State Directors of Teacher Education and Certification.

72. D

Let x be the number of people in the barn. Then, since each person and lamb has only one head, the number of lambs must be $30 - x$. Since people have two legs, the number of human legs totals $2x$. Similarly, since the number of legs each lamb has is 4, the total number of lamb legs in the barn is $4(30 - x)$. Thus, we have this equation: $2x + 4(30 - x) = 104$. To solve this equation, use the distributive property: $a(b - c) = ab - ac$.

We get: $4(30 - x) = (4 \times 30) - (4 \times x) = 120 - 4x$.

Our equation reduces to: $2x + 120 - 4x$ or $120 - 2x = 104$.

Now subtract 120 from both sides of the equation to get $-2x = 104 - 120 = -16$.

Dividing both sides of the equation by -2 yields $x = 8$. Therefore, there were 8 people, and $30 - 8 = 22$ lambs in the barn.

73. A

The 2 is in the hundreds place. If the number to the immediate right of the 2 (that is, the number in the tens place) is greater than or equal to 5, you increase the 2 to 3; otherwise, do not change the 2. In this problem, an 8 is in the tens place, so you must change the 2 to a 3, or 300.

74. A

The number 72104.58 is read "seventy-**two thousand**, one hundred four and fifty-eight hundredths." In other words, the 2 is in the thousands place.

75. B

Integrating another content area into the students' study of the American Revolution will develop a broader view of that period in history. Choice A is incorrect because although the teachers are integrating their lessons, they are each responsible for their own subject area. Choice C is incorrect because librarians are usually pleased when books are used by teachers and students. Choice D is incorrect because teaching integrated units does not mean that students will be doing homework for one subject during another's class period.

76. A

The correct answer is D: only the federal government can mint money. It would be disastrous for each state to mint money independently of the others. The state governments must, however, ratify A amendments to the Constitution before they become effective. It is the state governments that B provide for the local governments and that C regulate contracts and wills. Therefore, A, B, and C are powers reserved to the states; only D is a power reserved to the federal government.

77. C

An aside is a comment spoken directly to the audience that the other actors on stage are supposedly unable to hear.

78. D

This question relates to enabling teachers to document their teaching and to be aware of students' efforts, progress, and achievements. A portfolio is a purposeful collection of work that exhibits efforts, progress, and achievement of students and enables teachers to document teaching in an authentic setting. Standardized tests (choice A) are commercially developed and are used for specific events. A teacher-made test is used to evaluate specific objectives of the course, so choice B is not the best option. Observation is used only to explain what students do in classrooms and to indicate some of their capabilities; therefore, choice C is incorrect.

79. C

This question relates to evaluating specific objectives and content. Teacher-made tests are designed to evaluate the specific objectives and specific content of a course. Self- and peer evaluation (choice A) utilizes students' knowledge according to evaluation criteria that is understood by the students. A portfolio (choice B) is a purposeful collection of work that exhibits effort, progress, and achievement of students and enables teachers to document teaching in an authentic setting. Observation (choice D) is used to explain what students do in classrooms and to indicate to some degree their capabilities.

80. D

Standardized tests rate student performance against the performance of other students and report the scores in terms of percentiles, stanines, and scaled scores. A portfolio (choice A) is a collection of student effort, progress, and achievement. Teacher-made tests (choice B) evaluate specific objectives and content. Stu-

dents' classroom behaviors and capabilities are evaluated through observation (choice C).

81. C

The most efficient way to gain information about a new setting is to speak with someone who is familiar with the circumstances. Orienting oneself with the physical layout (choice A) would be helpful but will not provide information about the student population or materials. Although communication with the principal (choice B) is always a good idea, the principal usually will have little time to have an in-depth discussion and will not be able to tell specifically which books are available for teachers' use. Eventually Ms. Woods will need to match curriculum guidelines to the material available (choice D), but sitting in a closet will not introduce her to staff and student characteristics.

82. D

Only choice D includes all of the techniques that would be useful in improving and monitoring writing. The students have set goals toward which they will strive (item II) bit by bit until they reach them. The teacher and student have an opportunity to discuss good and bad points of the student's writing in a nonthreatening atmosphere (item III). It is always helpful to have a model of good writing (item IV), and allowing students to choose which paper to discuss enhances self-esteem. Forcing a student to write every night (item I) will do little to create quality work. Therefore, choices B and C are incorrect.

83. B

First, it is helpful to view the shaded area as the area of the square minus the area of the circle. With that in mind, you simply need to find the area of each simple figure, and then subtract one from the other. You know that the radius of the circle is 6 units in length. That tells you that the diameter of the circle is 12 units. Because the circle is inscribed in the square (meaning that

the circle fits inside of the square touching in as many places as possible), you see that the sides of the square are each 12 units in length. Knowing that, you compute the area of the square to be 144 square units (12 × 12). Using the formula for finding the area of a circle (πr^2), where $\pi = 3.14$, you get approximately 113 square units (3.14 × 6 × 6). Then subtracting 113 (the area of the circle) from 144 (the area of the square) gives you the answer of 31 square units.

84. B

If you can fold a two-dimensional figure so that one side exactly matches or folds onto the other side, the fold line is a line of symmetry. The following figure is a non-square rectangle with its two lines of symmetry shown:

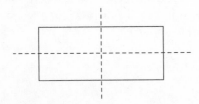

One might think that lines drawn from opposite corners are lines of symmetry, but they are not. The two halves would be the same size and shape, but they would not fold onto each other. Note that the question asks about nonsquare rectangles. Squares (which are rectangles) have four lines of symmetry.

85. A

To answer the question, you must recognize that triangles *ADB* and *AEC* are similar triangles, meaning that they have the same shape. Therefore, the corresponding angles of the two triangles are the same, or congruent, and the corresponding sides of the two triangles are proportional. Given that, you can set up the following proportion, where *x* is the distance from point *A* to point *C*:

$$\frac{3}{7} = \frac{5}{x}.$$

Solving the proportion by cross-multiplication, you see that the length of segment *AC* is about 11.7. Knowing that the length of segment *AB* is 7 feet, you subtract to find the length of *BC* (11.7 − 7 = 4.7).

86. B

Statement I is true because the winner could be Mr. Greenfield or it could be someone else. Statement II is not true, even though Mr. Greenfield bought many more tickets than any other individual. He still has a block of only 300; there are 700 ticket stubs in the drum that aren't his. This tells us that statement III is true. Finally, statement IV is false. Do not confuse the true statement "all tickets have an equal chance of winning" with the false statement that "all persons have an equal chance of winning."

87. C

Historical almanacs contain yearly data of certain events, including the time at sunrise and sunset along with weather-related data and statistics. A historical atlas is a collection of historical maps that may or may not include population data. Historical population data may best be found in government publications on the census. An encyclopedia article would contain a factual summary of the colonial period and the American Revolution; however, the article might not include an analysis of the role of Fort Mackinaw during the American Revolution because encyclopedias attempt to give overviews rather than interpretations or analysis. A secondary source on Michigan during the colonial period might better address that question. Information on when the first treaty was signed and the terms of the treaty would most likely appear in a history book.

88. A

Putting together or arranging elements to make a whole pattern or product is synthesis. Choices B, C, and D are examples of tasks requiring analysis, not synthesis.

89. A

Inductive reasoning involves making generalizations based on a particular fact or example. Students would use deductive reasoning (choice B) if they were to discuss the characteristics of romance and then compose a musical piece encompassing those characteristics. Oral interpretation (choice C) is a type of dramatic speech, and evaluation (choice D) involves judging the quality or merits of a work or product.

90. A

New technologies can be helpful to students in many ways. Choice B would stifle the student's creativity and result in less sophisticated writing. Choice C has not been proven effective as a technique to help students improve their spelling. Choice D means that the teacher would not be applying standards of good writing in evaluating the student's work.

91. D

In choice D, the teacher gives the student appropriate feedback and avoids simply stating the answer, giving the student a chance to think about the correct answer. The other choices are only partially correct.

92. A

The students have developed criteria against which they can decide or judge if someone is intelligent. The students were gathering characteristics, not examples (choice B), and the students have yet to test their criteria (choice C). Instead of creative thinking (choice D), in this activity, students are engaged in critical thinking.

93. B

A limited money supply and rising prices were major causes of the Great Depression. The money supply was most affected by the gold standard, and the Smoot-Hawley Tariff Act further affected consumer prices.

94. C

Different students respond differently to different kinds of stimuli. Choices A and B state basically the same idea in different words. Choice D is incorrect because even when teachers plan an activity that is different from the norm, an instructional principle or rationale should be behind the activity.

95. D

The task described in choice D requires analysis of the situation or problem. Choice A requires application, the level below analysis; choice C requires comprehension, the level below application; and choice B requires knowledge, the lowest level in Bloom's *Taxonomy*.

96. D

This question focuses on a basic musical concept, harmony. Harmony is the performance of two or more different pitches simultaneously. Therefore, when looking at the answer choices provided, it is good to begin by eliminating those that have nothing to do with pitch. A rhythm instrument (item I) is a nonpitched instrument in almost all cases, so choices A and B are eliminated. Because two or more different pitches must be performed simultaneously to have harmony, item III can also be eliminated, because there are two performers but not two different pitches. That eliminates choice C and leaves choice D as the correct answer.

97. A

By selecting books for the classroom library that match students' independent reading abilities, the teacher is recognizing that each student must improve his or her reading ability by beginning at his or her own level and progressing to more difficult materials. Choice B is incorrect because books that are challenging will most likely be frustrating to at least some of the students. Choice C is incorrect because the presence or absence of separate word lists should not be a determining factor in selecting books for a classroom library. Choice D is incorrect because all children need access to a classroom library regardless of their reading abilities.

98. D

Adding up Matt's scores, you get 522. Multiply 90 by 6 to compute the number of total points it would take to have an average of 90 ($90 \times 6 = 540$). Subtracting the points Matt earned (522) from the points he needed (540) to earn an A–, you find that he was 18 points shy of his goal.

99. B

The most basic definition of literacy is the ability to read and write.

100. C

Miscue analysis is designed to assess the strategies that children use in their reading. Goodman was interested in the processes occurring during reading, and he believed that any departure from the written text could provide a picture of the underlying cognitive processes. Readers' miscues include substitutions of the written word with another, additions, omissions, and alterations to the word sequence.

101.

Essay 1

Ms. Treen has an important opportunity to make new friends, find help for her students, and involve the adults in improving their own language skills. The first thing she needs to do—assuming she is not bilingual—is find someone who will help interpret for her during parent conferences and classroom visitation sessions.

Ms. Treen can give parents some important information: the best way for them to help the children learn to read is to read to them and with them. Because some parents cannot read themselves, she might provide this information orally with the help of the interpreter. She can provide a list of books for the children to take with them to the library; even though the parents may not be able to find the books, this way they can ask for help. If the adults are nonreaders, the teacher might suggest that the responsible adult just provide a time for the child to practice reading and actually sit and listen to the child read.

If the teacher and interpreter can make sure that the parents understand the importance of regular family visits to the library, they have achieved a major goal. The teacher might even

ask a librarian to come to the school and help the parents to take out a library card for themselves and their students. Perhaps the local library might even plan an event for children that might not be stressful for those families that have never used a library.

Teachers might collect magazines that children can check out and take home for the entire family to read. The teacher might also send home a list of some educational television programs that the families can watch together.

Analysis of Essay 1

The essay is an excellent example of a good answer. The essay answers each question asked in a simple, straightforward way. The solutions are feasible and reasonable. The writer uses both simple and complex sentence structure. The punctuation and grammar are certainly acceptable. The essay flows logically and is well organized. It is a model answer.

Essay 2

Ms. Treen should require parents to read to their children in the English language. She should check to make sure that the parents are using the library and should make sure that the children are doing so. Ms. Treen should send home a list of books for purchase that every home should have; by checking on this regularly, she can improve the learning of her students.

Analysis of Essay 2

The essay answers each part of the question, and the three-sentence answer is direct and to the point. The solutions proposed, however, are not feasible. The teacher cannot require the families to buy books for their home. She also does not take into account the fact that many of the parents may not be able to read aloud to their children in English. The writer does not consider the fact that the teacher may not be able to communicate with the families. Even though the answer is without errors, it is simplistic and unrealistic.

Essay 3

Ms. Treen should send home assignments for the families to do together that require the use of the library. She can sell encyclopedias for the parents to buy.

Analysis of Essay 3

A two-sentence essay is not appropriate for a three-part question. The content is debatable: it would be unethical for a teacher to sell encyclopedias to parents. The essay does not take into account that there are no library cards in some homes or that most parents do not or could not use the library. Can teachers really *require* the entire family to do assignments? This answer is clearly written, but the content is unacceptable.

Index

N

O

Look Up & Know

evaluation
analysis
comprehension
sythesis / synthesize
semantic map
inductive thinking & reasoning
deductive reasoning
hypothesis formation
pattern indentification
divergent thinking
mnemonic
antonym
synonym
homonyms
idioms
literal level comprehension
authentic reading

NOTES

NOTES

NOTES

NOTES

NOTES